SOCIAL, POLITICAL AND
CULTURAL CHALLENGES OF THE BRICS

SOCIAL, POLITICAL AND
CULTURAL CHALLENGES OF THE BRICS

Gustavo Lins Ribeiro
Tom Dwyer
Antonádia Borges
Eduardo Viola
(organizadores)

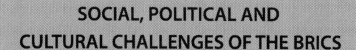

Associação Nacional de Pós-Graduação
e Pesquisa em Ciências Sociais

Langaa

First published in South Africa by
ANPOCS
Associação Nacional de Pós-Graduação e Pesquisa
em Ciências Sociais

Av. Professor Luciano Gualberto, 315 – 1º andar
Cidade Universitária – Butantã
05508-010 – São Paulo – SP – Brazil

(55 11) 3091-4664/3091-5043

anpocs@anpocs.org.br
www.anpocs.org.br

Langaa RPCIG
Langaa research and Publishing Common Initiative Group

P.O. Box 902 Mankon
Bamenda
North West Region
Cameroon

Langaagrp@gmail.com
www.langaa-rpcig.net

ISBN 978-9956-792-26-9 (e-book)
ISBN 978-9956-792-14-6 (paperback)

Dados Internacionais de Catalogação na Publicação (CIP)
(Câmara Brasileira do Livro, SP, Brasil)

Social, political and cultural challenges of the BRICS [livro eletrônico] / Gustavo Lins
    Ribeiro...[et al.]. – São Paulo : ANPOCS, 2014
    1 Mb ; ePUB.

Vários autores
Outros organizadores: Tom Dwyer, Antonádia Borges, Eduardo Viola
Bibliografia.
ISBN 978-9956-792-26-9

    1. Desenvolvimento econômico - Países em desenvolvimento 2. Economia -
Brasil 3. Economia mundial 4. Inclusão social 5. Globalização 6. Política - Brasil
7. Política mundial
    I. Ribeiro, Gustavo Lins. II. Dwyer, Tom. III. Borges, Antonádia. IV. Viola, Eduardo.

14-12893   CDD-338.9

Índices para catálogo sistemático:
1. Desenvolvimento econômico : Economia 338.9

Summary

Social, political and cultural challenges of the BRICS

A symposium, a debate, a book

....

Gustavo Lins Ribeiro

For the almost 40 years of its existence, ANPOCS has contributed to introducing or consolidating new thematic areas in the academic agenda of debates in the Brazilian social sciences. Commensurate with this history, at the 37th Annual meeting, hosted in Águas de Lindoia, São Paulo, in 2013, we organized a large International Symposium, *The BRICS and their social, political and cultural challenges on the national and international levels*. There were six sessions of debates, gathered under the umbrella of "Development and public policies," "Social inclusion and social justice," and "Emerging powers and transformations in the international system," followed by a final plenary session. Around 30 anthropologists, political scientists, sociologists and researchers in international relations from Brazil, Russia, India, China and South Africa, met over three highly productive days. As might be expected at ANPOCS, the encounter was marked not only by the diversity of countries and disciplines, but also by the theoretical and political diversity of the participants, something already apparent in the composition of the Brazilian coordinators of the Symposium.

The book we have the pleasure to present here is just one tangible outcome of the papers and dialogues emerging from this encounter. Like the Symposium, the volume is divided into three sections. Looking to address an international readership, it is published in Portuguese and English. The work may also be accessed via the ANPOCs portal, making it more readily available to researchers worldwide.

WHY UNITE 30 SOCIAL SCIENTISTS FROM THE BRICS AT THE ANPOCS MEETING?

This question relates both to the importance of the BRICS and to the importance of the social sciences in these countries and, in particular, in Brazil. First of all, while the state and business leaders of the BRICS have deepened their relations and agendas of mutual interests over the last few years, the intellectuals and academics from this consolidating international block still have a long way to go. The lack of mutual knowledge needs to be reduced quickly. In our view it is more than time to search for a strategic approximation between the *intelligentsia* of the BRICS countries, which contain important academic communities, beyond the government initiatives that very often suffer from the excesses of officialdom. The block needs to be understood as a whole and individually, in terms of each of its components, in order to inform the general public and intervene where necessary in the correlated processes in a qualified way. The more knowledge that opinion makers and qualified interpreters have concerning the problems in their countries, the easier it will be to develop the complex foundations needed for cooperation and reciprocal exchange.

We set out from the principle that the existence of a new block of global governance like the BRICS also creates the need for a closer approximation among their civil societies, a fundamental part of which are precisely academics and researchers, due to their capacity to produce and disseminate knowledge and information, influencing public opinion. In the academic world, as in other areas of social life, the interactions and exchanges inevitably become denser and more consolidated when we increase our levels of communication and exchange: in other words, when networks of mutual interests are constructed and maintained over time. The participation in congresses is an important step but needs to be accompanied by the exchange of students and the establishment of shared research interests capable of generating more perennial alliances, deeper exchanges and more differentiated knowledge.

We also wanted to stimulate a heterodox agenda as part of the internationalization of the Brazilian social sciences. Much has been said for and against South/South academic cooperation. This is a long debate in which I have participated for more than ten years through an initiative called "world anthropologies" (RIBEIRO and ESCOBAR, 2006, 2012; RIBEIRO, 2006). Contrary to what some may hastily suppose, this move does not express a wish to discard the important contribution made by the hegemonic social sciences. But it does involve criticizing and looking to escape the overwhelming American hegemony, the continuation of which threatens to install a monotonous set of agendas, theories and propositions. We need to move beyond this metropolitan provincialism and make room for a provincial cosmopolitanism, thereby investing in heteroglossic cross-fertilization as a source of innovation and creativity. All the BRICS countries have well-established academic communities representing complex loci of enunciation within the geopolitics of knowledge. What we can learn from them is a universe yet to be more widely explored.[1]

Another source of inspiration for an intra-BRICS academic dialogue is the potential represented by comparing this diverse set of countries which have problems traditionally explored by the social sciences. For example: the large contingents of their populations living in social exclusion; urban violence; ethnic, cultural and linguistic diversity; questions of national integration; the impacts and new relations formed by the globalized world; tensions between multicultural and intercultural proposals and national

---

1   In addition to the volume edited by myself and Arturo Escobar, the idea of exploring other academic traditions can also benefit from books such as those by Boskovic (2008); Das (2003); De L'Estoile, Neiburg and Sigaud (2002); Ntarangwi, Mills and Babiker (2006); Patel (2010); Uberoi, Deshpande and Sundar (2008); Yamashita, Bosco and Eades (2004), and the World Social Science Report (Unesco 2010).

homogenization; racial, interethnic and gender relations in tension; rapid social and cultural changes; environmental problems caused by economic growth; income concentration; economic growth and social inequality; public policies and social inclusion. The possibility of comparing the knowledge accumulated in the five countries undoubtedly has the potential to influence research agendas, favour the increase in mutual knowledge, as well as leave behind a problem typical of the social sciences that Norbert Elias (1989) called natiocentrism. The present volume represents a contribution in this direction. By stimulating us to think of unusual comparisons, the mere existence of the BRICS is already a stimulus to a heterodox interpretative imagination.

The project as a whole, Symposium and book, are indices of the undeniable importance and leadership of the Brazilian social sciences today at international level, thanks to the quality of the work of Brazilian scholars, increasingly present in congresses and prestigious international publications. It is worth highlighting our participation as presidents, vice-presidents or board members of international disciplinary associations like the International Sociological Association, the International Political Science Association, the International Union of Anthropological and Ethnological Sciences and the International Social Science Council. ANPOCS has also worked to demonstrate and amplify the cosmopolitanism of our social sciences and their capacity to intervene in contemporary processes, contributing to their organization at global level. The international protagonism of Brazilian social scientists introduces another twist to the hegemonic circuits of internationalization, typically controlled by the major traditional disciplinary centres, and enables the amalgamation of a more plural.

DIFFERENCES, POWER AND TAXONOMIES

Very often the differences between the BRICS are accentuated more than what they have in common. Indeed there are good reasons for this, linked both to the characteristics internal to each country and to their global interests. It is not impossible to imagine, for example, conflicts of interest between Brazil and China in the African continent where both countries are increasingly present through state and private companies. The BRICS contain a former world imperialist power, Russia, alongside a huge contemporary power with its own imperialist past, China. They are undoubtedly global players with their nuclear arsenal and their very often expansionist sense of grandeur. They are joined by India, also possessing military nuclear technology, equally distinguished by its own history and civilization, but with a common trait that makes it more immediately closer to South Africa and more indirectly closer to Brazil: its colonial past. The latter three countries are products of complex colonial histories and, in different ways, were the jewels in the crown of their respective empires in Asia, Africa and South America. The more recent political experience of the five countries is also distinct. China is a one-party State. South Africa carries the legacy of a regime that divided the nation, apartheid. India has an intense colonial memory in which the politically complex national unity is problematized by ethnic, cultural and linguistic factors. Russia, for its part, was one of the two great world powers until 1991. And Brazil, with its multifarious social problems, has undergone an important process of democratization since the 1980s.

If something unites all five countries beyond their identification as "emergent" nations – a euphemism to designate places where capitalism anticipates big returns – it is the presence of the State as a more or less central actor. All of them embrace a traditional development model that implies the degradation of the natural environment and, very often, the (re) production of social inequalities. Moreover they all have a visible economic, political and sometimes military influence in the regions in which they are embedded and a desire to be more proactive at international level (something that the formation of the block in itself illustrates). In fact various of the BRICS, if not all of them, reflecting their current role as the dynamos of the world capitalist system, have ambitions frequently interpreted as imperialist. Brazil is certainly no exception to this claim (FONTES, 2012; ZIBECHI, 2012). I believe that one of the missions of a critical approach to the social sciences of the BRICS must be to point programmatically to what

I call post-imperialism (RIBEIRO, 2003, 2014), that is, the prefiguration of a participation in the world order that does not involve the use of the imperialist mechanisms that we know and critique so well.

Undoubtedly the BRICS were an invention initially of interest to the big transnational capital based in Wall Street, one more taxonomic device of the powerful in their ceaseless search to establish a geopolitics that reflects their own interests. The expression "emerging markets", for example, long ago became the preferred classification rather than the Jurassic "underdeveloped countries" or its *aggiornamento,* "developing countries". These examples show that the classificatory systems change over time, including in response to the critiques to which they are subject. There is no doubt that the control of global taxonomies and their associated forms of verification, certification, interpretation and dissemination are part of the power of agencies of governance and, historically, of diverse forms of imperialism. However, it would not be the first time that categories invented by the powerful are given new meanings and put into circulation within other semantic and political circuits, sometimes for purposes radically different to the original. The appropriation of the BRICS label by the BRICS themselves appears to illustrate precisely this movement. In the end, like any other invention at political and symbolic level, it needs to be believed in and the fight to define its meaning becomes political. As an imagined, reappropriated and re-imagined invention, the BRICS are subject to diverse readings.

Of course the role of this still consolidating block should not be exaggerated. However the current conservative reaction to its presence as a global force is revealed strongly when the subject turns to the establishment of its own development bank. Are they challenging the hegemony of the Bretton Woods institutions, i.e. the World Bank and the International Monetary Fund? Will new circuits of capital, currencies, services and industrial goods be created beyond the control of the hegemonic centres? This reaction, widely divulged by the conservative global media and its spokespeople, shows, aside from the variations in the economic growth of each country, that the BRICS power platform bothers the central countries and transnational financial capital. The latter are not interested in changes or surprises to the hierarchy currently prevailing in the world system. Should the creature turn against its creator, it needs to be put in its place or be destroyed.

Irrespective of the success or otherwise of the BRICS, their mere presence and will to power indicate other geometries to the world system. Will it be a new vision of distribution of power in the world? It may well be that now, at the start of the 21st century, we are in a transitional phase that leads to a shift in the civilizational scale with the return of the centre of the world system to China. If this really does happen, it will be even more urgent for the BRICS countries to understand the new world that seems to be in its gestation stage.

FINAL REMARKS

We are faced with multiple challenges. These include preparing a new generation of researchers about the BRICS and the development of the block's own academic agenda. ANPOCS is contributing to meet these goals with the organization of the International Symposium in 2013 and the publication of this book in 2014. The Symposium would not have been possible without the sponsorship of the Banco do Brasil Foundation and the Social Service of Commerce (SESC). This book, meanwhile, would not have existed without the support of the National Economic and Social Development Bank (BNDES). Our thanks to these institutions for having understood the importance of our initiative and enabled its realization. I also wish to thank all the participants of the Symposium and the book who believed in this project and participated in it enthusiastically. Mentioning the name of Gabriela Rosa, tireless in her work, I wish to express my sincere gratitude to all the ANPOCS support staff who made the International Symposium an example of organization and friendliness.

Readers of anthropology, political science, sociology and international relations now have at their disposal a book that will certainly show the rich potential of working within the framework of the discussion on the BRICS. We hope that is followed by many other volumes, helping to deepen our exchanges and knowledge. Enjoy the read!

REFERENCES

BOSKOVIC, A. (ed.). (2008), *Other people's anthropologies. Ethnographic practice on the margins*, New York/Oxford, Berghahn Books.

DAS, V. (ed.). (2003), *The Oxford Indian Companion to Sociology and Social Anthropology*, Delhi, Oxford University Press.

DE L'ESTOILE, B., NEIBURG, F., SIGAUD, L. (eds.). (2002), *Antropologia, Impérios e Estados Nacionais*, Rio de Janeiro, Relume Dumará/Faperj.

ELIAS, N. (1989), *El processo de la civilización*, México, Siglo XXI Editores.

FONTES, V. (2012), *O Brasil e o capital-imperialismo*, Rio de Janeiro, Editora UFRJ.

NTARANGWI, M., MILLS, D., BABIKER, M. (eds.). (2006), *African Anthropologies. History, Critique and Practice*, London/New York, Zed Books.

PATEL, S. (ed.). (2010), *The ISA Handbook of Diverse Sociological Traditions*, Londres, Sage Publications.

RIBEIRO, G. L. (2014), *Outras globalizações. Cosmopolíticas pós-imperialistas*, Rio de Janeiro, EdUERJ.

_____. (2003), *Postimperialismo. Cultura y política en el mundo contemporáneo*, Barcelona, Gedisa.

_____. (2006), "Antropologias Mundiais: Para um novo cenário global na antropologia", *Revista Brasileira de Ciências Sociais*, 21, 60: 147-165.

RIBEIRO, G. L., ESCOBAR, A. (eds.). (2006), *World Anthropologies. Disciplinary Transformations within Systems of Power*, Oxford/New York, Berg Publishers.

_____. (2012), *Antropologias Mundiais. Transformações da disciplina em sistemas de poder*, Brasília, Editora da Universidade de Brasília.

UBEROI, P., SUNDAR, N., DESHPANDE, S. (eds.). (2008), *Anthropology in the East: Founders of Indian Sociology and Social Anthropology*, Calcutta/London/New York, Seagull Books.

UNESCO – United Nations Educational, Scientific and Cultural Organization and ISSC – International Social Science Council. (2010), *World Social Science Report. Knowledge Divides*, Paris, Unesco.

YAMASHITA, S., BOSCO, J., EADES, J. S. (eds.). (2004), *The Making of Anthropology in East and Southeast Asia*, New York/Oxford, Berghahn Books.

ZIBECHI, R. (2012), *Brasil potência. Entre a integração regional e um novo imperialismo*, Rio de Janeiro, Editora Consequência.

Part one

DEVELOPMENT AND PUBLIC POLICIES
IN THE BRICSS

Social sciences and the BRICS

Tom Dwyer

This introductory text recapitulates some important moments in the recent history of Brazilian social science exchanges with Russia, India, China and South Africa (BRICS). These acquired considerable impetus in September of 2013 when ANPOCS organized, under the direction of president Gustavo Lins Ribeiro, a series of discussions between social scientists from the five countries. This was a daring initiative, and this book gives us some idea of the enormity of the challenges lying ahead, not only for Brazilian social scientists, but those in each of the BRICS countries.

In this book a set of papers has been selected from our meeting in Águas de Lindóia that brought social scientists together to discuss a series of issues of common concern to all. Each chapter develops a perspective on national issues, but transmits them in a way designed to be relevant to readers in other countries. The authors have built their own interpretations of their own country's processes with reference to: development and public policy, social justice and social inclusion and emergent powers and transformations in the international system.

I find it useful to see globalisation as occurring in three relatively autonomous, but interconnected systems: commerce, supra-national relations and cultural exchange. In this chapter I shall concentrate on examining one specific area of cultural exchanges, scientific cooperation and, specifically, that between social scientists, and more especially sociologists.

CULTURAL EXCHANGE – SCIENTIFIC COOPERATION

Since the end of the Military Regime there has been growing Brazilian bilateral scientific cooperation with Russia and China. Scientific cooperation with Russia is governed by a joint declaration of Foreign Ministers, signed in 1997, this concentrates on the peaceful use of space, energy, military technology and an umbrella area that is both technological and scientific.

Today bi-lateral cooperation with China is conducted around bio-fuels and agriculture, and agreements have been signed in a number of areas including: forestry, hydro-electricity, health, new materials, biological engineering and nuclear energy. The most important and enduring cooperation with China has been in the aerospace programme which began in the 1980s and which resulted in the launching of the first "China-Brazil Earth Resources Satellite" in 1999, and others since then.

The Indian Ministry of Science and Technology established an agreement in 2003 with the Brazilian National Council of Scientific and Technological Research (CNPq) to cooperate principally in Biotechnology, Ocean Science & Technology, Building Materials and Technologies and Metrology.

During the military regime Brazil developed secret contacts with South Africa around nuclear cooperation.[1] In more recent years the "Brasilia Declaration identified Science and Technology as one of the key areas for greater trilateral interaction and cooperation, their implementation to be shepherded by the Science and Technology Ministers of India, Brazil and

---

1   <http://www.wilsoncenter.org/publication/brazil-south-africa-nuclear-relations>. Accessed on 3/5/14.

South Africa [IBSA] through annual meetings aimed at establishing the modalities of collaboration, identifying priority areas and flagship".[2]

There exists a research agenda that could be taken up by the sociology of science and that involve the reconstruction of the history of the agreements between our countries, to compare them to those made with developed countries, to evaluate their success, and also the conflicts that have emerged in such cooperation. Given that scientific activity is not dominated, in theory, by commercial interests, the study of barriers to communication among natural scientists who engage in cooperation are of special interest for learning about the conditions and circumstances under which relations of trust are built. Such research, which is in the line of the "sociology of the BRICS", should contribute to future generations, in science, business and government, because it helps people learn from the successes, mistakes and limits of the past.

However, we all understand that science is a field governed by power relations. When we step back and examine the agenda of scientific cooperation between the BRICS countries we find that there has been very little explicit official support in Brazil for research into topics identified with the social sciences. Given that globalisation is also a cultural process, where scientific and technological developments are intertwined with culture, values and social change, this appears to be an extraordinary silence.

SOCIOLOGY AND THE BRICS

As a sociologist, I see two types of BRICS sociology: "sociology of the BRICS" and "sociology in the BRICS". The former studies the interactions between actors in these countries as they make the BRICS a reality: through commerce, supra-national relations and cultural exchange. From a Brazilian viewpoint the intensity of such interactions

---

2   <http://www.nrf.ac.za/projects.php?filter_risa=13>. Accessed on 3/5/14.

have increased markedly over the last two decades, although uneven, they are subject to both conflict and concord, today they constitute an emerging field of academic research. The latter demands initially that we learn from each other about common social processes, and in this way we construct dialogue with fellow social scientists around common and uncommon points in development paths of the BRICS countries. The idea is to permit sociologists (and others) to establish insight into each other's processes of historical development and social change. This process will lead to the identification of common concerns and agendas among sociologists in the BRICS countries, and this is my wager, will contribute to changing the international face of the discipline. We can envisage long-term consequences for: (1) teaching curriculum, (2) scientific publication, (3) social theory and (4) scientific exchanges and research. As in this book texts from each BRICS country will be published to illustrate how social processes, many of which are today treated predominantly with reference to the industrialised or neighbouring countries, have been researched in five countries.

I shall illustrate with an example that may seem obvious, I sometimes hear young Brazilian sociology students complaining about how low industrial wages received by Indian and Chinese workers are a factor that gives firms in those countries unfair competitive advantages. When I ask them to describe how Brazil developed, they frequently ignore that criticisms that are similar to those they make of our BRICS partners were made about the process of Brazilian development in the industrialised countries. This is just a small example of how a modified teaching curriculum, which moves away from a perspective grounded in the developed countries can contribute to increasing understanding between BRICS partners and among university students.

Also, the translation of important texts from one BRICS language to another should help foster a scientific awareness of the social processes involved in the rapid changes occurring in our countries. Questions that are specific to the BRIC countries (without the "S") for example the twin dimensions of very large populations and open spaces and their contribution to the structuring state power appear as a subject that is unlikely to be of interest to so-called "international sociology". But it is not enough to translate important texts and to change the teaching curriculum, it is also necessary to produce new knowledge!

In the field of international academic sociology the long-term impact of and recognition of a BRICS sociology will depend on its theoretical ambitions. As we get to know each other's work better, to understand each other's countries better, emergent agendas should permit the production of knowledge with new theoretical ambitions.

To produce new knowledge, and to make scientific exchanges meaningful it is necessary to have financing. Up until now, as we saw earlier, most official funding has flowed into the natural sciences and to technology. Social scientists must find the arguments to convince the makers of scientific policy that the success of the development of the BRICS as an emerging force in the world power structures depends on building a capacity to establish a way of living together that avoids destructive conflicts. This appears to be a precondition for healthy commercial relations, international cooperation and even for successful cooperative research.

In the longer term one consequence of the development of BRICS social sciences will be on the development of expertise: it will be necessary to form a new generation of bi and multi-lingual researchers, of translators and interpreters specialised in the social sciences and the native languages of the BRICS countries. Also we shall need to form students who are capable of assembling the jig-saw puzzle of a BRICS social sciences-in-construction and, on this basis, to build theory.

Such an intellectual challenge forces sociologists, wherever they may be, and also other social scientists, to think about the moving terrain of their disciplines. It is my belief that national sociological associations (I am not qualified to talk for other disciplines) have a role to play in organising agendas of comparative research projects and meaningful scientific exchange. Especially in the building of agendas capable of confronting the complex intellectual challenges that the emergence of the BRICS poses.

CONCRETE STEPS IN DEVELOPING A SOCIOLOGY
IN AND OF THE BRICS

Exchanges between social scientists in our countries have been extremely limited up until quite recently. In 2005 the Brazilian Sociological Society (SBS) invited an Indian keynote speaker to its bi-annual conference in Belo Horizonte. (PATEL, 2006) In its 2007 conference in Recife, SBS sponsored a round table discussion on the BRICS, with invited representatives from Brazil, Russia, China and South Africa. An interesting exchange was held around basic diachronic and synchronic data about each country, emphasising both qualitative and quantitative dimensions and employing sociological, political science and demographic concepts to transmit basic information necessary in order to begin useful comparisons. One of the presentations drew attention to increasing contacts between the five countries, and suggested the interactions between the BRICS would be a fertile ground for study. This discussion not only provoked the public to think about Brazil in terms of new reference points, but also suggested new objects of study.

In 2009 Chinese Sociological Society's president, Li Peilin, made a presentation at the SBS conference in Rio de Janeiro (LI and LI, 2011), he also visited the IBGE and IPEA and convinced himself that Brazil-China comparative research could prove a fertile ground upon which to develop a new approach in sociology. The following year, as director of the Institute of Sociology of the Chinese Academy of Social Sciences (CASS), he reserved some of the resources allocated to finance the celebrations of his Institute's 40th anniversary and the commemorations of Fei Xiatong's 100th birthday, to organize a round table discussion which brought together presidents and ex-presidents of sociological associations from the BRIC countries. The Institute of Sociology's intention was to discover if there was any sense to building closer academic relations with India and Brazil, to complement those that were already developing between Russia and China.

At this CASS meeting I presented a paper from which I shall now draw upon. It pointed out four directions for social science research: (1) the mapping, documentation and theoretical analysis of conflicts that between the BRIC countries and their citizens, (2) the production of comparative analysis of our diverse development processes, (3) the changing values, perspectives, horizons of youth and also their views of other BRIC countries, and their capacity to absorb signs and cultural output from these countries and (4) to rewrite history. In Pointing out this last suggestion I cited Gilberto Freyre's (2003) "Tropical China," José Roberto Teixeira Leite's (1999) "China in Brazil" and Amaral Lapa's (1968) "Bahia and the Route of the Indias" as pioneering examples of works that permit a rethinking of Brazil's historical ties with its BRIC partners.

SOCIAL STRATIFICATION IN THE BRIC COUNTRIES

In 2010 an Integrative Session on Sociology in the BRIC countries, proposed by the sociological associations of each country, was held at the International Sociological Association's (ISA) World Sociological Congress in Gothenburg, Sweden. From this and the Beijing meeting held earlier in the year, an agenda developed around the second point made above. Just over a year later, in October of 2011, the first fruit ripened, a book on social stratification in the BRIC countries was launched under the title of "Jin Zhuan Guo Jia She Hui Fen Ceng: Bian Qian Yu Bi Jiao". A Forum was held at CASS to discuss its contents and to develop further plans. Celi Scalon, the editor of the Brazilian contributions, led a six member delegation, a Russian delegation of a similar size was also present.

This book consisted of a comparative study of social stratification in the BRIC countries – the general editor Li Peilin introduced the book: "I firmly believe this book would have significant influence after its publication. That's why I have devoted my enormous time and energy organizing this book. The influence not only results from the contents of the papers, but more from the impact of the rise of BRIC countries on the future global economic and political regime [...] analysing social structural changes, especially changes in the social stratification structures of the BRIC countries, is a special sociological perspective in the study and analysis of social issues.

This unique sociological perspective is necessary to help us achieve a better understanding of the economic growth and social development of the emerging economic powers. This very special perspective would also help us unveil the mystery that how these emerging powers with such dramatic differences in history, geography, culture, language, religion, etc., could in some instances share a common will and taken joint actions. In any event, it is the profound social structural changes in these countries that determine their own future and, to a large extent, will shape the socio-economic landscape of the future world" (LI, et al., 2013: xiii; xxiv-xxv).

In 2013 World Scientific Publishing Co. in Singapore published the volume in English under the title "Handbook of Social Stratification in the BRIC Countries". (LI, et al., 2013) This initiative was "self-managed", a representative of the sociological association of each of the four BRIC countries organised the contribution of specialist authors, very limited external funding was sought and no international research contract was signed. It was at the 2011 Beijing launching of this book that it was agreed to advance on the same lines with a second project which corresponded to the third suggestion made in 2010: "sociology of youth in the BRIC countries.". I shall return to this project later in this chapter, but before doing so I must mention one initiative that involved three of the BRICS countries and counted on government funding.

SOCIAL SCIENCE COOPERATION WITHIN THE IBSA FRAMEWORK

In 2008 the CNPq launched a call for research proposals that involved Brazil, India and South Africa,[3] the IBSA group. While more limited than any BRICS related initiative, because it involved only democratic countries, one project examined key questions related to democratic governance. It

---

3   See: <http://www.mct.gov.br/index.php/content/view/74666.html#vazio>. Accessed on May 3, 2014.

was observed that in all IBSA countries "the cases in which citizens raise legitimate yet contentious demand through protests and other forms of contestations are highly likely to meet state resistance. However, from the citizen's viewpoint, action is important, and despite the potential lack of state response, contributes to the sense of agency and empowerment that is crucial for democracy. Not letting the state off the hook [...] is in itself an empowering expression of citizenship and political identity" (MOHANTY, THOMPSON and COELHO, 2011: 3). I attended a seminar in February of 2011 that wound up the project "State Society Relations in India, Brazil and South Africa – IBSA",[4] and was quite struck by the difficulties of communication. While the legacy of British colonialism made for some isomorphism in administrative structures in South Africa and India, there was far less correspondence with Brazilian structures. This implied a higher degree of immediate mutual understanding between South African and Indian social scientists than was possible with their Brazilian counterparts. A second difficulty was linguistic, understandably Brazilian colleagues had much more difficulty in expressing themselves in the language of the seminar – English – than did their South African and Indian counterparts, so natural difficulties associated with understanding a different society and its conceptual terms were aggravated by considerable confusion around the precise meanings of words and pronunciation. A further point called my attention, what to my mind was destined to have been a direct dialogue between three nations, was intermediated by the Institute of Development Studies at the University of Sussex, England. This carried the risk of establishing British hegemony over dialogue. However, in spite of these reservations, what I was witnessing seemed to be the beginning of a process capable of leading to further cooperation. I am convinced that this has to take place directly between social scientists who work in the nations involved, and that in situations where only two languages are involved, translation

4 <http://www.cebrap.org.br/v2/news/view/39>. Accessed on 3/5/14.

appears to be more appropriate to guarantee a high level of inter-cultural dialogue than does the insistence of using English as a *lingua franca*.

SOCIOLOGY OF YOUTH IN THE BRICS COUNTRIES

The four BRIC countries together account for nearly one half of the world's youth population. In 2012 the ISA organised the World Sociological Forum in Buenos Aires, it was there that a round table discussion was held on this new book project. Given that South Africa had recently been incorporated as a member of the political BRICS, a representative of the South African Sociological Association was invited to participate. The method for developing this new project was simple, authors from each country would write about eight common issues. Writers would be recognised specialists in their own country and, as such, also familiar with international discussions on the issues under discussion, however, we assumed that most would be unfamiliar with the material from other BRICS countries. The aim of the book would be to raise the level of mutual comprehension about both sociology and youth in each of the countries. In a happy coincidence, a little before the Buenos Aires meeting, the Delhi declaration was launched at the BRICS' leaders annual meeting, and "youth policy dialogue" was elected as a new priority area for exchange.

A first draft of the book, involving on the four BRIC countries, was finished in September 2013, and discussed at a meeting financed by FAPESP at Unicamp, and subsequently at the Brazilian Sociology Conference in Salvador. The second draft of the book is currently undergoing revision before being submitted for publication.

The organisers of both volumes are united in seeing sociology as one of the few disciplines that permits the examination of processes of globalisation in their diverse dimensions: commercial, cultural and supra-national. They also understood that, through dialogue, new understandings can be developed and new theoretical categories and innovative analyses about youth in our countries which can potentially enrich the sociology of youth. This latter point was explicitly recognised by ISA's Research Committee 34 (Sociology of Youth), which has attributed a presidential session to the discussion of youth in the BRICS at the 2014 World Sociology Conference in Yokohama. Some suggestions about the future of youth research in our five countries will be raised on this occasion, and also cooperation in the production of materials for the educational system.

SOCIOLOGY OF THE BRICS

In my own view we are engaged in scientific dialogue – which requires a certain degree of elaboration and understanding, as we do this we examine the words of others and try to build a relation together – this process is worthy of analysis in itself, it is a component in making the BRICS. In my own work on developing a sociology of the BRICS a key focus is always the question of communication. My perception is based on three sources: (1) constant visits to China, conducting research with Chinese colleagues and the reception of Chinese delegations particularly at my university, (2) Participation in international dialogues under ISA sponsorship and also participation in BRICS-related initiatives in sociology conferences in Brazil, India and Russia, (3) the observation of administrative fiascos, where the desire to build the BRICS goes beyond the capacity to transmit basic information and to deliver on promises.

On this last point, by far the most embarrassing of these that I have personally witnessed was promoted in São Paulo in 2012 by the Minister of Education.[5] Some 400 people gathered in the *Parlatino* of the Latin American Memorial, among them were some 200 representatives of about forty

---

5 <http://portal.mec.gov.br/index.php?option=com_content&view=article&id=18245:bras il-e-china-intensificam-relacao-na-area-educacional-&catid=221>. Accessed on 3/5/14.

Chinese universities, invited to participate in an educational fair where they would be able to recruit up to 5,000 Brazilian students in the programme "science without borders". The opening session was full of officials and discourses about the importance of relations between our peoples. Minister Mercadante affirmed that education was the principal bridge of diplomacy, and emphasised the need to consolidate the historic partnership between the two countries. "Academic and cultural exchange between students is fundamental, with people going from here and coming from there, in a manner that is as strategic as the partnerships that we maintain with the Chinese in the fields of nanotechnology, agriculture and innovation". On this same day I walked around the educational exhibits, there was not one single Brazilian student! The next morning one of our research assistants from Unicamp made a similar observation. The Chinese educators who had flown a half way around the world to meet potential new students were unable to understand, and eager for explanations. Today, only 193 Brazilian students have been granted scholarships by the sciences without borders programme to study in China.[6]

All of those who involve themselves seriously with the question of the BRICS are conscious of the tremendous difficulties that lie ahead. We are at the precipice of a cultural disaster on a world scale, the "shock of civilizations" looks like it could extend to all parts of the world. Starting with fast developing trade, political and scientific relationships between Brazil and China we can see the necessity for mutual understanding especially when faced with the numerous potential conflicts that emerge. We simply know far too little about each other. Past efforts to cooperate have made for research terrains where the observation of interactions, both past and present, can serve as material for sociological reflection. If the BRICS are

6 <http://www.cienciasemfronteiras.gov.br/web/csf/bolsistas-pelo-mundo?p_p_id=mapabolsistasportlet_ WAR_mapabolsistasportlet_INSTANCE_Y7eO&p_p_lifecycle=0&p_p_state=normal&p_p_ mode=view&p_p_col_id=column-2&p_p_col_count=1&siglaPais=&nomePais=&codigoAr ea=&tituloArea=Todas&siglaModalidade=&nomeModalidade=Todas>. Accessed on 3/5/14. Of a total of 50,175 scholarships awarded, there were only: 12 Brazilian students in South Africa, 4 in Russia and 5 in India!

to establish themselves as a force on the world stage, this requires dialogue and mutual understanding.

Comprehension and dialogue are of course made far more difficult when one examines concrete preventable disasters, such as that promoted by Brazil's Minister of Education. Had Minister Mercadante been more cautious and less braggart he would have made a far more constructive contribution to student exchange and to building BRICS dialogue.

CONCLUDING NOTE

On the 18th and 19th of March 2014 the Sixth Academic Forum of the BRICS countries was held in Rio de Janeiro. Organized by IPEA it brought together nominees of each government to discuss a variety of issues in an effort to produce greater mutual understanding. Of particular relevance for theoreticians of development was the sharing of the idea that the adhesion to certain "universal standards" laid down by multi-lateral organisations, under the leadership of the industrialised countries, needs to be reviewed.

Even though a number of questions dealt with in the forum are normally considered as a part of the domains where sociology, political science and anthropology have expertise, the specialist participants in the ten sessions came principally from two disciplines: economics and international relations.

Brazilian social scientists frequently find it difficult to listen to some of their Russian and Chinese colleagues, they object to their "official technocratic discourses". What impressed at this meeting was the officialism of a number of the Brazilian presentations, many time-series began in 2003 as though nothing occurring before this year was seen as worthy of mention. For example, to produce a comparative understanding of urbanisation processes in Brazil that is relevant to China and India it is necessary to at least go back to the period when Brazil was a predominantly rural country. The Russian and Chinese men of system who were present at the forum (and both countries also sent scientists) may well have asked themselves if some of their Brazilian colleagues had adhered to a Soviet model in order to facilitate inter-cultural dialogue! Should these forums, held prior to the annual meetings of the BRICS heads of state, continue to be organised in this way they risk of producing not comprehension but incomprehension, and of weakening the potential benefits of autonomous academic dialogue.

It is in this context that it is necessary to reassert the importance to ANPOCS' initiative, and to justify scientific dialogue and research as a value as we seek to promote understanding between peoples.

REFERENCES

FEI, X. (1992), *From the Soil: The foundations of Chinese Society*, Berkeley, Los Angeles, University of California Press.

FREYRE, G. (2003), *China Tropical*, São Paulo/Brasília, Imprensa Oficial do Estado/ Editora da Universidade de Brasília.

LAPA, J. R. do A. (1968), *A Bahia e a Carreira da Índia*, São Paulo, Edusp/Companhia Editora Nacional.

LEITE, J. R. T. (1999), *A China no Brasil: Influências, marcas, ecos e sobrevivências chinesas na sociedade e na arte brasileiras*. Campinas, Editora da Unicamp.

LI, P., LI, W. (2011), "O status econômico e as atitudes sociais dos trabalhadores migrantes na China" *in* T. Dwyer, et al. (orgs.), *Consensos e Controvérsias. Sociedade Brasileira de Sociologia e Tomo Editorial*, Porto Alegre, p. 31-49.

LI, P., SCALON, C., GORSHKOV, M. K. E., SHARMA, K., et al. (orgs.). (2011), Jin Zhuan Guo Jia She Hui Fen Ceng: Bian Qian Yu Bi Jiao, Chinese Academy of Social Sciences, Beijing.

LI, P., SCALON, C., GORSHKOV, M. K., SHARMA, K. (orgs.). (2013), *Handbook of Social Stratification in the BRICs countries*, Singapore, World Scientific Publishing.

MOHANTY, R., THOMPSON, L., COELHO, V. S. (2011), *Mobilising the State? Social Mobilisation and State Interaction in India, Brazil and South Africa*, Brighton, Working Paper n. 359, University of Sussex, Institute of Development Studies.

PATEL, S. (2006), "Para além de um pensamento binário: Questões para uma Sociologia auto-reflexiva" *in* M. S. G. Porto & T. Dwyer, *Sociologia e Realidade: Pesquisa social no Século XXI*, Brasília, Editora da UnB. p. 37-50.

Development, social justice and empowerment in contemporary India

A sociological perspective

....

ticized
Abstract   Since Independence in 1947, the questions of social justice and empowerment have been haunting Indian society and the State, as development remains a lopsided process. India has been struggling to overcome its problems of poverty, unemployment and poor quality of education. Development comes neither from above nor from below. It has not brought about equitable capacity-building among the deprived sections of the society. The rich and those who hold positions of power and authority corner the fruits of India's democracy and development. Such a situation makes governance weak and plasticised. Inequality has increased, with new dimensions and parameters. The socio-economic dynamics of India do not mean egalitarianism and distributive justice. Indian political democracy has survived because of a small number of its alert and conscientious citizens.

Keywords   Capital, Caste/Casteism, Colonialism, Development, Distributive justice, empowerment, equality/Inequality, Feudalism, Freedom, Gendering, globalization, governance, Idea of India, liberalization, Social Justice/just society.

※ ※ ※

India's past before her Independence in 1947 was characterized by colonialism, feudalism and caste-based inequality. Such was the compound of these three elements that social justice was practically unheard of. Colonial rulers and feudal lords denied justice as they manipulated legal enactments and decisions in their own interests. The caste system extended a helping hand to these two institutions, namely, colonialism and feudalism.

Independence was a blow to colonial and feudal forces. However, B. R. Ambedkar felt that as a result of Independence the position of his own people had not altered much. He wrote: "the same old tyranny, the same old oppression, the same old discrimination which existed before, exists now and perhaps in a worse form" (AMBEDKAR, 1995: 1318-1322, quoted from PERRY ANDERSON, 2013: 138). It was too early to say just after less than a decade from India's Independence. Today, after sixty six years of India's liberation, the weaker sections have come a long way in seeking social justice. However, the questions of social justice and empowerment vis-à-vis the development remain there with new dialectics and dimensions.

Development can be viewed in terms of two perspectives: (1) the official view, and, (2) the social science view. As per the official view, development aims at target-oriented achievements through state-sponsored programmes, planning and economic growth. The State can, however, also allow the private sector to participate in the projects of economic development. In general, the nation as a whole gets benefited from development programmes, but it helps particularly the weaker sections, women, children, and both rural and urban poor. The main aim remains an attack on poverty, unemployment and illiteracy. The social science view focuses on the ethos and spirit of development in terms of its nature and direction as (1) socialist, (2) capitalist and (3) as an amalgamation of both. However, the two views are in no way unrelated as both refer to the same sections of society.

Abolition of feudal/colonial land-tenure systems, introduction of green revolution, nationalization of banks, facility for loans and subsidies and access to market, adult franchise, social reforms, rights to information, education, food, etc., social legislations, empowerment of weaker sections and women are examples of macro-structural development. Institutions to effect such structural changes have been created.

Gunnar Myrdal (1968, vol. 1) has pinpointed specific bottlenecks in the "modernization" of India. However, some scholars (SINGER, 1972; KOTHARI, 1970) are of the view that caste, religion and joint family have not been obstructive in development and social change. Recently, Amartya Sen (2000) has put forward the view that development is freedom, and the latter is "social". And "social" means social opportunity. Freedom implies "choice" for individuals to make available more than one opportunity. Sen refers to a deep complementarity between individual agency and social arrangements, and the latter include opportunities. For Sen, "social" implies "economic" and "political". Freedom is achievement, and unfreedom is inequality. In this way, "market" is social. The unfreedoms are multiple in terms of restrictions on access to opportunities based on caste, religion, social background, language, region, marginality, etc. Social structures generate mental structures as P. Bourdieu (1988) talks in the context of the elitist and hierarchical system of education in France.

Casteism, gendering and marginality pervade even today despite reforms, legislation, and movements. 'Female reason' and 'gender regimes' in regard to family, work, and state (CONNELL, 2002) obstruct empowerment or the equitable distribution/sharing of resources. Alienation and deprivation are writ large in everyday life. Bourdieu (1996) refers to such a situation of people being at the top and at the bottom as the Grand Pole and the Small Pole. Nobility is created and reproduced. This is happening in India too, through caste, class and education.

In a normal situation, economic development and social opportunity are interlinked, but this is not happening in India. Today, it is a well accepted view that economic growth is not being transformed into distributive justice/shares. Even in the late 1950s, it was pointed out that India had "dangerous decades ahead" (HARRISON, 1959). Later on, due to distortions in the functioning of Indian democracy, emanating "discontent" was highlighted. Ramchandra Guha (2007) talks of **Four**

Rs, namely, Rights, Riots, Rulers and Riches as the perpetual entities in post-independent India at the helm of affairs in economic, political and social spheres. One needs to know the nature, functioning and dialectics of these four components of India's post-independence formation. With some anguish, Dipankar Gupta (2009) considers India like a "caged phoenix", incapable of flying because of the strings/barricading created by the entrenched sections of the people.

India of today is suffering from "crisis of governability", and its roots are in the emergence of a new power elite, economic dominants and cultural overlords. A major portion of the fruits of development is cornered by a small minority of the new elite. Along with the top-ranking elite, the new middle class is also not far behind in sharing the spoils. Liberalisation and globalization have created software hubs at some places, and there one could see the modern age of a new tribe of engineers and managers, who are basically service-providers working for the multinational companies.

Sociologically speaking, "social governance" is under the control of select individuals, families and communities. This is so because of the systems of inheritance, family, caste and religion. We can also say that it is a sort of cultural dilemma of governance. Another point is also equally worth consideration, namely, the emergence of "demand groups" (RUDOLPH and RUDHOLPH, 1987). Rich peasants, urban youth, students, government functionaries and entrepreneurs have been demanding a lion's share in the state's resources.

❋ ❋ ❋

No development can be justified without "justice". In the absence of justice, questions about development come up, such as: What is development? Whose development? Who has planned/thought of a particular direction of development?

Justice has three main dimensions: (1) philosophy, ideology and society, (2) truth (theory and knowledge) and (3) practice and realization. Based on these dimensions one can see: What is a "just society"? Justice is the first function of institutions (RAWLS, 1999; SEN, 2009). Justice demands sacrifice. It is natural and not a matter of political bargaining. However, in India, "justice" has generally been gained through bargaining by pressure groups, political parties, ethnic groups, castes and their associations, religious and regional groups.

Justice guaranteed by the Constitution of India and legal enactments is also largely an outcome of socio-cultural and political movements before India's independence and in the succeeding decades after independence. To ensure a "just society", India has to make still a long march. Injustice is tolerated in India, fearing greater injustice. Justice is not absolute, it is seen as "fairness", against utilitarianism in real life.

The question is: How to pursue equality in the land of hierarchy? Can justice be done in a caste-ridden society? How to ensure ownership and control of resources to the actual claimants? Marc Galanter (1984) and Bina Agarwal (1998) have raised some of these questions with regard to the backward sections and women in Indian society respectively. Where are the institutions that can ensure a "just society" or a "desired type of society"? A public sense of justice can create civic friendship. However, there are also certain particularistic practices of social justice.

A couple of political parties have been advocating seeking benefits for certain castes and communities, who are their strong vote-banks. Socially speaking, opportunities and jobs for all, keeping in view the social needs of all, should be made available with a certain degree of social choice. However, on the contrary, gendering of opportunities and social choice persists, and child labour is also a rampant practice. A "just" or "good" society enshrines citizenship with rights and dignity. It grants enough space to "civil society". Culturally, there is no space for alienation, marginalization and social impediments in a just society.

✳ ✳ ✳

"Empowerment" is not a fixed phenomenon; it is an ongoing concern. At any point of time, empowerment keeps "man" and "culture" in the forefront. "Modernity" and "enlightenment" have created considerable space for both man and culture. Going by P. Bourdieu's viewpoint (1991), a society can be characterized by distribution of different kinds of resources of "capital". The positions and their interrelations are determined by access to and control of the "capital", which includes "economic capital", "cultural capital", and "symbolic capital". People in India do not have equal access and opportunities to resources of the society as they do not have resources to build capacities to compete with the privileged ones. Such a situation is indicative of incoherence between the proclaimed goals of the State and actual policies. There is also inconsistency between the stated goals and resource allocation.

Confusion between ends and means is generally there in regard to education and healthcare. Drop-outs in schools by the children of the poor families and inaccessibility to healthcare facilities are glaring examples of the underpowered people. They remain deprived of their legitimate shares in the resources and opportunities of the society. A large segment of the people suffers from socio-cultural alienation in spite of their participation in the political process (elections). A person may be a "voter", but not necessarily a citizen, in a true sense of the term. A person without any say in the affairs of his/her society is not an empowered one; hence he/she is less than a citizen. A person may also be a marginal one, if he/she is denied an opportunity. Alienation of people from socio-cultural activities and political processes is a clear yardstick of the lack of empowerment. Exclusion of women, weaker sections, and the poor from decision-making persists despite the official proclamations for equality and a just society. The questions are:

Who represents?

Who are represented?
Who are deprived?
Who are alienated?
Who are benefited?
Who are included/excluded?

Today, categories such as rich/poor, weak/strong, powerful/powerless, resourceful/resourceless, etc., have become pronounced weakening the conventional categories of caste, ethnicity, religion and language. This does not imply, however, that the conventional categories have become redundant and outmoded. The Scheduled Castes, the Scheduled Tribes and the Other Backward Classes have experienced a rise through the provisions for them to provide education, jobs and opportunity to contest elections at different levels. The rise of these sections has weakened the caste rigidities. Despite this, poverty or social disadvantage haunts the SCs, the STs and the OBCs to a considerable extent. A large number of landless workers are still there without substantial and enduring benefits from the official plans and programmes.

Gross Domestic Production (GDP) was quite high in the last decade with an average of 7.7%. Today, it is less than 5%. Per capita income in India is about a quarter of that in China, and inequality is also much higher. In India, just 66 resident billionaires control assets worth more than a fifth of the country's GDP (ANDERSON, 2013: 162-163). Capital is three times more concentrated than in the United States. Poverty has slightly declined, but in 2005 its average income was just $ 1.25 a day. Infant mortality, under-nourishment and ill-health continue to be there on a large scale. Two-thirds of all government subsidies for food, fuel, and electricity are taken away by rich farmers. Education and health are now largely in the private sector, depriving the quality in education and healthcare to the poor. The schemes like Mahatma Gandhi National Rural Employment Guarantee Act (MNREGA), Food Security, Pension for the old, etc., have given some relief to the poor.

❊ ❊ ❊

The "Idea of India" has been made out as a romantic image in terms of unity in diversity. But we can't ignore the ground reality of social inequality, gendered social relations, misery, poverty, unemployment, and a grand divide between village and city, rich and poor, strong and weak, elite and masses, etc. The "Idea of India" needs to be a comprehensive and representative of India's culture, economy, politics and people.

Indian pluralities of caste, class, ethnicity, language, religion, region, etc., have interrupted even distribution of the fruits of economic growth and development. Arvind Das (1994) observes that the very identity of India is becoming indistinct. Das (ibid. 7-44) discusses at length based on certain economic and socio-political happenings in post-independence period that India has been "invented, uninvented and reinvented". Now the question is: What is India today? There is a lack of unanimity on the answer to this question. Patrick French (2011: IX-XII) observes: "Nearly everyone has a reaction to India, even if they (foreigners) have never been there. They hate it or love it, think it mystical or profane; find it extravagant or ascetic; consider the food the best or the worst in the world". French focuses on three aspects to know India as an entity, namely, **Rashtra** or nation, **Lakshmi** or wealth, **Samaj** or society.

Construction of the "Idea of India" has been a popular theme in recent years, particularly based on the post-independence developments. Shashi Tharoor's **India: From Midnight To The Millennium** (2000), **Re-Imagining India and Other Essays** (Orient Blackswan, 2010), **A Possible India: Critical Essays in Political Criticism** (CHATTERJEE, 1998), **India: A Sacred Geography** (ECK, 2012), **Understanding Contemporary India: Critical Perspectives** (edited by VANAIK and BHARGAVA, 2010), Meghnad Desai's **The Rediscovery of India** (2009), **Imagining India: Ideas For The New Century** (NILEKANI, 2008), **Becoming Indian** (VARMA, 2010), **The Other India: Realities of an Emerging Power** (edited by CHAKRABARTY, 2009), **Handbook on Social Stratification In the BRIC Countries: Change and Perspective** (co-authored by LI PEILIN, GORSHKOU, SCALON and SHARMA, 2013), etc., are well-known writings. A couple of points from these titles clearly emerge regarding haziness in the conceptualization of India both as an idea and as a reality.

Diana L. ECK believes that both mythology and topography provide for people and cultures the "maps" of the world based on her study of Benaras. She says that "imagined landscape" is not to speak of something fanciful, as it is the most powerful landscape in which we live (op. cit., 39). A considerably different view is taken by Patrick French (op. cit., xii) as he observes: "With its overlap of extreme wealth and lavish poverty, its mix of the educated and the ignorant, its competing ideologies, its lack of uniformity, its kindness and profound cruelty, its complex relationships with religion, its parallel realities and the rapid speed of social change – India is a microcosm, and may be the world's default setting for the future". Ashis Nandi in his **foreword** to **Re-Imagining India** (op. cit.) considers culture, religion, economy, democracy, harmony, political flexibility, and globalization as parameters for defining Indianness. A similar view is given by Shashi Tharoor (op. cit., p. 5) as he writes: "I will argue that the only possible idea of India is that of a nation greater than the sum of its parts. An India that denies itself to some Indians could end up being denied to all Indians".

Pavan K. Varma's says that asymmetry and cooptation characterize the unfinished revolution of culture and identity (op. cit.). Varma writes: "Inequalities thrive in the field of culture because dominant cultures consider their domination normal, even morally good and uplifting, and have the means to project this image globally. Those at the receiving end are either positively co-opted or are ill-equipped to provide rejoinder. In this unequal transaction, the past and the present merge" (op. cit., p. 228). Inequality is not noticed, may be by a conscious design. The problem arises when equality is denied by the well-entrenched people to the new aspirants to those positions and statuses that have remained a sort of monopoly of selected few.

Nandan Nilekani (op. cit., p. 8) writes: "India in particular, for all its complexity is a country that is as much an idea as it is a nation". As a nation India can look for new strategies for equality and equal opportunities for those who have remained deprived and on sidelines. This takes us to Meghnad Desai (2009: 443-465), who says: "Whose India? Which India?". Desai's view is that the Indian success story (in the recent past) had been getting more and more hyped up. Eye-catching slogans were attributed to the short-lived economic growth and "globalization". India must not be defined by the "other", that is, by alien powers. India needs "a new start" every time. After Nehru, there was a new start, after Indira Gandhi, after the Janta Party, after Rajiv Gandhi, and now after Man Mohan Singh, we can earmark turning points in post-independent India. No other power, such as the US, should be a mirror for India. An Indian needs to be an individual citizen.

K. L. Sharma (2013: 37-57) has raised the following questions about contemporary India:

1. How are men and women shaped and reshaped in terms of socio-cultural, economic, and political considerations?
2. What criteria determine status?
3. How the criteria of shaping individuals, families, and groups undergo change?
4. How it has been possible for some people to have more income, better standard of living and access to higher jobs and positions?

Socio-economic contours of India do not fall in a progressive development pattern. Unevenness persists, distributive shares are unequal. Empowerment is also not uniform. Indian democracy has survived largely as a political phenomenon. Incongruence between political democracy, economic equality and social justice has become a stark reality of India. There is a sort of deadlock. Hopefully, it would end in the future. A semblance between democracy, equality and empowerment remains a dream only at this juncture.

REFERENCES

AGARWAL, B. (1998), *A Field of One's Own: Gender and Land Rights in South Asia*, Cambridge, University Press.

AMBEDKAR, B. R. (1995), "Writings and Speeches", vol. 14, Part Two, Bombay, p. 1318-1322, *in* P. Anderson, *The Indian Ideology*. 2012, Gurgaon, Three Essays, Collective, p. 138.

ANDERSON, P. (2012), op. cit.

BOURDIEU, P. (1988), *Homo Academicvs*, Cambridge, Polity Press.

_____. (1991), *Language and Symbolic Power*, Cambridge, Polity Press.

_____. (1996), *Distinction: A Social Critique of the Judgment of Taste*, London, Routledge and Kegan Paul.

CHAKRABARTI, R. (2009), *The Other India: Realities of an Emerging Power*, New Delhi, Sage Publications.

CHATTERJEE, P. (1998), *A Possible India: Essays in Political Criticism*, Delhi, Oxford University Press.

CONNELL, R. W. (2002), "Gender Regimes and the Gender Order", in *The Polity Reader in Gender Studies*, Cambridge, Polity Press.

DAS, A. (1994), *India Invented: A Nation in the Making*, New Delhi, Manohar.

DESAI, M. (2009), *The Re-discovery of India*, London, Allen Lane/Penguine Books.

ECK, D. L. (2012), *India: A Sacred Geography*, New York, Harmony Books.

FRENCH, P. *India: An Intimate Biography of 1.2 Billion People*, New Delhi, Allen Lane/ Penguine Books.

GALANTER, M. (1984), *Competing Equalities*, Delhi, Oxford University Press.

GUHA, R. (2007), *India After Gandhi: The History of the World's Largest Democracy*, London, Picador.

GUPTA, D. (2009), *The Caged Phoenix: Can India Fly*, New Delhi, Panguine/Viking.

HARRISON, S. S. (1960), *India: The Most Dangerous Decades*, Princeton, Princeton University Press.

KOTHARI, R. (1970), *Politics in India*, New Delhi, Orient Longman.

MYRDAL, G. (1968), *Asian Drama: An Inquiry into Poverty of Nations*, vols. 1, 2, Penguin Books.

NANDY, A. (2011), "The Past of All Possible Futures: A Foreword", in *Re-Imagining India and Other Essays*, New Delhi, Orient Blackswan.

NILEKANI, N. (2008), *Imagining India: Ideas for the New Century*, New Delhi, Penguine/ Allen Lane.

RAWLS, J. (1999), *A Theory of Justice* (revised edition), New York, Oxford University Press.

RUDOLPH, L. I., RUDOLPH, S. H. (1987), in *Pursuit of Lakshmi: The Political Economy of the Indian State*, New Delhi, Orient Longman.

SEN, A. (2000), *Development as Freedom*, New Delhi, Oxford University Press.

_____. (2009), *The Idea of Justice*, London, Allen Lane/Penguine Books.

SHARMA, K. L. (2013), *Handbook on Social Stratification in the BRIC Countries: Change and Perspective* (with Li Peilin, M. K. Gorshkov & Celi Scalon), Singapore, World Scientific.

SINGER, M. (1972), *When a Great Tradition Modernizes: An Anthropological Approach to Indian Civilization*, Praeger Publishers.

THAROOR, S. (2000), *India: From Midnight To Millennium*, New Delhi, Penguine Books.

VANAIK, A., BHARGAVA, R. (2010), *Understanding Contemporary India: Critical Essays*, New Delhi, Blackswan.

VARMA, P. K. (2012), *Becoming Indian: The Unfinished Revolution of Culture and Identity*, New Delhi, Penguine Books.

India's public policy

Issues and challenges & BRICS

....

P. S. Vivek

Abstract   India aimed at the socialist pattern of development since its independence in 1947. Emphasizing on uniform development and sustainable growth all over India and eliminating disparities in income to ensure equality of opportunity for all, Jawaharlal Nehru, the first Prime Minister of India enunciated the objectives of the public policy in India. He declared large dams and power plants to be the *temples of Modern India*, and treated them as *monuments to a nationalistic vision of modernization and growth*. Since its independence, India went on to build over 3000 dams which it believed would improve quality of life by providing drinking water to many, while supporting economic growth by diverting water for power and irrigation. And indeed, India's irrigation systems have enabled the country to be self-sufficient in food production since 1974.

Prime Minister Indira Gandhi, in 1969 nationalised fourteen commercial banks by promulgating an ordinance. This act was not only an instrument to bolster her image of being pro-people, but to give her a handle to acquire the wherewithal to finance social goals in the future. Prime Minister Narasinmha Rao's economic policies in 1992 marked the most radical break from policies the country had pursued since independence. It altered the course of India's economic and social structure, integrating the economy with the emerging world order and changing the way India's economy and economic institutions would look in times to come. Industrial production had been strengthened and diversified to actively foster the growth of new and progressive entrepreneurs and to create fresh opportunities for hitherto neglected and backward areas in different parts of the country.

With the passing of age of imperialism, development acquired a new meaning, Indian leaders, starting from the first Prime Minister of India, spoke to many of the world leaders in a bid to embrace development as the means to raise the standard of the masses, supply them with their basic needs, empower them to lead a decent life, and help them to progress and advance in life not only in regard to material things, but also culturally. By advancing higher education systems, India, like many other BRICS countries, is transforming itself from a regional to global player – be it in education, infrastructure, power generation, soft skill, manufacturing enterprises, agriculture or development of non-material culture. For the present, India may have to capitalise on its population (quality and number), if it has to make a distinct mark at the international level.

Keywords evelopment, dependency, Five year Plan, public policy, indigenous people, capability deprivation, marginalised community, Human development.

INTRODUCTION

The contemporary world is characterized by the simultaneous integration of economies and disintegration of societies. In between, national states must cope with the crisis of legitimacy of the political system as well as with the economic crisis of the developmental process.

Under such historical conditions the asymmetrical structural relationships between societies impact both the development process and sociopolitical movements. The current process of techno-economic restructuring, which is integrating and reshaping economies and societies throughout the world, has originated in the interests and values of the dominant centers of the system. The technological revolution has arisen from the scientific institutions and leading corporations of the major industrial countries, and taken shape in products and applications suited to the most profitable markets in these countries.

While science and technology are universal, their trajectories and applications are not. The process of socioeconomic restructuring that took place during the 1980s was a deliberate public and private response aimed at restoring the basis of profitable capital accumulation in the core countries, in the aftermath of the structural crisis of the 1970s in the global North. Yet it has actually reshaped the whole international economy and especially so of nation-states on the margins. The effects of these changes on dependent economies and societies were determined by the values, needs, and interests of the dominant societies, although mediated by the specific social structure of each country.

The response of each country to the restructuring was conditioned by its relative position in the international division of labor, itself the product of previous social situations marked by dependency. Countries (and the social forces within them) were greatly constrained by the need to deal with the major consequences of the broader process of techno-economic restructuring. It follows that dependency, understood in its original dialectical version, is a necessary starting point for analyzing the current processes of social domination and social change. It should be responsive to new historical processes, particularly the fundamental challenge represented by the current technological revolution.

There are serious political implications of the developing global situation. Forces struggling for social change in many nation-states have oscillated for decades between the dead end of populism and the artificial paradise offered by dogmatic readings of Marxism. In the second half of the twentieth century, when democracy was painfully and partially restored in most countries, a series of pragmatic reformist attempts tried to pave the way for the reconstruction of the social fabric, a precondition for development and social change. But the difficulties imposed by the broader process of international restructuring have halted most of these reformist efforts. This has endangered democratization, opening the way for the old cycle between demagoguery and repression.

Nevertheless, despite the limitations of current leaders and political parties, a program of cautious but deep social reforms, involving not only economic and technological aspects, but also political, institutional, and even cultural dimensions, seems the only way out in the midst of the dramatic transformation of the world system. The challenge for developing nations is certainly enormous considering that it comes when the region is weaker and more vulnerable than ever. To counteract the pernicious effects of the new dependency in a lasting historical perspective will require a new politics make up of social reform and technological modernization within a democratic framework. This new politics, alert to popular demands and expectations and open to the creative potential of social movements, also requires a leadership humble enough to learn the lessons of the emerging world.

INDIA AS A WELFARE STATE

In 1956, the first Prime Minister focused on industrialisation while speaking on the occasion of introducing the second Five year Plan to the Parliament of India. On may 23, 1956, Jawaharlal Nehru Said:

> We are engaged in shaping the future of India, with a burden of history and sense of humility, taking its millions forward. There is no journey's end when a nation is marching. The ultimate aim, as we envisage it (is) the objective of socialist pattern of society. We all agree that there should be a uniform development and that disparities between individuals (with) regard to income (and other) areas should be removed (to ensure) equality of growth and opportunity all over India.

The twentieth century has seen far-reaching changes all over the world.
There have been wars and revolutions. The tempo of change is very great.
Any plan we make is subject to great political, economic and technological
changes. Without some kind of philosophical and ideological approach, we
would have no yardstick to measure (these changes) (BETABYAL, 2007: 582).

Dedicating the Bhakra Nangal Dam to the nation, Jawaharlal Nehru on
July 8, 1954, called it the *temples of Modern India, monuments to a nationalistic
vision of modernization and growth*. After independence in 1947, India went
on to build over 3000 dams which it believed would improve quality of
life by providing drinking water to many, while supporting economic
growth by diverting water for power and irrigation to fields. And indeed,
India's irrigation systems have enabled the country to be self-sufficient in
food production since 1974 (BETABYAL, 2007: 587).

Indira Gandhi, as an assertive Prime Minister of India, had in July 1969
nationalised fourteen commercial banks by promulgating an ordinance to
that effect. This act was not only an instrument to bolster her image of
being pro-people, but also gave her a handle to acquire the wherewithal
to finance social goals in the future. This kind of step was articulated by
the radical section in the ruling party for a long time (1956, 1963). While
announcing the decision in the Parliament of India on July 21, 1969, the
Prime Minister said:

The government of India has taken several measures towards the
achievement of the (national) goal of a socialist pattern of society (so
far). Public ownership and the control of the national economy and of
its strategic sectors are essential and important aspects of the new social
order which we are trying to build in the country. We regard this as
particularly necessary in a poor country which seeks to achieve speedy
economic progress consistent with social justice in a democratic political
system in which opportunities are open to all. There has been a notable
breakthrough on the agricultural front, technologically and otherwise.
Our industrial base has been strengthened and diversified. It will be one of

the positive objectives of nationalized banks to actively foster the growth of new and progressive entrepreneurs and to create fresh opportunities for hitherto neglected and backward areas in different parts of the country". (BETABYAL, 2007: 596-598.)

Manmohan Singh's Budget Speech in the Parliament on February 29, 1992 marked the most radical break from economic policies the country had pursued since independence. It altered the course of India's economic and social structure, integrating the economy with the emerging world order and changing the way India's economy and economic institutions would look in times to come. He said:

We have to accept the need for restructuring and reform if we are to avoid an increasing marginalisation of India in the evolving world economy [...]. This budget represents a contribution to the successful implementation of great national enterprise, of building an India free of wars, want and exploitation, an India worthy of the dreams of the founding fathers of our republic (BETABYAL, 2007: 596-598).

Indian leadership thus was determined to plunge into the liberalisation, privatisation, globalisation (LPG) bandwagon. They did not waste time. Indian Economy is the twelfth largest in the world and fourth largest by purchasing power parity. In the 21st century, India is an emerging economic power having vast human and natural resources. Of late (since 1992) Indian public policy has sought qualitative improvement in the economic progress of a country. It shows not only a sustained increase in national and per capita income but also qualitative changes which lead to higher standard of living. Four factors in particular guided the Public policy in India:

- human resources (labour supply, health, education);
- national resources (land, minerals, water, forest cover);
- capital formation (machines, factories, roads);
- technology (science, engineering, management).

In an attempt to contain the desired objective political leadership in the country introduced a five year plan as a strategy from the very beginning of the independence of the country and self rule. The Harrod–Domar model, the post Keynesian model of economic growth was adopted to explain an economy's growth rate in terms of the level of saving and productivity of capital. Since the model also had implications for less economically developed countries like India; where labour is in plentiful supply but physical capital is not, slowing economic progress. A cursory look at the Five-Year Plan as a development policy may provide some insight to the trajectory of development of India as emerging nation.

FIVE-YEAR PLAN PROGRAMME

First plan (1951 to 1956): It was based on Harrod–Domar model. Community development programme was launched in 1952. It emphasised on technical development, price stability, power and effective public transport.

Second plan (1956 to 1961): Also called Mahalanobis plan after its chief architect. Its objective was rapid industrialisation, advocated the use of imports which led to emptying funds leading to foreign loans. It shifted basic emphasis from agriculture to industry far too soon. During this plan, price level increased by 30% against a decline of 13% during the first plan.

Third plan (1961 to 1966): At its conception time, it was felt that the Indian economy has entered its takeoff stage. Therefore, the plan was to make India a self reliant and self generating economy. Also, it was realised from the experience of the first two plans that agriculture could be given the top priority to suffice the requirements of export and industry. This plan was a complete failure due to unforeseen misfortunes viz. Chinese aggression (1962), Indo Pak war (1962), Indo Pak war (1965), Severest drought to 100 years (1965 to 1966).

Three annual plans (1966 to 1969): Annual plans were adopted for three years. The prevailing crisis in agriculture and serious food shortage necessitated the emphasis on agriculture during the annual plans. During these plans a whole new agriculture strategy involving the widespread distribution of highly-yielding varieties of seeds, the extensive use of fertilisers, exploitation of the irrigation potential and soil conservation was put into action to tide over the crisis in agriculture production. During the annual plans, the economy basically absorbed the shocks given during the third plan, making way for a planned growth.

Fourth plan (1969 to 1974): The main emphasis of this plan was on agricultural growth rate so that chain reaction could be seen. It fared well in the first two years with record production, but, during the last three years it failed because of poor monsoon in the country. India had to tackle the influx of Bangladeshi refugees before and after the 1971 Indo-Pak war. This is also the period when the OPEC increased oil prices leading to a huge trade deficit for India that finally culminated in the devaluation of its currency.

Fifth plan (1974 to 1979): the fifth plan proposed to achieve two main objectives viz *removal of poverty* (*Garibi Hatao*) and *attainment of self reliance*, through promotion of high rate, better distribution of income and a very significant growth in the domestic rate of saving. The plan was terminated in 1978 (instead of 1979) when the Janata Party government came to the power.

Rolling plan (1978 to 1980): there were two sixth plans. One by Janata Party government (For 1978 to 1983) which was in operation for two years only and the other by Congress government when it returned to power in 1980. The Janata government plan is also called Rolling plan.

Sixth plan (1980 to 1985): Objectives of this plan were to increase the national income, modernisation of technology, ensuring continuous decrease in poverty and unemployment, population control through family planning, etc.

Seventh plan (1985 to 1990): The seventh plan emphasized policies and programmes which aimed at rapid growth in food grains production, increased employment opportunities and productivity within the framework of basic tenants of planning. It was a great success, the economy recorded 6% growth rate against the targeted 5%.

Eighth plan (1992 to 1997): The eighth plan was postponed by two years because of political upheavals at the Centre and it was launched after a worsening balance of payment position and inflation during 1990–1991. The plan undertook various drastic policy measures to combat the bad economic situation and to undertake an annual average growth of 5.6%. It recorded a rapid economic growth, high growth in exports and imports, improvement in trade and current account deficit.

Ninth plan (1997 to 2002): This plan was developed in the context of four important dimensions: quality of life, generation of productive employment, a regional balance and self-reliance.

Tenth plan (2002 to 2007): Its objectives included achieving the growth rate of 8%, reduction of poverty ratio to 20% by 2007, universal access to primary education by 2007, increase in literacy rate to 72% within the plan period and to 80% by 2012.

Eleventh plan (2007 to 2012): Accelerate growth rate of GDP from 8% to 10% and then maintain at 10% in the 12th plan in order to double per capita income by 2016-2017. It proposed increase in the agricultural GDP growth rate of 4% per year to ensure a broader spread of benefits. It envisaged reduction of the dropout rate of children from elementary school from 52.2% in 2003-2004 to 20% by 2011-2012; increase the literacy rate for persons of seven years or more to 85%. It also proposed to reduce infant mortality rate (MR) and maternal mortality ratio (MMR) to 1 per 1000 live births, in the country. It had envisaged raising the sex ratio for age group 0-6 to 935 by 2011-2012, and, to 950 by 2016-2017; ensuring electricity connection to all village and BPL households by 2009 and the round-the-clock power by the end of the plan and increase forest and free cover by five percentage points in India.

The 11th plan document reveals the intricate nature of the dependency relationship that India has to enter in order to survive in the near future. The very move to liberalise and privatise the public sector meant the contraction of state power and legitimacy.

In keeping with the Millennium Development Goals (MDGs) adopted by the United Nations in 2001; the Government of India set itself the following targets to be achieved by 2015 for reducing poverty and other causes of human deprivation and promoting sustainable development:

• Achieve universal primary education.
• Reduce child mortality.
• Improve maternal health.
• Combat HIV/AIDS, malaria and other diseases.
• Ensure environmental sustainability.
• Develop a global partnership for development.
• Eliminate gender disparities in primary and secondary education, preferably by 2005, and in all levels of education by 2015.
• Halve the proportion of the people suffering from hunger.

SOME REASONED REFLECTIONS

Though India managed to increase food grain production over the years such that the country was no more dependent on food subsidies from outside, yet its food grain distribution became highly skewed. Those at the bottom of the pyramid were the most to suffer. The much hyped green revolution was successful in only parts of the country and this added to the problem of regional imbalance further. A new rich farmer lobby emerged at the regional level (in the states of Punjab, Haryana and Western Uttar Pradesh), leading to the organisation and articulation of new political interests (FRANKEL, 2005).

Similarly most of the poverty reduction programmes that were inaugurated as early as the decade of 1950 failed to meet expectations. The planners adopted a two-pronged approach for poverty alleviation since the 1950s:

a) Indirect intervention or Trickle down hypo-research – This approach believed that rapid growth of per capita income would trickle-down to the poor. Thus programmes such as 1952, Community Development Projects (CDP) and 1953, National Extension Service (NES), were introduced in the First Five Year Plan. Other programmes were Intensive Agricultural District Programme, 1959, High-Yielding Varieties Programme, 1966-1967 and land reforms had been introduced.

b) Direct intervention – This approach gave birth to some programmes such as beneficiaries oriented programmes like: 1969-1970, Small Farmers Development Agency (SFDA) and Medium Farmers and Agricultural Labourers (MFAL); Rural Works Programme (RWP, 1970), Drought Prone Area Programme (DPAP), Employment Guarantee Scheme (EGS) of Maharashtra, Minimum Needs Programme (MNP), Integrated Rural Development Programme (IRDP), National Rural Employment Programme (NREP) and Rural Landless Employment Guarantee Programme (RLEGP), Jawahar Rojgar Yojana (JRY) Indira Aawas Yojana (IAY) and recently enacted the Mahatma Gandhi National Rural Employment Guarantee Act (MNREGA, 2005).

In addition the planning commission proposed to establish village co-operatives and panchayats as the major instruments of agricultural development and poverty alleviation, to involve the majority of the small peasantry in labour intensive development schemes and community action programmes. The Nehruvian model that stressed top to bottom disbursement of resources failed as it relied heavily on the bureaucracy and the rural elite to carry out the reforms (BRASS, 1993; FRANKEL, 2005).

Even the land reforms did not beget the required result though they did lead to certain structural changes in the matrix of agrarian production. Internationally, an income of less than $ 1.25 per day per head of purchasing power parity is defined as extreme poverty. By this estimate, about 21.92% percent of Indians are extremely poor. Income-based poverty lines consider the bare minimum income to provide basic food requirements; it does not account for other essentials such as health care and education.

Currently, 55% of the GDP is contributed by the service sector when this section only constitutes 20%, and the agricultural sector constitutes

54% of the population and contributes around 17% to the total GDP. Even the secondary sector including manufacturing has come down to 6% from the earlier figure of 10%, leading to ever increasing informal sector 94% of the working population (Economic Survey, 2012-2013). Several issues can be highlighted with regard to the low industrial production in the country. It is pertinent to mention that much of the economy was state controlled prior to 1991 and therefore most of the problems related to the public sector enterprises. Many of the issues were inherent in the policy formation itself. The following could be enumerated as some of the obvious consequences of the industrial policy implementation.

Gap between targets and achievements: Excepting 1980s, the industrial growth in the country could not achieve its previous targets. This slow growth of the industrial sector had an adverse impact on the overall growth performance of the country. Specifically the failure of the industrial sector to generate adequate employment opportunity to absorb the labour force resulted in no substantial change in the standard of living of the people.

Under-utilisation capacity: A large number of industries suffer from under-utilisation capacity. The causes for this under-utilisation are many and varying from technical to shortage of raw materials, frequent power failures, labour disputes, govt. policies and the demand factor.

Concentration of economic power: Though the authorities have stressed reducing the concentration of economic power in fewer hands, the actual policy only tended to concentrate more and more resources in fewer hands. This is clear from the fact that big industrial houses have considerably increased their assets and sales turnover during the plan-periods.

Elite-oriented consumption: The industrial sector witnessed a rapid growth of consumer durable goods units designed for the elite sector of the economy. Particularly during the 1980s the production of motor-cycles, scooters, TVs, radios, air-conditioners and refrigerators, computers and cosmetics increased significantly.

Performance of public sector: The performance of public sector units in India has not been satisfactorily judged from the profit point of view. Most of the PSUs are running in losses. But their performance should not be judged from a profit yard-stick only as they have certain broader socio-economic objectives.

Growth of regional imbalances: Industrial development in the country has concentrated in the western regions of the country while the eastern and north eastern region has been totally neglected in the process. States like Maharashtra and Gujarat have received a major part of industrial licenses during the recent years while the entire north-east has not received its due share. Though substantial investments in the public sector were made in backward States like Orissa, MP and Bihar, the expected trickling down effects of industrial development were not found during the years.

Industrial sickness: A large number of industries particularly in the public sector have been sick during the plan periods due to bad and inefficient management. Further adequate attraction has not been given to improvement in technology and quality of the product in these units. At the end of 1992 there were 2.36 lakh sick industrial units involving an outstanding credit of Rs 12, 500 crores.

In fact, the Confederation of Indian Industry (CII), in a meeting with the Prime Minister of India (July 29, 2013) has strongly expressed the imperative to do much more at the policy level to revive and restore macroeconomic balance. Terming the very high Current Account Deficit (CAD) as the economy's biggest problem, it cautioned the government to resist helping it by financial support alone. Though India has developed a competitive manufacturing sector in certain industries, capable of meeting domestic demand and leveraging export markets; there is a need to allow these industries to scale up by freeing up the sector even more and create competitive manufacturing in other industries.

It is of deep concern that the share of manufactures in exports has been going down consistently over the years. There have been growing imports of coal, gold and iron ore despite the boasting of India as the second largest reservoir of the minerals in the world. India has to increasingly rely on imports to meet its coal demand. Similarly iron ore imports too have dramatically increased. The issue of concern for industry with respect to Rupee rates is its volatility rather than its value. What is also alarming is that overtime the Indian economy has ended up in a spiral of contractual labour relations. Of the total labour force 93% work in the unorganized sector.

Even the "temples" of modernity could not live up to expectations. For instance as of today 75% of the total energy is provided by thermal plants and hydroelectricity plants contribute only 24%, nuclear only 2.4% and renewable a paltry 7% (Economic Review, 2012). The question therefore is on what front the nation has marched ahead vis-à-vis development. There have been certain socially beneficial legislations that have been passed in recent times which I wish to dwell on.

HUMAN DEVELOPMENT

Growth though important cannot be an end in itself. Higher standard of Living as well as of development opportunities for all, stemming from the greater resources generated by economic growth, are the ultimate aim of development policy. This implies the need to bridge regional, social and economic disparities, as well as the empowerment of the poor and marginalised, especially women, to make the entire development process more inclusive. The draft Twelfth Five Year Plan's subtitle *Faster, More Inclusive and Sustainable Growth*, puts the growth debate in the right perspective. The government's targeted policies for the poor, with that prospect can help belter translate outlays into outcomes.

The global economic and financial crisis which has persisted for the last five years has not only exposed the vulnerability of almost all the countries over the globe to external shocks, but also has lessons for development planning. Countries need to have inbuilt social safety nets for facing such eventualities, which affect most the weak and vulnerable, and wipe out the fruits of growth for years. India with its focus on inclusive development and timely interventions has, however, been able to weather the crisis better than many other countries.

India is on the brink of a demographic revolution with the proportion of working-age population between 15 and 59 years likely to increase from approximately 58% in 2001 to more than 64% by 2021, adding approximately 63.5 million new entrants to the working age group between 2011 and 2015, the bulk of whom will be in the relatively younger age group of 20-35 years. Given that it is one of the youngest large nations in the world, human development assumes great economic significance for it as the demographic dividend can be reaped only if this young population is healthy, educated, and skilled.

The policy planners in India have, over the years, engaged themselves in making more inclusive growth and development policies, focusing on human development. This approach has been reflected in the substantial enhancement in budgetary support for major social-sector programmes during 2012-2013 like the Pradhan Mantri Gram Sadak Yojana (PMGSY), Backward Regions Grant Fund, Right to Education (RTE), Sarv Shiksha Abhiyan (SSA), Rashtriya Madhyamik Shiksha Abhiyan, National Rural Health Mission (NRHM) and rural drinking water and sanitation schemes.

INCLUSIVE DEVELOPMENT

Inclusive development includes social inclusion along with financial inclusion and in most cases the socially excluded are also financially excluded. Many segments of the population like landless agricultural labourers, marginal farmers, scheduled castes (SCs), scheduled tribes (STs), and other backward classes (OBCs) continue to suffer social and financial exclusion. The government's policies are directed towards bringing these marginalised sections of the society into the mainstream as it is also reflected in social-sector expenditures by the government.

Central support for social programmes has continued to expand in various forms although most social-sector subjects fall within the purview of the states. Central government expenditure on social services and rural development (Plan and non-Plan) has increased from 14.77% in 2007-2008 to 17.39% in 2012-2013 with an all-time high of 18% in 2010-2011 due to the combined effect of higher expenditure under the Pradhan Mantri Gram Sadak Yojana (PMGSY) and education. Expenditure on social services by the general government (centre and states combined) has also shown increase in recent years reflecting the higher priority given to this sector. Expenditure on social services as a proportion of total expenditure has been increased.

Among social services, the share of expenditure on education has increased from 43.9% in 2007-2008 to 46.6% in 2012-2013, while that on health has fallen from 21.5% to 19.2%. However, India's expenditure on health as a percent of GDP is very low compared to many other emerging and developed countries. Unlike most countries, in India private-sector expenditure on health as a percentage of GDP is higher than public expenditure and was more than double in 2010. Despite this the total expenditure on health as a percentage of GDP is much lower than in many other developed and emerging countries and the lowest among BRICS (Brazil, Russia, India, China and South Africa) countries.

INEQUALITY

Human Development Report (HDR) measures inequality in terms of two indicators. The first indicator is the income Gini coefficient which measures the deviation of distribution of income (or consumption) among the individuals within a country from a perfectly equal distribution. For India, the income Gini coefficient was 35.8 in 2010-2011. In this respect, inequality in India is lower that of many other developing countries e.g. South Africa (57.8), Brazil (53.9), Thailand (53.6), Turkey (40.8), China (41.5), Sri Lanka (40.3), Malaysia (46.2), Vietnam (37.6), as well as countries like USA (40.8), Hong

Kong (43.4), Argentina (45.8), Israel (39.2), Bulgaria (45.3), etc., which are otherwise ranked very high in terms of the human development index.

To estimate the rural-urban gap, the monthly per capita expenditure (MPCE) defined first at the household level to assign a value that indicates the level of living to each individual or household is used. According to the provisional findings (68th round in 2011-2012 of the NSS), the average MPCE is Rs 1281.45 and Rs 2401.68 respectively for rural and urban India, indicating rural-urban income disparities. However, monthly per capita rural consumption rose by 18% in real terms in 2011-2012 over 2009-2010, while monthly per capita urban consumption rose by only 13.3%. Thus the rate of increase in the MPCE of rural areas is higher than that of urban areas, indicating a bridging of the rural-urban gap.

EMPLOYMENT

The last decade, i.e. 1999-2000 to 2009-2010, witnessed an employment growth of 1.6% per annum. Employment growth in the second half of the decade was relatively modest. The labour force participation rate, which reflects the persons who express their willingness to work declined from 430 per thousand persons in 2004-2005 to 400 per thousand persons in 2009-2010. The LFPR declined particularly for rural females. The growth of those in the labour force declined possibly on account of greater number of persons opting for education/skill development.

There has been a steady increase in the ratio of students to total population from 20.5% in 1993-1994 to 24.3% in 2004-2005 and further to 26.6% in 2009-2010, and this largely explains the modest growth in employment in second half of 2000-2010. The students to population ratio increased faster in rural areas and more so for females. It may, however, be mentioned that the unemployment rate, according to UPSS criteria, in fact declined between 2004-2005 and 2009-2010, both in rural and urban areas, implying that relatively larger proportions of persons who were willing to work, were actually employed.

An increased intensity of employment is also reflected by an overall increased availability of employment to workers based on current daily status (CDS). One development of interest is the loss in female employment in rural areas and loss in female employment in urban areas as well. One of the reasons for this is that a significant number of women (137 million in 2009-2010) opted not to work to continue education. But total employment (rural and urban combined of males and females combined) is positive.

UNEMPLOYMENT

The unemployment rate decreased slowly from 1993-1994 to 2004-2005. Despite negligible employment growth, the unemployment rate fell from 8.2% in 2004-2005 to 6.6 per cent in 2009-2010. The decline in the unemployment rate implies a decline in unemployed people. The fall in unemployment despite marginal growth in employment in 2009-2010 could be due to the demographic dividend, as an increasing proportion of the young population opts for education rather than participating in the labour market. This is reflected in the rise in growth in the enrolment of students in higher education from 492,500,000 in 1990-1991 to 1,697,500,000 lakh in 2010-2011. Enactment of the Right to Education and programmes like the Sarva Shiksha Abhiyan could also have contributed to this.

Employment in the Organized Sector: Employment growth in the organized sector, public and private combined has increased by 1.0% in 2011, as against 1.9% in 2010. The annual growth rate of employment in the private sector in 2011 was 5.6% whereas that in the public sector was negative. The share of women in organized-sector employment was around 20.5% during 2009-2011 and has remained nearly constant in recent years. The impact of the economic slowdown on employment in India indicates that the upward trend in employment since July 2009 has been maintained.

POVERTY AND EMPLOYMENT GENERATION PROGRAMMES

The Planning Commission estimates poverty using data from the large sample surveys on household consumer expenditure carried out by the National Sample Survey Office (NSSO) every five years. It defines the poverty line on the basis of monthly per capita consumption expenditure (MPCE). It has estimated the poverty lines at all India level as an MPCE of Rs 673 for rural areas and Rs 860 for urban areas in 2009-2010. Based on these cut-offs, the percentage of people living below the poverty line in the country has declined from 37.2% in 2004-2005 to 29.8% in 2009-2010. Even in absolute terms, the number of poor people has fallen by 52.4 million during this period. Of this, 48.1 million are rural poor and 4.3 million are urban poor. Thus poverty has declined on an average by 1.5% per year between 2004-2005 and 2009-2010. Infant mortality rate (IMR) which was 58 per thousand in the year 2005 has fallen to 44 in the year 2011. The number of rural households provided toilet facilities annually have increased from 6.21 lakh in 2002-2003 to 88 lakh in 2011-2012. The improvement in these social indicators is also a reflection of fall in deprivation.

The government is following a focused approach through various flagship schemes in the areas of poverty alleviation and employment generation to achieve inclusive development. Some important poverty alleviation and employment generation programmes are as follows:

Mahatma Gandhi NREGA: This flagship programme of the government aims at enhancing livelihood security of households in rural areas by providing at least one hundred days of guaranteed wage employment in a financial year to every household whose adult members volunteer to do unskilled manual work with the stipulation of one-third participation of women. The MGNREGA provides wage employment while also focusing on strengthening natural resource management through works that address causes of chronic poverty like drought, deforestation, and soil erosion and thus encourage sustainable development. The MGNREGA is implemented in all districts with rural areas. About 4.39 crore households have been provided employment of 156.01 crore person days of which 82.58 crore (53%) were availed of by women, 34.56 crore (22%) SCs, and 24.90 crore (16%) by STs.

At national level, with the average wage paid under the MGNREGA increasing from Rs 65 in FY 2006-2007 to Rs 115 in FY 2011-2012, the bargaining power of agricultural labour has increased as even private sector wages have increased as shown in many studies. Improved economic outcomes, especially in watershed activities, and reduction in distress migration are its other achievements.

Wages under the MGNREGA are indexed to the consumer price index for agricultural labour (CPI-AL). While some initiatives have been taken recently, with better planning of project design, capacity building of panchayati raj institutions (PRIs), skill upgrading for enhanced employability, and reduction of transaction costs, gaps in implementation could be plugged to a greater extent and the assets so created could make a much larger contribution to increasing land productivity.

National Rural Livelihood Mission (NRLM)-Aajeevika: The Swarnjayanti *Gram Swarozgar Yojana* (SGSY)/NRLM a self-employment programme implemented since April 1999 aims at lifting the assisted rural poor families (swarozgaris) above the poverty line by providing them income-generating assets through a mix of bank credit and government subsidy. The rural poor are organized into *self-help groups* (SHGs) and their capacities built through training and skill development. Approximately 168.46 lakh swarozgaris have been assisted with bank credit and subsidy. The SGSY now restructured as the NRLM has been renamed Aajeevika and implemented in mission mode across the country since 2011. The main features of Aajeevika are:

a) one woman member from each identified rural poor household to be brought under the SHG network;

b) ensuring 50% of the beneficiaries from SC/STs, 15% from minorities, and 3% persons with disability while keeping in view the ultimate target of 100% coverage of BPL families;

c) training for capacity building and skill development;

d) ensuring revolving fund and capital subsidy;

e) financial inclusion;

f) provision of interest subsidy;

g) backward and forward linkages;

h) promoting innovations.

Swarna Jayanti Shahari Rozgar Yojana (SJSRY): The SJSRY launched on 1 December 1997 aims at providing gainful employment to the urban unemployed and underemployed, by encouraging them to set up self-employment ventures or creating wage employment opportunities. The scheme has been revamped w.e.f. April 2009. A total of 4,06,947 people have benefited from this scheme during 2012-2013.

SOCIAL PROTECTION PROGRAMMES

The coverage of social security schemes has been expanded to provide a minimum level of social protection to workers in the unorganized sector and ensure inclusive development. Such schemes include the following:

Aam Admi Bima Yojana (AABY): *The Janashree Bima Yojana* (JBY) has now been merged with the AABY to provide better administration of life insurance cover to the economically backward sections of society. The scheme extends life and disability cover to persons between the ages of 18 and 59 years living below and marginally above the poverty line under 47 identified vocational/occupational groups, including "rural landless households". It provides insurance cover natural death, death due to accident, or permanent disability due to accident. The scheme also provides an add-on benefit of scholarship of Rs 100 per month per child paid on half-yearly basis to a maximum of two children per member studying in Classes 9 to 12. A total of 289.94 lakh live under the JBY and 178.67 lakh live under the AABY and had been covered till December 2012.

Rashtriya Swasthya Birna Yojana (RSBY): The scheme provides smart card-based cashless health insurance cover of Rs 30,000 per family per annum on a family floater basis to BPL families in the unorganized sector with the premium shared on 75:25 basis by central and state governments. In case of states of the north-eastern region and Jammu and Kashmir, the premium is shared in the ratio of 90:10. The scheme provides for portability of smart card by splitting the card value for migrant workers. As on 31 December 2012, the scheme is being implemented in 27 states/ UTs with more than 3.34 crore smart cards issued.

The Unorganized Workers Social Security Act 2008 and National Social Security Fund: The Act provides for constitution of a National Social Security Board and State Social Security Boards which will recommend social security schemes for unorganised workers. The National Social Security Board was constituted in August 2009. It has made some recommendations regarding extension of social security schemes to certain additional segments of unorganised workers. A National Social Security Fund with initial allocation of Rs 1000 crore to support schemes for weavers, toddy tappers, rickshaw pullers, beedi workers, etc. has also been set up.

Social Security Agreements (SSAs): SSA, a bilateral instrument to protect the interests of Indian professionals as well as self-employed Indians working in foreign countries, was initiated by signing an SSA between India and Belgium on 3 November 2006. So far India has signed 15 SSAs with Belgium, Germany, Switzerland, France, Luxembourg, Netherlands, Hungary, Denmark, Czech Republic, Republic of Korea, Norway, Finland, Canada, Sweden, and Japan. These SSAs facilitate mobility of professionals between two countries by exempting them from double payment of social security contributions and enables them to enjoy the benefits of exportability and totalisation.

RURAL INFRASTRUCTURE AND DEVELOPMENT

Rural infrastructure and development programmes for achieving a higher degree of rural-urban integration and an even pattern of growth and opportunities for the poor and disadvantaged sections of society include the following:

Bharat Nirman: Launched in 2005–2006 by the government to provide basic amenities and infrastructure to rural India has six components: irrigation, roads, housing, water supply, electrification, and telecommunication connectivity.

Indira Awas Yojana (IAY): The IAY is one of the six components of Bharat Nirman. During 2012–2013, as against a physical target of 30.10 lakh houses, 25.35 lakh houses were sanctioned and 13.88 lakh had been constructed as on 31 December 2012. The unit assistance provided to rural households for construction of a dwelling unit under the IAY is being revised from April 2013. Eighty-two left–wing extremism (LWE) – affected districts have been made eligible for a higher rate of unit assistance. Under the Homestead Scheme, the unit assistance for purchase/acquisition of house sites for those rural BPL households who have neither land nor a house site will be enhanced from Rs 10,000 to Rs 20,000 from April 2013, to be shared by the centre and states in a 50:50 ratio. For effective monitoring of the IAY, MIS software Awaasoft' has been put in place.

Pradhan Mantri Gram Sadak Yoyana (PMGSY): The PMGSY was launched in December 2000 as a fully funded centrally sponsored scheme with the objective of providing connectivity to the eligible unconnected habitations in the core network with a population of 500 persons and above in plains areas and 250 persons and above in hill states, tribal areas, desert areas, and in the 82 selected tribal and backward districts under the IAP. A total of 3,63,652 km road length has been completed and new connectivity has been provided to over 89,382 habitations by the states. Work on a road length of about 1,07,739 km is in progress.

Rural Drinking Water: About 73.91% of rural habitations are fully covered under the provision of safe drinking water in rural areas as measured by habitations with the provision of at least 40 litres per capita per day

(Ipcd) of safe drinking water. The financial outlay for rural drinking water supply increased considerably under *Bharat Nirman* in 2012-2013. Census 2011 reported 84.2% rural households as having improved drinking water sources with tap water, hand pumps and covered wells constituting the major sources. Therefore ensuring safe drinking water for the remaining 15.8% of rural households with unimproved sources and 22.1% of rural households that have to fetch water from beyond 500 m is the major challenge.

Rural Sanitation – Total Sanitation Campaign (TSC): "According to Census 2011, only 32.7% of rural households have latrine facilities. The TSC renamed the *Nirmal Bharat Abhiyan* (NBA) aims to transform rural India into *Nirmal Bharat* by adopting a community saturation approach and achieve 100% access to sanitation for all rural households by 2022. NBA projects have been sanctioned in 607 rural districts. Under the NBA, the provision of incentives for individual household latrine units has been widened to cover all above poverty line (APL) households that belong to or are SCs, STs, small and marginal farmers, landless labourers with homesteads, physically challenged, and women headed along with all BPL households.

Since 1999, over 8.97 crore toilets have been provided to rural households under the TSC/NBA. A total of 12.57 lakh school toilet units and 4.24 lakh *Anganwadi* toilets have also been constructed. With increasing budgetary allocations and focus on rural areas, the number of households being provided toilets annually has increased from 5.96 lakh in 2002-2003 to 88 lakh in 2011-2012. A total of 28,002 gram panchayats, 181 intermediate panchayats, and 13 district panchayats have been awarded the *Nirmal Gram Puruskar* (NGP) in the last seven years.

URBAN INFRASTRUCTURE, HOUSING, AND SANITATION

The central government has been assisting state governments by way of various centrally sponsored schemes through national financial institutions providing better urban infrastructure, housing, and sanitation in the country. Some of the initiatives in this area are as follows:

Jawaharlal Nehru Urban Renewal Mission (JNNURM): The JNNURM, a flagship programme for urbanization launched in December 2005, provides substantial central financial assistance to cities for infrastructure, housing development, and capacity development. The two out of four components under the JNNURM devoted to shelter and basic service needs of the poor residing in urban areas are:

- *Basic Services to the Urban Poor* (BSUP) for 65 select cities and.
- *Integrated Housing and Slum Development Programme* (IHSDP) for other cities and towns.

Rajiv Awas Yojana (RAY): The RAY was launched in June 2011 with the vision of creating a slum-free India. Phase I of the RAY (preparatory phase) is for a period of two years from the date of approval of the scheme and is currently under implementation. Phase II of the RAY shall be for the remaining period of the Twelfth Five Year Plan. An amount of Rs 50 crore has been allocated for the year 2012-2013.

Integrated Low Cost Sanitation Scheme (ILCS): The ILCS aims at conversion of individual dry latrines into pour flush latrines thereby liberating manual scavengers from the age-old, degrading practice of manually carrying night soil. The allocation for the scheme for 2012-2013 is Rs 25 crore.

SKILL DEVELOPMENT

Education and skill development play a pivotal role in economic development and growth of any country as they provide an environment for creating jobs and help in reduction of poverty and other related social fallouts. A new strategic framework for skill development for early school leavers and existing workers has been developed since May 2007 in close consultation with industry, state governments, and experts.

The *National Skill Development Corporation* (NSDC) approved 24 training projects in 2012, for imparting skill training in a wide array of sectors like healthcare, tourism, hospitality and travel, banking, financial services and insurance (BFSI) retail, Information Technology, electronics, textiles, leather, handicrafts, automotive, agriculture, cold chains and refrigeration, tailoring, carpentry, and masonry. Besides formation of Skill Councils for seven sectors, proposals related to food processing, telecom, agriculture, plumbing, logistics, capital goods, and construction sectors have also been approved during this period.

The NSDC has been able to get some of India's biggest corporate groups interested in the private sector-led skills training programme for graduates and post-graduates in Jammu and Kashmir called Udaan. Scaling up of this initiative is targeted to make 40,000 people in Jammu and Kashmir skilled and placed in jobs over a five-year span. In the north-east region, the NSDC is partnering the Ministry of Youth Affairs and Sports in the Youth Employability Skills (YES) project. Till December 2012, NSDC partners established its presence in 25 states and three Union Territories and covered 312 districts in India.

UNIQUE IDENTIFICATION AUTHORITY OF INDIA (UIDAI)

After successfully completing Phase I enrolments, the UIDAI is actively engaged in Phase II in which 40 crore residents are to be enrolled before the end of 2014. By the end of 2012, 24.93 crore Aadhaars had been generated and approximately 20 crore Aadhaar letters dispatched. The UIDAI has also established infrastructure to generate 10 lakh Aadhaars per day and process 10 million authentication transactions a day. Apart from meeting targets related to enrolments, significant amount of effort were spent on enabling service delivery of government schemes with Aadhaar online authentication and Aadhaar-enabled benefits transfers to bank accounts of beneficiaries.

The government has decided to initiate direct transfer of subsidy under various social schemes into beneficiaries bank accounts. The transfer will be enabled through a payments bridge known as Aadhaar Payment Bridge (APB) wherein funds can be transferred into any Aadhaar-enabled bank account on the basis of the Aadhaar number. This eliminates chances of fraud/error in the cash transfer process. The Aadhaar number will be linked to the beneficiary database so that ghosts/duplicates are weeded out from the beneficiary list.

To make withdrawal of money by the beneficiaries easier and more accessible and friendly, micro ATMs will be set up by banks/post offices throughout the country in an open manner particularly with the help of SHGs, community service centres (CSCs), post offices, grocery stores, petrol pumps, etc. in rural areas and accessible pockets. Pilots on direct benefit transfer (DBT) have also been successfully conducted in the states of Jharkhand, Tripura, and Maharashtra to transfer monetary benefits related to rural employment, pension, the IAY, and other social welfare schemes. Important pilots are the fair price shops in East Godavari and Hyderabad districts of Andhra Pradesh which are being enabled to carry out online Aadhaar authentication. In another important pilot with oil marketing companies (OMCs) in Mysore, delivery of LPG gas cylinders is being done only after Aadhaar online authentication of customers.

EDUCATION

To reap the benefits of the demographic dividend to the full, India has to provide education to its population and quality education. It also stresses the need to build capacity in secondary schools to absorb the pass outs from expanded primary enrolments. Many schemes have been initiated by the government for elementary and secondary education. Some are as follows:

Sarv Shiksha Abhiyan (SSA) Right to Education (RTE): The Right of Children to Free and Compulsory Education (RTE) Act 2009, legislating Article 21A of the Constitution of India, became operational in the country on 1 April 2010. It implies that every child has a right to elementary education of satisfactory and equitable quality in a formal school which satisfies certain essential norms and standards.

The achievements till September, 2012 include opening of 3,34,340 new primary and upper primary schools, construction of 2,84,032 school buildings, 16,42,867 additional classrooms, 2,17,820 drinking water facilities and 6,18,089 toilets, supply of free textbooks to 8.32 crore children, appointment of 12.46 lakh teachers, and imparting of in-service training to 18.64 lakh teachers. Significant reduction in the number of out-of-school children on account of SSA interventions has been noted.

Mid-day Meals (MDM): Under the MDM, cooked midday meals are provided to all children attending Classes I-VIII in government, local body, government-aided, and National Child Labour Project (NCLP) schools. Education Guarantee Scheme (EGS) alternate and innovative education centres including madarsas/maqtabs supported under the SSA across the country are also covered under this programme. At present the cooked midday meal provides an energy content of 450 calories and protein content of 12 grams at primary stage and an energy content of 700 calories and protein content of 20 grams at upper primary stage.

Adequate quantity of micro-nutrients like iron, folic acid, and vitamin A are also recommended for convergence with the NRHM. About 10.54 crore children (7.18 crore in primary and 3.36 crore in upper primary stages) benefited under the programme during 2011-2012. The MDM-MIS has been launched to monitor the scheme and annual data entries for about 11.08 lakh schools have been completed. The MDM-MIS will be integrated with the Interactive Voice Response System (IVRS) meant to capture the information from the schools within a span of 1 hour on a daily basis to monitor the scheme.

Rashtriya Madhyamik Shiksha Abhiyan (RMSA): The RMSA was launched in March 2009 with the objective of enhancing access to secondary education and improving its quality. It has helped in the construction of new school buildings and repair to existing secondary schools for strengthening of infrastructure, payment of regular salary of teachers and staff sanctioned under the RMSA, learning enhancement programmes, equity interventions, etc.

Model Schools Scheme: A scheme for setting up of 6000 high quality model schools as a benchmark of excellence at block level at the rate of one school per block was launched in November 2008 to provide quality education to talented rural children. The scheme has two modes of implementation:

1. 3500 schools been set up in as many educationally backward blocks (EBBs) through state governments;
2. the remaining 2500 schools are to be set up under public private partnership (PPP) mode in blocks which are not educationally backward.

Saakshar Bharat (SB) Adult Education: The National Literacy Mission, recast as SB, reflects the enhanced focus on female literacy. The Census of India 2011 shows that the literacy rate improved sharply among females as compared to males with the latter increasing by 6.9% points from 75.26% to 82.14% and the former by 11.8% points from 53.67% to 65.46%. Literacy levels remain uneven across states, districts, social groups, and minorities. The government has taken focused measures for reducing the disparities in backward areas and target groups. By March 2012, the programme had reached 372 districts in 25 states and one Union Territory covering over 161,219 gram panchayat.

By the end of March 2012, about 16 lakh literacy classes enrolling about 174 lakh learners were functioning. Since the Mission has been envisaged as a people's programme, stakeholders, especially at grassroots level i.e. PRIs, have due say and role in its planning and implementation. Despite the efforts of the government to provide primary and elementary education, there is a lot more to be done in terms of quality. The declining levels of educational achievement are a cause for concern, though it is unclear how much of the decline is because of lower levels of learning, and how much is because schools are reaching out to enroll students with lower preparation than they did earlier.

HIGHER AND TECHNICAL EDUCATION

The Indian higher education system is one of the largest in the world in terms of the number of colleges and universities. While at the time of Independence, there were only 20 universities and 500 colleges with 0.1 million students, their number has increased to 690 universities and university-level institutions and 35,539 colleges upto 2011-2012. Of the 690 universities, 44 are central universities, 306 state universities, 145 state private universities, 130 deemed universities, 60 institutes of national importance plus other institutes, and 5 institutions established under state Legislature Acts.

A number of initiatives have been taken during the Eleventh Plan period with focus on improvement of access along with equity and excellence, adoption of state-specific strategies, enhancing the relevance of higher education through curriculum reforms, vocationalisation, networking, and use of IT and distance education along with reforms in governance in higher education. The major initiatives are as follows:

- During the Eleventh Plan, 16 central universities were established which include conversion of three state universities to central universities. Seven new Indian Institutes of Management (IIMs), 8 new Indian Institutes of Technology (IITs), 10 new National Institutes of Technology (NITs), 5 Indian Institutes of Science Education & Research (IISERs), and 2 Schools of Planning and Architecture (SPAs) were also established.
- The *National Mission on Education through ICT* (NMEICT) which aims at providing high speed broadband connectivity to universities and colleges and development of e-content in various disciplines is under implementation. Nearly 404 universities have been provided 1Gbps – connectivity or have been configured under the scheme and 19,851 colleges have also been provided VPN connectivity.

Over 250 courses have been completed and made available in the National Programme on Technology Enhanced Learning (NPTEL) Phase I and another 996 courses in various disciplines in engineering and science are being generated in Phase-ll of NPTEL by IIT Madras. The low cost access-cum-computing device Aakash 2 was launched on 11 November 2012. Using the A-View software developed under the NMEICT, several programmes for teachers empowerment have been conducted for batches of 1000 teachers at a time by IIT Mumbai.

- A Scheme of Interest Subsidy on Educational Loans to economically weaker sections (EWS) students was introduced from 2009-2010.
- To address the increasing skill challenges of the Indian IT industry, the government has approved the setting up of twenty new Indian Institutes of Information Technology (IIITs) on public private partnership (PPP) basis. The project is targeted for completion in nine years from 2011-2012 to 2019-2020. The Government of India also provides financial assistance to the states to meet the costs of establishing new government polytechnics in un-served districts.

HEALTH

Improvement in the standard of living and health status of the population has remained one of the important objectives for policymakers in India. In line with the National Health Policy 2002, the NRHM was launched in April 2005 with the objective of providing accessible, affordable, and quality healthcare to the rural population. It seeks to bring about architectural correction in the health systems by adopting the approaches like increasing involvement of community in planning and management of healthcare facilities, improved programme management, flexible financing and provision of untied grants, decentralized planning and augmentation of human resources.

The combined revenue and capital expenditure of the centre and states on medical and public health, water supply and sanitation, and family welfare has increased from Rs 53,057.80 crore in 2006-2007 to Rs 1,18,295.78 crore in 2011-2012. This outlay will be directed towards building on further initiatives and extending the outreach of public health services, ultimately leading towards the long-term objective of establishing a system of universal health coverage. Despite the efforts by the government to provide affordable access to the decentralised public health system, its expenditure on public health as a percentage of GDP is very low.

The government has launched a large number of programmes and schemes to address the major concerns and bridge the gaps in existing health infrastructure and provide accessible, affordable, equitable healthcare. The details of some major programmes and developments are as follows:

National Rural Health Mission (NRHM): The NRHM which provides an overarching umbrella to the existing health and family welfare programmes was launched in 2005 to improve accessibility to quality healthcare for the rural population, bridge gaps in healthcare, facilitate decentralised planning in the health sector, and bring about inter-sectoral convergence. Better infrastructure, availability of manpower, drugs and equipment, and augmentation of health human resources in health facilities at different levels have led to improvement in healthcare delivery services and increase in outpatient department (OPD) and inpatient department (IPD) services.

Accredited social health activists (ASHAs): Have been engaged in each village/large habitation in the ratio of one per 1000 population. Till September 2012, 8.84 lakh ASHAs had been selected in the entire country, of whom 8.09 lakh had been given orientation training. Further, 7.96 lakh ASHAs had been provided drug kits. As part of the infrastructure strengthening under the NRHM, 10,473 sub-centres, 714 primary health centres (PHCs), and 245 community health centres (CHCs) have been newly constructed. A total of 8199 PHCs have been made functional as 24X7 services across the country. Further, nearly 2024 vehicles are operational as *mobile medical units* (MMUs) in 459 districts in the country under the NRHM. The total plan outlay for the year 2012–2013 under the NRHM is Rs 20,542 crore.

Janani Suraksha Yojana (JSY): The JSY launched in 2005 aims to bring down the MMR by promoting institutional deliveries conducted by skilled birth attendants. The beneficiaries have increased from 7.38 lakh in 2005-2006 to more than 1.09 crore in 2011-2012. The number of institutional deliveries has increased from 1.08 crore during 2005-2006 to 1.75 crore during 2011-2012. The number of institutional deliveries during 2012-2013 (up to September 2012) was 80,39 lakh.

In addition, Janani Shishu Suraksha Karyakram (JSSK): A new initiative which entitles all pregnant women delivering in public health institutions to absolutely no expenses delivery covering free delivery including Caesarean, free drugs, diagnostics, blood and diet, and free transport from home to institution including during referrals, is also in operation.

National Vector Borne Disease Control Programme: To control and prevent vector-borne diseases such as malaria, dengue, chikungunya, Japanese encephalitis, kala-azar. and lymphatic filariasis in the country, a National Vector Borne Disease Control Programme has been launched. Of these six diseases, kala-azar and lymphatic filariasis have been targeted for elimination by 2015. With this initiative, malaria has shown a declining trend with 0.95 million cases and 446 deaths reported out of the 94.85 million persons screened in 2012 (up to November) compared to 1.31 million cases and 753 deaths of the 108.97 million persons screened in 2011.

Dengue in the recent past has been reported from almost all lire states and UTs except Lakshadweep. During 2011, 18,860 cases and 169 deaths were reported, whereas during 2012,47,029 cases and 242 deaths have been reported. Chikungunya cases have shown a declining trend after its re-emergence in 2006.

Human Resources, Infrastructure Development/upgrading of Tertiary Healthcare: To strengthen government medical colleges, land requirement norms and infrastructural requirements for opening new medical colleges have been revised. However, to further increase availability of doctors, it is proposed to set up new medical colleges attached to district hospitals and strengthen and upgrade existing ones to add 16,000 new MBBS seats during the Twelfth Plan period.

In order to meet the shortage of nurses, a scheme is under implementation for opening of 132 ANM schools and 137 general nursing and midwifery

(GNM) schools in districts where there are no such schools. Opening of six nursing colleges at the sites of AIIMS-like institutions is also under implementation. The scheme for strengthening/upgrading of state government medical colleges envisages a one-time grant to be funded by central and state governments in a 75:25 ratio. 72 medicals colleges have been funded until March 2013.

To augment the supply of skilled paramedical manpower and promote paramedical training, one *National Institute of Paramedical Sciences* (NIPS) at Najafgarh, Delhi, and eight *Regional Institutes of Paramedical Sciences* (RIPS) are being set up at a cost of Rs 804.43 crore. Besides, State Government Medical Colleges are being given provided support for conducting paramedical courses through one-time grant.

Pradhan Mantri Swasthya Suraksha Yojana (PMSSY): The PMSSY aims at correcting regional imbalances in the availability of affordable/ reliable tertiary health-care services and augmenting facilities for quality medical education in the country. For the year 2012-2013, Rs 1544.21 crore has been earmarked under the PMSSY, which aims at:

1. construction of 6 AIIMS-like institutions in the first phase at Bhopal, Bhubaneswar, Jodhpur, Patna, Raipur, and Rishikesh and in the second phase in West Bengal and Uttar Pradesh;
2. upgrading of 13 medical colleges in the first phase and 6 in the second phase. The academic session for 50 MBBS seats has commenced at the six new AIIMS like institutions in September 2012 and hospitals are likely to be operational by September 2013.

Ayurveda, Yoga and Naturopathy, Unani, Siddha and Homoeopathy (AYUSH): The Indian system of medicines is also being developed and promoted by involvement/integration of the AYUSH system in national healthcare delivery through an allocation of Rs 990 crore Plan outlay in 2012-2013. To integrate AYUSH healthcare with mainstream allopathic healthcare services, the states are provided financial support for co-location of AYUSH facilities at PHCs, CHCs, and district hospitals and supply of essential drugs to standalone AYUSH hospitals/dispensaries.

WOMEN AND CHILD DEVELOPMENT

Women lag behind men in many social indicators like health, education, and economic opportunities. Hence they need special attention due to their vulnerability and lack of access to resources. Since national budgets impact men and women differently through the pattern of resource allocation, the scope and coverage of schemes for women and child development have been expanded with progressive increase in Plan expenditure under various Plan schemes, increased employment for women under the MGNREGA and *gender budgeting* (GB). The allocations for GB as a percentage of total budget have gone up from 2.79% in 2005-2006 to 5.91% in 2012-2013. Some of the important schemes and policy initiatives for economic and social empowerment of women and child development are as follows:

Integrated Child Development Services (ICDS) Scheme: The objective of the ICDS scheme is holistic development of children below 6 years of age and proper nutrition and health education of pregnant and lactating mothers starting with 33 projects and 4891 *anganwadi centres* (AWCs) in 1975. This has now been universalised with cumulative approval of 7076 projects and 14 lakh AWCs including 20,000 anganwadis "on-demand". Greater emphasis is being laid on awareness generation, convergence with the MGNREGA, and MIS-based monitoring.

Rajiv Gandhi Scheme for Empowerment of Adolescent Girls (RGSEAG): *Sabla*: Sabla now operational in 205 selected districts aims at all-round development of adolescent girls in the age group 11-18 years and making them self-reliant with a special focus on out-of-school girls. The scheme has two major components, nutrition and non-nutrition. Nutrition is being given in the form of "take home rations" or "hot cooked meals" to out-of-school 11-14 year old girls and all adolescent girls in the 14-18 age group.

The non-nutrition component addresses the developmental needs of 11-18 year old adolescent girls who are provided iron – folic acid supplementation, health check-up and referral services, nutrition and health education, counseling/guidance on family welfare, skill education, guidance on accessing public services, and vocational training. The target of the scheme is to provide nutrition to 1 crore adolescent girls in a year.

Indira Gandhi Matritva Sahyog Yojana (IGMSY): The IGMSY is a conditional cash transfer scheme for pregnant and lactating women implemented initially on pilot basis in 53 selected districts in the country from October 2010. As on 31 December 2012, more than 3 lakh beneficiaries had been covered and Rs 27 crore released to states. The scheme is now covered under the Direct Benefit Transfer (DBT) programme with nine districts being included in the first phase. In 2012–2013, the scheme has a budgetary outlay of Rs 520 crore and targets covering 12.5 lakh pregnant and lactating women.

National Mission for Empowerment of Women (NMEW): This initiative for holistic empowerment of women through better convergence and engendering of policies, programmes, and schemes of different ministries was operationalised in 2010–2011. Under the Mission, institutional structures at state level including State Mission Authorities headed by Chief Ministers and State Resource Centres for Women (SRCWs) for spearheading initiatives for women's empowerment have been established across the country.

Rashtriya Mahila Kosh (RMK): The RMK provides micro-credit in a quasi-informal manner, lending to *intermediate micro-credit organizations* (IMOs) across states. It focuses on poor women and their empowerment through the provision of credit for livelihood-related activities. With a corpus fund of Rs 31 crore, the RMK has grown to over Rs 180 crore including reserves and surplus due to credit, investments, and recovery management with an additional budgetary allocation of Rs 69 crore. From its inception in 1993 over 7.19 lakh women have been the beneficiaries of RMK.

Policies to address violence against women: Addressing violence against women is another area which has received a lot of recent attention. Following the recent tragic incident of sexual assault in New Delhi

(December 2012), a committee of eminent jurists, headed by former Chief Justice of India Justice J. S. Verma, was constituted to review existing laws and examine levels of punishment in cases of aggravated sexual assault and it has submitted its recommendations. An ordinance has also been issued on sexual assault against women [Criminal Law (Amendment) Ordinance, 2013] based on the recommendations of the Justice Verma Committee.

New initiatives are being taken like one-stop crisis centres for providing shelter, police assistance, legal, medical and counseling services with public hospitals as focal point. A scheme for providing restorative justice through financial assistance and support services to victims of rape will be implemented in the Twelfth Plan as per the directives of the Supreme Court of India.

WELFARE AND DEVELOPMENT OF SCHEDULED CASTES (SCS), SCHEDULED TRIBES (STS), AND OTHER BACKWARD CASTES (OBCS)

Economic and social empowerment and educational upliftment of socially disadvantaged groups and marginalized sections of society is necessary for achieving faster and more inclusive development. Programmes are being implemented through states, government's apex corporations, and NGOs for the upliftment of disadvantaged and marginalised sections of society.

Special Central Assistance (SCA) to the *Scheduled Castes Sub Plan* (SCSP) is a major initiative for lifting SCs above the poverty line through self–employment or training. The amount of subsidy admissible is 50% of the project cost, subject to a maximum of Rs 10,000 per beneficiary. Another recent measure is increasing the existing rates of relief to victims of atrocities, their family members, and dependents as per the Scheduled Castes and the Scheduled Tribes (Prevention of Atrocities Amendment) Rules 2011. A number of schemes to encourage SC students to continue higher education studies are also under implementation. Some of them are as follows:

- *Pre-Matric Scholarship Scheme* for SC Students studying in Classes IX and X was introduced from July 2012 to support parents of SC children in education of their wards so that the incidence of drop-out, especially in the transition from elementary to secondary stage is minimised. Students with parental income not exceeding Rs 2 lakh per annum are eligible for this scheme. An amount of Rs 777 crore had been released to states upto December 2012 for scholarships to an estimated 35 lakh beneficiaries.

- Under the revised *Post-Matric Scheme* for SCs an amount of Rs 1269.73 crore has been released to states. The number of beneficiaries during 2012-2013 is estimated at 40 lakh.

- Under the Rajiv Gandhi National Fellowship Scheme which aims at providing financial assistance to SC students pursuing MPhil and PhD courses, Rs 125 crore has been allocated for 2000 new/renewal fellowships during 2012-2013.

- Under the National Overseas Scholarship Scheme, financial support to students pursuing Master's level courses and PhD/Post-Doctoral courses abroad, 30 awards are given per year.

- Under Top Class Education, eligible students who secure admission in notified institutions like the IITs, IIMs, and NITs, are provided full financial support for meeting the requirements of tuition fees, living expenses, books, and computers.

SCHEDULED TRIBES (STS)

For the welfare and development of STs, an outlay of Rs 4090 crore has been made in the Annual Plan for 2012-2013 to provide *Special Central Assistance* (SCA) to *Tribal Sub-Plan* (TSP). The SCA to TSP is a 100% grant extended to states as additional funding to their TSP for family-oriented income-generating schemes, creation of incidental infrastructure, extending financial assistance to SHGs, community-based activities, and development of forest villages.

For economic empowerment of STs, financial support is extended through the *National Scheduled Tribes Finance and Development Corporation* (NSTFDC) in the form of loans and micro-credit at concessional rates of interest for income-generating activities. Market development of tribal products and their retail marketing is done by the *Tribal Cooperative Marketing Development Federation of India Limited* (TRIFED) through its sales outlets.

There are also many schemes for helping ST students. Under the Post-Matric Scholarship Scheme, 100% financial assistance is provided to ST students whose family income is less than or equal to Rs 2 lakh per annum to pursue post-matric-level education including professional, graduate, and postgraduate courses in recognised institutions. The Top Class Education Scheme for STs provides financial assistance for quality education to 625 ST students per annum to pursue studies at degree and post-degree level in any of 125 identified institutes.

Financial assistance is also provided to 15 eligible ST students for pursuing higher studies abroad in specified fields at Master's and PhD level under the National Overseas Scholarship Scheme. A scheme for Strengthening of Education among ST Girls in Low Literacy Districts is also being implemented to bridge the gap in literacy levels between the general female population and tribal women.

MINORITIES

The five communities-Muslims, Christians, Sikhs, Buddhists, and Parsis – notified as *minority communities* constitute 18.42% of the total population of the country. The Multi-sectoral Development Programme, a special areas development initiative to address the "development deficits" especially in education, skill development, employment, health and sanitation, housing, and drinking water in 90 *minority concentration districts* (MCDs), was launched in 2008-2009. The authorised share capital of the *National Minorities Development and Finance Corporation* (NMDFC) has been raised from Rs 650 crore in 2006-2007 to Rs 1500 crore in 2010-2011 for expanding its loan and micro-finance operations to promote self-employment and other economic ventures among backward sections of the minority communities. An amount of? 99.64 crore has been released to the NMDFC during 2012-2013. The Prime Minister's New 15 Point Programme for Welfare of Minorities which earmarks 15% of targets/outlays for minorities in many important schemes aims at ensuring the equitable flow of benefits of education, employment, and basic infrastructure schemes to minorities.

With the enhanced corpus (of Rs 750 crore till March 2012) the *Maulana Azad Education Foundation* (MAEF); three scholarships schemes, Pre-Matric, Post-Matric, and Metric-cum-means based, which are being implemented exclusively for the notified minorities. Two schemes: (1) the Maulana Azad National Fellowship for Minority Students and (2) Computerization of Records of State Wakf Boards, are under implementation since 2009-2010. There is also a scheme for Leadership Development of Minority Women.

OBCS

Central assistance is provided to states for educational development of OBCs. Under the Pre-Matric Scholarship for OBCs Scheme, against an allocation of Rs 50 crore during 2012-2013, Rs 35.45 crore was released to states up to December 2012. Under the Post-Matric Scholarship Scheme, the target is to provide scholarship to 17.25 lakh OBC students. To provide hostel facilities to OBC students studying in middle and secondary schools, colleges, and universities and enable them to pursue higher studies.

PERSONS WITH DISABILITIES

Persons with disabilities are a valuable human resource for the country. For the physical rehabilitation, educational and economic development, and social empowerment of differently-able persons many schemes are in operation. According to Census 2001, there were 2.19 crore persons with disabilities in India comprising 1.26 crore males and 0.93 crore females, who constitute 2.13% of the total population; with 75% living in rural areas; 49% literate; and only 34% employed. Some important schemes for the welfare of disabled persons include the following:

- Schemes of *Assistance to Disabled Persons for Purchase/Fitting of Aids/Appliances* (ADIP): The ADIP was launched to assist needy disabled persons in procuring durable, sophisticated, and scientifically manufactured, modern, standard aids and appliances that can promote their physical, social, and psychological rehabilitation, by reducing the effects of disabilities, and enhance their economic potential. Every year around 2 lakh persons with disabilities are provided assistive devices.
- *Deendayal Disabled Rehabilitation Scheme* (DDRS): The DDRS includes projects for providing education, vocational training, and rehabilitation of persons with orthopaedic, speech, visual, and mental disabilities. It provides for 18 model projects covering various services provided by voluntary agencies which are supported through grants-in-aid that include programmes for pre-school and early intervention, special education, vocational training and placement, community-based rehabilitation, manpower development, psycho-social rehabilitation of persons with mental illness, and rehabilitation of leprosy-cured persons.
- Incentives to Employers in the Private Sector for proving Employment to Persons with Disabilities: This Scheme incentivises the private sector to employ persons with disability with the government providing the employer's contribution to the *Employees Provident Fund* (EPF) and *Employees State Insurance* (ESI) for three years, for employees with disabilities employed on or after 01 April 2008 with a monthly salary up to Rs 25,000.

SOCIAL DEFENCE

The social defence sector includes schemes/programmes which aim at the welfare, security, healthcare, and maintenance especially of indigent senior citizens by providing them productive and independent living and schemes for victims of substance abuse aimed at drug demand reduction through awareness campaigns and treatment of addicts and their detoxification so that they may join the mainstream. The *Integrated Programme for Older Persons* (IPOP) aims at covering 64,000 beneficiaries during 2012-2013. Grants-in-aid are provided to NGOs for running integrated rehabilitation centres for addicts, regional resource and training centres, and other projects through the Assistance for the Prevention of Alcoholism and Substance (Drugs) Abuse scheme.

There are three national-level financial institutions which also help in the upliftment of the weaker sections of society. The *National Scheduled Castes Finance and Development Corporation* (NSCFDC), *National Safai Karamcharis Finance and Development Corporation* (NSKFDC), and *National Backward Classes Finance and Development Corporation* (NBCFDC) provide credit facilities to their target groups at concessional rates of interest for various income-generating activities. Micro-finance beneficiaries of the NBCFDC and NSKFDC have increased by 23.79% and 54% respectively, while those under the NSCFDC have fallen by 66% in 2012-2013 (April-December) over the corresponding period of the previous year.

THE CASE OF FOOD SECURITY PROGRAMME

In the aftermath of the ghastly tragedy in Chhapra (State of Bihar, North India) where 22 children lost their lives after they consumed a government-provided school meal containing organophosphate pesticides, we must demand of the State a far greater commitment to administering large-scale welfare programmes that are meant to improve, not destroy the life of citizens. What we, however, cannot do is cynically use such tragedies to question the very need for such services. But this is precisely what has already begun to happen. Under the National Food Security Ordinance (NFSO) issued earlier this month, the national mid-day meal scheme (MDMS) will become part of the larger national food security programme and self-serving critics have already started using Chhapra as a weapon with which to beat back this new initiative (EPW, 2013: 7).

Six decades since the commencement of planned growth and after a quarter of a century of being one of the fastest growing economies in the world, India still bears the shame of seeing close to half its children suffering from under-nutrition. If "growth" by itself has had such a limited impact on malnourishment then it surely is time for a national emergency programme to frontally attack such a fundamental deprivation. Now, food intake is not the only determinant of nutrition but inadequate food certainly does have an impact on nutritional status; and that is why it is unquestionable that we need a massive programme that ensures and operationalises the citizen's very basic right to food. The legislation ensuring this right has been four years in the making and over time it has been watered down bit by bit so that what the NFSO provides for is not a universal right to food but a very modest movement in that direction which may yet bring down calorie deficiency and the horrendously high levels of under-nutrition.

Under the NFSO, the central and state governments commitment to food security will cover four broad areas: provision of (1) monetary benefits to pregnant mothers, (2) cooked meals to children under six, (3) cooked meals to school-going children and (4) subsidised grain of 5 kg per capita per month through the public distribution system (PDS) to 75% of the rural and 50% of the urban populations. This supply of rice/wheat/millets could meet up to half of total monthly cereal consumption. The second and third components of the new programme incorporate the MDMS and a part of the Integrated Child Development Services. It is the supply of grain through the PDS that has attracted the most attention, and criticism, from the proponents of what can be called a "growth-not-subsidy" approach.

Three major criticisms are labelled against the food security programme. The first, obvious given who the critics are, is that it will lead to a fiscal disaster. The more carefully prepared estimates of costs point out that as against the Rs 1,20,000 crore now being spent every year on the ongoing schemes, the new costs will be Rs 1,50,000 crore a year. This is no more than 1.5% of gross domestic product and much lower than the scare-mongering which throws up costs in the range of Rs 4,00,000 to Rs 5,00,000 crore a year. The argument that this is a massive hand-out conveniently ignores the much larger volume of concessions (called "incentives") now being given to industry and finance, not to mention the state-sponsored loot of public resources.

The second criticism is of colossal waste since it is based on the PDS which has been shown to be ineffective and wasteful. The PDS has in the past indeed been a byword for corruption and leakage. But it is not sufficiently acknowledged that states which have overhauled their system – Tamil Nadu is one but not the only example – have made a remarkable achievement in delivering grain where it is needed and reducing leakages. There is indeed much that remains to be done to reform the PDS but condemning it when it has shown the potential to work is irresponsible and motivated criticism.

The third and most bizarre criticism is that the new PDS is "anti-farmer". In 2011-2012, total cereal procurement was 63 million tonnes (mt), in 2012-2013 it was 71 mt. Total distribution was 55 mt and 56 mt in the two years, respectively. The new PDS is expected to see distribution go up to 62 mt. So how is the demand of the new PDS going to take procurement to impossible levels and turn agriculture upside down by pushing aside all non-cereal crops?

The more substantive criticism against the NFSO is that after dragging its feet for four years the United Progressive Alliance (UFA) government took the ordinance route with an obvious eye on deriving electoral benefits in the next Lok Sabha polls. The UFA mistakenly thinks that Mahatma Gandhi National Rural Employment Guarantee Act (MGNREGA) won it the 2009 elections, and that the direct benefit transfer scheme and the new food security programme will help it win 2014. If it thinks it has found the tickets to electoral success, the UPA is more likely to be chasing a chimera. A rushed roll-out is also likely to damage the NFSO implementation. As it is, the states have not been sufficiently consulted; the NFSO makes no mention of the guidelines to be followed for selection of beneficiaries; the shift from household to per capita entitlement is fraught with administrative risks and other than in select states a major reform of the PDS has not been undertaken.

Is the very worthwhile national food security programme going to be short-changed then at the altar of the Congress Party's electoral ambitions?

Chhapra asks if we have to be careless in administering public services and if we cannot show more commitment in providing services for the needy and the most vulnerable. The food security programme asks us to acknowledge the scale of one major and basic social problem around us and demonstrate a willingness to address it head-on, even if belatedly.

DEMOGRAPHIC DIVIDEND OF INDIA!

Countries with high levels of political capacity experience the sharpest declines in birth and death rates as well as the greatest gains in income. Politics indirectly and directly affects the environment within which individuals make decisions about the size of families; these decisions, in turn, change the future economic dynamics of a country. We find that political capacity ensures that rules are evenly applied, allowing investment for long-term gain. Our projections show that under conditions of high political capacity, anticipated demographic and economic transformations will allow China to supersede the dominance of the United States by the end of this century and will also enable the rise of India into the ranks of the dominant powers. We assess the consequences of these changes in world politics.

India was one of the first nations to adopt a population control policy, which it did in 1952. Having recognized rapid population expansion as a serious national concern (National Population Policy 2000), successive policies have emphasized not only the provision of basic needs such as sanitation, immunization, reproductive health, and family planning services but the enhancement of women's education and employment opportunities as well. While these policies have led to rapid reductions in mortality, particular maternal and infant mortality rates as well as fertility and birth rates have lagged behind and resulted in a rapid expansion of the population.

India's birth rate now stands at approximately 23 births per 1,000 population. The total fertility rate (TFR) is at 2.98. By contrast in 1970, the birth rate was approximately 40.6 and the TFR was 5.88. Thus, India has undergone much of the demographic transition process and experienced a sharp decline of approximately 48% in its TFR over the past 30 years. India's mortality rates have declined even more sharply from approximately 17 deaths per 1,000 population in the early 1970s to 8.5 in 2000 (representing a 50% decline). Consequently, India's population, despite dramatic improvements in life expectancy, continues to grow rapidly, inhibiting economic development.

These changes in vital rates at the aggregate level mask a greater degree of variation at the sub national level (ZACHARIAH and PATEL, 1984). These patterns are consistent with those of economic growth – in general, the lower the fertility rate, the higher the economic growth. Furthermore, declines in aggregate mortality and fertility in India have been relatively smooth and not as steep as seen in the case of China detailed later in this essay. This pattern potentially has a connection to economic growth as aging populations enter the picture in the mid-twenty-first century.

The effect of politics in reducing fertility in some 15 Indian states is well noted (ROUYER, 1987). It is observed that politically capable governments can successfully implement policies leading to an improved quality of life, greater control for women over marriage decisions, and availability of and access to family planning alternatives. Improved quality of life tends to reduce infant mortality rates, while legislation increasing the marriage age tends to reduce the number of children in households. He adds that, while the effects of contraception cannot be denied, the ability of a government to provide such services has a significant effect on reducing fertility in societies at relatively low levels of development.

The effects of political capacity on births are robust. Higher political capacity generates sharp declines in fertility. Forecasts suggest that these effects are expected to continue over the next 50 years. Note that the decline in fertility is steeper under conditions of high political capacity. Assuming high political capacity will be maintained, estimates suggest that India can fully complete the demographic transition within the next half-century. In the interim, India will continue to experience an expanding population, given the large cohort in the reproductive age (KUGLER and SWMINATHAN, 2006: 586).

The implication is that by increasing its political ability, India can achieve significant acceleration in the reduction of birth rates. Our estimate suggests that with higher political capacity, India can lower its birth rates to about 17 births per 1,000 in the next 50 years. By way of contrast, the low-capacity forecast suggests that birth rates will remain around 25 births per 1,000 over the same time period.

While these forecasts incorporate a certain degree of uncertainty, the high growth scenario is plausible given the experiences of China and Japan, and predicts a growth rate of approximately 8% until 2050 (BAJPAI, 2001). It may be recalled that the implementation of economic reforms in 1991 helped India attain a 6% GDP per capita growth rate. This economic opening has also produced greater opportunities in key sectors including information technology and biotechnology. These gains have been accompanied by high political capacity that seems critical for India to continue the current pace of economic reforms.

The most dramatic effects of higher political capacity are observed in individual productivity. Consensus has now emerged among successive Indian governments that the processes of deregulation and liberalization need to deepen. Examples of such commitments to reforms include reduction in the fiscal deficit and federal subsidies to agriculture, continuing reforms in the banking sector, large-scale disinvestments in the public sector, product dereservation for small-scale industry, elimination of price control mechanisms, reform of the power sector, and so forth. Successful reorientation of governmental spending toward high-priority areas of health, education, and infrastructure development is also likely to lead to higher rates of economic growth (BAJPAI, 2001). In addition to continuing reforms, demographic stability will also likely propel India into the stages of higher economic growth.

It may be argued that demographic transitions and economic expansions are associated with political changes. India is entering this demographic and economic transition. And, because of its size, India may develop the potential to challenge the global dominance of the rising power/s.

CONFRONTING ODDS

Moving towards a comprehensive framework of sustainability, along with human security and equity, is obviously not easy a task for India. A number of serious obstacles and challenges will need to be overcome by the Government in India, which include:

Knowledge, capacity and expertise gaps: Despite the enormous strides in science, our understanding of the ecological dynamics of our world is still limited. The chasm between modern and traditional knowledge has meant that the insights and information of the latter are not available to today's decision-makers, and the capacity to deal with the huge ecological problems we have created is limited. There are major problems with data generation, reliability and access. Clearly, a major effort is needed to harness all forms of knowledge, generate new information and understanding, build capacity to move into new pathways of sustainability, and put all knowledge and data on these aspects into the public domain.

Political apathy and hostility: Current political governance systems mostly centralise power in the hands of a few, even in countries with universal suffrage that are called democratic. There is an inherent resistance to major change in centralised political systems, and often those in power are either themselves profiting from the current economic system, or heavily influenced by others profiting from it. All this creates a major hurdle to the sort of change needed. However, such apathy and hostility is slowly changing, and will change faster as public mobilisation creates greater pressure from below, global agreements create pressure from above, and political leaders themselves realise the benefits of change.

Corporate power: The enormous profits that corporations make from the currently unsustainable economic system, coupled with their hold on most nation states and their lack of accountability to the public, are a major source of resistance to change. People's movements and responsive governments have to move to reduce the clout of corporations, facilitate alternative, people-based production, business, trade and exchange, and regulate/incentivise corporations towards practices of sustainability.

Military interests: The military is a powerful influence in most countries, is not known to be particularly interested in or sympathetic towards issues of ecological sustainability, and indeed has a strong vested interest in continuing the status quo. It is important for ecological and justice-equity movements to have a strong peace and demilitarisation angle, along with ongoing dialogue on how ecological and socio-economic security are much better ways to secure populations than the military.

Public apathy and attitudes: Decades of the current system have created a sense of apathy or helplessness, or worse, have co-opted the public into believing that salvation lies in unending consumption. Much sensitisation work is needed by civil society and governments to create mass public awareness of the abyss we are falling into, and of the need to explore different pathways towards genuine human well-being.

To move towards a post-2015 framework that integrates ecological sustainability, human security and equity, the Government of India may have to consider the following steps:

1. Assessment of various visions and frameworks being proposed globally or in individual countries, from which India could learn, adopt and evolve its own framework as suitable for its ecological, cultural, economic and political context.

2. Consolidation of information already available on trends in sustainability and unsustainability (such as those on use of agricultural chemicals, or air pollutants, in ROY and CHATTERJEE 2009; on forest cover, carbon emissions, drinking water and sanitation in GOI, 2011; on energy intensity of industries in RAO, et al., 2009, and so on).

3. Initiation of public discussions and consultations involving all sections, particularly local communities, in rural and urban areas to expand the understanding of the fundamental problems with the current system,

as also to generate inputs to the post-2015 framework at both national and global levels.

4. Review of current macroeconomic and political governance structures, assessment of current levels of ecological unsustainability, and related human insecurity and inequity, using tools such as those listed above, and delineation of specific macroeconomic and governance changes needed to move towards a framework of sustainability.

5. Discussion on new framework at political levels, including in relevant parliamentary standing committees, towards a political commitment in the National Development Council to conceptualise the Thirteenth Five-Year Plan within this framework.

It is very unlikely that the Indian government will on its own move towards a radically different framework than the one currently in operation. There is a crucial role for people's movements, civil society organisations, academic think tanks, and progressive political leaders to push it in this direction (KOTHARI, 2013: 152).

Moreover, it should be obvious that India cannot forge such paths alone, not least because of the incredibly complex ways in which it is already intertwined with other nations and with the earth as a whole. It will need to do so in partnership with other countries, and within the context of evolving global frameworks. Still, it cannot simply be a recipient of these frameworks. It must be one of the champions of new global processes towards sustainability and equity, pushing especially the vision of earth, and within that, humanity, as one, even while respecting the diversity of peoples and communities within this whole. Without a simultaneous transformation at the global level, an exposition of which is not the purpose of this paper, its own efforts, even if comprehensive and strong, are likely to be undermined by wider economic and political forces.

So even as the above exercise is carried out for domestic purposes, at the international level India and its communities must also advocate a central focus on sustainability, along with human security and equity for the global post-2015 framework. Given that ecological collapse and global inequities will have the most serious impact on people in countries like India, such advocacy is not only to show its responsibility towards the earth, and indeed all humanity, but also to safeguard the interests of the peoples and nature it harbors.

OUTLOOK AND CHALLENGES

The global recession of 2008 and the recent global slowdown have squeezed the fiscal space for most countries and consequently the purse for social-sector spending. However, India's social sector spending has seen a continuous increase even during these crisis-ridden years. India needs to balance the dual imperatives of growth and inclusion. This can happen only if growth leads to higher and better jobs. While the government's flagship programme, the MGNREGA, is intended to fill this "job deficit" in the interregnum to focus on longer-term inclusive growth strategies. The $ 1 trillion Infrastructure opportunity is one such example. Even in the interregnum, schemes like the MGNREGA should move towards more production – and growth-generating activities.

The draft Twelfth Five Year Plan has emphasized faster, more inclusive and sustainable growth. A special effort is needed in two areas of human development in India – health and education. These will help translate our demographic advantage into a real dividend. There is also need to address delivery-related issues in a mission mode to ensure optimum utilisation of funds and to convert outlays into outcomes. For this, good governance is critical.

A number of legislative steps have also been taken to secure the rights of people, like the *Right to Information Act*, the *MGNREGA*, the *Forest Rights Act*, and the *RTE*. Thus the funds are in place, rights constitutionally guaranteed, and many achievements recorded, but there are also pressing issues like leakages and funds not reaching the targeted beneficiaries. While the *Direct Benefit Transfer* (DBT) system with the help of the DID can help in plugging many of these leakages, there is enough scope for expenditure reduction even in social-sector programmes through convergence (integration and combining).

Economic Survey 2011–2012 had pointed out that there are many schemes like the AABY, JBY, and RSBY with significant overlap and catering to the same or similar categories of the population, with *Shiksha Sahyoga Yojana* (SSY) as an add-on benefit under the former two schemes. A welcome development this year is the merger of the JBY with the AABY. There are many other such areas where convergence can take place. For example the JSY, Janani Shishu Surksha Karyakram (JSSK), and Indira Gandhi Matritva Sahyog Yojana (IGMSY) have many overlapping features and the same beneficiaries.

This calls for a careful exercise in identifying overlapping schemes and weeding out or converging them. A threshold level could also be fixed for the schemes as a critical minimum investment or outlay is needed for any programme to be successful. The Committee on "Restructuring of Centrally Sponsored Schemes" has suggested that new centrally sponsored schemes should have a minimum Plan expenditure of Rs 10,000 crore over the Five Year Plan and should be included under flagship schemes.

Another area needing attention is decentralisation. While Plan programmes are designed with a bottom-up approach and are panchayat – and PRI-centric, they are actually implemented in a top-down manner and do not effectively articulate the needs and aspirations of the local people, especially the most vulnerable. With the 73rd Constitutional Amendment, several functions were transferred to PRIs and since 2004 there has also been massive transfer of funds to PRIs, especially after the enactment of the MGNREGA. But institutionally the PRIs remain weak and do not have the required capacity to plan or implement programmes effectively. The Twelfth Five Year Plan proposes a complete break from the past and provides sizeable resources to the Ministry of Panchayati Raj. These higher outlays should be converted into outcomes. This calls for greater focus on empowering PRIs through training and awareness generation coupled with social audit of all social-sector programmes. Cash transfers to the intended beneficiaries can also help empower citizens, even while giving them choice of provider. This too can help improve the quality of service delivery.

PUBLIC RESPONSE TO DEVELOPMENT IN INDIA

Basically, "development" has become a mask for extremely gross forms of exploitation and corruption in Tribal dominant regions of India. An objective sociological analysis majority of the development projects in India would probably conclude that it is a vital expression of civil society against forced dispossession of the indigenous people. As Sainath observes in his book *Everybody Loves a Good Drought* (1996), huge amounts of money are allocated for "tribal development", very little of which benefits or even reaches the Adivasis. So movements against these projects must be understood as in the words of Kishen Patnayak:

> The politicians, social workers and pro-people intellectuals should start thinking in this direction: are mines a bane or a boon to the indigenous people? They must take a clear stand. Have they any evidence for the idea being propagated that leasing out mines to the companies will benefit and make the people and the state prosperous? (PADEL, 2010: 13).

Ongoing movements against excessive industrialisation in tribal inhabited regions in India have tended to follow Gandhian principles of ahimsa (non-violence), and an alternative view of industry and development, in which the dignity of labour and village life are valued above profit.

Mining project supporters are deeply mistaken when they label protestors "anti-national", "anti-social", "anti-government", "anti-industry" or "anti-development". The movements against aluminium and steel projects in India are a response to basic injustice and prick the nation's conscience. But how open are government officials when it comes to listening to this conscience?

All over the world, Gandhi is still an inspiring model of resistance to the multiple injustices of government repression and financial manipulation.

Movements like those in Odisha (state situated on the east coast of India) may yet show the way to the rest of the world, helping all to resist the ungroundedness of modern life and its power structures, which threaten the quality, if not the very existence, of human life on earth. These movements represent the interests of the poorer, more exploited sections of society. They are no more "anti-social" or "anti-national".

Gandhi's ideals were subverted much too soon. Shortly before his death, he had an exchange of letters with Nehru concerning a fundamental difference in their outlooks. For Gandhi, village life and "industry", in the sense of self-sufficiency in producing one's own food, clothes and other needs, formed the core of civilised living. He thought that the rush towards machine-based industrialisation and city life was making the human race rush headlong on a path to collective suicide.

Since the US dropped aluminium-detonated atom bombs on Japan in 1945, we live perpetually on the edge of an abyss of self-destruction. The military-industrial complex has aluminium at its core. As Chomsky says (2003: 58):

> The reality is that under capitalist conditions – meaning maximisation of short-term gain – you're ultimately going to destroy the environment: the only question is when.

The mass use of aluminium as a symptom of the ungroundedness and speediness of modern-life, in which business, economics and politics, and all the systems that make up the modern power structure, are alienated from an awareness of where things, including ourselves, come from. Our whole civilisation is spinning out of control, driven by a financial system that recognises only short-term profit. Cleverness of mind tends to, be channelled into the profit motive, split off from consciousness of the results of one's actions. This cleverness manifests in repeated promises to share the profit with people whose labour and resources "are exploited" – promises that are invariably broken. Nowhere is this clearer than in the modern mining industry and its impact on indigenous people.

The villagers and the indigenous people in India (like in other parts of the world) have survived enormous exploitation and marginalisation. With their sense of community living; they could demonstrate to the world a better way of living together. As the then President of India, K. R. Narayanan, said in his Republic Day speech on 25 January 2001, alluding to the Maikanch police killings (in Odisha state) just five weeks earlier:

> The mining that is taking place in the forest areas is threatening the livelihood and survival of many tribes [...]. Let it not be said by future generations that the Indian Republic has been built on the destruction of the green earth and the innocent tribals who have been living there for centuries.

The first prerequisite for real development for tribal people is the protection from exploitation, not to allow the source of their community livelihood and civilization to be a resource for some individual or government's greed and profit motive. The money, which is poured into tribal areas of India in the name of development (be it the construction of Tehri Dam in Uttarakhand – north India; the bauxite mining in the state of Odisha – eastern coast; nuclear plant in Jaitapur, Maharashtra; or Coca Cola factory at Plachimada in Kerala – south India), it reaches into the hands of contractors and others who perpetuate the cycle of exploitation (VIVEK, 2013).

Most of the "development" projects have proved to be failures to bring about development of the common people – the tribals and the marginalised. These "failed" development projects serve the interests of power itself; by uncompromisingly reducing poverty to a technical problem and by promising technical solution to the sufferings of the powerless and oppressed people (FERGUSON, 1990). The hegemonic problem of development is the principal means through which the problem of poverty is depoliticized in the world today. The prevailing discourse on development is emanating principally from the World Bank and other models of development (Singapore, Shanghai, New York, Tokyo, Kawasaki, Toronto, and Stuttgart) from the developed countries at the beginning of 21st century and American social science supports it.

The ideas of development which has many interpretations (and therefore become confused) are quite often powerful in "policy-making" because they provide spacious kind of hanger for different persuasions to hook on (Railway Station walking plazas, Dept Stores/malls, flyovers, etc.). The idea of social capital has been one of such ideas. It has been subject of number of symposia and prestigious academic gatherings.

Borrowing from Pierre Bourdeau, the concept of *social capital* was used by Robert Putnam (Harvard Professor) in 1993 to define government in Italy to talk about trust, norms and networks that can improve the efficiency of society by facilitating coordinated action (PUTNAM, 1993: 167). Put it simply, it refers to the familiar everyday notion that "it is not what you know (that counts, but) it is who you know". Yet it has come to be described by one of the World Bank experts as "the missing link" in development (GROOLAERT, 1997).

It must be noted that the work of often very clever and well intentioned social scientists derives from and contributes to a hegemonic social science that systematically obscures power, class and politics. It may be said that social capital and closely related idea of *trust and reciprocity* and the ideas of activities of *civil society* (held to be sphere of association outside the state, in which people freely participate) participation and non government organisations have come to constitute new weapons in the armoury of the anti-politics machine that is constituted by the practices of "international development". They are clever ideas which suit the interests of global capitalism because they represent problems that are rooted in differences of power and in class relations as purely technical matters that can be resolved outside the political arena.

INDIA IN LATIN AMERICA

There was scarcely any migration from India to Latin America, historically. After the abolition of slavery in the early 19th century, the British "indented" Indian labour for their colonial plantations all over the world. In the LAC region, Indian indentured labour was shipped mainly to the Caribbean: the former British colonies of Trinidad and Tobago and Guyana. The French overseas territories Martinique and Guadeloupe, and the Dutch colony of Suriname also received migrant Indian labour in this period. There were subsequent migrations by Indian businessmen and professionals to other countries of the region, but these were scanty, as mentioned in the Report of the High Level Committee on the Indian Diaspora, submitted to the Indian government in January 2002 (BHOJWANI, 2013: 40).

India has also been little known in most of the LAC. Those populations tended to regard it as a distant, benign entity, with admirable spiritual and cultural traditions. It is also seen through the kaleidoscope of contrasting images of poverty and progress. Though there were important cultural encounters in the early 2oth century, they did not result in durable and expanded contacts, apart from some features which are little known, such as the establishment of the Ramakrishna Ashram in Argentina in 1933. Jawaharlal Nehru's meetings with Latin American delegations, at the International Congress of Oppressed Peoples in Brussels in 1927, ignited interest on both sides. India's leading communist ideologue, M N Roy played an important role in the creation of the Mexican Communist Party in 1917.

The first Indian embassies were opened in Brazil and Argentina in 1948, and in other major countries over succeeding years. Argentina provided a famine-hit India with a shipment of 1,40,000 tonnes of wheat as early as 1946. The first high LAC dignitary to visit India was Argentine President Arturo Frondizi in December 1961. In 1968 Prime Minister Indira Gandhi made an extensive tour of the region, visiting Brazil, Uruguay, Argentina, Chile, Colombia, Venezuela, Trinidad and Tobago and Guyana.

Political and economic interaction, however, was still relatively limited. Latin America was absorbed with the us and Europe, and India focused on Asian-African unity and the Non-Aligned Movement. Being a relatively closed economy, foreign trade and investment did not figure prominently in India's priorities. From the 19505 till the 19805 most LAC economies were looking inward. The wave of liberalisation that swept India since the 19905 and the corresponding opening up of Latin America around the same period created a self-confidence that enabled and spurred both to venture beyond their traditional space. The inherent economic complementarities began to be discovered and examined by a tentative official establishment. A more important campaign was under way, led by intrepid Indian business enterprises in search of alternative sources of fuel and raw materials, as well as markets for their booming automobile, pharmaceutical, textile, software and other industries.

India's diplomatic footprint in LAC expanded gradually in recent decades, but to a lesser extent than in other parts of the world. Significant countries, such as Ecuador, Bolivia, Uruguay, Paraguay, and the Dominican Republic still do not have resident Indian missions, despite having embassies in India, and the presence of Indian business in those countries. Nineteen Latin American and Caribbean countries have resident missions in India. Some have consulates and commercial offices in important Indian cities. India has 14 resident embassies in that region, a few cultural centres in the Caribbean, Mexico and Brazil, and a consulate general in Sao Paulo, Brazil.

Attempts at composite political dialogue with the region date back to September 1995, when India's external affairs minister (EAM) met the foreign ministers of the then "Troika of the Rio Group" in New York. It was decided to have an annual structured dialogue, which was unfortunately not followed up. An agreement for Political Consultation and Cooperation was signed with the Andean Community during the visit of the EAM to lima, Peru in June 2003. There was little follow up on this, as on related efforts towards economic cooperation.

An agreement was signed between India and the CARICOM to establish a Standing Joint Commission for Consultation, Cooperation and Coordination, during the visit of the foreign and trade minister of Jamaica, then chairman of the CARICOM Community Council, in November 2003 to India. The first and only meeting of India – CARICOM foreign ministers was held in February 2005. Foreign ministers of the eight-member Integrated System for Central America (SICA) met the EAM in Delhi in 2004 and again in 2008. There was a meeting on the sidelines of the UN General Assembly in September 2010 in New York, and further meetings are planned.

CONTEXTUALISING BRICS

Why look at these BRICS countries? One reason is that they all seem to possess a range of economic, military and political power resources; some capacity to contribute to the production of international order, regionally or globally; and some degree of internal cohesion and capacity for effective state action. Particularly in the cases of China and India, increased attention has followed from their high levels of economic growth and from projections of their future economic development and its possible (although usually underspecified) geo-political and geo-economic implications (WILSON and PURUSHOTHAMAN, 2003; VIRMANI, 2004). A second reason is that all of these countries share a belief in their entitlement to a more influential role in world affairs.

Challenges to the legitimacy of international order have rarely resulted from the protests of the weak; they have come more often from those states or peoples with the capacity and political organization to demand a revision of the established order and of its dominant norms in ways that reflect their own interests, concerns and values. The reason for considering the BRICS countries together flows from the development of relations between and among them.

These moves from a traditional pluralist view of international society to one characterized by greater solidarism have undoubtedly represented a substantial challenge to countries such as Brazil, Russia, India, China and South Africa. They interacted in problematic ways with the complex processes of economic and political liberalization taking place in all of these states, more importantly, with the limits and contested character of that liberalization. And they challenged traditional modes of conducting foreign policy, privileging new kinds of soft power and rewarding new kinds of diplomacy.

The changing norms of international society have had a significant impact on the character of the great power club. Being a great power has never been solely about the possession of large amounts of crude material power. It has been closely related to notions of legitimacy and authority.

There are, of course, substantial differences among BRICS in terms of their power and geopolitical importance; in terms of their economic weight and degree of integration into the global economy; in terms of their distinctive cultural and historical trajectories; and in terms of their domestic political systems. Yet considering them together provides one useful way of opening up a series of questions about the pathways to power that have been, or might be, available to them.

There are two theoretical narratives that constantly recur in discussions of how the international system influences the foreign policies of BRICS countries. The crucial feature of any system is the distribution of material power, and hence the dominant political reality of the post-Cold War order is the preponderance of the United States. Great powers are determined on the basis of their relative military capability. To qualify as a great power, a state must have sufficient military assets to put up a serious fight in an all-out conventional war against the most powerful state in the world (MEARSHEIMER, 2001: 5).

A second cluster of theoretical approaches highlights not the continuity of conflict and power-political competition but rather powerful changes under way in both international and global society, especially those associated with globalization. The central claim is that new kinds of systemic logic have gathered a force that will enmesh and entrap even the most powerful. A new raison de systeme is developing that will alter and ultimately displace old-fashioned notions of raison d'etat. Since the end of the Cold War liberal versions of these well-established arguments have dominated the field.

Denser networks of transnational exchange and communication create increasing demand for international institutions and new forms of governance. Institutions are needed to deal with the ever more complex dilemmas of collective action that emerge in a globalised world. As large states expand their range of interests and integrate more fully into the global economy and world society, they will be naturally drawn by the functional benefits institutions offer and pressed towards more cooperative patterns of behaviour.

BRIC countries, Africa and other candidates

Development indicators	BRIC countries				South Africa	Sub-Saharan Africa	Other BRIC candidates	
	Brazil	Russia	India	China			Indonesia	Nigeria
Population (2009)	194 mil.	142 mil.	1.15 mil.	1.33 mil.	49 mil.	840 mil.	230 mil.	155 mil.
GDP (US$, 2009)	1,573 bil.	1,232 bil.	1,310 bil.	4,985 bil.	285 bil.	956 bil.	530.3 bil.	173 bil.
GDP per capita (PPP, current intl. $, 2009)	$10,499	$14,913	$3,015	$6,778	$10,278	$2,162	$4,151	$2,203
GDP avg. Growth rate (1990–2009)	25%	0.3%	6.3%	10.1%	2.5%	3.3%	5.0%	4.5%
GDP projected avg. Growth rate (2011–2014, as of April, 2011)	4.2%	4.5%	8.1%	9.5%	4.0%	Not available	6.6%	6.5%
Merchandise exports (US$, 2009)	153 bil.	303 bil.	162 bil.	1,201 bil.	62.6 bil.	251.7 bil.	119.5 bil.	52.5 bil.
HDI % change (1990–2010, for Brazil only 2000–2010)	7.6%	3.8%	33.3%	44.2%	−0.5%	Not available	31.0%	Not available

Gobal Sherpa, 2011 (www.globalsherpa.org). Data source: World dataBank, International Monetary Fund (IMF), UNDP Human Development Report.

These systemic arguments have implications for the analysis of Brazil, Russia, India, China and South Africa. First, it implies that these countries will come under increasing pressure to adapt, and that the theoretical logic of this adaptation can be best captured either by notions of rational adaptation, learning and technical knowledge, or by notions of emulation, normative persuasion, socialisation and internalisation. Second, it implies that the sources of resistance to change are likely to be found within these societies in "blocking" coalitions, made up of the interest groups that grew powerful under previous economic and political models, or in the continued power of older ideas and ideologies, often embedded within state institutions (HURRELL, 2006: 5).

In all of the BRICS nations, the imperatives of economic development are starkly evident, both in their relative salience within overall government policy and in the importance of specific objectives – the importance of raw materials and energy in Chinese foreign policy; Brazil's desire to diversify export markets; the importance of increasing US and western foreign investment in India; or the role of energy exports as one of the most crucial bargaining tools within Russian foreign policy (PAYNE, 2005: 97).

In all of these cases powerful external pressures for change have come up against very deep-rooted sets of domestic social, cultural, political and economic structures and very distinctive national traditions, leading to developmental trajectories that continue to vary very significantly.

This duality speaks to the tension between an aspiration to international influence and a continued sense of vulnerability, and to the difficulty of having to defend oneself against an increasingly intrusive world that challenges old-established national ways of acting and thinking. It also speaks to the contested, and as yet unfinished, debates as to how far these countries should embrace a liberal, globalised order and what the actual space for autonomy might be in the face of the changing character of the global economy on the one hand, and US hegemonic power on the other.

REFERENCES

BAJPAI, N. (2001), *Sustaining High Rate of Economic Growth in India*, Working Paper, Harvard University, Centre for International Development.

BATABYAL, R. (2007), *The Penguin Book of Modern Indian speeches (1877 to the Present)*, New Delhi, Penguin Books.

BHOJWANI, D. (2013), "India and Latin America: Forging Deeper Ties", in *Economic and Political Weekly*, vol. XLVIII, n. 30, p. 39-42.

BRASS, P. (1985), *Caste, Faction, and Party in Indian Politics*, vol. II, New Delhi, Chanakya Press.

_____. (1993), *The Politics of India since Independence*, Cambridge University press.

CARDOSO, F. H., FALETTO, E. (1979), *Dependency and Development in Latin America*, Berkeley, University of California.

CASTELLS, M., LASERNA, R. (1989), "The New Dependency: Technological Change and Socio-economic Restructuring in Latin America", in *Sociological Forum*, vol. 4, n. 4, December, Special Issue: Comparative National Development: Theory and Facts for 1990s, p. 535-560.

CHOMSKY, N. (2003), *Understanding Power*, London, Penguin.

Economic Survey. (2012-2013), *State of the (Indian) Economy and the Prospects*, Union Budget 2013-2014, Government of India, New Delhi, Ministry of Finance.

EPW. (2013), "Case for a Food Security Programme", in *Economic and Political Weekly*, vol. XLVIII, n. 30, p. 7-8.

_____. (2013), "Not a Closed Chapter", in *Economic and Political Weekly*, vol. XLVIII, n. 30, p. 7-8.

FERGUSON, J. (1990), *The Anti-Politics Machine: "Development" Depoliticization and Bureaucratic Power in Lesotho,* Cambridge, Cambridge University Press.

FRANKEL, F. (2005), *India's Political Economy 1947-2004:The Gradual Revolution*, Reprint, New Delhi, Oxford University Press.

Government of India. (2011), *Millennium Development Goals: India Country Report 2011*, Central Statistical Organisation, New Delhi, Ministry of Statistics and Programme Implementation.

GROOLAERT, C. (1997), "Social Capital: The Missing Link", in *Expanding the Measure of Wealth: Indicators of Environmentally Sustainable Development*, Washington, D.C., World Bank.

HARRISS, J. (2001), *Depoliticizing Development*, 3rd ed., Delhi, Left Forward Books.

HURRELL, A. (2006), "Hegemony, Liberalism and Global Order: What Space for Would-Be Great Powers?" in *International Affairs* (Royal Institute of International Affairs 1944-, vol. 82, n. 1, January, p. 1-19).

KOTHARI, A. (2013), "Development and Ecological Sustainability in India: Possibilities for the Post-2015 Framework", in *Economic and Political Weekly*, vol. XLVIII, n. 30, p. 144-154.

KUGLER, T., Swaminathan, S. (2006), "The Politics of Population", in *International Studies Review*, vol. 8, p. 581-596.

MEARSHEIMER, J. J. (2001), *The Tragedy of Great Power Politics*, New York, Norton.

NARAYANAN, K. R. *President of India, Republic Day* speech delivered on 25 January 2001.

National Population Policy. (2000), *National Population Policy*, New Delhi, National Population Council.

PADEL, F., DAS, S. (2010), *Out of This Earth: East India Adivasis and the Aluminium Cartel*, New Delhi, Orient Blackswan.

PAYNE, A. (2005), The Global Politics of Unequal Development, Basingstoke: Palgrave.

PUTNAM, R. (1993), in *Making Democracy Work: Civic Traditions in Modern Italy*, Princeton New Jersey, Princeton University Press.

RAO, N., SANT, G., RAJAN, S. C. (2009), *An Overview of Indian Energy Trends: Low Carbon Growth and Development Challenges*, Pune, Prayas.

ROUYER, A. (1987), "Political Capacity and the Decline of Fertility in India", in *American Political Science Review*, vol. 81, p. 453-470.

ROY, J., CHATTERJEE, B. (2009), *Sustainable Development in India? Who Should Do What?* at website <http://www.indiastat.com/article/drjoy/fulltext.pdf>. Accessed on July, 19, 2013.

SAINATH, P. (1996), *Everybody Likes a Good Drought: Stories from India's Poorest Districts*, Delhi, Penguuin.

VIRMANI, A. (2004), "Economic performance, power potential and global governance: towards a new international order", Working Paper, n. 150, *Indian Council for Research on International Economic Relations*, New Delhi.

VIVEK, P. S. (2013), *Social Capital: Politics of Development and Displacement*, Research Paper presented at a National Seminar, on January 10, organised by Gandhigram Rural Institute – Deemed University, Gandhigram, Dindigul, Tamilnadu, India.

WILSON, D., PURUSHOTHAMAN, R. (2003), *Dreaming with the BRICs: the Path to 2050,* in *Global Economics*, Paper n. 99, New York, Goldman Sachs.

ZACHARIAH, K. C., PATEL, S. (1984), "Determinants of Fertility Decline in India", Working Paper n. 699, Washington, World Bank.

From the minority points of view

A dimension for China's national strategy

....

Naran Bilik

Abstract   China has been proud of itself for its preferential treatment of minorities, especially for its National Regional Autonomy. However, such preferential policies are now under sustained attack from nation-building intellectuals.[1] I try to argue that preferential treatment of minorities in China is still justified when we approach it from the common notions of justice, ethics, and subjectivity. I also argue that history shows that China consists of different cultures, languages and ethnicities; it is absolutely not a homogenous entity as many would imagine.

Keywords   preferential treatment nationalism justice ethics subjectivity.

---

1   Discrepancy exists between the government's attitude toward Han elites and those of minorities in terms of political criticism. Han elites are allowed more space for such criticism while their minority counterpart is not.

DEBATING "MINORITY PROBLEMS"

New China has established a national regional autonomy system for more than half a century now. More than a century ago, Dr. Sun Yat-sen was thinking of establishing a Han-only nation-state known as *Zhonghua*, but later had to recognize the reality that the land and the peoples he and his comrades were going to govern were so diversified that the Han-only nation-state could not be justified and was not workable. He and his followers recognized that the newly built state should be more culturally inclusive in the beginning though non-Hans should be assimilated eventually into Han. Contrary to Sun's successor Chiang Kai-shek who did not recognize most national minorities and regarded them only as sub-branches of the Han, Mao and his communist party recognized national minorities and had won their support in the Civil War. A large number of minority members have joined the communist party and the People's Liberation Army with utmost devotion. Altogether 55 national minorities have been "identified",[2] or in some cases, reconfirmed,[3] between the 1950s and 1970s. From 1949 to 2000, minority population increased from 6% to 8% of the total population resulting from multiple factors, including "identity switch".[4] The national regional autonomy system is the foundation for all preferential

---

2   Professor Qin Heping argues that the 55 minorities were in existence long before the CPC "Identification Project". The CPC did not "identify" the 55 minorities; instead it reconfirmed the 55. Cf. Qin Heping, *56 ge minzu de laili bingfei yuanyu minzushibie – guanyuan zubie diaocha de renshi yu sikao*. Paper presented at the sixth Southwest China Forum, June 16-18, 2013.

3   While cultural communities in South China are nominally confusing in the Chinese record, such traditional communities such as the Mongol, the Uyghur, and the Tibetan have been well established in history. Even Dr. Sun Yat-sen, the leader of the 1911 revolution, successfully launched under the slogan of driving out the Manchu and revive China, recognized the coexistence of the Han, the Manchu, the Mongol, the Muslim, and the Tibetan after the revolution. From recognizing only four minorities to exactly 55, it took more than half a century. New China has reconfirmed the traditionally well-known national communities of Mongols, Manchus, Uyghurs, Tibetans, with the later addition of the Miao and the Yao, while "identified" the rest.

4   Many Han people "joined" Minorities for preferential benefits such as social promotion and university enrollment.

policies, and is the result of longtime negotiation between majority Han and minority non-Hans over political and other interests.[5] The national regional autonomy guarantees that quotas are kept for minority members to fill governmental posts to guarantee their full participation; minority languages and culture are allowed or even encouraged to develop. At the same time, central government has the right to develop minority areas, opening up mines and oilfields, or establishing lumbering industries. A huge number of Han population have moved into minority regions and has brought with it technology and Chinese education and culture. Such minority preferential policies has been implemented since the 1950s up till now though there was suspense during the Cultural Revulsion. The majority Han Chinese generally accepted such policies since the targeted minority populations were so small that no one would take a serious look at the issue.

However, since the opening up and especially since China developed into an economic superpower, nationalism has also surged, a phenomenon facilitated by the popularization of internet and other digital technologies. Nation-building elites feel the need of having a spiritual and moral support strong enough to match the state's economic might. Several forces combined to challenge the national regional autonomy system:

- Marketization prefers equal opportunity for individuals and groups.
- High-speed economic development needs to be matched with nationalism for spiritual support.
- Reconfiguration of geopolitics demands national security and mainstream politicians tend to regard minority issues as a threat or a burden.

---

5   Through negotiation leading national minorities such as the Mongolian, the Tibetan and the Uyghur gave up their independence claims and agreed to join the Han to form a unified modern state. The government has relocated a huge number of Han population to minority areas and opened up mineral mines and oilfields. In return, the major national minorities were allowed to establish autonomous regions, autonomous prefectures, and autonomous counties or banners.

- The old-style nationalism calling for linguistic and cultural assimilation is revived to fill in "the spiritual void" after the Cold War.

The first argument gives full support to absolute equality of right to every citizen, disregarding their background of language, culture, history, gender, or feeling. Despite the fact that people who hold such views would also embrace China exclusionist view in the worldwide ideological confrontation between China and the West, saying that China's culture and history makes it too special to be included in the list of free nations. Statism-cum-nationalism is the core ideology of mainstream elites, and they have no reservation for holding such a view. When the interest of the state is at issue, nothing should prevent the Leviathan from suppressing anything that threatens its rightful execution of "duties". "For the national interest", or "the interest of the state overrides all", is the principle. Actually, this version of a statist view is quite nationalistic considering the historical encounters between China and the West. National humiliation is remembered in both the official and folk discourses,[6] solidifying the nationalist foundation for the unity of the whole nation. In folk knowledge "foreigners" are usually defined by languages, cultures, and oftentimes, phenotypical appearance. It seems natural that minorities can easily be categorized as "semi-foreigners" analogically since they also speak a different language, have a different culture, and sometimes look quite different. Therefore, the present version of statist nationalism is quite exclusive linguistically, culturally, and sometimes phenotypically. The culminating economic and political might puts a high stake in on nationalism. Consequently, along this line of thinking, minorities have become a "burden" if not "a threat" for the nation-builders.

While minority opinions with a nationalist bent are under strict control, Han intellectuals who hold nationalistic views are outspoken and are less

---

6   Paul A. Cohen has described such humiliating experiences and their remembering in detail. Cf. Cohen, Paul A. 2003. *China Unbound: Evolving Perspectives on the Chinese Past*. London and New York: Routledge.

restrained: they demand that government give up the old-style national autonomous system, and some even call for quick assimilation of minorities. One argument stands out salient: according to the author of a paper there are three geographic factors vital for China – the land inhabited by the minorities takes up more than half of the territory; minorities in the western regions are distributed along the national borders; those minority regions abound in natural resources. She claims that due to three factors minority regions are full of risk since cultural and linguistic factors can cultivate nationalist feelings and help motivate separatism; national autonomy can structurally encourage separatism; and such risk increases when the minority population is more than half of the total.[7]

Minority's response, however, is prompt and strong. They are supported by some intellectuals who oppose the assimilationist approach. One scholar argues that multiple cultures in China are the social capital that enables China to develop peacefully and are the corner stone for building a harmonious society.[8] The same author points out that anti-minority advocators advocates have forgotten the tragedy of holocaust. A Mongolian professor wrote a series of 13 articles to refute the anti-minority views.[9] Chen Jianyue wrote that such views have neglected the international practice of helping minorities, and have confused the differences in nature of colonialism, majority nationalism, chauvinism, and national liberation movement.[10] While the central government, with an untypical ambiguous attitude, reconfirms the legitimacy of the National Autonomy System, it allows dissident views to be aired.

---

7   Sun Yan. *Leizui haishi yinhuan?* (in Chinese). <http://www.21ccom.net/articles/zgyj/gqmq/2011/0520/35913.html>.

8   Zhang Haiyang. 2006 *Zhongguo de duoyuan wenhua yu zhongguoren de rentong* (in Chinese). Beijing: Minzu Chubanshe.

9   Amongst others, *Zhongguo minzu zhengce de hexin yuanze burong gaibian – pingxi "dierdai minzu zhengce shuo zhiyi* (in Chinese), <http://site.douban.com/154036/widget/notes/13133662/note/269501671/>.

10 Chen Jianyue. 2005. *Duo minzu guojia hexie shehui de goujian yu minzu wenti de jiejue – ping minzu wenti de "qu zhengzhihua" yu "wenhua hua"* (in Chinese), *Shiejie Minzu*, n. 5.

Nationalism echoes well in the heartland of China where national minorities are much less exposed except to popular images of beautiful minority girls in colorful dress dresses or minority boys showing their dark skin and strong muscles. Complaints are readily expressed: Why those minorities are given so much? And why they are they so ungrateful and create instabilities instead? According to the opinion of many, strong measures should be taken to assimilate national minorities so that they can communicate in the same language and practice the same custom.

HISTORY REMEMBERS

However, taking history into account, the issue is not as simple as yes or no.

The idea of nation-state came to China at the end of the 19th century. Following the model of "One nation, one state" Dr. Sun Yat-sen imaged a Han-state without Manchus, Mongols, Muslims and Tibetans. Though he changed his expression, though he never gave up his assimilationist approach, after the 1911 revolution that guaranteed the reestablishment of the Han-state and took an inclusive stand toward minorities, his original idea of assimilation has left an indelible mark in Chinese history. The Communist Party of China (CPC) supported the Soviet model of political recognition of minorities though a great deal of modifications have been made to it. After the founding of Communist China in 1949, the central government "recognized" (or reconfirmed, rather, in some cases) not only the four "nationalities" (Manchus, Mongols, Muslims and Tibetans) but also other 50 national minorities. As a result China has now become a multi-nationality state, further legitimizing its vast expanse of sovereign land.

Looking back at the time before the 1911 revolution, the failure of the Qing government in the Sino-foreign wars has provided momentums for Han nationalists led by Sun Yat-sen and Zhang Taiyan who were devoted to "throwing out the Tartar caitiffs and reviving China". Sun Yat-sen believed that defeating foreign imperialist forces was secondary to ousting the Manchus, a core idea that provided ideological support for exclusionist nationalism: creating a nation-state of cultural and "racial" homogeneity. While members of our "race" should be included, the others should be excluded. According to the fictive genealogy that was imagined and mapped out by Han elites such as Liang Qichao, who categorized Han and Manchu into one "race" (*zhong*) while others into five different *zhong*, that is, Mongolian, Turkic, Donghu (Tongusic), Di-Qiang, and Man-Yue.[11] While Manchus used to be a different *zhong* close to "untamed beasts", they had already been civilized or considered as Han. Other Han elites, however, refused to accept the version of a presumed Manchu, amongst whom Zou Rong (Tsou Jung) was the most extreme. He stated in his popular pamphlet *Gemingjun* (The Revolutionary Army): "Unfair! Unfair! What is more unfair and bitter in China today is to have to put up with this inferior race of nomads with wolfish ambitions, these thievish Manchus, as our rulers".[12] The rise of Han nationalism reached its highest point during the 1911 evolution, which brought into being the Republic of China. "In a China so defined, the Manchus, simply because they were non-Han, had no rightful place; they should be, according to the manifesto of the revolutionary alliance, 'expelled'".[13] At first Republicans identified China as a Han nation with common descent, common territory and culture, "which was also politically sovereign".[14] Later, the revolutionaries found this racialist strategy unworkable[15] and had to switch to a much compromised version of territorial nationalism. In order to lay claim to the frontier

11 Liang, Qichao. 2001. *Yinbinshi wenji dianjiao*, p. 3214. Kunming: Yunnan Jiaoyu Chubanshe.

12 Tsou, Jung. 1968. *The Revolutionary Army: A Chinese Nationalist Tract of 1903*, p. 65. Trans. John Just. The Hague: Mouton.

13 Rhoads, Edward J. M. 2000. *Manchus and Han: Ethnic Relations and Political Power in Late Qing and Early Republican China, 1861-1928*, p. 293. Seattle: University of Washington Press.

14 Harrell, Stevan. 2001. *Ways of Being Ethnic in Southwest China*, p. 29. Seattle: University of Washington Press.

15 A Han China would lose over half the land and the abundant deposit of natural resources besides strategically losing buffer zones in dealing with adjacent foreign countries such as Russia and India.

territory inhabited by non-Han peoples, which had been under imperial rule, Sun Yat-sen and his comrades had to include, rather than expel, the Manchus and other non-Han, to form a "Republic of Five Nationalities" (*wuzu gonghe*) of Han, Manchu, Mongolian, Muslim, and Tibetan.[16] This reformulation of strategy was vital: Sun Yat-sen planned to relocate 10 million Han people over a span of 10 years in Southwest China, Inner Mongolia and Xinjiang.[17] This long-term plan for colonizing Mongolia and Xinjiang was designed for demobilized soldiers in the future.[18] In Sun's vision ethnic minorities in China could not stand on their own and should be assimilated into the Han, forming a big *minzu*[19] and therefore a homogenous nation-state. That means, instead of making the cultural and national boundaries coincide by expelling non-Hans from "China Proper," they had to start with laying claims on the same expanse of land as the Qing rulers, and then tried to assimilate non-Hans to unify cultural and territorial boundaries, a grand project that would take much longer

---

16 Zhao, Suisheng. 2004. *Nation-State by Construction: Dynamics of Modern Chinese Nationalism.* p. 67-68. Stanford: Stanford University Press.

17 Sun Zhonghsan, *The International Development of China,* written between 1918 and 1919, became the second part of *Jianguo fangliie* (Nation-building Strategies, 1998).

18 Sun, Zhongshan (Sun Yat-sen). 1998. *Jianguo fanlüe* [The International Development of China], p. 175-176. Henan: Zhongzhou Guji Chubanshe.

19 There is no proper translated equivalent for the Chinese word *minzu*. The word is so polysemous that it often carries conflicting meanings. First of all, China is one *minzu* (nation); second, this *minzu* contains again 56 different *minzu* (previously nationalities, or, recently, ethnic groups). The word *minzu* is still being redefined pragmatically through negotiation over "stakes" or "capitals"_ between the Han and the non-Han communities. Though scholars in China differ over the English translation of *minzu* (ZHOU, 1998), I would agree with Kymlicka (1995) and Bulag (2002) that a "multinational state", which involves "previously self-governing, territorially concentrated cultures" were incorporated into "a large state" and cultural diversity was created as a result and to which China is a fit, is different from a "polyethnic state", in which case "cultural diversity arises from individual and familial immigration". Hence, in the former case, the incorporated cultures are "national minorities", and I would rather use the Chinese *pinyin* "*minzu*" to avoid complications due to different ways of translation and disputing interpretations. I cannot, however, overlook another critical point for further understanding China's *minzu*: their identification and recognition depends, in the final analysis, on the State's will (It is hard for the State, for example, to recognize more than the present 56 *minzu* though many more are yet to be identified or recognized).

time. This territoriality-first-assimilation-second strategy has been the gist of the Chinese nation-state though it was occasionally overwhelmed by Marxist-Leninist class modeling of revolutionary discourses and practice. But even during the Cultural Revolution, such nationalism-cum-patriotism has never disappeared altogether.

The multi-nationality state came as a result of a great compromise: the minorities such as Mongols and Uyghur's agreed not to secede from China, and the Chinese central government rewarded them with autonomous status. The areas sparsely inhabited by national minorities are abundant in natural resources and are ideal for Han migrants; the central government gives them preferential treatment and support them with financial aid and tax priority. National minorities are also allowed quotas for political promotion in the local autonomous government. Before and after the communist takeover in 1949 the CCP has carried out nationality policies that encourage Minzu education and cultural expressions, and even allows political assertions. Between 1950s and 1970s the Chinese government has identified 55 officially recognized national minorities or *Shaoshu Minzu* in Chinese pinyin.

JUSTICE, ETHICS, AND SUBJECTIVITY

At present the mainstream discourse of on the national question is mostly of a cultural assimilationist nature without taking into account such modern notions as justice, fairness, virtue and happiness. To address such imbalance the anthropological approach of engagement and subjectivity is necessary indeed. The American anthropologist Clifford Geertz once joined a group of prominent academics and intellectuals to rebut then President Ronald Reagan who was said to have brought harm to liberal democracies. In his Trilling Memorial Lecture at Columbia, delivered in 1977, he brought forward some important principles that he cherished for life: "the integrity of other cultures; the sanctity of all human life [...]; the principle of equality as between men and women, supremely, but also as between classes, races, and generations; and the always mixed but largely brutal and desolate legacy of colonialism".[20]

I agree with John Rawls who states:

> [...] [J]ustice denies that the loss of freedom for some is made right by a greater good shared by others. It does not allow that the sacrifices imposed on a few are outweighed by the larger sum of advantages imposed on a few are outweighed by the larger sum of advantages enjoyed by many.[21]
> [...] the persons in the initial situation would choose two rather different principles: the first requires equality in the assignment of basic rights and duties, while the second holds that social and economic inequalities, for example inequalities of wealth and authority, are just only if they result in compensating benefits for everyone, and in particular for the least advantaged members of society.[22]

Sympathy for the weak and poor has almost become a universal principle accepted even by such real-idealist as Charles Peirce who in his late years, poverty-stricken, finalized his ordering of the normative sciences as aesthetics, "followed by ethics and logic".[23]In a similar vein, almost a century later, Michael Herzfeld pointed out that we need to surpass the old model of "applied anthropology" or "practical anthropology", which are largely platforms built for collaboration between government agencies and financial organizations such as the World Bank and anthropologists.[24]

---

20 Clifford Geertz, 2010, *Life among the Anthros and Other Essays,* Kindle Edition, Loc 72-91, ed., Fred Inglis, Princeton and Oxford: Princeton University Press.

21 Rawls, John, 1971, *A Theory of Justice*, p. 4. Cambridge, Massachusetts & London: The Belknap Press of Harvard University Press.

22 *ibid.,* p. 14–15.

23 Brent, Joseph. 1998 (1993). *Charles Sanders Peirce: A Life*, Revised and Enlarged Edition, p. 312, 333, 347. Bloomington and Indianapolis: Indiana University Press.

24 The anthropologist Michael Herzfeld came to Fudan University in Shanghai to deliver a speech, entitled "Engaged Anthropology"The talk was given on 29 March, 2013, <http://news.fudan.edu.cn/2013/0408/33025.html>.

The engaged anthropology is quite straightforward in stating that it works for the benefit and interest of the local communities who are usually weak and vulnerable politically and economically.

In China's case, as far as minority issues are concerned, statism or nationalist statism, can only lead to further turmoil and increased hatred between national minorities and the national majority, who were otherwise getting along quite well in the past. They first should be treated as "life forms" with dignity and subjectivity. Their languages and cultures deserve high respect. National harmony would be realized unless the wishful thinking of "one nation, one state, one language, one culture" be abandoned. Though I am not going as far as Lee Whorf in believing that patterns of language influence those of thinking, I insist that language does have strong connections with local material and spiritual life; it deserves in every way respect from the majority. Cultural plurality and political unity belong to difference planes or levels, and diversity at the level of social life does not deny the possibility of reaching an "overlapping consensus" at the higher level. While linguistic and cultural diversity are the social fact and defy any non-recognition, political communities can be imagined, designed, and constructed by nationalist elites who disregard reality. However, history has shown what human disasters such non-recognition of linguistic and cultural diversity could bring to the world. Embracing justice, engaging ethics, and evoking subjectivity can help open a new chapter in dealing with "nationality issues" in China since the trichotomy of justice, ethics, and subjectivity can serve as a common tie that binds peoples of different languages and cultures together without coercion and forced assimilation. When people are united to work for the realization of "the ecology of the mind", when the unity of material forms, communicative energy, and spiritual life have become the content of the public imagination instead of the content of wishful assimilationist thinking. Minorities are not "threats" or "burdens"; they are as much as "life forms" as the majority, who are like everybody else, husbands, wives, sons, daughters, grandparents, grandchildren, and so on. Human beings can live together without giving up their linguistic and cultural identities. This is history as well as reality though it may not agree with the strategy of those radical nation-builders. Listening to local voices in local languages and dialects in order to understand the minority points of view can bring real dialogue between the minority and the majority, and can diagnose what is at stake in nationality relations taking account of the claims of both the minority and the majority. There is no alternative for China but striving for political unity without linguistic and cultural assimilation. This is a new national strategy that many leaders and officials have realized but are hesitant to adopt and practice. Now it is high time.

Liquid modernity, mevelopment Trilemma and *ignoledge* governance

A case study of ecological crisis in SW China

Zhou Lei

Abstract   In this paper, a Mundellian "development trilemma" is proposed by the author as a globalization conundrum and an impossible trinity, in order to describe three elements of "development" running afoul with each other that deteriorated into a vicious circle (a triangle of impossible trinity), and occasioned a Southwest China development case.

The three elements of impossible trinity can be summarized as followed:

A: development based on infinite growth and material abundance presupposition – a free flow of "modernity" and a "civilized juggernaut".

B: prosperity accessible to all (fantasy) and one "fluid" development/ modernity paradigm fits all – "development by the people, for the people and of the people"; an ever-lasting exchange process between nature resources and artificial knowledge concoctions.

C: nature conservancy and continuity of cultural heritage – a "stateless" global village where miscellaneous cultures converge and intermingle versus a myriad of "sovereign tribes" where culture "fossilized" and encrusted by incremental development sugar coats.

In order to use network analysis, anthropological method and holistic approaches to unravel the *imponderabilia* of global interconnectedness and liquid modernity, this research intends to analyze the development failure in SW China through a few concepts stemmed from Chinese contexts, such as textual governance, political bi'an and *ignoledge*.

Keywords Liquid modernity; development trilemma; *ignoledge*; environmental anthropology; textual governance; China.

In macroeconomic management, policy makers must face a trade-off of simultaneously choosing two, not all, of the three policy choices: monetary independence, exchange rate stability, and financial openness. This famous hypothesis in international finance is a fundamental contribution of the Mundell-Fleming framework, which is better known as "impossible trinity", or the "Trilemma".

As it could be problematic when we move around concepts from one sphere to another, disassociating/disembedding them from the intertwined and jargons-specific contexts; this paper intends to be more vigilant on the concept's expansion of "trilemma" (rather than) in a strict economic sense, focuses more on using this Mundellian triangulation method to re-examine some ethnographic phenomenon collected from Southwest China.

Starting from 2005, first as an environmental journalist for Chinese government-funded news organizations, I have produced enriched news data over a three-year, full-time journalistic career (about 200,000 Chinese characters, consisting of news wire services, newspaper stories, diagnostic reports for governmental officials, news commentaries, investigative reports for news websites, etc.) concerning environmental degradation in SW China, specifically evidenced by *Dianchi* Lake[1] pollution, water-

---

1 To a great extent, Yunnan's prosperity and the development of its capital city Kunming are both dependent upon Dianchi Lake, which claims to be the sixth largest freshwater lake in China and the biggest in the high-plateau region of south – western China. Dianchi Lake resembles

transfer projects, flawed development strategies, destructive urbanization models and industrialized mono-culture. In 2008 I began to re-examine the environmental degradation in SW China, mainly focusing on Dianchi Lake, from anthropological perspectives, through one year of fieldwork in a lakeside village and for the following three years I frequented a few other villages and city dwellings in Kunming – capital of Southwest China Yunnan province, in order to understand an ecological crisis case that includes issues of development, modernity, governance, knowledge dissension and social suffering.

"LIQUID" SYNDROME AND "SOLID" GOVERNANCE MEGALOMANIA: AN INTRODUCTION

In his thought-provoking book *Liquid Modernity*, Bauman offers a novel way of analyzing modernity, based on Beck's "second modernity", by pointing out that the essence of "liquid modernity" can all be boiled down to the fact that, "Fluids travel easily. They "flow", "spill", "run out", "splash", "pour over", "leak", "flood", "spray", "drip", "seep", "ooze"; unlike solids, they are not easily stopped – they pass around some obstacles, dissolve some others and bore or soak their way through others still".[2]

As in this case, the environmental crisis of *Kunming* is manifested as a "liquid syndrome", signifying massive-scale degradation in water resources, auguring an ominous future for both development and livelihood. Alongside with this liquid crisis, what also happening in *Kunming* is the consolidation

---

an ear in shape, and covers an area of 309 square kilometers, with a length of 40 kilometers from south to north and a width of 12.5 kilometers from west to east. The entire shore line is 163 kilometers long. According to the latest statistics, the overall volume of fresh water in this lake amounts to 1560 million cubic meters. Geographically, the lake is demarcated by an embankment which splits the lake into two parts; the southern part is called the "outer sea" (wai hai), and covers 96.7% of the entire lake, and the northern part is called the "grassed sea" (cao hai).

2 Bauman, Z. (2000) Liquid Modernity. Malden, MA: Polity Press. p. 3.

of "solid" governance dominion, inflicted upon the society as a concrete and immediate menace.

Kunming city is built around the *Dianchi* Lake and its urban area lies to the north, which has proven to be one of the major reasons for *Dianchi*'s ecological degradation, for all the waste, either from households or industrial plants, flows southward into the lake – 60% of it being unprocessed. In 2000, *Kunming* had a 2,920 square kilometer water-receiving area and a population of 3,099,000, including 2,594,000 urban residents; this figure increases to 6,432,212 in 2011 due to a drastic urbanization process.

However, it will be problematic to contemplate, that once upon a time, there was an "eco-lifestyle", when contaminated water was well managed, preventing them from polluting a sacrosanct lake. Ethnographic evidences have shown that even until now, many dragon temples still dotted along the coastline of lake, with myriads of them destroyed or dilapidated due to heretic urbanization movements from 1980s onwards. On the one hand, the lake has nourished a waterborne group who is highly "superstitious", treating the lake as a sacrosanct void habited by deities and dragons; on the other hand, the lakeside villagers have never stopped to explore and use the lake environment as a major means to earn a livelihood, such as fishing, irrigating, land reclamation for agriculture and mining. During this process, the lake has been objectified and profaned as mundane resources, used and contaminated as such (villagers told me that, even prior to 1930s, when they possessed no arable land but a small boat –abode afloat for a whole family – they drank from the water, at the same time, pissing and dumping rubbish into the lake; more evidences have shown, over a very long period of time, that people living nearby the lake have been polluting the lake on a regular basis). Having said that, we cannot deny that prior to "modernity time", people nearby *Dianchi* produced a variegated spectrum of ecological knowledge, mores, commune regulations, myths, folklores, admonitions and social rules on lake environment conservation. (Nearby North Village – a pseudonym for protection of privacy – where I conducted fieldwork, I found one stone tablet with characters carved in 1880 and embedded on the wall of a dragon temple, which specified that all villagers should respect the lakeside environment; any activities such as slashing lakeside wetland plants or pollution of lake water should be restricted and punished by the commune governance entity.)

From this perspective, it is wrong to examine the water crisis in Kunming only as a consequence of "liquid modernity". When we follow Bauman's approach, starting to analyse "transgressive, boundary-breaking, all-eroding modernity", we need to realize that as the liquifying powers move from the "system" to "society", from "politics" to "life-politics", more emphasis should be given to the details human beings have been constantly confronting, especially in relation to the balance/imbalance of the "Trilemma". To put it in a nutshell, a free flow of modernity or developmental motivation, material abundance and reckless wastefulness, in opposition to the continuity of cultural heritage inherited by individuals and idiosyncratic communities.

In its master plan, the local government intends to turn *Kunming* into a super-modern city (with four districts: southern, western, eastern and northern *Kunming*), as I will explain in more detail later, but here I will merely sketch-out the basic concepts behind the urban constructions taking place in the city. According to authoritative knowledge, *Kunming* is to be an "Oriental Geneva" within the environs of the lake; its special functions being as a regional manufacturing center, an industrial base, a center for tourism – and culture-related industries and an Asian flower producing center. All the counties belonging to *Kunming* are to be redeveloped into an urban area, replacing the rural areas with landmarks, high-rise and modern buildings.

Like many other provincial capital cities in China, which have been rebuilt based on model metropolises in China such as *Shanghai* and *Beijing*, the most audacious piece of architecture in *Kunming* city, in my personal view, is a hotel located in the center, which mimics a spiral, not unlike the Babel Tower as visualized in the Bible. Since the founding of the People's Republic of China, urban areas have changed significantly; few old streets and houses have survived unscathed and many more have simply disappeared completely. In 2007, the city was still pushing forward with its redevelopment plan to transform a decades-old flower market surrounded by phoenix trees into a brand new international flower-trading center.

Meanwhile, public parlance and authoritative knowledge, as represented in voluminous government files and political statements, brag about the long history that *Dianchi* Lake and the city has enjoyed. When you wander around the city, people familiar with the history of *Kunming* will point out that some street names can be traced back hundreds and even thousands of years; but that they are just a name, nothing else.

Jin Ning county, which is a part of Kunming located on the west bank of *Dianchi* Lake, was once the home town of the "Great Navigator" *Zheng He*, or Cheng Ho, who lived during the Ming Dynasty (1368-1644), and who is alleged to have conquered the ocean and circled the globe before Columbus. According to Gavin Menzies in his book, "1421: The Year China Discovered the World", "On the 8th of March, 1421, the largest fleet the world had ever seen sailed from its base in China. The ships; huge junks nearly five hundred feet long and built from the finest teak, were under the command of Emperor Zhu Di's loyal eunuch admirals. Their mission was to proceed all the way to the end of the earth in order to collect tribute from the barbarians beyond the sea, and then unite the whole world in Confucian harmony".[3] This narration has inspired time and again the residents of *Dianchi* Lake to pursue new seafaring dreams. In *Jin Ning*, the local residents are still used to addressing *Dianchi* Lake as *Kunyang* Ocean (*Kunyang Hai*; *Kunyang* being the ancient name of *Jin Ning*), and they truly believe that it was the vastness of *Kunyang* Ocean that inspired Zheng's dream of circumnavigation. To hear a proud and pompous narration of Yunnan's past is not uncommon, and especially of *Dianchi* Lake, and in such narrations *Dianchi* is not simply a lake, but a civilization. Late in 2012, and sponsored by the Yunnan provincial government, *Jin Ning* marshaled a new ambitious

3   <http://www.1421.tv/the_book.asp>. Website of Gavin Menzies book, 1421: The Year China Discovered the World.

reconstruction project in an effort to resurrect the Ancient Dian Kingdom, investing 22 billion RMB in a tourism-oriented, ancient Dian town.

However, due to the unscrupulous activities that have been taking place over a two-decade period – since the beginning of the 1990s – *Dianchi* Lake, the *Kunyang* Ocean and the Dian Civilization, have instead been turned into a green, polluted nightmare.

Among other observations, after I had finished pouring over the large number of pages produced by the mass media regarding the pollution of *Dianchi* Lake, the most salient features and important analyses to be drawn from the rhetoric-laden media narratives concerned the concept of textual governance, which in this context is a term I have coined to describe how severe social problems and environmental worst-case scenarios are being addressed textually by Chinese government figures at various levels. My analysis and exploration of textual governance is based on an analysis of twenty-years worth of media data, as produced by the Chinese government's key mouthpiece and propaganda apparatus: the "X"[4] news organization (by gaining access to X's news database, I was able to track all the journalistic pieces related to *Dianchi* Lake published between 1987 and 2007), meaning I had to sift through texts often exceeding 200 pages and covering various critical stages of the pollution control and treatment process. Prior to my research, I had been preoccupied with the hypothesis that the mass media in China must have undergone an evolutionary process in its narratives. First, there had been an awakening in terms of environmental awareness, with an ensuing barrage of reporting that depicted China as enmeshed in an eco-disaster. Second, there had been responses from the meritocracy and grass roots level, as well as the delineation of a collective brain-storming process at the government and community levels and in the public sphere, and third, a litany of measures and milestones had been put in place by the government on various levels. However, my in-depth

---

4   In this paper, many names have been replaced by pseudonyms for the purposes of displaying the impartiality and neutrality of the author.

reading of X's reports dissuaded me from drawing any conclusions regarding these these afore mentioned views; because, since the very beginning of 1987 when X first gained access to digital reports regarding *Dianchi* Lake, the agency's writing has been embedded in a self-explanatory circle, meaning it has kept repeating itself almost every year and shows no signs of slowing down. In the agency's late 1980s narratives, the public was presented with an all-encompassing description of the *Dianchi* problem: the degradation of the ecology, the problematic urban drainage system, the various counter-measures being put in place, new endeavors aimed at securing clean water, the new, deeply-flawed urban plans, and also the new political expressions and political statements. To put this another way, although the level of seriousness assigned to pollution might have varied over different political epochs, the public sphere, the governmental apparatus and also *Dianchi* Lake as a subject, have already been incorporated into a *fin-de-siecle* narrative. For more than two decades, people have been lamenting the same losses, making the same insightful decisions, phasing in the same "new-fangled" policies, expressing the same complaints and criticizing the same phenomena.

These observations may lead us to the conclusion that the pollution of *Dianchi* Lake has been addressed only symbolically by the government rather than as a real social and environmental problem, using environmental "newspeak" invented as part of the governance process. This textual governance, however, has failed at its core to address the environmental constraints experienced at the praxis level, representing merely a form of "eco-spin", as embedded within the government's process. This explains why *Dianchi* Lake was drained during the Great Leap Forward period (*da'yuejin*, in the 1960s), used as farmland for agriculture, pumped as an industrial water source and filled with highly polluted waste water by industries located around the lake in the 1990s, and reconstructed to serve the booming tourism industry since 2000. During all these phases, and up to the present, *Dianchi* Lake has remained a key source of drinking water – serving as a large "drainage tank" for the ever-expanding *Kunming* urban area. As a result, *Dianchi* Lake can be viewed to some extent as a "virtual bank", one the government has been able to utilize at any time to serve its textual governance aims.

Rarely in real life I think, do people review news articles written in the past, but if they did so about *Dianchi* Lake, they would be stunned by the fact that everything written in 2007 was simply a repetition – an authentic representation (*zhenshi zaixian*), of stories written in the 1980s and 1990s.

Although covered in slime since the mid 1980s, people have never given-up fashioning new exotic expressions for *Dianchi* Lake, reincarnating it as something sublime or politically aesthetic. In journalistic narratives, *Dianchi* Lake has time and again been referred to as the "Shining Pearl of the High Plateau" (*gaoyuan mingzhu*, a phrase coined by the late premier *Zhou Enlai* and still used by government figures, the media and historians, even though today the "pearl" is smeared by slime, silt and "phlegm"), the birthplace of the ancient Dian Kingdom (*Gudian Wenming*) and the "hometown of dinosaurs" (*konglong zhixiang*). On February 13th 1989, according to one X news story, "a new dinosaur fossil was excavated in *Kunming*, around the *Dianchi* Lake region, one dated to the Jurassic period around 200 to 145 million years ago, and due to its unique characteristics, the dinosaur was named the *Kunming Dinosaur*, making its birthplace – a small village in the environs of *Dianchi* Lake – the 'village of dinosaurs'".

On August 15th 1993, another story from X news stated that "new scenery has appeared around *Dianchi* Lake", due to an infamous tourism and ethnicity case that has had widespread repercussions in the anthropological field since. In order to create a new tourism destination and enhance the cultural heritage of the reclaimed land around *Dianchi* Lake, the local government built an ethnic minority village (*minzu cun*) by the lakeside; often referred to by anthropologists as the "human zoo" – the prototype of many "zoo" projects in trans-border areas around the Mekong. In this village, the local tourism developers intended to show Yunnan's diverse minority culture within a tree-clad, artificial village dotted with exotic dwellings; and with all the typical minority architectural styles and geographical icons described in poorly written tourist brochures; replicated and brought to life in the village in miniature, in an attempt to create an "exotic" *Dianchi* Lake (and in the journalistic narratives, the village has since been addressed on numerous occasions as, the "flower of minorities", or *minzu zhi hua*). Many "villagers" were hired from diverse ethnic groups scattered across Yunnan Province and upon recruitment became contract workers who now cannot go back to their home villages for family reunions, even during the important festive seasons. The responsibility of the villagers in this miniature ethnic village is to provide "authentic" cultural performances and be prepared to deal with a volley of questions from the tourists. Many pictures representing the cultural and festive celebrations performed by these "ethnic flowers" have been taken by news organizations over the years in the village. At first, when major government policies were phased in, local news organizations were taxied to the village in order to interview ethnic villagers from varied backgrounds – to show their consensus on the immediate necessity of these policies. On February 3rd 1988, one news story ran regarding the building of tombs for people still alive, stating that since 1987, 68 tombs had been built by workers from the Southwestern Apparatus Factory on a mountain facing *Dianchi* Lake, saying that "due to the beautiful lake's view and good geomantic position, a "stone city mountain" (*shi cheng shan*) has been strewn with tombs built for people who are still alive; people pay one or two thousand Yuan for a sixteen square meter graveyard, which is believed to hold propitious *fengshui* (geomancy)".

Bauman mentioned that "In modernity, time has history, it has history because of the perpetually expanding 'carry capacity' of time – the lengthening of the stretches of space which unites time allow to 'pass', 'cross', 'cover' – or conquer".[5] However, in this case, we can see how people manage past and present, tangible and intangible, time and space, through rather complicated strategies. In a strict Panopticon power sense, both the supervisor and supervised, governing figures and downtrodden, all relish chances of embracing a prosperous and rich present or future, at the same time, trying to preserve some idiosyncratic individual or endemic

---

5   Bauman, Z. (2000), Liquid Modernity. Malden, MA: Polity Press. p. 9.

signatures (such as unique fauna and flora, ethnic origin, lifestyle, *Dianchi* landscape, worship system, etc.).

As a journalist, I worked for the X news organization between 2004 and 2008, during which time I found that much of the exoticism and many of the fantasies concerning *Dianchi* Lake had not been pushed to the periphery, but had actually been strengthened and brought to the center. In 2005, I myself wrote many news stories pertaining to the new "exotica" of *Dianchi* Lake, including the new relics excavated providing archaeological evidence of a prosperous and sophisticated Dian Civilization, and because one of the most important propaganda topics in 2005 was the 60-year anniversary of the Anti-Fascist War (during which Japan invaded China). I personally accompanied four groups of veterans from the US, paying homage to the *Dianchi* Lake into which several fighter jets had plunged. In 2007, I attended another anniversary ceremony, this time for the National Level *Dianchi* Tourism Resort Region, during which one of the most important events was a gala party held in the "Human Zoo" or "Minority Village", to which were invited famed divas and an orchestra from Beijing – the event was broadcasted live on China Central Television (CCTV). In 2005, another great Chinese historical figure, one who has a close connection with *Dianchi* Lake, dominated the Chinese media for almost an entire year – *Zheng He* (Cheng Ho) – the legendary navigator from the Ming Dynasty. To many researchers and those sharing his birth place, the vastness of *Dianchi* Lake re-kindles his seafaring dream, and the phrase, "600 Year Anniversary of Zheng He's Journey to the West Ocean" (*zheng he xia xi yang*), was a recurring one among the Chinese media at that time. My responsibility as a journalist was to visit the great navigator's hometown in *Jin Ning*, on the west bank of *Dianchi* Lake. However, before I went to *Zheng He*'s home town, I interviewed many experts, historians and government figures, all of whom were obsessed by *Zheng He*'s charisma and his mystic maritime achievements, and especially the powerful Ming Dynasty he was a part of, believed by many local people to have been on a par with the USA in its apogee, though less belligerent. As one of my interviewees stated, "The Ming empire was ten-times as prosperous and rich as the USA is now, but it was still peace loving". Another expert told me, at a symposium to commemorate the spirit of *Zheng He*: "*Zheng He*'s spirit and heritage will definitely resonate and be passed down from generation to generation. Our Chinese government should make good use of this specific period of history and present an alternative China to the world – a powerful and at the same time peaceful China, and the local Yunnan government should put more effort into publicizing itself as the hometown of this great navigator".[6] In Zheng's home town, I visited his tomb, which has been redeveloped as a garden atop a mountain facing *Dianchi* Lake, and followed the soot-covered narrow streets to his progeny's house, conversing with the eighteenth generation of the *Zheng He* family for two hours, and wrote up a short story as follows:

"It was not until 1995 that the descendants of *Zheng He* – who lived in the fifteenth century and circled the world 88 years before Christopher Columbus – began to acknowledge his identity. Serving as a eunuch for the Ming Dynasty (AD 1368 – AD 1644), his identity has ensured". His achievements have been mentioned little, both in the national history records and the chronicles of related counties. In the official historical records of the Ming Dynasty, only fourteen Chinese characters are used to describe the identity of this great explorer: "*Zheng He*, born in Yunnan, so called Sanbao eunuch". His progenies, those passed down from *Zheng He*'s adopted son, were also hesitant to acknowledge their origins, first as a result of *Zheng He*'s embarrassing "masculinity" situation and later out of political considerations. "Because *Zheng He* was a eunuch, most of our progenies feel reluctant to recognize that fact", said *Zheng Enliang*, an eighteenth generation descendent of *Zheng He* who now lives in *Jin Ning*, a suburb of *Kunming*. "Until my relatives from Thailand, the fifteenth generation, came to visit us in 1995, I did not acknowledge publicly [...] my identity", said Zheng.

Between 1405 and 1433, *Zheng He* allegedly made seven journeys to Xi Yang, the Chinese name for the South China Sea and beyond, as well

6   Excerpt from interview conducted in 2005 by the author.

as to a wider area stretching as far as Africa, a global tour still grand in our time. However, for *Zheng Enliang*, it has taken a long time for him to be acknowledged as a relative of the great explorer from 600 years ago.

According to Zheng, the first time he became aware of his ancestry was several decades ago when he was still an eight-year-old schoolboy. "I was attending primary school in the Chang Kai-shek era and there was one chapter in my history book titled "Sanbao eunuch's maritime odyssey'", said Zheng. "I was curious about his surname, which is the same as mine and so rushed back home to ask my elders about it".

His grandfather, *Zheng Tiancai*, from the sixteenth generation of the *Zheng He* family, responded flatly, "You are the eighteenth generation descendant of *Zheng He*". The answer proved to be a surprise, but not a fact to brag about. During most of his life, he tried very hard to avoid mentioning his ancestral history and even adopted a pseudonym, *Ma Guangbi*. "After the liberation (the founding of PR China in 1949), for quite a long time people were all covering up their family history, facts that could be related to overseas relatives (then a shame bordering on sin)", said Zheng. "I never mentioned to anybody about my ancestral origins and denied it to many around me who actually knew".

The situation has now changed. Zheng prides himself on his ancestry and tells his son and grandson time and again about the glorious achievements of their ancestor. Their family photo, taken in front of the statue of *Zheng He* in *Jin Ning Zheng He Garden*, is sometimes used by the local government as propaganda material for the *Zheng He* Memorial Hall.

Zheng still remembers a poem his grandfather taught him about his ancestry:

> New spring of lunar month
> Outbound to avoid enemies' hunt
> Bid adieu to old home in Kun Yang
> Moving to new shelter in Yu Xi small town
> Although life is hard and rough
> Thou shalt not forget you are Zheng He's son

When I juxtaposed my writing with another news story regarding *Zheng He* from 1992, I found that the narrative and motivation presented fifteen years before had been better oriented and politically structured. Entitled "By commemorating 587 years since *Zheng He*'s navigation, *Kunming* expresses its ambition of opening up to the outside world", the story contains many facts and political clues that help to decipher the *Dianchi* Lake fantasizing process. First, in 1992, the State Council approved *Kunming* as a "coastal opening-up city", and the local government intended to use this hard-won opportunity to build *Kunming* into a trade and international tourism center in southwestern China – within the Southeast Asia economic sphere. As a result of this, many strategic urban plans were to be enforced, including the creation of a high-tech development zone and three international corridors linking the area to Europe, America and Southeast Asia. Also, there was a plan to merge the ethnic village, the *Dianchi* Tourism Resort Region and the West Mountain Garden together to form an international Southeast Asian tourism center. This story was written in 1992. As I combed through the news produced by the X news organization over two decades, it gradually occurred to me that dinosaurs, archaeological evidence, *Zheng He*, the Flying Tigers, the Southern Silk Road, and many other news elements, were all exotica and fantasies created in order to show the government's ambitions, political strategies and post-development conceptualizations. This approach has now been in place for more than twenty years, during which time *Dianchi* Lake has become polluted, as new waste water processing factories have been built and rebuilt, new water resources have been secured, new urban development plans fashioned, and new public concerns mirrored by the media in headlines – numerous times.

When looking at the annual National Environmental Protection Proceedings Reports written since 1992, I noticed many phrases used repeatedly, which together form an "environmental grammar" within the government's official reports and political statements, both reflexive and auto-explanatory. In order to explore this observation, I provide here excerpts from many official news narratives written between 1993 and 2007. However, I would first like to clarify that this verbatim translation of quotes does not represent elaborative obfuscation, but simply an attempt to document the quantitative nuances, political willingness and representations contained within the textual governance framework:[7]

> Environmental protection is a concern to all humanity. We should adhere to the policies of economic urban and rural construction, the synchronized environmental construction plan and its enforcement, in order to realize comprehensive environmental treatment both in cities and villages. We should strengthen the environmental justice system, reinforce environmental supervision and administration; actively address industrial pollution to protect and utilize natural resources, including the land, minerals, oceans, forests, grasslands and water, according to the law.

In 1994, the National Environmental Protection Bureau stated:

> Based on macro-management of the overall volume of waste, the National Environmental Protection Bureau will enforce a master plan entitled the "China Cross-century Green Project", investing 180 billion Yuan in 1300 projects focused on the "Three Rivers" (Huai, Liao and Hai Rivers) and the "Three Lakes" (Dianchi, Chaohu and Taihu Lakes).

In 1996, Xie Zhenghua,[8] President of the National Environmental Protection Bureau, said:

---

7   All the quotes and figures, whether officials speeches or government reports, are taken from the X News Agency database, and can all be found on the internet as news stories.

8   Xie stepped down in a scandalous environmental pollution case regarding Songhuajiang River in 2003 – a major international river in northern China that ends in Russia. The biggest petroleum company in China built a refinery near the Songhuajiang River and in the incident, black industrial waste from the factory poured into it, creating panic among nearby residents and also international concern. At the time, the public vehemently criticized the efficacy of Chinese rhetoric-laden measures and plans. Xie finally resigned under great pressure from both within and outside government.

We should focus on the treatment of pollution in the "Three Rivers" and "Three Lakes" areas; on acid rain and sulfur dioxide, whilst at the same time taking into account all pollution treatment projects designated by other regions and industries".

In 1996, in the document, "Regarding Decisions upon Several Problems Concerning Environmental Protection",[9] the State Council said:

We have decided that governments at various levels should strengthen their water pollution prevention and treatment strategies, with an emphasis on the protection of drinking water sources. We should emphasize the treatment of pollution in the "Three Rivers" and "Three Lakes" areas; bolster the prevention and treatment of water pollution in other rivers, lakes, reservoirs and coastal regions.

On March 8th 1997, China's then President Jiang Zemin, addressing the Central Family Planning and Environmental Protection Symposium, stated:

The "Ninth Five-year Plan" and "The Synopsis of the Future Development Plan to 2010", have brought forward the requirements for the next fifteen years; so up to the year 2000, we should control the tendency towards environmental pollution and ecological degradation, with parts of cities and regions improved in terms of their environmental conditions. Then, up to 2010, we should alter the trend towards ecological and environmental aggravation; improving the environment, both in the cities and in the villages [...]. We should focus on reducing pollution in the "Three Rivers" and "Three Lakes" in terms of acid rain and sulfur dioxide [...].

---

9   The colloquial wording of the report title is not a perfunctory translation of the original text; on the contrary, the awkwardness of the wording is famed political grammar and a political willingness statement – a style used in many critical government reports by top Chinese political figures, including the epilogue for the Cultural Revolution and the reports ushering in the "Opening-up and Reform" policy era.

In 2004, Zeng Peiyan, Vice Premier of the State Council, said:

> The Chinese government places a high premium on environmental
> protection endeavors and will strengthen its judicial framework, developing
> a strong economy and making technological breakthroughs to build an
> economized society [...] to strengthen the treatment of pollution in the
> "Three Rivers" and "Three Lakes", reduce acid rain and sulfur dioxide
> levels, improve Beijing, the Bohai Ocean, the Three Gorges Dam area
> and the South-North Water Transfer regions.

It is worth mentioning that the media entities (from X news organization
in this case) and narratives that I quote here in great detail are of great
importance within the Chinese political circle which, more often than not,
is symptomatic of the subtle changes and adjustments taking place within
the Chinese government policy framework. Many official reports and
government gazettes are transmitted and promulgated by X unabridged,
and national government newspapers are all required to carry original
reports, or only slightly edited articles, to the designated time and even the
designated page. Accordingly, in this sense, any analysis of the reports and
narratives produced by X helps accurately portray the hidden narratives
and implications found within government and official texts, revealing
textual governance in action; however, the phraseology used is based on
the following two theoretical considerations:

First, the environmental milieu, public opinion, the media and
government counter – measures, plus the enforcement of these measures
and their effectiveness, are all incorporated within an enclosed narrative
which may be reproduced at any time, and in which facts may be reinvented,
lies become the truth and the truth become lies, with the resulting media
constructed scenarios representing an external form of the aforementioned
textual governance process.

Second, once the texts, newspeak and phrases have been invented, they
are not changed or rephrased, but simply regurgitated as official, political
statements (known in Chinese as *tifa* – new points made by officials), even

though in reality these approaches may have already failed. As a result, one is constantly witnessing slightly different *tifa* – as one version is replaced, mentioned less or fades out once its shelf life has expired or as the textual governance (its structure and content) is rearranged. Within the Chinese political arena, much attention is paid to minutiae in terms of any changes in tone or nuance of the wording used, rather than any "real" changes introduced, and in this sense, the textual governance ebbs and flows like water, changing in volume, color and sound, and yet not changing in any meaningful sense; it is simply marked with different temporal notes and demarcations.

As described by James Joyce in his *A Portrait of the Artist*:

> And from here and from there through the quiet air the sound of the cricket bats: pick, pack, pock, puck: like drops of water in a fountain falling softly in the brimming bowl.

In this sense, we can approach the textual governance as a new governmental technique; people who govern as liquid modernity prevails can use this to negotiate the way out from the "Impossible Trinity Trilemma". The textual governance somehow created a new dimension of space and time, which could be used for media exposure, public deliberation, manipulation of the future and virtual social capital accumulation. When people visit government funded Urban Planning Museums in Kunming, or read media coverage of socialist construction, all they are really gazing at is a theoretical and conjectural development *doxa* (the unexamined/self referential frame for all further cognition), an ideal metropolis existed in bi'an (the other shore) and an *imaginaire*. Through textual governance, an imaginary line, people who wield "solid" powers can evade the theorem of liquid modernity, so the modernity of fluid can sustain a tangential or shearing force when at rest/reality descends.

In order to explore this textual governance process in more detail, I will now discuss the case of the water hyacinth, as grown on *Dianchi* Lake.

CASE STUDY: THE PLIGHT OF A "POLITICAL" PLANT

First introduced to *Dianchi* Lake as a form of ecological knowledge, to address the decades-old pollution problem, water hyacinths dominated the lake's waters for many years – representing an invasive species. Here I investigate one very "political" plant used within Chinese environmental governance and the knowledge contestation that led to its use. Generally speaking, water hyacinths are perceived as an ecological nightmare by *Kunming* locals, especially those in their thirties who still remember harvesting these plants during their high-school years. The use of water hyacinths to clean up the lake's pollution is a manifestation of the government's "ecological management" and textual governance approach, with the flourishing of the plant highlighting the lake's poor water quality and the inefficacy of environmental governance. However, after some subtle but highly political maneuvering, this plant has now been transformed into a highly publicized cash crop, as well as an innovative bio-treatment tool grown widely and harvested regularly around Dianchi. So, ecologically, what led to this water hyacinth enigma developing?

THE "NEW WATER HYACINTH DEAL" FOR DIANCHI LAKE

By the end of 2009, a cumulative twelve billion RMB had been poured into the restoration of *Dianchi* Lake, in response to the twenty-year pollution problem. The medium – to long – term *Dianchi* management plan has set aside more than RMB100 billion for the period 2008 to 2020, and under this plan, the provincial government has deployed large amounts of of labor and materials, and extensive financial resources, plus has gathered together proposals from a range of disciplines, and this is reflected in the partial progress that has been made towards achieving improved environmental health and a promising future, one yet to be attained.

One of the new ecological management activities introduced has come under fire from both the experts and the public since it was introduced in late July 2012. The pollutant – absorbing water hyacinth is expected to turn garbage into treasure, covering a vast cultivation area of 26 square kilometers within three to five years, according to local government sources. Concurrently, the large-scale production of vegetables around *Dianchi* is expected to purify the water through the extraction of contaminants.

The water hyacinth, cherished as a pollution fighter and a cash crop, has spread quickly around *Dianchi*, with activities covering its entire production supply chain, from seedlings growth and hydroponics, through to aquaculture management, harvesting, transportation, post-processing, bio-fertilizer production and agro-ecological applications. All these steps, all industrialized, have already matured and merged into an entire water hyacinth economy. As a result, the previously disputed pollution and pollutants have been converted into a "factory of raw materials", one which has been transformed into an all-new, scientific solution to the environmental problems that exist. However, the public continues to doubt the efficacy of other, more critical and fundamental measures, such as urban planning, the underground pipe system, water recycling, sewage treatment, water-efficient farming, an ecologically-friendly design for the *Dianchi* city area and the sustainability of cross-regional water transfer activities.

Given that the water hyacinth-dependent eco-fertilizer industry is subject to a profit margin and the sustainability of its raw materials supply, a remedy for Dianchi Lake's illness other than the water hyacinth must be found – since the "landscape of pollution" (like the blue algae) – as recalled by local people, is in stark contrast to the healthy and picturesque waterscape that once existed:

"*Fish (including Sinocyclocheiluses – a rare local species) swam in crystal clear water dotted with seaweed (Ottelia acuminatas); the aroma of lotus flowers mixed with the glistening pearls of Dianchi clams*". (All these should be counted as manifestation of herbal sovereignty and endemic ecological idiosyncrasy, which constituted one dimension of the impossible trinity.)

WHAT ON EARTH IS INSIDE THE WATER HYACINTH BOX?

Nicknamed eichhornia – a "water purifier", the water hyacinth grows fast on the surfaces of rivers and lakes; endangering transportation, suffocating fish and harming health. Once decomposed, it pollutes water, stunts the growth of other plants, and so creates an imbalance in the ecology of a given area. The plant is also known as "German weed" in Bangladesh – due to its German origins, as "Florida devil" in South Africa – because it was introduced from the state of Florida in the USA, as "Japanese trouble" in Sri Lanka – since it was imported from Japan, and as the "purple devil" in India. It has been named one of the top ten most detrimental grass species worldwide, and by the Chinese Ministry of Environmental Protection as one of the top sixteen most dangerous invasive species. In 2003, it was included in the "List of the First Batch of Invasive Species in China". As well as around *Dianchi*, the plant was also introduced to Taihu Lake in 2007 and 2008, leading to a dramatic reduction in a variety of water pollutants (based on repeated observations), but also the near total elimination of water-dissolved oxygen, leaving the lake unable to self-purify and the aquatic animals there being unable to metabolize – creating a vicious chain reaction for which the water hyacinth, like a double-edged sword, has been blamed.

I surveyed *Dianchi* at three separate locations around the edges of *Haigeng* District (north side of lake) – from the foothills of the West Mountain to *Fubao* village – and toured *Daguanlou* Park and the city waterways that connect to *Dianchi*, seeing virtually no water hyacinths due to the harvest carried out not long before. Yet, along the scenic path between *Hongta* road and *Fubao* village, and along the waterway from the "seven kilometer" road to the Yunnan office of Xinhua News Agency, the area is covered with a dense carpet of water hyacinths, with hardly any spaces in-between. Prior to commercialized cultivation, the water body of the lake fluctuated in terms of quality, with the color varying between black and green. Now, the surface looks like a lawn.

All the local residents understand that the reason for this is the thick layer of sediment which has built-up on the lake floor due to the long-term dumping of city sewage and agro-chemical residues, both of which have severely hindered the cleaning efforts. Due to the nurturing of these water hyacinths, sedimentation has led to eutrophication of the water in the lake, and given the current rate at which the water hyacinths are "eating pollutants", the public is skeptical about the feasibility of the approach. Many local residents and environmentally-conscious citizens know full-well that this plant, having been introduced to China as a cure for its environmental problems, has actually led to the deterioration of water quality and to a bio-invasion since the 1980s.

Acclaimed as a scientific breakthrough, the water hyacinth, from the government's perspective, has excelled at its job, as has the accompanying industrialization approach, including intensified cultivation activities, reclamation and salvage activities, and resources exploitation. To sum up; therefore, the current "green nightmare" is the result of a scientific experiment based on a "water hyacinth recycling" economy.

Hang Yaping, a Senior Engineer at the Institute of Ecology of *Dianchi* in Kunming, told me that the implementation of the project "research into and demonstration of the utilization of nitrogen, phosphorus and other resources by water hyacinths in *Dianchi*" between 2009 and 2010, proved that scientific cultivation, collection and disposal is one of the most fruitful ways to avoid the eutrophication caused by nitrogen and phosphorus build-up.

The sponsors of the project also justify the water hyacinth economy based on a simple eco-formula; that since a water hyacinth contains 6.777% nitrogen and a phosphorus content of 1,885.5mg/kg, 1,700 tons of nitrogen and 490 tons of phosphorus will have been extracted from the lake if the growing area reaches 22 hectares. According to a recent analysis by the *Dianchi* Management Authority, the post-processing cost of dealing with the water hyacinths is RMB 75 per ton, with RMB 7,500 million spent on post-processing activities alone, on top of equipment acquisition plus plantation, management and protection costs for the existing 33,000 acre area, all of which is expected to produce nearly one million tons of water hyacinths.

To be fair, it is a biological fact that the water hyacinth is inherently able to absorb pollutants; however, the rationale behind the bold project, one which has gone against public criticism, lies in the promoters problematic logic and lack of awareness of eco – management issues.

SELF-CIRCULATION OF POLLUTION BEHIND
THE WATER HYACINTH ECONOMY

Once fully commercialized, any plant will become an economic object and its growth be turned into an industry, one which involves cost and investment analyses and with profit margins as the key consideration. In this sense, *Dianchi* has been transformed into a manufacturing base – a water hyacinth factory– one transforming pollutants into raw materials. As a result, *Dianchi* will soon become a "green monster" waiting for a "magnificent recovery"; but only in three to five years. Even if the water quality has not improved by then, experts will ascribe this failure to the overwhelming difficulties faced by them, and so bring in new investments and bio-technologies to deal with the pollution; starting the process all over again.

When surveying the "water cropland" in *Fubao* village, I was told by a local farmer who was contracted to grow dozens of acres of water hyacinths, that he and other contractors, in order to mark the boundaries of their growing areas, had divided *Dianchi*'s surface into huge "water hyacinth fields", setting up rows of eucalyptus trees every few meters.

Meanwhile, according to some contractors, these plants are accidentally sprayed with bio-fertilizers from the surrounding fields, in which vegetables such as leeks and chives are grown, as well as flowers, and that it is these actions that are the real cause of the agro-chemical pollution in the area; the fertilizers run-off the fields and into *Dianchi* Lake during irrigation periods and the wet season. Added to this, the pollutants used are self-circulating, meaning *Dianchi* has inadvertently become a factory for such anti-environmental products, with its waters unlikely to improve in quality any time soon.

One should also ask: On what basis did the local government come up with the figure of 26 square kilometers of growth within the next three to five years? Obviously, to arrive at this figure in pursuit of purification, the ecologists failed to take into account the total quantity of pollutants in the water body that would need to be absorbed by the water hyacinths; it would be simply too complex a task to tackle such an immense amount of data produced by the ever-changing flower and leek plantations, plus the expanding agro-chemical pollution and sewage coming from an ever-expanding Kunming. When addressing public concerns at a press conference in mid-July, 2012, the Kunming municipal government announced that the central government had demanded it resolve the pollution problem in Dianchi by 2015 – asking for water quality to reach "class V" (according to the Chinese government, this is water to be used for agriculture and landscape work only) in Cao Hai (a lakeside swamp) and "class IV" (water for industrial use, not for human consumption) in Wai Hai – around the outer reaches of the lake.

Now it may be understood why previous efforts have been so inefficient, costly and unproductive, with as much as ten billion RMB spent already. While unable to predict whether the new scientific solutions will be effective or not, we may at least be able to "brainstorm" the subject and verify within the next three to five years the efficacy of the high-tech solutions of all kinds introduced with respect to *Dianchi* Lake – the "big pollution black hole".

Although bio-technology has its merits, we have to examine eco-management as a whole, and pay close attention to the following questions:

- Is pollution in Dianchi a mere ecological problem and an economic subject, or is it a topic that demands a more sociological and anthropological analysis?
- Is the pollution related to the urbanization of Kunming, which has become a tremendous supplier of polluting materials?
- Since the pollution is the result of extended periods of eco-mismanagement, imbalanced industrial growth and the side effects of urbanization, have we addressed the real sources of the eco-degeneration taking place?
- Have we ever reflected upon the over-consumption and financial indulgence inflicted upon our ecosystem?
- Have we fully studied the ecological chain linking new Kunming with *Chenggong* City (a new district developed as new engine of New Kunming, comparable to "la defense" in Paris; in July, 2013, this city has been reported

as "ghost city" – gigantic urban sprawl with few dwellers – by Foreign Affairs Magazine.), and the lake-surrounding suburban regions?

• Will the constantly expanding Kunming be able to continue to provide a fresh – water supply to its citizens?

• What will the city do in terms of finding a freshwater supply once the water diverted from the *Jinsha* and *Zhangjiu* Rivers and *Qingshui* Lake is exhausted?

• How can Chenggong sustain its flower-based economy and its growth status, as Kunming marches towards becoming a gigantic chemical-driven city based on the benefits provided by the Sino-Burmese oil pipeline? (This oil pipeline, originating in the Andaman Sea, will end in Kunming, and in March 2013, news of the construction of a Para-Xylene factory in An'Ning – around twenty kilometers from downtown Kunming, created alarm and unrest among *Kunming's* citizens, who feared this would end up as another *Dianchi* Lake nightmare, but of the air).

Chenggong is supposed to be transformed into a new city of flowers, with gardens in bloom all year, rather than the agro-chemical and fertilizer-dependent low-end "vegetable" fields that exists now. It is meant to be a shining example of biodiversity on the plateau – an urbanity of varied flora – a city described by such vocabulary as ecology, tourism, culture, recreation and ethnicity; an example of de-growth, with a structure related to health and quality of life rather than a number-driven economy. In fact, many who have been to *Changgong* have been disturbed by the sight of eccentric buildings, agricultural mismanagement, bizarrely designed colleges and industrial parks, and lengthy commuter roads between the old and new districts, in essence – an urban planning disaster.

ECO-MANAGEMENT DISORDER AROUND DIANCHI LAKE

No different from its predecessors going through the process of urbanization, Kunming is still cursed by such words as "size, landmark and modern" – a monotonous and rigid duplication of a "foreign paradigms" that is quite popular, in particular, among emerging municipalities that are still following the outmoded urban sprawl process, involving inappropriate construction projects, an indiscriminate quest for size and exoticism, the use of inefficient underground drainage facilities, messy and congested traffic systems, plus ubiquitous CBDs and high-tech parks. All these blunders have already ripped the traditional culture and "cultural vitamins" out from this old city.

Unlike the neatly and uniformly planned *Beijing* and other large northern Chinese cities, *Kunming* has a capillary-like, irregular and slightly tortuous road system, as well as a large number of hybrid communities on its outskirts, owing to rapid urbanization and the resulting real estate boom. The burden imposed by such concepts as *Big Kunming, New Kunming,* the "South Asian City" and the "Central city in Southwest China", has centralized many of the city's functions and resettled a large proportion of the farming population into lakeside villages, paving the way for huge city malls and international trade centers. To relieve the extremely severe traffic congestion, the local government has tried to decentralize the transportation system by building several transportation centers around the city. However, as a result, its citizens have to pay exorbitant prices to get from a congested downtown, on to the suburban stations, and finally to their prefectural destinations such as *Yuxi, Mile, Gejiu, Pu'er and Xishuangbanna* (people have to pay an extra 30 to 40 RMB on taxis, one way, just to reach the transportation system linking downtown with the suburban stations).

Having lost its traditional landscape to demolition and then development activities, *Kunming* is searching for a new candidate; enter *Chenggong* – the new Kunming. As mentioned above, the planners, rather than shaping an intelligent and eco-friendly city in terms of its functions, structures, details and services, have messed it up, getting stuck in the same urban logic as other initiatives; renovating material centers, building materials stores, supermarkets, agricultural produce markets, salons (for sex services), snack bars and food stalls.

The irony of the new water hyacinth deal is the planners' failure to identify the fundamental issues and reluctance to respect the traditional wisdom behind building new habitats.

Kunming's previous and future aesthetic uniqueness lies in the concept of *feng shui* (geomancy). The old *Kunming* is built on a propitious *feng shui* image, with a tortoises back as its downtown and a reclining snake wrapped around the tortoise, symbolizing the serpentine mountain close by. *Kunming* used to be a city encircled by lakes while the water system of *Dianchi* and the city waterways interacted with tributaries cascading down from the mountains and slopes. The city and its local countryside were separated by transitional temples, wilderness and farmland. These landscape features lasted for hundreds of years, until they were disrupted by the advent of the 1940s.

Also, a cityscape should respond to its people's multifarious needs, and those needs should be allowed to rise and grow with the environs. In traditional Cuihu District, the remaining pleasant cityscape is the product of a natural fusion of coin and textiles businesses, the washing of clothes, embroidery, study rooms, shops, a vibrant social life, educational facilities and scholars, all gathered together and representing a natural, coherent and responsive cityscape. Therefore, the design and building of a new Kunming (or "flower city" called Chenggong) should involve the participation of ecologists, environmental organizations, designers, agronomists, poets, a range of shop owners, bio-genetic researchers, soil scientists, entomologists, craftsmen, weavers, fruit and vegetable farmers, gastronomists, floral-food specialists, folklore experts, and a range of other native inhabitants who wish to adapt an eco-friendly lifestyle, one which will suit their own customs and cultivate a spontaneously mature and intelligent community, naturally, modestly and efficiently, rather than end up with fragmented and "centralized politic-like urbanities", those with administrative functions positioned at the center and with industries and education centers kowtowing at the periphery.

What on earth is at the heart of the water hyacinth initiative? The plausible answer is that it is yet another "administrative and political plant", one that will help enforce executive orders and legitimize pollution; the superficial, inefficient and weak representation of a poorly focused form of eco-management centered in textual governance.

CONCEPTUALIZING THE "POLITICAL OTHER SHORE" (BI'AN): THE ADVENT OF THE POST-ECOLOGICAL ERA IN WHICH *IGNOLEDGE* IS STRENGTH

In Contesting Spatial Modernity in Late-Socialist China, Li Zhang explores the "cultural logic and politics of late – socialist restructuring in the context of China's transition to a pro-growth, commercialized consumer society".[10] Using her hometown, *Kunming*, as an example, she presents the reader with an ethnographical analysis of a city struggling to achieve spatial modernity. According to Li, "*Kunming* is just one of many Chinese cities undergoing the massive demolition of the old and the hasty construction of the new in an effort to become modern [...] but spatial and architectural re-configurations do not merely reflect recent socio-economic changes in China; they also transform the very modes of social life, local politics, and cultural identities".[11] Remarking on Li's conclusion regarding the spatial modernity of *Kunming*, which emphasizes the observation of "how the wide spread sense of being late and the desire to catch up with the modern world is transferred to the spatial realm and plays a decisive role in shaping the late-socialist city space",[12] Christoph Brumann makes one particularly interesting remark, asking "why is the modernist, automobile-centered city embraced so enthusiastically in China? Could it be that western modernity reaches Kunming in a mediated version, via Hong Kong, Shanghai or

---

10 Li Zhang. 2006. Contesting Spatial Modernity in Late-Socialist China. Current Anthropology 47 (3), June.

11 Ibid. p. 461.

12 Ibid. p. 475.

Tokyo, rather than directly from London, Paris, or New York?"[13] What is mentioned by both Li Zhang and Professor Brumann here, concerning modernity, post-socialism, displacement and disorientation, constitutes the background to my analysis and discussion here, that is, that through water management and its interaction with the political paradigm, *Dianchi* Lake is, to a large extent, closely connected with both local, urban planning and the entire metamorphosis taking place in China. Without first elaborating on the background to *Dianchi* Lake, any analysis and conclusion in relation to it would lack legitimacy, so in this chapter I apply three phrases – "political other shore", "post-ecological" and *ignoledge* – in order to address what Li refers to only superficially in her illuminative article. Meanwhile, my analysis will also attempt to answer the question Christoph Brumann posed in his remarks.

In the first place, I would like to say that the term "political other shore" or political bi'an is not a complete invention by any researcher or scholar. If one observes attentively enough, many government files and gazettes in China are full of jargon and acronyms, such as the word bi'an, or similar concepts and permutations of this word, which have been mentioned frequently at the central government level and then trickled down to the micro-political arena. As a journalist, researcher and anthropologist, I have spent much time familiarizing myself with all the phrases used in government texts and speeches regarding development and *Dianchi* Lake, and one of the most important observations I have made relates to the fundamental importance of a combination of speeches and articles produced at different times by the government. In the context of this research, we need to bear in mind that much writing with a temporal dimension has been produced, such as the Provincial Five-year Plan (which has been published eleven times consecutively; the Provincial Level Five-Year Plan is based on the National Five-Year Plan and the different items and projects contained

---

13   Ibid. Comments section, page 476. (Christoph Brumann, Institute fü r Vòlkerkunde, Universitate Zu Koln, Germany.)

therein conform to the latter's general conceptualization within a given five year period), the 1999 Kunming World Horticultural Fair (both the central government level and local level have used this as an opportunity to show a modern China, and as a result, much money has been spent and many preferential policies promulgated, including the great urban construction plan for *Kunming*, as part of which many old streets and buildings have been toppled and replaced with green meadows, horticultural settings and high-rise buildings.), and the year 2000 ("end of the Millennium"), year 2001 ("beginning of the new millennium"), year 2008 (year of the "Green Olympics" in Beijing) and year 2020 projects (a master plan for provincial development spanning a decade and based on a prototype created by the central government). When I was a child at school, my teachers reinforced in us a strong and almost exhaustively charismatic regard for the year 2000, and I can still vividly recall this unprepossessing shard of time being described by my teachers and in the media as a solution to the many problems plaguing me as a primary school student, or plaguing China as a backward (luo hou) country. Bauman wittily observed that in the era of liquid modernity, "the task of constructing a new and better order to replace the old and defective one is not presently on the agenda – at least not on the agenda of that realm where political action is supposed to reside".[14]

Later on, when I was gradually and socially constructed by my "environment", I found that the "year 2000 syndrome" or "year 2000 phenomenon" never slid into disillusion, and was never cast away by those people (and the public) whose duty was to mobilize others. When we analyze social suffering, political upheaval and democratic undercurrents in the case presented here, the concepts of "power, post-development, post-socialist, modernity, discipline and punishment", as invented by Weber, Foucault, Daniel, Benjamin and many others, seem too general. In the Chinese case, the concept of a "political other shore" (*zhengzhi bi'an*) would seem to apply, in which a collective brainwashing process is used – for which

---

14 Bauman, Z. (2000), Liquid Modernity. Malden, MA: Polity Press. p. 5-6.

every goal mentioned within the governance texts is bound to come to fruition. This textual governance is given credence by the authoritative knowledge production system, which, once it has been endorsed by the government, can be repeated in the media, engrained in political parlance and can encroach upon the daily conversations of Chinese citizens. As a result of this, all suspicions, worries and concerns should be put to one side and considered both redundant and counter-constructive, or as "not evolving with the time" (*yushi jujin*), because all the possibilities and details have already been considered within the conceptual maps and strategies, those based on a scientific development perspective (*kexue fazhanguan*). Even though the government tends not to deny the complexity of development, modernity and urbanization issues, it believes that its textual governance is self-correcting and should be followed from the beginning to the very end.

In The Dialectics of Modernization,[15] Tong addresses many quintessential concepts concerning modernization through the use of Habermas's theory, including among them *ti* (substance), *yong* (function), tradition and modernity, science and democracy, and constitutional solidarism. By delving into the historical background, Tong maps out the genealogy of modernity in the Chinese context – from *Liang Qichao*'s western learning of qi (instrument) to the studying of ti (Chinese learning), Liang Shuming's locating of eastern and western cultures within the developmental logic of human culture as a whole, *Mou Zongshan*'s developing of "new kingliness-without" from "old sageliness-within", to Chinese Marxists – in order to make the past serve the present and foreign things serve China.[16] The modernization, urbanization and in this case, pollution of *Dianchi* Lake, should all be included in the official Chinese modernization process according to Tong – but as socialist modernization with Chinese characteristics. Tong also states that the most important thing is "not the formulation but the interpretation of the

---

15 Tong Shijun. 2000. "The Dialectics of Modernization; Habermas and the Chinese Discourse of Modernization". Canberra, Australia: The University of Sydney East Asian Series 13, Wild Peony, National Capital Printing.

16 Ibid. p. 162

program of modernization".[17] To a great extent, I agree that the political bi'an, as I have defined here in this chapter, is completely intertwined with the modernization of Chinese society, a concept that has enthralled and perplexed the Chinese ever since the early 1900s. Ironically, these ultimately philosophical and cultural goals have been reincarnated as an incentive to follow the collective modernization endeavour, which may prove hazardous in the end.

Ulrich Beck, in his book *Reflexive Modernization: Politics, Tradition and Aesthetics in the Modern Social Order*, delineates reflexive modernization as something that is "supposed to mean that a change of industrial society which occurs surreptitiously and unplanned in the wake of normal, autonomized modernization and with an unchanged, intact political and economic order, implies a radicalization of modernity, which breaks up the premises and contours of industrial society and opens paths to another modernity".[18] However, in the *Dianchi* pollution and the Three Parallel Rivers cases, the modernization effort has been planned and has occurred "unsurreptitiously", that is, it has broken up the old contours of industrial society and opened paths to another "political bi'an", without self – destruction. All the political bi'an and modernization strategies put in place are reinforced and justified by scientific and democratic discourse; written down by experts with technological expertise from numerous knowledge backgrounds, and then deliberated through long term and exhaustive democratic discussions. During this process, voices from the common people (*min jian*) and the public sphere (*gong gong kong jian*) are selectively harkened by the decision makers, and as a result, this modernization is motivated, reinforced and supported by neo-socialist *ignoledge*.

Concerning the word *ignoledge*, I have to admit that it is directly influenced by George Orwell's widely read novel 1984, in which it is

---

17 Ibid. p. 315

18 Beck, Ulrich; Giddens, Anthony and Scott Lash. 1994. Reflexive Modernization: Politics, Tradition and Aesthetics in the Modern Social Order. Stanford, California: Stanford University Press.

said "War is peace, freedom is slavery and ignorance is strength", and *ignoledge* is therefore an audacious assemblage by me of two words – ignorance and knowledge. When people discuss China, or any other country struggling in a post-modern, post-development and post-socialist environment, no one either dismisses or denies the long-term efforts these countries have exerted, especially China, in attempting to modernize and "civilize" their countries, or to elevate their countries to a level where all people are created equal and have the inalienable right to pursue freedom and happiness and; thus, are treated equally by all other countries who bear the hallmarks of modernization, democracy and modernity. However, the most disturbing fact is that, as the government officials' capability to construe modernity and development has grown, they have become increasingly incapable of approaching problems in a holistic and comprehensive manner. Their pursuit of knowledge began with ignorance, which is fine, but has ended in another form of jargon-laden and techno-centric ignorance, which is a disaster, and the saddest part is, they have never awakened to the fact that this is not in fact knowledge, but ignorance. In The Eleventh Five-Year Provincial Development Concepts and Future Goals in 2020,[19] which will be enforced as a quasi-constitution and development plan in Yunnan for the next five to fifteen years, among the 25 odd pages, less than half a

---

19 Compilation of governmental files. I gained access to Yunnan Provincial Library's (Yunnan *Sheng Tu Shu Guan)* government files section and procured the full text of this strategic plan. The strategic plan was written by the Yunnan Provincial Policy Research Center, which is a government think-tank and has immense influence upon the knowledge circle in Yunnan, including universities, research centers, NGOs, companies and research institutes in different governmental departments. This strategic plan will be submitted to the provincial government leaders and finally approved as a quasi-constitution. It is worth mentioning that, although this is a provincial strategic plan, it is a basic political and administrative requirement demanded by the central government, so all provinces in China have to prepare a strategic plan before they can carry out their own, future plans. The strategic plan is analogous to the central government edition in format and its basic concerns with economic and social life. It is common for provincial governments to invite a cohort of experts from all around China to write the strategic plan, and in this regard, the strategic plan is symptomatic of the overall *ignoledge* status of the country in this specific sphere.

page is devoted to addressing the government's plans for environmental protection. The remaining space is left for the conceptualization of a regional, manufacturing and international logistics center, a gigantic new *Kunming* Urban Circle with an overall population of over ten million, an economic "engine" stretching to *Guangxi, Guizhou, Chongqing, Tibet, Vientiane, Bangkok* and *Yangon,* an international railway hub linking with the "three Asias" and "two oceans" (*san ya and liang yang,* meaning Southeast Asia, South Asia and East Asia; the Indian and Pacific oceans), and a hydropower center tapping into the Three Parallel Rivers to the fullest degree – in essence an urbanized Yunnan with 24 million citizens by 2020. In the introductory part of this strategic plan, the planners provide a general background to provincial development: "The new scientific development concept will clash drastically with the old development paradigms, institutions and interests sharing patterns in which social conflicts run more conspicuously [...] these pressures and challenges will not necessarily all worsen into imminent problems, even though the materialized problems will all be addressed by our methods. What's most important is that we shall take advantage of new opportunities and strive upward amid difficulties, to maintain the momentum of economic development with all possible measures, trying to realize the second and third strategic steps for constructing a "well-off society" (*xiaokang shehui*). Only through these measures, can we promise that the ship of provincial development, will sail through treacherous shoals and into a prosperous, rich and blissful bi'an".[20]

"Ci'an" or temporality is a word I will use throughout this section, and as I should have mentioned earlier, the concepts of bi'an and ci'an ("well-off society" – *xiaokang shehui*: the most quoted phrase in the Chinese media), are derived from the two pillars of thought woven into the texture of Chinese civilization: Buddhism and Confucianism, and have proven to represent an integral step towards the Chinese utopia of "Great Unity"

20 Ibid. Compilation of governmental Files, p. 127.

(Great Community) or its modern socialist version, solidarism. Tong testifies that *Kang Youwei*'s ideas heavily influenced *Mao Zedong*, saying "The idea of Great Unity (*da tong*), therefore, corresponds with the Confucian idea of the world, which is central to the traditional form of cultural nationalism in China".[21] Both to the authoritative knowledge and general public, the well-off society rarely materializes in actuality, partly due to the political and philosophical difficulties that arise, plus the unpredictable nature of all individuals. As a part of traditional Chinese political knowledge, at least two elements should be focused upon in order to realize the Great Unity and ci'an; first, that people who govern are benevolent (*ren*), and, second, that people are blessed with an illuminating consciousness (*ming jue*), innate knowledge (*liang zhi*) and reason (li).

In *The Dialectics of Modernization: Habermas and the Chinese Discourse of Modernization*, Tong Shijun discusses Habermas's views on socialism, adding that "Habermas understands socialism in terms of its contrasts with both social atomism (individualism) and social holism (the utopia of totality). Differentiating these two forms of socialism from each other, socialism in the first sense here corresponds to society as a structural component of the life-world – and is called "constitutional solidarism", while socialism in the second sense corresponds to society as the life-world – and is called "self-limiting societalism". The Chinese experience of modernization supplies an instructive background for understanding these two senses of socialism".[22] From the aforementioned statement, what is particularly relevant to the discussion in this chapter is the interconnectedness of the concept of bi'an with the "Great Unity" mentioned in Tong's book, for as he remarks, this utopia (and the political other shore, bi'an and the well-off society can be considered different forms of utopia), "has been attractive to modern Chinese thinkers such as Kang Youwei, Sun Yat-sen and Mao

---

21   Tong Shijun. 2000. The Dialectics of Modernization: Habermas and the Chinese Discourse of Modernization. In The University of Sydney East Asian Series 13. Wild Peony Pty, Ltd. p. 279.

22   Ibid. p. 250. Tong Shijun. 2000.

Zedong [...] and the idea of the Great Unity (Great Harmony, or Great Community) of the world, comes from the Confucian book titled The Book of Rites."[23] Once one juxtaposes the narratives of these thinkers with the conceptualizations displayed in the Chinese government's strategic plans, one will find an interesting inter-textuality within the government's imagination; for example, Chinese President Hu Jintao has summoned all of China to strive for a "harmonious society", championing a new moral tenet entitled the "Eight Glories and Eight Stigmas" (a post-socialist version of the Ten Commandments) or Ba Rong Ba Chi (八荣八耻).

In reality, the public has parodied the Eight Moral Tenets, coming up with hu shuo ba dao (胡说八道), which can mean either "Hu's eight principles" or "Hu said something nonsensical". According to Tong, Kang Youwei describes in detail the utopia of the Great Unity, whereby all living creatures seek happiness and wish to avoid sadness, and that all the sufferings of mankind would be eliminated by eradicating the nine spheres from which suffering originates. This analysis explains why the "political other shore" has become an important concept within the theoretical and attitudinal weaponry of Chinese governments. If you do not acknowledge the sufferings of temporality or ci'an as reasonable and unavoidable, there will not be a bi'an or Great Unity in the future, as all the problems, sadness and sufferings are destined to be eradicated.

Once this transitional stage is completed; therefore, ultimate happiness will be achieved. As we can see in the Kunming urbanization case, the meritocracy and authoritative knowledge groups have followed two paths of historical construction simultaneously. The first path dismisses the past as ci'an, listing all the sadness and sufferings that have occurred at different historical times and that have subsequently been eradicated by more recent efforts and endeavors, while the second romanticizes the past by focusing on its long vanished and forlorn prosperity and glory; most of the time through literature and anecdotal rhetoric. However, these paths both

---

23 Ibid. p. 279

attempt to salvage a past that never existed; recount a historical sadness — a time when people were denied the chance to live as they wished. This strategy may be seen as negating the past by referring to the present, so as to legitimize the current regime.

IGNOLEDGE: A CRITICAL VIEW

Drawing on the aforementioned concepts of textual governance and political bi'an, *ignoledge* can be addressed using a three-dimensional approach, and before I elaborate on the details of this, allow me to delineate the basic structure of this concept. First of all, *ignoledge* is a power that goes to the core and is convoluted with such concepts as modernity, development, politics, ecology, eco-politics and environmentality. Second, textual governance involves the manipulation of temporal and spatial dimensions through the juxtaposition of different decisions and strategies by the ruling powers and political entities, and third, political bi'an is a socially synchronized imaginative praxis which amalgamates the local, the meritocracy and authoritative knowledge together, eventually contributing to the realization of textual governance and the genesis of *ignoledge*.

As Steven Lukes describes in his book *Power: A Radical View*, the "three-dimensional view of power as a critique of behavior focuses on (a) decision-making and control over the political agenda; (b) issues and potential issues; (c) observable (overt and covert) and latent conflict and; (d) subjective and real interests".[24] To contextualize this analysis, *ignoledge* is also a power that cannot be dissociated from decision-making and control over the political agenda, and can be used to address contestations between different countries or interest groups within countries. Moreover, it is oriented towards an effort to revive a past prosperity, to erase a historical

24 Lukes, Steven. 2005. *Power: A Radical View*. Second expanded edition published by Palgrave Macmillan, New York, USA.

stigma and to usher in a socialist renaissance in a comprehensive way, and all current and potential issues, and overt and latent conflicts, may be addressed through this packaged "knowledge". In the end, the use of *ignoledge* realizes many goals, these being:

1. the domination of power and its manipulation over resources;
2. the capability to harness organizational and physical power to its own ends;
3. the compliance of previously discordant voices from the non-governmental sphere;
4. the production of power.

According to Foucault, when compared to repression, "production" is positive in the sense that it "traverses and produces things, it induces pleasure, forms knowledge, produces discourse and more specifically, it produces "subjects", forging their character and normalizing them". The transfer of water from the Three Parallel Rivers area might eventually be conducive to the expansion of Kunming and the "Dian civilization", strengthening their influence within the Greater Kunming region and realizing the seafaring dreams of Zheng He and his journeys across the Kunyang Ocean (Dianchi Lake) and beyond, a mentality which lives within local people and local political ambitions. In "The Anthropology of Power", Angela Cheater summarizes the inconsistency of Foucault's descriptions of power, by drawing-upon another definition of power given by Foucault; "Power in the substantive sense, le pouvior, doesn't exist [...] power means [...] a more-or-less organized, hierarchical, co-ordinated cluster of relations". Coincidentally, we can see in the structure of *ignoledge,* a combination of the following, opposing elements:

a) local knowledge;	authoritative ambition
b) indigenous narratives;	technological narration
c) regional contestation;	intra-organizational competition
d) historical glory;	socialist narration
e) community-based profit;	collective good and urban prosperity

f) grass-roots rural economic prosperity;	non-governmental knowledge subordination
g) governmental knowledge production;	non-governmental knowledge subordination
h) backwardness;	modernization
i) pastoral nostalgia;	socialist ecological civilization
j) *ti* (agriculture as "substance");	yong (high technology as "function")
k) communal well-being;	socialist harmonious society and great unity

All the listed elements follow Foucaultian principles; that is, the organization, hierarchical structure and co-ordination of different binary relations and oppositions, as demanded by "the power" and held within the organizational and governmental system, are never alienable or transferable, and this leads us to the textual governance seen here in relation to the environmental problems of *Dianchi* Lake and the local use of political bi'an. Here, all the different strategies used, those which correspond to different and even contradictory goals, may be accomplished simultaneously, based on a collective utopia in which, theoretically, everyone is happy with the results.

By creating the new phrase and concept of political bi'an, I can describe the large amount of scientific and endemic knowledge being incorporated into a final theoretical structure, that which constitutes the essential fiber of *ignoledge*. In addition, the construction of political bi'an allows for, at least superficially, community participation, peer review, empowerment, and a "people-focused approach [...] listening to the voices of the poor", as described in Empowering Ambiguities by Wendy James,[25] who points out that "on the evidence of the Oxford English Dictionary (1971), 'empower' as a verb is, in itself, not new, but well established, having, since the seventeenth century, meant 'to invest legally or formally with power or authority; to authorize, license', or 'to impart or bestow power to an end or for a purpose;

---

25 Ibid. Lukes, Steven. 2005. Power: A Radical View: p. 13. Second expanded edition published by Palgrave Macmillan, New York, USA

to enable, permit'".[26] The political bi'an, in this circumstance, is also used to empower the public, to justify the *ignoledge* and to facilitate the textual governance; it imparts or bestows power to *ignoledge* and enables textual governance. Those suspicious of *ignoledge* are particularly alarmed by the "hazards versus providentiality" situation, as defined by Ulrich Beck in Risk Society and the Provident State, hazards resulting from the decisions made (in a residual risk society).[27]

> The entry into a risk society occurs at the moment when the hazards which are now decided and consequently produced by society undermine and cancel the established safety systems of the provident state's existing risk calculations.[28] As Ulrich Beck has said, with the advent of a risk society, it is critical to adopt reflexive modernization, which contains two elements:

1. the reflex-like threat to industrial society's own foundations, through a successful further modernization which is blind to dangers;
2. the growth of awareness and the reflection on this situation.[29]

The most problematic part of *ignoledge* is the fact that it is not self-critical, but self-worshiping and self-reverential. Political bi'an strengthens *ignoledge* as a power through moral and aesthetical justification, and the "scientific" aspects of textual governance merely reinforce *ignoledge* through technocratic and theoretical calculation.

Drawing on Charles Perrow, Ulrich Beck demonstrates that "science is no longer an experimental activity without consequences, and technology is no longer the low-risk application of secure knowledge. Science and

---

26 Ibid. p. 14

27 Edited by Scott Lash, Bronislaw Szerszynski and Brian Wynne. 1996. Risk, Environment and Modernity: Towards a New Ecology: p. 32. London: SAGE Publication Ltd.

28 Ibid. p. 31

29 Ibid. p. 34

technology produce risks in carrying out the experiments and thereby burdens society as a whole with managing the risks".[30]

The desire for a secure future, as envisioned by the downtrodden, is held at bay by the irrefutable political bi'an and knowledge of the meritocracy, as manifested in innumerable strategies and as represented in textual governance, and in this sense, the advent of *ignoledge* is when the "darkest darkness prevails".[31]

First motivated and empowered by a prosperous and glorious history that can be dated back over 2000 years, and by a seafaring hero who allegedly circumnavigated the globe in 1421, it seems that the New Urban Kunming Plan, interwoven with a multi-centered, multi-dimensional Yunnan, will definitely embark on a voyage of magnificent grandeur. However, the vessel on which these dreams are carried may be a rocket or simply a "Ship of Fools" (narrenschiff).

CONCLUSION: LIQUID MODERNITY, TRILEMMA AND *IGNOLEDGE*

In this paper a Mundellian "development trilemma" is proposed by the author as a globalization conundrum and an impossible trinity, in order to describe three elements of "development" running afoul with each other and deteriorated into a vicious circle, and occasioned in a Southwest China development case:

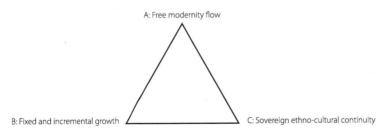

A: Free modernity flow

B: Fixed and incremental growth   C: Sovereign ethno-cultural continuity

---

30 Ibid. p. 36

31 Ibid. p. 38

A: development paradigm based on infinite growth and material abundance – a free flow of "modernity", fluid modernity and a "civilized juggernaut". In this case, we have noticed that in SW China, people who possess more power and alternatives have chosen textual governance as a special governmentality technique, in order to carve out a visionary time/space through an imaginary dotted line.

Bauman argues that "At the threshold of the modern conquest of space Descartes, looking forward, identified existence with spatiality, defining whatever exists materially as res extensa". (As Rob Shields wittily put it, one could rephrase Descartes' famous cogito, without distorting its meaning, as "I occupy space therefore I exist".).[32]

Through examining the possessed and dispossessed group in Kunming case, the local authoritative and totalitarian group customarily transformed "nouns" into "verbs", in the sense that first delineate a liquid political bi'an, then occupy real space/time through transformative performance. They transgress boundaries; evade obstacles, traverse different liminal states, in order to maximize the occupation of space, time and material abundance.

B: prosperity accessible to all and one "fluid" development/modernity paradigm fits all – "development by the people, for the people and of the people"; an ever-lasting exchange process between nature resources and artificial knowledge concoction. As a consequence, what we are witnessing is not a fixed and incremental growth based on infinite growth proposition and accessible to all – manifested by some promises – but a bizarre "pollution democracy", pollution by the people, for the people and of the people.

In the field site, for local villagers and the dispossessed/disenfranchised mass, although they have denied the chances of mapping out future development plans together with the policy makers, unscrupulously using any resources at their disposal for material abundance accretion is

---

32 Bauman, Z. (2000), Liquid Modernity. Malden, MA: Polity Press. p. 113.

tolerated by the government (and villagers) to some extent. Therefore, I found that almost every villager in my field site have used the misuse/ overuse of resources to amass their material abundance, generating rather sinister effects of environmental degradation. In this sense, the dispossessed are beneficiaries and victims of pollution. Their livelihood is depended on building more properties (both for real use and as a means to acquire compensation money from government when the whole villages are destroyed for the political bi'an transformation plan, such as a ring road highway sweeping around the "Oriental Geneva Lake", linking all satellite counties into a solid New Kunming cityscape); growing more Chinese leeks and flowers through overusing fertilizers and pesticides; harvesting as much fish as possible from the lake, etc.

Accordingly, the fixed and incremental growth is gained at the expense of environment and human health, through exploiting all resources, in a liquid modernity context, no matter in what space/time they reside: past (Zheng He, archeological excavation of dinosaurs), present (lake pollution, urbanization, political regime legitimacy) and future (development of doxa that could occupy more space and time, be it virtual, real, or surreal).

C: nature conservancy and continuity of cultural heritage – a "stateless" global village where miscellaneous cultures converge and intermingle versus a myriad of "sovereign tribes" where culture is "fossilized" and encrusted by an incremental development sugar coat (a sovereign ethno-cultural continuity).

The solid powers and liquid modernity abhor vacuum and obstacles, in order to achieve the effect of oversaturation. At the same time, the self-acclaimed post-socialist state in a liquid modernity era needs a historical corporeality and transcendental avatar to accredit its sovereignty, ethno-centric identities, cultural and moral telos. This explains why the concepts of ti (substance), yong (function), datong (great unity) have been used in producing key tropes of political bi'an and *ignoledge*.

Out of these liquid "trilemma", the *ignoledge* should be treated as darkening light and concealed *aletheia* when memory persists and time melts, turning lithe, supple and fluid-like: as powerfully captured by Salvador Dali in his *La persistencia de la memoria*.

REFERENCES

ANDERSEN, N. A. (2003), *Discursive Analytical Strategies: Understanding Foucault*, Koselleck, Laclau, Luhmann, The Policy Press.

BAUMAN, Z. (2000), *Liquid Modernity,* in M. A. Malden, Polity Press.

BECK, U. (1986), *Risk Society: Towards a New Modernity*, Thousand Oaks, CA, Sage.

_____. (2000), *What Is Globalization?* London, Blackwell.

_____. (2005), *Power in the Global Age,* in M. A. Maiden, Polity Press.

BECK, U., GIDDENS, A., LASH, S. (1994), *Reflexive Modernization: Politics, Tradition and Aesthetics in the Modern Social Order*, Stanford, California, Stanford University Press.

BEIDELMAN, T. O. (1959), *A Comparative Analysis of the Jajmani System*, New York, Association for Asian Studies.

BENSHU, X. (1993), *Jin Dai Kunming Cheng Shi Shi.* (The Modern History of Kunming City). Kunming, China, Yunnan People's Publishing House.

BERGER, P. L., LUCKMANN, T. (1966), *The Social Construction of Reality: A Treatise in the Sociology of Knowledge*, New York, Doubleday.

BERNAL, J. D. (1939), *The Social Function of Science*, London, G. Routledge and Sons.

BOURDIEU, P. (1992), *Language, Symbolic Power*, Edited and introduced by John B. Thompson, translated by Gino Raymond & Matthew Adamson, Polity Press.

BROSIUS, J. P. (1999), *Analyses and Interventions: Anthropological Engagements with Environmentalism.* Current Anthropology n. 40, 3: 277-309.

BURTON, M., SCHOEPFLE, G., MILLER, M. (1986), *Natural Resource Anthropology*, Human Organization, n. 45, 3: 261-269.

CHEATER, A. (1999), "The Anthropology of Power: Empowerment and Disempowerment", in *Changing Structures*, p. 5, London, Routledge.

CROLL, E., PARKIN, D. (eds.). (1992), *Bush Base, Forest Farm: Culture, Environment and Development*, London, Routledge.

ELLEN, R., HARRIS, H. (2000), "Introduction", *in* R. Ellen, P. Parkes, A. Bicker (eds.), *Indigenous Environmental Knowledge and its Transformations: Critical Anthropological Perspectives*, Amsterdam, Harwood Academic Publishers, p. 133.

FABIAN, J. (1984), *Time and the Other: How Anthropology Makes its Object*. New York, Columbia University Press.

FISCHER, E. F., BENSON, P. (2006), *Broccoli and Desire: Global Connections and Maya Struggles in Postwar Guatemala*, Stanford, Stanford University Press.

GAOLIN, Z. (2007), *The Basic Trend of Food Consumption of Chinese Residents: From 1957 to 2004* (《中国城镇居民食品消费的基本趋势: 1957-2004》). China Renmin University Press Resource Center. Issue January. Category, History of Economy.

GELLNER, E. (1983), *Nations and Nationalism*, Ithaca, Cornell University Press.

GIDDENS, A. (1984), *The Constitution of Society: Introduction to the Theory of Structuration*, Berkeley, University of California Press.

GRAFTON, R., ROBIN, L., WASSON, R. (eds.). (2005), *Understanding the Environment: Bridging the Disciplinary Divides*, Sydney, NSW, University of New South Wales Press.

GRAGSON, T., BLOUNT, B. (eds.). (1999), *Ethno-ecology: Knowledge, Resources, and Rights*, Athens, GA, USA, University of Georgia Press.

GRIFFITHS, T. (2001), *Forests of Ash: An Environmental History*, Cambridge, Cambridge University Press.

HEAD, L. (2000), *Cultural Landscapes and Environmental Change*, London, Arnold.

HEAD, L., TRIGGER, D., WOODWARD, E. (2004), "Nature, Culture and the Challenges of Environmental Sustainability: Bridging the Science/Humanities Divide", in *Report on ARC Research Network Special Initiative Seed Funding*.

HENNING, A. (2005), "Climate Change and Energy Use: the role for anthropological research", in *Anthropology Today*, 21, 3: 8-12.

HIRSCH, E., O'HANLON, M. (eds.). (1995), *The Anthropology of Landscape: Perspectives on Place and Space*, Oxford, Clarendon Press.

HONG, L., FAN, L., ZHANG, W. (2007), *Conceptualization: Linking 21 countries in Europe, Asia and Africa*. News of Yunnan Daily, November 13th.

INGOLD, T. (2000), *The Perception of the Environment: Essays on Livelihood, Dwelling and Skill*, London, Routledge.

JINGYU, Z. (1997), *Old Kunming. Compiled by the Kunming Daily*. Kunming, China, Yunnan People's Publishing House.

KNIGHT, J. (ed.). (2000), "Natural Enemies: People-Wildlife Conflicts", in *Anthropological Perspective*, London, Routledge.

KNOWLES, J. (1997), *Traditional Practices in the Tasmanian World Heritage Area: A study of five communities and their attachment to the area. Hobart, Tasmania, Unpublished Report for the Steering Committee of the Traditional Practices in the World Heritage Project*.

KOTTAK, C. (1999), "The New Ecological Anthropology", in *American Anthropologist*, 101: 23-35.

LASH, S., SZERSZYNSKI, B., WYNNE, B. (1996), *Risk, Environment and Modernity: Towards a New Ecology*, London, SAGE Publication Ltd.

LUKES, S. (2005), *Power: A Radical View. Second expanded edition*. New York, Palgrave Macmillan.

MUNDELL, R. (1963), "Capital mobility and stabilization policy under fixed and flexible exchange rates". in *Canadian Journal of Economics*, 29, 475-485.

NICKUM, J. E. (1998), "Is China Living on the Water Margin?", in *The China Quarterly*, p. 886, Johnston, B., 1994. "Human Rights and the Environment". in *Practicing Anthropology*, 16, 1: 8-12.

_____. (1995), "Towards an Environmental Anthropology", in *Practicing Anthropology*, 17, 4: 29-31.

SHIJUN, T. (2000), *The Dialectics of Modernization Habermas and the Chinese Discourse of Modernization*. The University of Sydney East Asian Series Number 13, Wild Peony. Canberra, Australia, National Capital Printing.

ZHANG, L. (2006), "Contesting Spatial Modernity in Late-Socialist China". in *Current Anthropology*, June, 47, 3: 465.

ZHANG, Y. (2007), "The birth of nanke (men's medicine) in China: The making of the subject of desire", in *American Ethnologist*, 34, (3). Accessed through LSE data-base on April 2nd 2009.

The global position of South Africa as BRICS country

Freek Cronjé

Abstract   The formation of the **BRICS contingent** opened up new political and economic debates and discourses. The BRICS members are all developing or newly industrialised countries, and they are distinguished by their large, fast-growing economies and significant influence on regional and global affairs. The Group has received overwhelming global attention since its inception in 2009 and it has been playing a critical role across the globe.

Following the BRICS countries' emerging economies with rapidly increasing GDP's, these countries also create high environmental impacts, raise ethical practice issues, exacerbate social justice inadequacies, and bring different **political and economic issues** strongly to the fore.

In 2010, **South Africa** was the last country to join the BRICS and currently holds the Chair of the Group. Against this background, as well as South Africa's strategic position in Africa, the **political and economic systems** of the country are constantly, from all over the globe, under the magnifying lens.

Consequently, this article aims to critically analyse the political and economic sectors of South Africa. **Macro level issues**, for example good governance, economic growth, development programmes and projects, and issues related to sustainability will be touched on. Conceptually the paper will be structured and guided by **Dependency and World System theories**. In the investigation of these two sectors (political and economical) an attemp is also being made to determine the country's **global position** in terms of the classical concepts of core, periphery and semi-periphery.

Keywords BRICS; Dependency Theory; Economic Sector; Global; Political Sector; South Africa; World System Theory

INTRODUCTION

The formation of the **BRICS contingent** opened up new political and economic debates and discourses. The BRICS members are all developing or newly industrialised countries, and they are distinguished by their large, fast-growing economies and significant influence on regional and global affairs. The Group has received overwhelming global attention since its inception in 2009 and it has been playing a critical role across the globe.

Following the BRICS countries' emerging economies with rapidly increasing GDP's, these countries also create high environmental impacts, raise ethical practice issues, exacerbate social justice inadequacies, and bring different **political and economic issues** strongly to the fore.

In 2010, **South Africa** was the last country to join the BRICS and currently holds the Chair of the Group. Against this background, as well as South Africa's strategic position in Africa, the **political and economic systems** of the country are constantly, from all over the globe, under the magnifying lens.

This article will critically analyse the political and economic sectors of South Africa. **Macro level issues**, for example good governance, economic growth, development programmes and projects, and issues related to sustainability will be touched on. Conceptually the paper is structured and guided by **Dependency** (as propounded by FRANK, 1969) **and World System** (proposed by WALLERSTEIN, 1974) **theories**. In the investigation of these two sectors (political and economical) an attemp is also being made to determine the country's **global position** in terms of the classical concepts of core, periphery and semi-periphery.

Frank and Wallerstein are of course not the only proponents and writers of dependency theory and world system theory. In this regard, Graaff and Venter (2001: 78) also refer to the so-called *dependistas*, for example Raul Prebisch, Paul Baran, Paul Sweezy and Fernando Cardoso; other world system theorists include for example Samir Amin and Ernst Mandel. Nevertheless different theorists, amongst others, one common characteristic of both theories are the explanation of underdevelopment due to exploitation of the so-called Third World countries by the so-called First World Countries.

Systems theory is the underlying base of both the dependency and world system theory. Before commencing with a brief description of each theory, the essence of systems theory – especially in view of the later argumentation and discussion (*Point 3*) – can be stipulated (GRAAFF and VENTER, 2001: 78-79):

- Firstly, a system implies that the parts are inter-connected and inter-dependent.
- Secondly, systems are not homogeneous networks; there are powerful nodes that dominate the areas around them.
- A third implication of systemness is that the whole is greater than the sum of the parts.
- Finally, societies combined may form a world system.

THEORETICAL CONCEPTUALISATION

A brief description of the two relevant theories will now follow.

Dependency theory

According to Frank (GRAAFF and VENTER, 2001: 81-83), capitalism and modernisation from First World countries had a negative and destructive influence on Third World countries. As a matter of fact wealthier countries – the core – actively under-develop the poorer countries – the periphery. Frank actually uses the concepts "metropolis" (for core) and "satellite" (for the periphery), but in line with world system theory to come, only the concepts "core" and "periphery" will be used. Modernisation theory (e.g. Rostow) reflects the viewpoint that the inability to develop under-developed countries is simply due to a lack of exposure to capitalism and Westernised thinking. Under-developed countries must fully enter into the free market system in order to get competitive, and in so doing, make rapid progress along the developmental pathway.

Dependency theory clearly showed, against the background of systems theory, that this kind of development is simply not possible along these lines, especially because of **economic positions** of countries in a structured system, as well as the **power dimensions** accompanying this structuralism. The systems logic is implied here: development and under-development are two sides of the same coin; one country's advantage is another country's disadvantage. Furthermore, it is thus not possible for under-developed countries to progress alongside the developmental evolutionist trajectory (e.g. spelled out by Marx, Rostow (again), Parsons and Giddens – *see* LE ROUX and GRAAFF, 2001: 48-58) in the same way and at the same pace.

Frank highlighted the extended chain of exploitation; reaching from the core deep into the rural areas of peripheral countries. He also refers to "surplus extraction" through the market; exploitation is conducted through unequal conditions of trade. An example to illustrate is that peripheral countries at a certain stage exported cheaper (often unprocessed goods) and bought more expensive (often manufactured goods). This resulted for peripheral countries in a chronic payment problem, as well as the fact that capital was continually being transferred from the periphery to the core (*also see* GRAAFF and VENTER, 2001: 82). This exploitation was made possible by the distortive mindset of the periphery to serve the needs of the core.

World system theory

Dependency theory is one of the most important building blocks of world system theory (together with the *Annales* School in Paris, and of course the work of Marx – *see* MARTÍNEZ-VELA, 2001: 2). As already indicated, the similarity between dependency theory and world system theory is embodied in the idea of a strong differentiation between **core** and **peripheral** countries (world system lexicon, but basically the same typology as Frank's "metropolis" and "satellite" countries). Core countries have a very central and direct role to play in relation with peripheral countries; core counties have integrated economies, which include primary, secondary and tertiary sectors, whilst peripheral countries lack backward (production) and forward (marketing and markets) linkages between sectors. Distinctive, however, from dependency theory, world system theory allows more space for "globalised powers and dynamics", as well as the "in-between" category of course, being introduced by Wallerstein, namely **semi-peripheral countries**. This category implies an intermediate position for these countries in terms of economics and politics. The "buffer" role being played by the semi-periphery ensures stability in the world system. In practice, according to Wallerstein, core countries exploit semi-peripheral countries, and semi-peripheral countries in turn, exploit peripheral countries (*also see* GRAAFF and VENTER, 2001: 87-88). Interestingly, and maybe not so well-known, Wallerstein also proposed a fourth category, namely **external areas**. External areas in theory maintain their own economic systems, and managed to stay outside the modern world economy. Earlier Russia (in the late nineties) can serve here as a good example; currently, maybe some countries in the Middle-East (HALSALL, 1997).

According to Wallerstein, the world capitalist system is differentiated in two ways, namely **horizontally** and **vertically** (GRAAFF and VENTER, 2001: 87-89). Horizontally the system is composed – as already mentioned – of core, semi-peripheral and peripheral countries. The world system is also vertically divided, since countries at every horizontal level, differ qualitatively from other countries at the same level; *all are equal, but some are more equal than others* [...].

Along the lines of the conceptualisation of Frank and Wallerstein, a "rough" schematic illustration of the world system today might look like this (note the BRICS contingency, as well as the possible expansion of BRICS).[1]

Figure 1 The world system

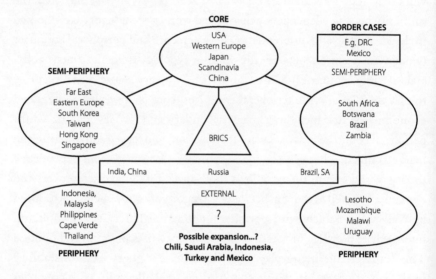

SOUTH AFRICA'S POSITION IN THE WORLD SYSTEM

Contextualisation

For the bigger picture, it is imperative to very quickly look at some historical moments. Most people, when positioning South Africa in the world

---

1 Placing of countries within the system is of course not exact and rigid; overlapping and "moving" of countries into different sectors due to world trends and other factors are highly "volatile" and central to this specific debate.

system, start with the colonial era, unfortunately ignoring the pre-colonial trade linkages between Eastern Africa and the Middle and Far East which affected Southern Africa, as well as Africa's role in early Greek, Roman, Asian, and Muslim world systems. World system theorists are of the opinion that South Africa formed part of the periphery during the colonial era, but was drawn into the semi-periphery around the time of the Second World War. Contributing factors in this regard include: a global depression in the world economy, rivalry between the USA and Britain, the emerging role of South Africa as a gold producer, and the coming to power of a white minority (*see* GRAAF and VENTER, 2001: 89-90). South Africa also dominated the peripheries in Southern Africa.

However, there is little doubt that *Apartheid* increasingly disadvantaged the potential of the country during the 1970's. Against the importance of politics and economics for Wallerstein in his typology, it is clear that the political machinery of the time (*Apartheid*), as well as economic sanctions from outside – in reaction to the very same regime – solidly contributed to our "new" peripheral and "skunk" status.

Consequently, the country's current position within the conceptual borders set out by Frank and Wallerstein will now be assessed.

For setting up the conceptual framework for the analysis, the four core pointers within systems theory will be the point of departure, namely, a system implies that the parts are inter-connected and inter-dependent, there are powerful nodes that dominate the areas around them, the whole is greater than the sum of the parts, and that societies combined may form a world system. Derived from these systemic assumptions, the article will consequently highlight in the next sections to come – in a simple Functionalist way – some critical **structural components** (institutions) in the system.

Institutional sectors

The two main "peripheral indicators" for the dependency and world system are of course the **political** sector and the **economic** sector, and these two sectors of South Africa will now be put to the order.

Political sector

Despite the miraculous political transition in the country in 1994, the political system currently is highly unstable and loaded with volatility. Bad governance, in-fighting, corruption, poor service delivery and financial management, and one disastrous policy decision after the other seems the order of the day.

An excellent example in this regard is the mining sector. With an already staggering mining industry, one would expect real support and guidance from government. However, when looking at the revised Act on Mineral and Petroleum Development (MPRDA), it is clear that the government will further force money out of the industry, and is going to make operational conditions in the industry even tougher. This will have a negative effect on investment in the sector, less tax will be earned, and less people will have a job. Lorimer (2013: 17) points out that the most severe critique against the previous Act was namely too much discretionary decision-making powers in the hands of the minister and departmental officials; in the previous Act there were 26 cases where the minister had the discretionary powers. In the new Act, it is even worse; a thorough assessment reveals that there are now 34 cases where the minister can simply act according to his/her discretion.

Numerous high profile African National Congress (ANC) members are part of an inner-circle class; they have got strong ties with government, *tenderpreneurs*, comrades, and in practice our new ruling class; the *power elite*, according to C. Wright Mills, and just the *circulation of another elite group*, in the words of Pareto [...]. In song with this, Mick Moore (2011: 1759-1760) refers to *political elite revenues*; these include arms deals, steal money from the public purse through the misuse of authority or take effective control of parts of the economy. Coincidently, or not, that some of the most serious mining scandals in the last few years involve some of the aristocratic ANC families. Prominent examples are the cases of Aurora where workers have been robbed to say the least, and of course Imperial Crown Trading; a company with no observable assets, but with strong links with the Zuma, Mandela and Motlanthe families. The latter company is all the way being supported by government, even up to the Constitutional Court. Dr. Mamphela Ramphele, former chair person of Goldfields, revealed shocking facts regarding empowerment beneficiation being pushed down in Goldfields' throat by government (LORIMER, 2013: 17). Linking on to this, Gunder Frank rightly points to a class of Third World political leaders who, especially through cooptation and corruption are sympathetic to the interests and values of core countries and in the process support the exploitative relationship between the core and periphery in a post-colonial era; in this process they are completely out of touch with the people on the ground. During tough times, your leaders must be in the townships, not in their offices or at media conferences; this is the viewpoint of Bobby Godsell, chair of Business Leadership South Africa (LAMPRECT and BLUMENTHAL, 2013: 6). Frank coined this grouping the *comprador bourgeoisie*, and they are strengthening the position of the capitalist system, and especially the transnational corporations (GRAAF and VENTER, 2001: 83). Wallerstein (1976) in turn is of the opinion that a state machinery is always strong; anyway, strong enough to protect their interests, guaranteeing their property rights, assuring various monopolies and spreading losses among the larger population.

It is indeed a sad state of affairs that empowerment for mine workers (even illegal workers) and communities are simply not a priority for government, especially sad when thinking of the Marikana massacre that happened in August 2012. Furthermore, it is no surprise that one protest and unrest action after the other are taking place; most of it has to do with labour issues (especially in the mining sector), and quite a lot of course with basic service delivery. When looking at the bigger picture and system, these kinds of unrests are of course not unique to South Africa; the recent unrest and protest actions in Turkey, Brazil and Chile is a case in point.

Reference to the mining sector is merely an example; these tendencies are of course also prevalent in other sectors as well, and occur also at provincial and local levels of government. The national elections will be held in 2014; it will defintely be an interesting, unstable, unpredictable and challenging period.

Economic sector

Although South Africa experienced some modest economic growth over the last few years (latest figures seem like a growth of 1%), there is no doubt that the country's economy is currently in serious trouble; this alarming situation reflects much more than just the aftermath of a global crisis since 2008/09. Two indicators reflect this situation, according to the chief economist of Standard Bank, Goolam Ballim (interviewed by DU TOIT, 2013: 3): **Firstly**, the economic growth rate during the last few years – in comparison with other emerging economies, and Africa – was nominal poor. **Secondly**, an increased number of the urbanised poor are demanding entry into the formal economy, jobs, and municipal services. In 2013 the Rand burst through the psychological level of ZAR 10 for one USD, the lowest value level of the Rand since 2009, and about 14% of the South African population live below the international poverty line per day – according to the UN $ 1, 25 – about ZAR 12.60 (NEL, 2013: 2). Towards the end of January 2014 the Rand weakened even more against the dollar, and the interest rate was adjusted upwards. Ballim (interviewed by DU TOIT, 2013: 3) furthermore states that the country lost about 42 million worker days in terms of productivity over the past five years; South Africa is seemingly the "strikers capital" of the world. It is clear that investors are currently wary to invest in the periphery and semi-periphery (so-called emerging economies), due to numerous reasons; the investment trend – according to economists – is to turn back to developed countries, the core.

A weaker Rand will lead to the increase of almost everything that is being imported: clothes, iPads, books and chemical products, to mention a few. Expenses of local enterprises that need to import steel and textile for the manufacturing of their products, will also escalate. If these enterprises don't increase their selling prices, the situation would inevitably lead to losses in terms of employment. Fuel prices will also rise and the cost of the infra-structure projects of government (e.g. the enormous expansion project of Transnet), will also be higher. As some consolation, it can be mentioned that the Australian Dollar as well as the

Brazilian Real also reached during the same time (middle June 2013) their lowest value against the USD in three and four years respectively (BlUMENTHAL, 2013: 1).

The statement of the economist Iraj Abedian – quoted by the Financial Mail (LAMPRECT and BLUMENTHAL, 2013: 6) – that the South African economy has not since 1994 being so without any direction, is alarming. Two thirds of the South African platinum mines are being operated at a loss, and the Platinum Index has reached its lowest mark in seven years. Mining production decreased in 2012 with 12,7%, and South Africa slipped down another ten (10) places within the Fraser Institute's Index regarding attraction for mining investment. South Africa is now the 64th most attractive country for mining investments; about one third from the bottom (LORIMER, 2013: 17). According to a Report of Nomura International (ANON, 2013a: 12), 145 000 workers at platinum mines in the country may lose their jobs by 2015 if the platinum price stays at around ZAR 15,00 and inflation at 8%.

The gross domestic product (GDP) can be hugely misleading, according to the Research Institute of Community Affairs at the University of the Witwatersrand in Johannesburg; wrong and "unhealthy" indicators, e.g. chronic diseases and motor accidents are stimulating the GDP. The Wits Report shows that the reality – despite economic growth – is that eight out of ten families in South Africa can't afford a healthy basket of food on a daily basis (TEMPELHOFF, 2013: 2).

According to the world system theory, it is possible for peripheral countries with strong state institutions to better their situation and perform themselves into the semi-periphery. That was probably the case with South Africa five years ago. However and also linked on with the issues being raised under the political sector, it is not that easy to escape underdevelopment. Wallerstein reiterates the important fact that countries cannot change their position in the hierarchy simply by the exploitation of their natural and human resources (GRAAF and VENTER, 2011: 89). Elements of dependency theory can also be spotted within the current economic dispensation: here we may refer to transport systems; or the lack thereof; labour systems – especially in the mining sector – still, since the *Apartheid* era, based on rural-urban migrancy; and signs of political suppression that are found within the governance sphere (*see* GRAAF and VENTER, 2001: 82-83).

On the positive side, there is some light at the "periphery" of the tunnel. Let us put our economic hopes on the BRICS (Brazil, Russia, India, China and South Africa) economic initiative (where South Africa is currently, without doubt, the weakest link), the bilateral agreement being signed with Japan in June 2013, as well as the recent research agreement between the aircraft company Boeing and the CSIR (Council for Scientific and Industrial Research) for the refinement of titan (South Africa is worldwide one of the biggest sources for un-refined titan ore). According to the Minister of Science and Technology, Derek Hanekom, "[...] it will create numerous work opportunities and ensure the economic growth of the country". The first plant is expected to be operational in 2017 (VAN ROOYEN, 2013: 18). Still on home turf, if the National Development Plan (NDP) becomes more than just a policy, it may lead to greater economic stability. According to Raymond Parsons, special advisor to the business organisation, Business Unit South Africa (Busa), the organised business community has ZAR 500 milliard to invest if there is absolute certainty regarding the smooth implementation of the NDP (JOUBERT, 2013: 2).

Within the context of a globalised world system, a free trade agreement between Europe and America – a strong agenda point at the recent G8 Summit in 2013 – might change the economic game globally in a significant way, and can render economic benefits to all; however, a cumbersome process and it might take years to be finalised (ANON, 2013: 18).

An important point of critique against world system theory (GRAAFF and VENTER, 2001: 91), is that the theory overemphasises the economy, and neglects other sectors or dimensions. Other important sectors, such as education and health are thus also critical, but the analysis within this article will be limited to the political and economic sectors.

CONCLUSION

The question then: Where does South Africa as BRICS country find itself between the core, periphery and semi-periphery in the global system? After the arlier analysis of the political and economic sectors, it is difficult to determine the position by either using a calculator, or a weighing scale. If South Africa is to be positioned within the **semi-periphery**, Wallerstein (1976) rightly warns that "[t]he semi-periphery, however, is not an artifice of statistical cutting points, nor is it a residual category. The semi-periphery is a necessary structural element in a world economy". The answer is not clear [...] what can be said is that South Africa's position is very complicated and challenging, definitely not static, and that the bigger picture (in South Africa, but also internationally) must be looked at, which is of course not so easy. Regarding this, Wallerstein (MARTíNEZ-VELA, 2001: 1) rightly states that "[m]an's ability to participate intelligently in the evolution of his own system is dependent on his ability to perceive the whole". New economic alliances e.g. BRICS and other economic initiatives (like the NDP) being referred to earlier in the article, generate different dynamics and hopefully some growth, but to remain in any sector is of course also not beyond challenge (clearly proven by the current position of the "West" – Wallerstein's point of regular cyclical rhythms), and the competition is stiff; again, in the words of Wallerstein (1976): "The hounds are ever to the hares for the position of top dog".

On an academic level, all over the world, despite core or periphery, social scientists are confronted – to a large extent – with the same issues; maybe with different angles to it or different interpretations, or new solutions. It must be remembered that **meta-theoretically** and **methodologically** Wallerstein can also be embedded within **interpretive Sociology**; also – again – keep Wallerstein's "cyclical rhythm" in mind.

Lastly, the sketched system (of South Africa and globally) is defintely a very **challenging and intriguing laboratory for the Social Sciences**.

REFERENCES

ANON. (2013a), Nommerpas: 145000 [*Exact number: 145000*]. *By* in *Beeld*, 12, Jun. 22.

_____. (Bloomberg). (2013b),Vryhandel-pakt bepleit [*A plea for a free trade agreement*]. *Beeld*, 18, Jun. 18.

BLUMENTHAL, M. (2013), Rand swakste in 4 jaar [*Rand at its weakest in 4 years*]. *Beeld*, 1, Jun. 12.

DU TOIT, P. (2013), Brunch met Goolam Ballim: Iets moet gedoen word [*Brunch with Goolam Ballim: Something has to be done*]. *By* in *Beeld*, 3, Jun. 22.

GRAAF, J., VENTER, D. (2001), "Understanding the world system", in Coetzee, J. K., Graaff, J., Hendricks, F. & Wood, G. (eds.), *Development: Theory, Policy, and Practice*, Cape Town, Oxford University Press. p. 77-95.

HALSALL, P. (1997), "Summary of Wallerstein on World System Theory", in *Internet Modern History Sourcebook*.

JOUBERT, J.-J. (2013), R 500 miljard kan kom: "Sakelui sal belê as ontwikkelingsplan ingestel word", in *R 500 milliard can come: Business people will invest if development plan is implemented*, *Beeld*, 2, Jun. 24.

LAMPRECT, M., BLUMENTHAL, M. (2013), Ekonomie: "Politici moet op grond wees", in *Economy: Political leaders must be on the ground*, *Beeld*, 6, Jun. 7.

LE ROUX, P., GRAAFF, J. (2001), "Evolutionist thinking", *in* Coetzee, J. K., Graaff, J., Hendricks, F. & Wood, G. (eds.), *Development: Theory, Policy, and Practice*, Cape Town, Oxford University Press. p. 45-61.

LORIMER, J. (2013), "Kontant vir kamerade", in *Cash for comrades*, *Beeld*, 17, Jun. 5.

MARTÍNEZ-VELA, C. A. (2001), "World Systems Theory", in *ESD*, 83: 1-5. *Fall*.

MOORE, M. (2011), "Globalisation and Power in Weak States". in *Third World Quarterly*, 32, 10: 1757-1776.

NEL, J. (2013), 14% van SA leef op R12 'n dag, in *14% of SA live on R12 a day*. *Beeld*, 2, Jun. 3.

SEIDMAN, S. (2008), *Contested Knowledge: Social Theory Today*. 4th. ed., Oxford, Blackwell Publishing.

TEMPELHOFF, E. (2013), "Al groei ekonomie, het 80% nie kos", in *Despite economic growth, 80% don't have food*, *Beeld*, 2, Jun. 6.

VAN ROOYEN, F. (2013), "Boeing, WNNR kyk saam na titaanplan", in *Boeing, CSIR look together at titan plan*, *Beeld*, 18, Jun. 12.

WALLERSTEIN, I. (1976), *The Modern World-System: Capitalist Agriculture and the Origins of the European World-Economy in the Sixteenth Century*. New York, Academic Press.

Development public policies, emerging contradictions and prospects in the post-apartheid South Africa

Sultan Khan

Abstract   After almost three and half centuries of economic exploitation through international capitalist pursuits through colonialism and apartheid, South Africa has emerged as a democratic country. The liberation mandate for South Africa's post-apartheid reconstruction and development was translated into a popular development policy called the Reconstruction and Development Programme (RDP) based on redistributive ideals framed in the historical document – the Freedom Charter. Such an ideal was compromised within two years of democracy as the reality of eradicating high levels of under-development amongst the vast majority of the previously disenfranchised Black populace became contingent on growth and development programmes that will create opportunities for their socio-economic advancement. Adoption of a neo-liberal economic development policy called Growth Employment and Redistribution (GEAR) was considered the most strategic approach for the state to deliver on its development mandate. Hence, participation in the international market driven economy was perceived as an inevitable option to meet the development woes challenged by the state. However, such an economic approach to development has been proven to come with a wide range of contradictions perceived to be the source of slow and unsustainable pace of delivery challenged by a restless civil society. Notwithstanding its domestic development challenges, it has succeeded in becoming an important political and economic actor both in the continent and on the international arena. In being afforded entry to BRICS in 2010 it has committed to new sets of multilateral agreements to solidify its south-south strengths so that it will enjoy mutual benefits from such an arrangement to meet its development challenges. It is against this context that this paper tests out South Africa's relative position and status within BRICS as a new entrant, highlighting some potential contradictions followed by prospects for engagement on a diverse set of development oriented programmes and projects within this multilateral arrangement.

Keywords Development Policy, Reconstruction and Development, Social Movements; National Development Plan, Growth Employment and Redistribution.

INTRODUCTION

South Africa has a history of almost three and a half century of colonialism and apartheid. The colonial period under the British was largely characterised by the extraction of raw materials in a quest to accumulate capital for the Crown whereas for almost half a century under apartheid rule, racial segregation was used as a means for both capital accumulation and to exercise political hegemony over the majority of the indigenous population. South Africa is not a homogenous country given its socio-political and historical context with the majority being African indigenous people (79.2%), Coloured (8.9%), Indians (2.9%) and White (8.9%) and other (0.5%) (RSA, Census 2011). Although Christianity is the dominant faith group in the country, other faith groups Islam, Hinduism, Judaism and indigenous African religions makes it a "rainbow nation" – a political reference to foster a sense of nationhood given the legacy of racial fragmentation and lack of social cohesiveness given the decades of discrimination, exclusion and material exploitation of the majority of the black populace.

Since the dawn of democracy in 1994, several attempts have been made by the state through policy reform and reformulation to ensure that the country is on its way towards sustainable forms of development breaking away from the underdevelopment and dependency created by apartheid amongst the majority of the Black population. South Africa as a developing economy entering the global stage after years of political isolation has not come to grips with its developmental goals simply because it had to make compromises from its strong socialist ideals enshrined in the Freedom Charter, considered as the most politically sacred mandate for liberation of the country (SUTTNER, 2006). It had to bow to the forces of internationalisation and global market forces to resuscitate its economy so that it could meet the development mandate to the majority of the people excluded from the economic benefits of the country. However, to a certain extent development has been skewed in favour of the vast majority of the white populace who stood to benefit both during and after the demise of apartheid. In so far as the Black populace is concerned, there has been an emerging middle class through a strategic Black Economic Empowerment programme (IHEDURU, 2004: 2) but only for those who have had strong political connections with the ruling party. For the vast majority, the benefits of development have not trickled down to make a difference in their quality of lives.

This paper examines the socio-historical evolution of South Africa since it has been colonised and later subjected to the inhumane apartheid policy to minister to the capitalist needs of the minority white ruling class spanning over thirty five decades. It examines the relationship between the state and the economy from the colonialist era, apartheid to the post-liberation phase of the country. The paper highlights the diversity in experiences at the macro-level in the country touching on distinct programs, national agencies, and specific development projects as well as on the micro level, bringing into focus particular scenarios that highlight the accomplishments, mistakes and dilemmas involving a wide range of social actors. It highlights that the development agenda of the country is replicated on the classical neo-liberal economic lines of the west which has compromised development for the vast majority of the population confined to the periphery of the economy due to is inability to innovate on the grounds of its country specific particularities. The roles of the state, the market, the civil society, and social movements in the processes involved in setting up the development agenda and engaging with it, are expounded.

BRIEF OVERVIEW OF SOUTH AFRICA'S SOCIO-POLITICAL HISTORY AND DEVELOPMENT CONTEXT

South Africa was first colonised by the Dutch in 1652. The Cape of Good Hope was an important and strategic maritime trading post for the Dutch East India Company (DEIC). At first most of the Europeans worked for the DEIC, but later, more and more Europeans chose to come to the Cape to settle. They moved away from Cape Town and established farms and little towns to the north and east of the country. When the Europeans came to the Cape, they came into contact with the native Khoikhoi people. The two groups had very different ways of life, and there were many violent clashes between them (Bank, 2007). In 1806 Britain took over the Cape from the Dutch East India Company. This caused unhappiness among the Dutch farmers and they started to penetrate the inner parts of the country (Transvaal) which is known as the Great Trek. The Great Trek resulted in contact with indigenous people and they occupied fertile land for agricultural and other commercial business. The discovery of gold in 1886 in the Transvaal (Witwatersrand) and diamonds on the banks of the Orange River in 1867 became the main driving force behind the first capitalist economy in the country and development of Africa's most advanced and richest economy. It also set the foundation for on-going feuds between the British and Boers for political control of the natural resources of the country to extract capital (MARKS and TRAPIDO, 1979: 52).

In 1877 the British took control of the Transvaal which is recorded as the first Anglo-Boer War – a battle between British and Dutch for control and expropriation of valuable, economically productive land. The second Anglo-

Boer War broke out in 1899 and the British took over the Orange Free State from the Boer. In Natal the coastal belt provided the British an ideal agricultural opportunity for sugar and other commercial agricultural production. Hence, all four provinces, Cape of Good Hope, Transvaal, the Orange Free State and Natal became colonies of the British who extracted valuable minerals and agricultural products in a quest for capital accumulation (BRINEY, 2007).

Under the political conquest of the British, racial segregation was enforced by creating and designating certain areas known as Native reserves for the indigenous Black people under the control of Tribal Authority structures based on ethnic division characterised by traditional forms of social stratification and organisation. A significant piece of legislation enforced by the British was the 1913 Land Act which alienated and designated land for residential, commercial and agricultural purposes to both British and the Boer. The alienation of land from the indigenous people amounted to almost 90% of the surface area of the country (ALIBER, 2003: 474-475) which is depicted in Figure 1 and 2 which illustrates the exploitation of the natural resources of the country by the minority white ruling class.

In 1948 the Boer in a historical political election won over the British which then led to the formation of what was called the Nationalist party which enforced stricter racial segregationist policies and the control and movement of local indigenous people in urban centres and towns who became dependent on the wage labour having given up the prospect of surviving from an agrarian economy. Having being confined to ten percent of the land, 90% of the indigenous people were confined to land which had very little economic value, migration to and from the industrial hubs of the country posed a menace to white culture and threatened the exercise of their political hegemony. Inorder to appease the local indigenous people, the apartheid government established bantustans or homelands as self-governing states. The idea was that the homelands would resemble a state within a state where Black indigenous people could live and vote for their own governments, led by chiefs who were controlled and administered by the apartheid Government. There was a homeland for different language groups like Venda and Xhosa in South Africa. These groups were referred to nations with a complex bifurcated governance structure, and all Black South Africans were made citizens of one of these "homeland" or "countries", without any consideration in respect of where they were born or where they lived. This meant forcing millions of people, who became non-citizens of South Africa, to these far off places. Each homeland had its own leader, installed by the apartheid government. They depended on white South Africa for economic survival and so could never challenge the Government. The world refused to recognise the homelands as independent countries. The homelands were Ciskei, Transkei, KwaZulu, Venda, Bophuthatswana, Gazankulu, KaNgwane, KwaNdebele, Lebowa and Quaqua.

Figure 1   Apartheid South Africa and Dispossession of Land

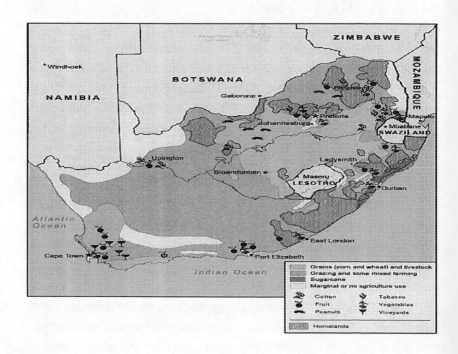

Figure 2 Mining and industrial nodes in the colonial and Apartheid era

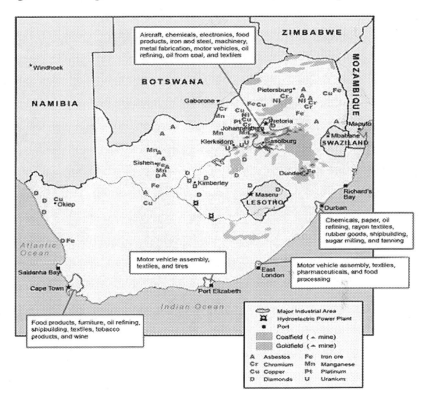

Many people had never even been to the place which they were now supposed to call home. They now had to get permission to come and work in the white South Africa as if they were foreigners. These "homelands" were home to the workers and served as a reservoir for cheap black labour. They were small territorial spaces making up less than a tenth of the whole country but accommodating almost 90% of the people. The land could not support all these people and was of the worst quality so that people were forced to work on mines and in factories in the towns to earn an income. This separated families as fathers left for long periods to work far away from home (BUNDY, 2004: 373-375).

igure 3   Location of the former Apartheid homelands

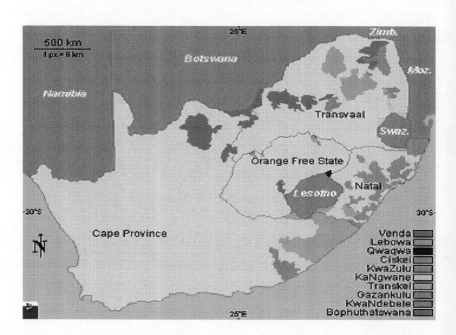

In 1958 the Freedom Charter was drawn which was a conglomeration of different political actors from the disenfranchised Black population comprising indigenous Africans, Coloureds and Indians. This Charter was a mandate for liberation of the country and in 1960 the ANC resorted to armed struggle against the apartheid regime resulting in the arrest of the late Nelson Mandela and the famous Rivonia Trial. Many went into exile whilst a significant number were incarcerated on Robben Island which is now an international iconic tourist site.

In the urban centres of the four provinces some 3.5 million people were forcibly removed and resettled in state built public housing estates known as townships under the notorious Group Areas Act of 1959. These were strategically located a distance from the predominantly white sanitized cities to ensure continuous supply of cheap labour for the burgeoning white capitalist classes. Local people migrating from these independent homelands were housed in state built hostels and were required to carry work permits called the dompass. Those not economically active in the city centres had to return to their respective homelands and native reserves (WALKER, 1982: 2).

After a short lull, in the 1970s the struggle against apartheid was pursued by ordinary working class people, civics and students. By late 1980s the country became ungovernable due to resistance and mass protests and in 1992 a negotiated settlement commenced leading to CODESA resulting in the transition to democracy.

THE DEVELOPMENT AGENDA OF THE POST-APARTHEID STATE

At the dawn of democracy in 1994, the Government of National Unity (GNU) comprising the African National Congress (ANC), the South African Communist Party (SACP) and the consolidation of the labour movement into the Congress of South African Trade Unions (COSATU) attempted to redress the historical imbalances of the past through the Reconstruction and Development Programme (RDP) (RDP 1994). It was basically a translation of the Freedom Charter formulated in 1956 into action which was the political mandate for liberation (ANC, 1956: 1). Although the RDP was designed to promote the development needs of those historically disadvantaged, the South African Constitution does not include the explicit right to development, but does recognize the right to human dignity, equality, equity, democracy, and justice. The Bill of Rights in the Constitution provides for social and economic rights, such as the right to basic services and health care within certain limits (RSA, 1996). Hence in this phase of democracy, South Africa came to be seen as a developmental state to eradicate the social inequality perpetrated by colonialism and apartheid.

Notwithstanding the grandeur principles enshrined in the RDP it had a short life span of two years and in 1996 the GNU switched to GEAR (Growth Employment and Redistribution) (Department of Finance, 1996) a neoliberal macro-economic policy founded on the principles of economic growth to support the development backlog inherited from the past (HABIB and PADAYACHEE, 2000: 253). GEAR emphasized that economic development would be led by the private sector, there would be privatization of state owned enterprises, government expenditure (especially social services) would be reduced, exchange control regulations would be relaxed, and there would be a more flexible labour market. GEAR was basically an American driven economic programme recolonizing South Africa making it a dependent satellite of its economic dominance of the world. Given it sense of security arising from its economic dominance within the South African economy it is least perturbed about any other bilateral and multi-lateral economic agreements that the country might engage with in the future (FAROUK, 2012).

According to Professor Sampie Terrrelanche an authority on the historical evolution of poverty and equality issues of South Africa for the past twenty five years, GEAR was born out of closed door meetings with the ANC and the ruling nationalist party before the transition to a democratic political dispensation. He highlighted that GEAR was a compromise between the late Nelson Mandela and the white business classes at which the ANC was convinced to forget about their socialistic ideals upon ascension to political power and the promise of large scale government intervention as enshrined in the RDP translated into action from the Freedom Charter. The ANC document "Ready to Govern" in 1992 in preparation for a transitional government had to pander to the typical American approach to growth through a trickle-down effect based on a loan of US$ 850mn to ensure the transitional period to democracy. Such a position according to Prof Terreblanche was contained in a document "Statement on Economic Policy" formulated in 1993 under a Transitional Executive Committee comprising the ANC and the National Party representatives that secured the loan based on a neo-liberal macro-economic policy called GEAR (FAROUK, 2013). The RDP office was abandoned and GEAR became the dominant programme of the ANC led government in 1996.

The GEAR macroeconomic strategy was summarised clearly by the Centre for Development and Enterprise.

> GEAR is consistent with the present strong international consensus on
> the efficiency of the market system. Recognising the importance of a
> globalised world economy, it stresses the need for a market-oriented
> growth strategy, fiscal discipline and investor confidence [...]. It sees
> job creation through greater labour market flexibility [...]. The strategy
> proposes a reduction of the budget deficit from 6% to 3% of GDP;
> financial liberalisation; a programme of privatisation; and a 6% annual
> growth rate [...]. (CDE, 1997: 6).

Under the policy of GEAR the development mandate post-apartheid was
devolved to the local government level with emphasis on people centred
development. As consequence, local authorities would be forced to generate
a larger proportion of their own revenues, and there was a strong emphasis
on public-private partnerships. Within an urban setting, this would mean
privatisation and the promotion of the principle of cost recovery which will
reflect in inadequate subsidies targeted at the poor. With regard to the provision
of basic infrastructure, services and development, there was consensus in the
ANC government circles that users should pay full cost-recovery, standards
should be relatively low, and privatisation should be regularised.

From a developmental perspective the transition to neoliberal GEAR
orthodoxy encountered an aberration with the basic needs-oriented RDP.
Rationalisation of the wasteful, fragmented and centralised administration
system resulted in the re-demarcation of the boundaries of the country
leading to the formation of nine provinces which included those homelands
and townships that were considered independent governing states during
the apartheid era. Figure 4 illustrates the new shape of South Africa by
provinces which includes former homelands and townships as part of social
integration, rationalisation of administration, and redressing the material
disadvantages of the past experienced by black people.

Each of these provinces operate within a three tier government structure
with the national sphere performing policy and resource allocation functions
whilst the local government sphere engages directly with service delivery
issues. The political and administrative systems of these three spheres are

founded on principles of inter-governmental relations with local government being the closest to citizens. During apartheid there were approximately 843 municipalities at the date of the first local democratic ballot of 1994. However the number of South African municipalities reduced to 284 at the time of the December 2000 poll to ensure conditions for their viability and continuity. Drastically reducing the number of municipalities was necessary to concentrate the insufficiently large human resources necessary and create economies of scale in local administration. It was especially necessary to increase the municipal area's size in order to have use of a larger area that could constitute the geographic outlines of a homogeneous local economy. Combining urban centres with their rural hinterlands appeared to be one of the means of reaching this objective. With the re-demarcation of municipalities, they are given greater responsibility for service delivery with very little support from the provincial and national government. At the local government level, they are expected to raise their own resources through taxes. Only national or provincial infrastructure programmes are funded by the state (KHAN and LOOTVOET, 2002: 299).

Figure 4   Post-apartheid demarcations into nine provinces

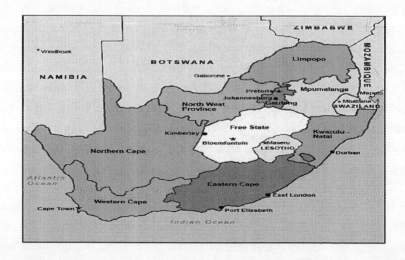

GEAR's neoliberal orientation was criticized, as it would only address the needs of big business and foreign investors in the big cities, the gap between the rich and poor would widen, and socio-spatial inequalities distinctive of the apartheid era would be reproduced, perpetuating unsustainable practices. In fact, the virtual abandonment of the RDP would mean that the poor would occupy the lowest rung on South Africa's new non-racial urban hierarchy (BOND, 2004; DESAI, 2005 and HART, 2005).

RESPONSE OF THE WORKING CLASS TO THE STATES NEOLIBERAL DEVELOPMENT POLICIES

Upon implementation of GEAR the working class through new social movements (NSMs) opposed the states programme of privatisation. The Washington Post on the 6 November 2001 carried news on South Africa's post-apartheid struggles for social justice, suggesting that for all the wretchedness of the apartheid regime it never disconnected people from basic services. The poor were exposed to the negative effects of privatisation and were becoming disillusioned by the lack of progress made by government to change their material conditions filtering from the dark days of apartheid. The political impact made by the New Left social movements had led to some analyst dubbing it as "South Africa's New Revolution" (Jon Jeter cited in COCK, 2003: 1-2) and more recently Adam Habib (2013: 87-88) in his book titled "South Africa's Suspended Revolution" asserts that the implementation of GEAR had a devastating consequence not only for the citizenry but also for the political evolution of the country. The ANC accused all those who were actively critiquing and opposing its neo-liberal economic policies of being ultra-left, waging a counter-revolutionary struggle against it and its democratic government (MADLINGOZI, 2007).

The political stir created by these NSMs was glorified to such an extent by the media that it appeared as a re-enactment of the violent struggles that took place between defenceless communities and law enforcement agencies as witnessed in the politically volatile days of apartheid. Virtually every week, thousands of demonstrators and unionised workers rallied on the streets to denounce the neo-liberal macro-economic policies contained in GEAR (Growth, Employment and Redistribution) and the ANC ruling party. To illustrate, in 2006 alone, there were 920 recorded cases of unrest related to poor service delivery that occurred in South Africa (HOUGH, 2008: 7). State force in the form of tear gas, rubber bullets and stun grenades, water cannons, armoured military vehicles and the unleashing of police dogs to demobilise angry protesting crowds engaged in protest actions was a frequent occurrence. Social movements such as the Soweto Electricity Crisis Committee, Landless Peoples Movement, the Anti-Privatisation Forum and Abahlali Basemjondolo have had planned marches banned.

A City Press article dated 29 May 2002 "Now the New Left rises to fight on" best describes this new social movement's potential to be the new political voice for the poor in South Africa on matters relating to development and basic service delivery:

> The New Left are stoically purist in their ideals of true liberation. They are gradually gaining momentum, much like in the heyday of the former radical left, which is now in government. They feel they are causing the new government discomfort and indigestion.

A leader of the Anti-eviction Movement in Durban, quoted in the City Press, commented on the goals of the new movements: "[...] is about fighting the capitalists who want to debilitate the efforts of the poor".

Ceruti (2007) in her paper titled "South Africa: Rebirth of mass movement" confirms the emerging class divide emerging between the rich and the poor that provides justification for the emergence of NSMs. She asserts that, between 2005 and 2006 alone, executive pay rose by as much as 34% with executives in South Africa enjoying the bulk of company wealth, while the gap between remuneration of CEOs and that of workers runs by a factor of over 50 to one. In other words, remuneration for the average CEO is more than 50 times that of the average worker in the country.

The prominence gained by the New Left on poverty, development and service delivery issues indicating that the "the New Left is here and slowly taking charge of day to day politics by waging the struggle for the working class and the proletariat on various issues" raised alarm in the political corridors of the ruling party (City Press, 29 May 2002. "The New Left rises to fight on"). It prompted analysis around whom and what this social movement was about, the risks it posed to the new democracy and the challenge it posed to the government's neo-liberal development agenda.

A cursory analysis of the character and profile of these movements in their early evolution suggests that it was a loose association of former activists that banded together to champion the cause of the poor that were challenged by the new neo-liberal economic policies of the government. Organisationally they were not hierarchical and lacked visible leadership resulting in the masses taking it upon themselves to determine course of action they wished to pursue (City Press, 29 May 2002. "The New Left rises to fight on"). This was in sharp contrast to apartheid day social movements which had a distinct leadership structure, organisational form, aims and objectives. The lack of concrete organisational form, made the state believe that it was a conglomeration of a third force group that set out to undermine the new democracy. Given that these movements were in their formative stages, it was not atypical for them to lack a clear organisational form. Moreover, social movements by their very nature, tend to have temporary and loose organisational structures as they mobilise around a social issue and disband once they have been addressed or resolved. Instead of formulating a deeper insight into the processes and dynamics of these new social movement formations, the state chose to lead a tirade of ugly exchanges and standoffs against those leaderships it has identified, accusing it of being *"counter revolutionary," "ultra-leftists" "playing to the right wing agendas"* and festering *"plots"* to destabilise the new democracy. Jeff Radebe the former Minister in the Department of Public Enterprise which pioneered privatisation policies as part of the neo-liberal agenda described the grass roots Soweto Electricity Crisis Committee as *"gangs of criminals"* that must be dealt with decisively (Mail and Guardian, 21 February 2002. "South Africa – The New Apartheid").

Reacting to the extreme resistance from social movements to the state's development policy, both the ANC and the SACP claimed that they *"are not threatened by the New Left"* and have instead raised their discontent about the manner in which the New Left was conducting itself. The then ANC spokesperson Smuts Ngonyama criticised the methods used by the new social movements in their opposition to the state's privatisation programme with contempt. He described their approach as:

> [...] something we cannot describe. They go out and destroy property
> and threaten the privacy and security of people. They are desperate for
> attention. They are gaining momentum by attacking the ANC and
> government (City Press, 29 May 2002. "The New Left rises to fight on").

The SACP, a strong alliance partner of the ANC also joined the berating ceremony of the new social movements. The party claimed that;

> [...] the people who regard themselves as the New Left are essentially a
> collection of ultra-left forces and have no common programme. What
> brings them together is their hatred of the ANC and disagreement with
> the SACP, and wanting to hive off COSATU (City Press, 29 May 2002.
> "The New Left rises to fight on").

The SACP further claimed that the New Left wanted a socialist leap and believed that socialism will be attained overnight. It reaffirmed its commitment to remain in the mainstream of socialist politics and confirmed its "hegemonic programme for the working class". At the same time, the SACP claimed that the so-called New Left would always remain outside the mainstream of socialist thought (City Press 29 May 2002 "The New Left rises to fight on"). This latter statement by the SACP provokes some deeper analysis. One needs to ask firstly what is it that makes these former comrades to form themselves into new social movements that operate outside "mainstream socialist thought"? Have they grown tired of the ANC and its alliance partners intellectualising on the speed with which developmental promises were being delivered to the poor in the country? Are the actions of the so called New Left social movements a simple expression of frustration against government's failure to change the material conditions of the poor or was it indeed an attempt to undermine the democracy and freedom that all oppressed South Africans have struggled for?

Habib (2003) provides a somewhat balanced response to the above mentioned concerns. He asserts that given that South Africa just walked the road to freedom, such contestations from new social movements should be perceived as an attempt to consolidate democracy instead of identifying them as a threat. The state response to these new social movements and their engagement with critical and important social issues may be perceived as an overreaction to political criticisms which in the long term provides checks and balances for mature democracies all over.

Despite Habib's social-democratic analysis on the role of NSMs to deepen democracy, GEAR has polarised the nation in monetary and political terms. In 2012 sixteen years after the implementation of GEAR one finds that that 20% of the South African population comprise the rich elite, 30% the petite bourgeoisie and 50% are very much impoverished. This translates to the top 20% comprising 10 million people receiving 75% of the total income constituting 3.7 million people classified white and 6.3 million blacks with whites making the richer part of that group. The lower 50% of the population in the same period received only 8% of the nation's total income (FAROUK, 2013). In post-apartheid South Africa it is common to hear the voices of the academic left and the grass roots movements that the rich are getting richer whilst he poor are getting poorer. Under the macro-economic policy of GEAR in spite of the great recession in America, the capitalist sector has performed well on the markets as the global geo-politics has shifted substantially which is illustrated in the flow of heightened tax revenues to the state. The budget deficits reduced to 6.5%, 4.2% and 4.8% in 2009, 2010 and 2011 respectively (National Treasury, 2012a). This is especially so in light of South African business corporations having become transnational corporations in different parts of the globe with a substantial share in the South African Stock exchange but with little engagement in the local economy resulting in mass unemployment rates, poverty and disillusionment amongst the majority of the working classes.

SHIFTING HUMAN FACE OF GEAR

The negative effects of GEAR and confrontation from the organs of civil society on the slow pace of development to fifty percent of the excluded citizenry lead the ANC government in the late second term of office to make a gradual shift in its macro-economic policy. Primarily, social movements in this period had an unsettling effect on political elites prompting the state towards a pro-poor policy especially those marginalised in the economy (BALLARD, et al., 2006: 415).

As a pro-poor measure the state increased social expenditure to serve as a safety net in the form expanded social-support grants for those excluded from the economy and development initiatives in the country. It is estimated that 22 million people (over 50%) of the population live in poverty, that is, on an income of less than R160 per month (DU PLESSIS and CONLEY, 2007: 49).

As will be noted from the Table 1 just more than fifty percent of the 22 million living on income less than R160 per month are in receipt of grants. The remaining are excluded.

for a variety of reasons due to the lack of documentation to access grants, not meeting the eligibility criteria and bureaucratic delays in the investigation and awards of grants.

The states interventionist strategy to ameliorate poverty through social assistance has been substantial. The Intergovernmental Fiscal Review reports that 88.5% of social development spending went to social assistance grants in 2004/05. This percentage was expected to decrease slightly to 87.6% in 2007/08. The most recent medium-term expenditure framework provides for social security allocations of R57,7 billion in 2006/07; R62,6 billion in 2007/08; and R68,3 billion in 2008/09 (National Treasury, 2005b). Whilst such an interventionist approach may have impacted on the lives of the just more than 50% of the population that are marginalised from the South African economy, it is questionable as to whether such dependence on the states social security grants are sustainable for those in receipt of these. This in many respects is likely to cause dependency and perpetuate the culture of poverty in the absence of more sustainable forms of development programmes and projects where the poor are empowered to take charge of their social welfare. The rationale for such a hefty investment on social security grants was perhaps to calm the waters amongst the restless masses who took to the streets daily crying out for basic service delivery and development for their social well-being which stood the threaten the political hegemony of the ruling ANC.

Table 1   Number of adult and child beneficiaries of
social assistance grants by end July 2006

Grant type	Number of adult recipients	Number of child recipients
Old Age Pension	2 162 990	
War Veterans Grant	2 624	
Disability Grant	1 356 937	
Grant in Aid	28 441	
Child Support Grant		7 410 760
Foster Child Grant		351 702
Care Dependency Grant		92 853
Total	3 550 992	7 855 315

Source: Department of Social Development (2006), SOCPEN, database).

At a more concrete level, deviating from the dependency caused by hefty hand outs on social security grants, there has been a rethink on the part of the ruling party on more sustainable ways to eradicate poverty and inequality. In this respect the government's adoption of the Industrial Policy Action Plan (IPAP) between 2011 – 2014 and the New Growth Plan in 2010 is aimed at creating employment and growth. The Industrial Policy Action Plan is a platform programme of the Department of Trade and Industry which aims to create 2.4 million jobs by 2020. In pursuit of this plan engagement with public finance institutions such as Industrial Development Corporation, the Development Bank and Khula Enterprise the state aims to ensure support for development projects by targeting the business sector with a view to creating jobs. The plan targets stimulating growth in the production of automotive components, minerals beneficiation, pharmaceuticals, tourism, business services, clothing and textiles, metal fabrication, transport equipment, green forms of energy, agro processing linked to food security, aerospace and nuclear materials and components (Department of Trade and Industry 2011). One of the criticisms against IPAP is the lack of skills to support the different sectors identified for investment given the state of the public schooling system and flight of skilled labour from the country.

The New Growth Path aims to reduce the levels of inequality prevalent amongst South Africans and targets those at the bottom of the economic ladder and regulates the income of the upper and middle classes including the elites. Small business enterprise development through development finance is one of the platform projects. It acknowledges that Black Economic Empowerment (BEE) has enriched those that are politically connected at the expense of the majority of those excluded from participating in the formal economy (Department of Economic Development, 2010: 33-34). However, one of the criticisms of a wage freeze on higher income earners has the potential of driving away skilled executives and investors.

More recently in 2012 the government embarked on a more enthusiastic development agenda by establishing the National Development Planning Commission (NPDC) which aims at creating a million jobs by 2030.

It is no different to the objectives contained in the New Growth Plan (National Planning Commission, 2012: 145-155). A criticism of the NPDC is that it does not address the wage caps on high income earners and such a silence is not atypical given the wide range of stakeholders including business representatives.

From the discussion on interventionist approaches put in place by state through social security safety nets for those excluded from the economy and the changes in economic policies to promote development, it appears that the state is concerned on the low levels of development achievement since democracy and has accordingly put in place new development policies to promote economic growth. Notwithstanding the deviation made by the state through a reinvigorated development policy for economic growth beyond the dominant neo-liberal macro-economic policy of GEAR, there are many challenges and obstacles that policy makers have to surmount if they are to deliver on their mission and vision with any measure of success. Various programmes have been experimented with over the years to kick-start development that will benefit those that are excluded from the economy with low levels of success.

Considering that only 25% of South Africans are engaged in the formal labour market, with almost 40% of the population dependent on state social security grants, low standard of education in public schools hardly preparing the youth for the labour market, backlogs in infrastructure development, failing health care system, poor levels of service delivery to those on the periphery of the economy, weak public administrative system, corruption and high levels of crime to mention a few, presents enormous challenges to this reinvigorated development policy. The political stability in the country is another factor that poses a risk to development policy implementation and its ability to meet its stated goals. There are signs of lower levels of political confidence expressed in the ruling parties ability to govern and take the country forward from the doldrums of underdevelopment perpetrated by apartheid.

CONCLUSION

The paper provides a snapshot of South Africa's socio-political and economic evolution in the different epochs of its history that shaped its present form as a developing nation. It highlights how colonialism and apartheid expropriated capital to benefit the minority white populace of the country leaving behind a devastating effect of underdevelopment amongst the majority of the Black population especially the indigenous populace of the country. In the post-apartheid era, South Africa has embarked on a Reconstruction and Development Programme to rehabilitate the previously disenfranchised populace with little success and bowed to a neo-liberal macro-economic policy as part of its development agenda. This macro-economic policy was perceived as a panacea to eradicate the development ills of the past only to find a small section of the Black population benefitting from it. As an emerging economy it has deviated from its developmental agenda and embraced policies that continue to benefit international capital by creating opportunities for trade in anticipation of a trickle-down effect that will benefit those that are excluded from the national economy. Hence, large segments of the population are excluded from participating actively in the economy and have become dependent on state grants and welfare services. Given the slow pace of development a variety of development programmes have been tried and tested to correct the historical socio-economic imbalances of the past, but with marginal success. As consequence, nineteen years post democracy a large segment of the South African population continue to live in poverty and squalor giving rise to new social movements that challenge the state aggressively on basic development issues. Development programmes and projects initiated by the state have been subjected to innumerable policy revisions and reformulation only to find that the desired objective of alleviating the plight of the poor on a sustainable basis is being further delayed resulting in a cycle of intergenerational underdevelopment perpetuating itself.

REFERENCES

African National Congress. (1956), *The Freedom Charter. Congress of the People*. Kliptown. South Africa. <http://www.anc.org.za/ancdocs/history/charter.html>. Accessed on May, 20, 2013.

ALIBER, M. (2003), *Chronic Poverty in South Africa: Incidence, Causes and Policies in World Development*, 31, 3: 473-490.

BALLARD, R., HABIB, A., VALODIA, I. (2006), *Voices of Protests: Social Movements in Post-Apartheid South Africa*. Pietermaritzburg, University of KwaZulu-Natal Press.

BANK, A. (1997), "The Great Debate and the Origins of South African Historiography", in *Journal of African History*, 38 p. 261-281.

BOND, P. (2004), *Talk Left, Walk Right: South Africa's Frustrated Global Reforms*. Pietermaritzburg, University of KwaZulu-Natal Press.

BRINEY, A. (2007), *Geography of South Africa – The World Fact book*. Retrieved from <https://www.cia.gov/library/publications/the-world-factbook/geos/sf.html>. Accessed on July, 15, 2013.

BUNDY, C. (1972), "The Emergence and Decline of a South African Peasantry", in *African Affairs*, 71, 285, p. 369-388.

Centre for Development Enterprise. (1997), "Getting into GEAR. The Assumption and Implications of the Macro-Economic Strategy", in *CDE Round Table*, N°1, 16p.

CERUTI, C. (2007), "South Africa: Rebirth of a mass movement International Socialism", in *Quarterly Journal of Socialist Theory*, issue 116.

COCK, J. (2003), *A Better Or Worse World? The World Social Forum, Porto Alegre. Centre for Civil Society*, Durban, South Africa. Research Report 5. <http://www.choike.org/documentos/wsf_s312_cock.pdf>.

Department of Economic Development. (2010), *The New Growth Path: The Framework*, November, South Africa.

Department of Finance. (1996), *Growth, Employment and Redistribution: A Macro-Economic Strategy*, published by the on 16 June 1996).

Department of Social Development. (2006), *Social Pension database*.

Department of Trade and Industry. (2011), *Industrial Policy Action Plan 2011/2012/2013/2014: Economic Sectors and Employment Cluster*, February, South Africa.

DESAI, A. (2005), "Uprooting and Re-Rooting Poverty in Post-Apartheid South Africa: A Literature Review", paper prepared for the *SANPAD Poverty Alleviation Workshop*, 24-25 May.

DU PLESSIS, P., Conley, L. (2007), "Children and Poverty in South Africa: The Right to Social Security" in *Educational Research and Review*, vol. 2, 4: 49-59.

FAROUK, F. (2013), Interview with Professor Sampie Terreblanche Prof. "White South Africans Will Have to Make Some Sacrifices", in *Civil Society Information Service (SACSIS)*, Aug., 7, 2013, University of Stellenbosch.

HABIB, A. (2003), "State-civil society relations in post-apartheid South Africa", *in* J. Daniels, A. Habib & R. Southall (eds.), in *State of Nation 2003-2004*, Pretoria, HSRC & Zed.

_____. (2013), *South Africa's Suspended Revolution: Hopes and Prospects*, Wits University Press, South Africa.

HABIB, A., Padayachee, V. (2000), Economic Policy and Power Relations in South Africa's Transition to Democracy, in *World Development*, 28, 2: 245-263.

HART, G. (2005), "Beyond Neo-Liberalism? Post-Apartheid Developments in Historical and Comparative Perspective", *in* V. Padayachee (ed.), *The Development Decade – Social and Economic Change in South Africa*, Capet Town, HSRC Press.

HOUGH, J. (2008), "Violent Protests at Local Government Level in South Africa: Revolutionary Potential?", in *South African Journal of Military Studies*, 36, 1: 1-13.

IHEDURU, O. C. (2004), "Black economic power and nation-building in post-apartheid South Africa", in *Journal of Modern African Studies*, 42, 1: 1-30.

KHAN, S. (2002), Infrastructure, Service Delivery and Local Development: A Few Considerations from Durban, South Africa in Governance, Urban Dynamics and Economic Development: A Comparative Analysis of the Metropolitan Areas of Durban, Abidjan and Marseilles by Bouillon A, Freund B, Hindson D and Lootvoet B, Plumbline Publishing, Durban, South Africa.

MADLINGOZI, T. (2007), *Post-Apartheid Social Movements and the Quest for the Elusive "New" South Africa*, Pretoria, University of Pretoria.

MARKS, S., Trapido, S. (1979), *Lord Milner and the South African State in History Workshop*, n. 8, p. 50-80.

National Treasury. (2005b), *Intergovernmental Fiscal Review*, Pretoria, National Treasury.

_____. (2012a), *Budget Review*, 22 February.

Republic of South Africa. (1996), *The Constitution of the Republic of South Africa*, n. 108, Pretoria.

SUTTNER, R. (2006), "Talking to the ancestors: national heritage, the Freedom Charter and nation-building in South Africa in 2005". in *Development Southern Africa*, vol. 23, n. 1, March 3-27.

WALKER, C. (1982), "A Process of Dispossession: An overview of relocation in Natal", in *Special Report*, n. 3, 1982.

Part two

CONTEMPORARY TRANSFORMATIONS
AND RE-ASSIGNMENT OF POLITICAL
AND CULTURAL MEANING IN THE BRICS

Political-economic changes and the production of new categories of understanding in the BRICS

Antonádia Borges

Brazil, Russia, India, China and South Africa together add up to more than an acronym for a set of countries that have recently started to collaborate economically. Neither is their relevance limited to the fact that, combined, they are home to 3 billion people. Despite the more or less lengthy and sophisticated debates that have already taken place on the BRICS countries, the last annual meeting of ANPOCS showed us how the interlocution between academics from these different nations, or conducting research in them, can inject some much needed fresh air into the social sciences, stimulating new analytic approaches, other possibilities for comprehension and new knowledge.

The theme of *justice and social inclusion* provides fertile terrain for revitalizing the social sciences in these nations by enabling a multi-way dialogue between academics from diverse backgrounds. Both notions – justice and inclusion – took root in the clash between modern and mostly Euro-American ideals of welfare and equity. As we know, these concepts became established as the patrimony of these societies and served as a parameter for observing the rest of the world, classifying and hierarchizing other regions in order to dominate and exploit them. Knowing the other through these parameters of justice and inclusion became a hegemonic form of producing knowledge about inequality.

The limits and paradoxes of this predominant model of analysis and intervention are many. For now we can focus on just two. On one hand, the modern scientific parameters of measurement presume common values taken to unite us all as Humankind. This homogeneity of the population under analysis – despite their myriad individual histories – supposedly assures the relevance of the method employed: that is, an approach that judges and classifies everyone according to the "same" parameters. On the other hand, the history of Euro-American colonial and imperial expansion under modernity is not considered to be itself responsible for producing an inherently asymmetric form of contact, a situation where the Other scrutinized by science is allowed no opinion on the pertinence of the criteria adopted in its analysis.

Returning to the question of renewing the social sciences, it is worth recalling that academics from the BRICS countries were never immune, of course, to this asymmetric model of knowledge production, which, though flourishing initially in Euro-America, gradually spread to every corner of the planet, becoming the "universal" form of doing science. The novelty and hope that emerge at this precise moment are linked to the pursuit of a transversal dialogue seldom encountered in previous decades: a dialogue without the explicit intermediation of Euro-American spaces and languages.

In a sense, it is as though we had met each other without interpreters, and this absence of intermediaries, in principle disconcerting, provides us with the space and time for longer observations and less hasty judgments. To take the Brazilian case, we always assumed that Russia, India, China and South Africa formed part of the Other, of the Orient even. Seldom though, or perhaps never, have we had such a clear opportunity as now – during these interactions between the BRICS nations – to recognize ourselves as the Other. In fact we continuously somewhat misguidedly located ourselves at the Euro-American pole of the relation, failing to realize that we were repeatedly classified as Other, as the Orient. Despite the many subtle singularities that mark each of the countries, a common condition of otherness never perturbed those who investigated us with their analytic models, taken as universally applicable and valid.

Directly related to this homogenizing analytical perspective is the observation that our countries have soaring rates of injustice and exclusion. Irrespective of the diversity of situations involved, what is highlighted by such macro-approaches is the fact that the inequality between members of the elite and the rest of the population is an outrageous fact which combined with widespread hunger and mass imprisonment (to mention just two of the tribulations assailing our contemporaries) often leads to a common "diagnosis" of our hopeless common future. What is at stake here is that this "commonality" is neither linked to a wider configuration beyond the borders of the nation states nor sustained by a committed understanding of local historical configurations. Therefore we urgently need to be capable of (1) rejecting the alien, exogenous and normative analytic models to which we have been exposed over decades or centuries; and (2) inventing new forms of understanding so that the clash between diverse senses of justice and inclusion can itself become a challenging source of ideas for transforming the atrocious world in which we live.

Our Symposium held in Águas de Lindoia in 2013 brought together investigators from a variety of academic traditions and disciplines, dedicated to researching questions related to justice and social inclusion. With us were our colleagues Elena Zdravomyslova and Mikhail Chernysh from Russia, Praveen Jha from India, Gao Bingzhong and Jiannan Guo from China, and Elaine Salo and Francis Nyamnjoh from South Africa, as well as the Brazilians Pedro Lara de Arruda and Maria Paula Gomes dos Santos.

Representative of our debates at the symposium, this section provides a wider audience with a rich set of texts in which the quality of the data is closely linked to the approaches adopted in their production. In all the works the scope and depth of the argument reveal each author's close engagement, combined with their insertion in a highly complex field of discussions.

The five texts included here can be divided into two general themes.

The first theme concerns a prior understanding of the cultural differences and transformations experienced in the BRICS countries, presuming that our aim is a meaningful dialogue in which all of us must become engaged if we wish to overcome the barriers of predictable reactions and exoticism.

The texts show that we have a great deal to learn over the course of our proposed dialogue, including in relation to the contemporary transformations and politico-cultural resignifications occurring in the BRICS.

The second theme suggests that there are aspects of local life within each nation state that can be comprehended, albeit superficially, by interlocutors from other countries. These are problems "known to everyone", that is, problems of an economic nature whose language imposes itself imperiously across the planet. In examining political-economic changes, the authors focusing on these issues invoke the need to produce new categories of understanding in the BRICS.

The first group contains articles by Nyamnjoh, Bingzhong, and Lara and Ashleigh, while the second contains those by Santos, and Jha and Chakraborty.

✻ ✻ ✻

On April the 27th South Africa commemorates the first direct elections in the post-apartheid era, which in 1994 anointed Nelson Mandela as president. In his chapter, Nyamnjoh sets out from the debates on the local radio on this day, in 2012, to talk about the problems assailing contemporary South Africa, reflected in the opinions of the general public who took part in the radio station phone-in. As the title of his text reveals, South Africa is living through a period of hope and fear. The democracy and freedom achieved in the constitution are not being felt in everyday life. For those who know even a little about the country, reading Nyamnjoh's article will confront them with an extremely complex reality. On one hand, everyone is aware of the legacy of apartheid and its impact on the present. On the other, though, how to deal with such a historical burden when the dominant groups, at least, seek harmony? How to keep alive the memory without igniting resentment? Nyamnjoh raises serious questions concerning the appeal for tolerance and appeasement in a society whose majority black population lacks the basic means for exercising its citizenship (the hurling of shantytown chemical toilets onto the express routes leading to Cape Town is just one of the most recent uprisings indicating the revolt over a paper tiger democracy, where half the population lives without basic sanitation). For the author, how do we adequately analyze a society where inequality becomes deeper every day, despite the effort of South Africans to "reinvent themselves"? Nyamnjoh backs the power of contestation of those who fight to demonstrate that consensus, equality and equity, enshrined in the Constitution, silence dissonant voices: whether that of President Zuma and his rival Malema, whether those who fight for reparation, to have their usurped land back, and resent the obliteration of philosophies of social action and the construction of the person – like Ubuntu – found prior to colonial occupation and exploitation.

Similar questions are evoked by Bingzhong Gao in his contribution to this volume. The transformations recently experienced in China are approached through an analysis of issues involving ancestrality, identity, legibility and legitimacy. Based on the Longpaihui case, Gao explores the vicissitudes of intangible cultural heritage (ICH). Despite the different relations between State and Society experienced among the BRICS countries, we can note that ideals of secularization taken as a cornerstone of modernity for decades have provided the bases for state action against cultural practices perceived to revive what is taken as backwardness or superstition. The destruction of innumerable temples in China would never suggest that ceremonies around the Dragon tablet would recently become re-established in the village of Fanzhuang in Hebei. In this town of a little over 5,000 inhabitants, today more than 100,000 people flock to the annual festival. Although the demographic scale of China might suggest that these people and their experiences are entirely "negligible", considering merely the numerical size of the "population", what Gao tries to show in his text is precisely the political and analytic impact that a study of the actions of these "small" grassroots social movements in the region may have on the social sciences. Pursuing a detailed analysis of their clandestine dedication to the Dragon tablet over the decades, along with their continual dialogue with academics and activists, he shows how the residents of this village successfully campaigned for the introduction of a cultural recognition policy that can now be encountered across the country. The political and semantic shift from "religion" (banned during the communist era for its alienated and alienating character) to "culture" implied not only the construction of museums (since temples were undesirable) but also the consolidation of a demand from those considered "backward" (as rural inhabitants, religious followers, etc.) for full belonging within the hegemonic society. If in China, as Gao explains to us, everything is named by the State before coming to exist in the world (from a child due to be born to a house under construction), the constitution of a contemporary political vocabulary to respond to such demands indicates controversies over the ways in which diversity is comprehended – including tensions between the traditional and the modern and between the elites and the general population – present in all our countries and to which we cannot close our eyes.

In Lara and Ashleigh's text we return to the dilemmas experienced in the present in dealing with historical burdens inherited from the colonial past. If in South Africa we have apartheid and racism, in India we still have "casteism". In both cases, although banned after independence, the two forms of discrimination and prejudice remain very much alive in everyday life. Aware of the complex narratives produced to explain the history and meaning of the caste system, the authors provide a careful synthesis of the topic, especially useful for those less familiar with the context in question. Legal changes achieved both at national level and in international forums by the anti-caste movements of various strains (some Hindu, others secular, others nationalist) demonstrate a long and slow process of achieving equal rights. In India the anti-caste movement has inspired the struggle of other majoritarian minorities, such as women, or people with disabilities, and their detailed investigation collaborates towards the understanding of other social phenomenon of contestation and historical transformation. The struggle for policies that include historically subjugated, exploited and disregarded populations shows that, despite the historical singularity, we need to challenge the parameters for constructing welfare developed by the elites of our countries through the exclusion of the majority of the population from decision-making spheres. As the authors show, studies in social sciences on such topics become more preeminent in contexts in which the vacuum of reliable data is directly connected to the hegemonic disdain of the theme under investigation.

The first three chapters of this section suggest that, despite their distinct histories, the clashes between the majoritarian minorities and the elites in South Africa, China and India have led to long and arduous battles in which those demanding rights have only made a few advances in gaining equality. In Santos's article, though, an apparently similar object – social protection – provides us with a way of thinking about the differences between social policies in Brazil and South Africa, their history and their implications for the present. Here too the major challenge seems to be the sources on the phenomenon under study (in this instance, basically quantitative in kind): namely, the systems of income generation and social security existing in Brazil and South Africa. Supported by diverse authors and research formats, the author argues that, in the absence of contemporary welfare programs such as the "Bolsa Família" in Brazil or the child support grant in South Africa, practically half the population of these two countries would immediately fall into the social space defined as "below the poverty line". This in turn would have a devastating impact on their current insertion in the networks of social transformation from which they had been excluded for two decades. Although this observation applies to both contexts, Santos ponders the meaning of the current policies in the two countries, taking into account a fundamental difference: the absence, in South Africa, of a system of social welfare similar to that existing in Brazil – that is, one extended to all citizens, irrespective of their participation in the work market and their contribution to social security funds. This distinction suggests that despite an apparently common form – the reparation of inequality through public income distribution policies that lead to an apparent social "levelling" through mass consumption – the relations between society, State and market in the two countries take on distinct features, leaving, in his assessment, the poor and mostly black South African population more vulnerable to the liberal political and economic winds than their Brazilian counterparts.

The absence of consolidated long-term policies focused on combatting inequality and the enthusiastic investment in the economic growth of countries like Brazil, Russia, India, China and South Africa also form the central lines of the argument developed by Jha and Chakraborty. Focusing on the themes of (in)justice, (in)equality and social inclusion, the authors enhance what their colleagues in this section have indicated, inviting us to reflect on the meaning and the implications of the liberalization – both political and economic – experienced in our countries, especially over the last three decades. Looking beyond the absolute values of the economic growth of the BRICS country, they argue the need to take into account the production of these indices and figures within a highly fluid global context and, especially, the intimate relations between this growth and the persistent, if not increasing, levels of inequality, rooted in badly remunerated work and the absence of social rights. In a word, the much-celebrated wealth of our nations is founded on the misery of – literally – billions of people, whose lives continue to be disdained in the name of a capitalist ideal of accumulation and development. Comparing indices of economic growth and inequality, the authors succeed in demonstrating in striking fashion that it is precisely hunger – yes, this is the real issue, notably in India, but not only there – and the physical annihilation of thousands of citizens on which the Eldorado experienced by the BRICS actually feeds. The analytic perspective adopted by the authors in the face of the endless elaboration of statistical data suggests an urgent need to deepen our debate on the limits of the hegemonic ideology of development, associating the latter with the low human development indices that – perhaps much more than the economic indices – are the real common trait to the contemporary realities in our countries.

*＊＊

The set of texts making up this section faithfully depict the complexity of the real-world situations experienced in countries like ours. In all of them we can clearly perceive the potential of the social sciences to contribute to an equally multifaceted, refined and critical understanding of the effects produced by this entanglement of elements in everyday lives, in conceptual frameworks and, especially, in the innumerable projects of transformation glimpsed locally. Without these efforts, homogenizing perspectives, disconnected from particular historical dynamics and oblivious to the fertile dialogues that mark the collaboration between the BRICS and other countries of the south, tend to undermine the numerous projects under way for constructing freedom – like those approached in the chapters presented to us here. Projects like those developed by people dedicated to thinking and transforming the countries in which we live – among whom we can include academics – shape a landscape often disregarded by Euro-American sensibilities and conceptual tools.

The BRICS countries, more than an unproblematic aggregate, constitute a contemporary event, an occasion that enables the exchanging of roles, shifts in perspective, and challenges to commonplace notions that we have tended to privilege precisely because we lacked – until the present moment – intellectual and political relations like those flourishing now. For this reason, we, the editors of this collection, are immensely grateful to all our colleagues who, with their enthusiasm and dedication, contributed towards this new initiative in search of mutual comprehension.

South Africa

Hopeful and fearful

....

Francis Nyamnjoh

Abstract   Inequality in South Africa based on racial discrimination is legally a thing of the past. However, inequality is not confined to race and does not disappear simply because it has been legislated against. Attitudes and relations are important additional indicators of the extent to which South Africa has effectively transformed its institutions and practices. This paper examines the continuities and discontinuities in social institutions, attitudes and relations as South Africans negotiate and navigate the challenges of forging a new egalitarian, convivial and interdependent "rainbow" society. The paper draws extensively on the discussions that took place on Freedom Day (Friday, 27 April 2012) on *SAfm*, a nationwide radio station of the South African Broadcasting Corporation, to probe the hopes and fears of a society seeking to re-invent itself.

Keywords   South Africa, apartheid, freedom, democracy, inequality, poverty, corruption, tradition.

INTRODUCTION

Inequality in South Africa based on racial discrimination is legally a thing of the past. However, inequality is not confined to race and does not disappear simply because it has been legislated against. Attitudes and relations are important additional indicators of the extent to which South Africa has effectively transformed its institutions and practices. This paper examines the continuities and discontinuities in social institutions, attitudes and relations as South Africans negotiate and navigate the challenges of forging a new egalitarian, convivial and interdependent "rainbow" society.

CONTEXT

It is Freedom Day on Friday, 27 April 2012 in Cape Town, South Africa. I am sitting behind my laptop in my study, listening to *SAfm* radio, determined to draw on the views of South Africans to write on the state of their nation, 18 years since the historic elections of 1994 that marked the end of apartheid, with the dawn of a new democratic dispensation. These reflections are based, in great measure, on notes I took listening to *SAfm* on that day, an experience that immediately begs questions. How representative of South Africans in their rainbow entirety are the views expressed on this particular station? What about South Africans who do not listen to the radio for whatever reason? And what about the views of non-South Africans, resident and non-resident, who feel just as entitled to constitutional protection, socio-economic comfort, human rights and dignity as their South African hosts? My answer is simple: These views are not necessarily insignificant, unrepresentative though they may be. The fact that some South Africans hold them at all means they should be taken seriously, for, as Archbishop Desmond Tutu has observed, no South African lives in a vacuum: "Each one of us is a constituent part of a greater organism: our community, our country, our continent, our world".[1] Every opinion counts even if it cannot be counted. I endeavour to supplement these *SAfm* voices, however, where possible, with views from academics and public figures drawn from other sources such as newspapers, books, internet and scholarly papers. This introduction is meant to provide a plural and general context as an entry point to the six contributions that follow.

FREEDOM DAY WITH *SAFM*

The questions of the day on Freedom Day at *SAfm* included: What were the expectations of South Africans when they cast their votes 18 years ago? How have those expectations been met? What disappointments might there be? What, according to them, have been the achievements of the past 18 years? What has worsened? What remains unfinished? What are the priorities going forward? South Africans called and texted the station and Tweeted and posted on Facebook to express their views.[2]

Opinions were rich and varied, passionate and analytical, and as much a reflection of the rainbow nation as of the diversity and multiplicity of experiences from different geographical, racial, class, cultural, gender and generational positions. It was apparent from the discussions and messages that perceived racial differences remain as important in shaping views and outlooks as class, place (rural, urban, township, city, neighbourhood, etc.), gender, generation, culture and political differences. There is an unfortunate tendency in some circles, argued one female studio guest, to deny that

---

1   Tutu D, Each one of us must help the miracle happen, *Timeslive*, 29 April 2012. Accessed on April 2012, <http://www.timeslive.co.za/local/2012/04/29/each-one-of-us-must-help-the-miracle-happen>.

2   Admittedly, in a rigorous survey, I would have systematically documented who the guests were, as they would also have particular leanings or opinions on the matter based on their social positions and affiliations.

race as a social construct continues to be effective. She called on fellow South Africans not to shy away from talking about social differentiation, as this remains an important indicator for who South Africans are. Race, she insisted, continues to be part of systemic and structural inequality, as it determines how South Africans experience their freedoms and relate to one another in real terms. To claim equality is not necessarily to provide for and to ensure equality in one's relationships and attitudes. As Phylicia Oppelt has written, "For some in our free SA, 'freedom' has still not arrived". They are not privileged enough to discard the shackles of race because they are reminded of it in every aspect of their lives".[3] Inadequate socio-economic transformation, according to others, limits tangible changes in race relations. Instead social and spatial apartheid is reproduced – the very apartheid that the proclamations and policies of racial equality of the new South Africa were supposed to have undone over the past 18 years. Another female studio guest argues that slow socio-economic transformation has trapped South Africans in their own ethnic and racial communities.

HAS ENDOGENOUS SOUTH AFRICA NOTHING TO OFFER?

Similarly, the re-introduction of traditional authorities in rural areas, far from being seen as an attempt at much more culturally accommodating forms of government vis-à-vis black South Africans repeatedly made to feel culturally inferior under apartheid, is being met with misgivings by a South African black elite all too keen to graduate from apartheid, even at the cost of throwing the baby of cultural diversity out with the bathwater. Faced with slow socio-economic transformation, growing criminality

---

3   Oppelt P, For some in our free SA, "freedom" has still not arrived, *Timeslive*, 29 April 2012. Accessed on April 2012, <http://www.timeslive.co.za/opinion/columnists/2012/04/29/for-some-in-our-free-sa-freedom-has-still-not-arrived>.

and the fact of more and more people being trapped in particular ethnic cultural geographies that are still mainly rural, administrative structures premised around shared cultural values such as the philosophy of ubuntu are ignored, with the attendant risk of social tensions and jeopardised inter-generational and inter-gender relationships. Although the empowerment of traditional authorities might make some anxious about a possible return to the bantustans of the apartheid era, where chiefs were divorced from their people and turned into high-handed dictators in the service of the dominant administration (NTSEBEZA, 2005; OOMEN, 2005),[4] there is little reason to suggest that chiefs, like the rest of South Africans, are incapable of re-inventing themselves in post-apartheid South Africa.

It would appear the platinum-rich Bafokeng Tswana nation of the North West province, known as the "Royal Bafokeng Nation", with kings who brand themselves as CEOs of "Bafokeng, Inc." – to cite one example only – just might have some lessons on creative improvisation and adaptation with changing circumstances that belie sweeping assumptions about the supposedly inherent fixation with the past and autocracy of systems of governance inspired by endogenous philosophies of personhood and leadership (COMAROFF and COMAROFF, 2009: 98-116). If chiefs are individuals with agency like every other individual in society, there is nothing inherently dictatorial about them as people or chieftaincy as an institution, just as there is nothing inherently democratic about presidents as people or the institution of the state (Fokwang 2009; Nyamnjoh 2003). The tendency to focus analysis "almost exclusively upon institutional and constitutional arrangements" assumes "the classical dichotomy between ascription and achievement" and "takes as given that stated rules should actually determine the careers of actors in the public arena" (COMAROFF, 1978: 1).

---

4   See Dr Mamphela Ramphele's critique of the Traditional Courts Bill (This is apartheid by another name, *Sunday Times*, 25 March 2012).

Institutions and individuals mutually constitute one another, at different points in history, depending on the relationships we choose to privilege. Thus, instead of uncritically diminishing current efforts by government to make rural South Africa governable by seeking to re-activate culturally informed administrative structures instrumentalised in myriad ways under apartheid, South Africans should collectively harness their energies and intellects to ensure a fair, balanced, representative and accountable outcome to current consultations on a Traditional Courts Bill.[5] It is not because rural South Africa is not urban South Africa that urban-based intellectuals, civil society activists and politicians should not actively participate in getting things rural right. Government can only be as effective and sensitive as the strength of the interest and commitment citizens and nationals collectively bring to bear on government action or inaction.

If South Africans are indeed a unique people, living testimony to the unconquerable spirit of humankind, as President Zuma claimed in his Freedom Day speech,[6] they are not to dismiss a priori, everything bequeathed by apartheid, for no other reason than that it served or benefited from the apartheid regime. To diminish chiefs and chieftaincy on these grounds would beg the question about myriad other continuities in post-apartheid South Africa. The failure to radically transform society socio-economically for most but an elite black minority has resulted in the reproduction of the apartheid past, where particular groups dictated by perceived hierarchies of humanity continue to be privileged to the detriment of others, without this having to be a conspiracy of any kind. The same is true for hierarchies between places, genders and generations, where those traditionally favoured under apartheid have seen their advantages reproduced in post-apartheid South Africa, by the failure to enforce significant socio-economic transformation.

---

5   See Weeks SM, Traditional Courts Bill contradicts Constitution: Singular power given to traditional leaders, *Cape Argus*, 30 April 2012. See also Gasa N, Proposed Traditional Courts Bill undermines the supremacy of the Constitution, *The Sunday Independent*, 25 March 2012.

6   See <http://www.info.gov.za/speech/DynamicAction?pageid=461&sid=26952&tid=65956>. Accessed on August 2012.

TENDERPRENEURSHIP, BUSINESS AS USUAL
AND THE POLITICS OF CONSUMPTION

It was argued, by many who called or texted, Tweeted or posted on Facebook in response to the questions posed by *SAfm*, that there has been too much focus by government on top-level socio-economic transformation initiatives, targeting an elite minority to the detriment of the majority trapped in poverty. The economy is still dominated by white South Africans and black empowerment has only meant the crystallisation of the black middle classes and a culture of *tenderpreneurship*. According to Terry MacKenzie-Hoy, a "tenderpreneur" in South Africa:

> [...] is a person who has made an extraordinary sum of money from a contract (usually a national government, provincial government or municipal tender) that has been awarded for some sort of service. The reason why such a lot of cash flows from the contract is that the award value significantly exceeds the cost of the services, and the surplus goes into the pockets of the contractor and the officials who award the contract.[7]

According to the general secretary of the Congress of South African Trade Unions (Cosatu), Zwelinzima Vavi, a "tenderpreneur" is one "who through political connections wins tenders unfairly and provides shoddy services to communities while more genuine entrepreneurs are side lined as well as their skills and proper services".[8] Tenderpreneurship is thought to have mostly benefited corrupt politicians and top civil servants seeking

---

7   See McKenzie-Hoy T, Tenderpreneurs frustrating legitimate contractors, *Engineering News*, 5 March 2010. Accessed on April 2012, <http://www.engineeringnews.co.za/article/tenderpreneurs-frustrating-legitimate-contractors-2010-03-05>.

8   See South African Press Association (Sapa), Cosatu warns against tenderpreneurs, *Business Report*, 4 March 2010. Accessed on April 2012, <http://www.iol.co.za/business/business-news/cosatu-warns-against-tenderpreneurs-1.812852>.

shortcuts to riches and to ostentatious consumption (FORDE, 2011; POSEL, 2010; SHAPIRO, 2011).[9]

According to Winnie Madikizela-Mandela, if VS Naipaul (2010) is to be believed,

> Black economic empowerment is a joke. It was a white confidence measure made up by local white capitalists. They took malleable blacks and made them partners. But those who had struggled and had given blood were left with nothing. They are still in shacks: no electricity, no sanitation and no sign of an education.

While affluent blacks can now send their children to posh schools historically exclusive to white students, it is not clear the extent to which this is a justification of time spent on death row, long solidarity confinement and struggle heroes who died seeking a better future for all and sundry. Even Nelson Mandela, she continues, who went to jail a revolutionary, came out preaching peace and compromise, and all too ready to accept "a freedom based on compromises and concessions".[10]

If media reports are anything to go by, it would appear Julius Sello Malema best epitomises these growing trends among politicians in the new South Africa.[11] Until his expulsion from the ANC on 29 February 2012,[12]

---

9 Corruption is supposedly so rife that Zwelinzima Vavi allegedly warned the ANC of the risk of South Africa becoming a "banana republic" because of its "predatory elite" (Ngalwa S and Majavu A, Vavi stuns ANC, *Sunday Times*, 12 June 2011). Vavi criticised the rise of "a culture of impunity" and of "me-first-and-to-hell-with-everybody-else" and called on South Africans to "remain true to the fundamental principles and culture of [...] struggle – selflessness and sacrifice" (Vavi Z, The Malema debate: Let us get rid of the "me-first" culture, *City Press*, 31 July 2011).

10 Wounds that will not heal, an excerpt from VS Naipaul's *The Masque of Africa: Glimpses of African Belief*, *Sunday Times Review*, 3 October 2010.

11 See, for example, Staff reporter, How Julius Malema pulls tender strings, *Mail & Guardian*, 5–11 August 2011; Forde F, How Malema amassed his millions, *Mail & Guardian*, 18–24 May 2012; Hofstatter S, Wa Afrika M & Rose R, Juju's jackpot, *Sunday Times*, 20 May 2012.

12 Found "guilty of portraying the ANC government and its leadership under president Jacob Zuma in a negative light, and for making statements on bringing about regime change in

Malema provided another example of a public figure privileging the rhetoric of exclusion over actively exploring cohesion among all and sundry in the rainbow nation. In 2010 Malema, then leader of the Youth League of the ANC (ANCYL), identified white South Africans as the enemy within and nationalisation and land restitution as his favourite themes. While he invited his mostly unemployed supporters among black South Africans to aspire to be like the whites in comfort and consumption, he particularly targeted Afrikaners in his choice of public choral performance to drive his message home. On 3 March 2010, for example, at his birthday party in Pholokwane, Malema, sang *Ayesab' Amagwala* – a popular Zulu anti-apartheid, liberation struggle song that contains the words "*dubul'ibhunu*", which translate into English as: "Shoot the *boer*". *Boer*, "farmer" in Dutch, refers to white South Africans from Dutch, German or Huguenot descent who speak Afrikaans, and are also known as Afrikaners. Malema sang the song repeatedly and supposedly provocatively – including in April 2010 during a visit to Zimbabwe, where he openly supported Robert Mugabe's land restitution programme – causing much uproar in the media and the wider South African society.

A debate ensued as politicians and others discussed whether the song should be allowed as part of South Africa's heritage and history, or prohibited as hate speech. The choice was between prioritising heritage to the detriment of harmony, or harmony to the detriment of memory,[13] in a context where equality and redress were much more a constitutional provision than a real-life experience for the bulk of those dispossessed and dehumanised by apartheid. The ANC's reaction was similar to Jacob Zuma's reaction to the controversy around his singing of *Umshini Wami* (Bring Me My Machine Gun). "If you

---

Botswana, at an ANCYL press conference on July 31, 2011", Malema was defiant and vowed to appeal: "I will die with my boots on, and I will die for what I believe in [...] I have not done anything wrong [...] I am persecuted for speaking on behalf of (the) ANCYL [...] I've never been a sell-out and I'm not going to sell out today". (Sapa, political bureau & own correspondent, Malema expelled, *Cape Times*, 1 March 2012). He eventually lost the appeal and the suspension was confirmed on 24 April 2012.

13 However, it should be noted that both memory and heritage are contentious and coloured by specific worldviews as post-apartheid nation-building is still in its infancy.

erase the songs, you erase the record of history", said Zuma of the anthem (GUNNER, 2009).[14] His shortcomings notwithstanding, it is difficult to ignore the weight of Malema's pronouncements. He speaks sense, as much as he speaks nonsense, and is as much a champion as he is a politician. To undo the wrongs of the past, there needs to be greater redistribution or division of wealth. However, what he is arguing is not always acknowledged, because of his self-image and the way he is portrayed in the media. Controversies and perceptions that his practices appear at variance with his preaching seem to sweep the substance of his argument under the carpet.

The controversies and tensions between heritage and harmony in the rainbow nation were only further enflamed by the death of Eugène Terre'Blanche – founder and leader of the Afrikaner Weerstandsbeweging (AWB, in English, Afrikaner Resistance Movement), an organisation formed in 1973 by right-wing extremist Afrikaners to resist what they saw as the weakening of apartheid regulations at the time – killed on 3 April 2010, allegedly by two of his black workers on his farm in Ventersdorp over unpaid wages. Tensions rose as some sought to link Malema's singing of "Shoot the boer" and Terre'Blanche's murder. Right-wing extremist groups such as the AWB and the Suidlanders, for long quiescent, conducted protest marches in Ventersdorp and threatened to avenge the murder. Other groups became involved, including AfriForum and the Transvaal Agricultural Union (TAU SA), who lodged a complaint with the Equality Court against Malema, accusing him of hate speech. On 18 March, a "Prosecute Malema" online campaign was launched to gather signatures for a letter directed to President Zuma; by 25 March, the South African Human Rights Commission had received 109 complaints against Malema for singing the song; and on 26 March and 1 April, the song had been ruled unlawful and unconstitutional by the North and South Gauteng High Courts, respectively, much to the dissatisfaction of many an ANC member (RODRIGUES, 2011: 1-4).

---

14 See also Mangena I, Umshini Wami echoes through SA, *Mail & Guardian*, 23 December 2007. Accessed on May 2012, <http://mg.co.za/article/2007-12-23-umshini-wami-echoes-through-sa>.

Malema, whom Xolela Mangcu qualifies as having come of age in the age of looting,[15] may live in Sandton, Johannesburg and cherish flashy designer clothes and shoes, big Breitling watches and gold, diamond-studded rings, the choicest wines and sushi off the belly buttons and nipples of naked beautiful girls (FORDE, 2011; SHAPIRO, 2011)[16] – indeed, he may share the same appetites and material comforts of the richest of those who systematically and actively excluded him and those he claims to represent from the old South Africa – but somehow he feels more legitimately entitled to the new South Africa, and to a culture of victimhood, and of consumption with reckless abandon, even at the risk of consuming the dignity and humanity of fellow South Africans. Belonging is an unending cycle of ever-diminishing circles, just as the results of liberation struggles are not measured in material terms exclusively.

Although a lot has been achieved materially for a small group of people, not enough has been done for the majority. Worse still, there is the stubborn feeling, even among economically empowered black people, that their collective memories of the struggle against apartheid are being muzzled by powerful minorities who are all too eager to consider apartheid dead and buried and to divorce the present from its history. With little consensus beyond a savage commitment to inflame tensions, while hoping for salvation from the constitution, South Africa appears to be a country of everyone-for-themselves-and-God-for-us-all. Little wonder that, for many, the God of all South Africans – *The State* – has become a scapegoat and a punch bag for its inability to do more than help those who help themselves. Abandoned and weakened by the competing and warring factions and interests called "South Africa", *The State* finds itself unable to achieve little more than reproducing social geographies of apartheid.

---

15 See Mangcu X, The Malema debate: Coming of age in the age of looting, *City Press*, 31 July 2011.

16 See also Ritz C, The emperor has no clothes, *The New Age*, 1 March 2012.

THE DIGNITY OF CITIZENSHIP

According to President Jacob Zuma, the government has provided more than three million units of subsidised housing since 1994.[17] However, while Reconstruction and Development Programme (RDP) houses, for example, might offer shelter, they do so at the expense of humaneness and the humanity of those who take up these houses, constructed at the periphery of almost everything relevant to their lives, as occupants find themselves having to live far away from their places of work and from the social amenities on which they depend daily, yet without affordable transportation. As poor and impoverished South Africans desperately seek to make ends meet at the margins, an informal economy develops around the RDP houses, as some end up renting out parts of the homes to make extra income and selling their electricity illegally to neighbours who still live in shacks. Many are abandoned to a precarious and degrading existence in makeshift homes at temporary and forgotten spaces such as Blikkiesdorp in Cape Town (SMITH, 2011). This, in addition to the continued existence of informal settlements without basic facilities, such as running water or decent public toilets, electricity, or decent sanitation, and with mass unemployment and millions still living below the R422 per month poverty line, means the majority of South Africans is yet to experience in real terms the comforts of freedom, human rights, democracy, citizenship and dignity promised by their unique Constitution. Basic facilities, such as running water and decent toilets, complementary to the comforts of freedom, for example, are luxuries that some informal settlement residents rarely experience. Many of these residents find alternative means of "comfort" in this regard, using buckets to both harness water from (functional) communal taps and to relieve themselves. One student researcher describes her experience of using a bucket in this way for the first time during her fieldwork in Langa township:

---

17   See <http://www.info.gov.za/speech/DynamicAction?pageid=461&sid=26952&tid=65956>. Accessed on August 2012.

While standing in the middle of the shack I realized that I had to use the bathroom [...]. There was no bathroom. This was not a house. It was a shack. The bed, kitchen and sitting room were all one in the same. Where did I expect a bathroom to be? There were several women in the house and one of them motioned to another to get the bucket [...]. There was a light yellow liquid already in the bucket. It did not look like urine though. My guess was that it was a cleaning detergent diluted with water. She placed the bucket on the floor in the middle of the shack. There was too short a window between the time the bucket was placed on the floor and when the other women began turning their backs to give me privacy before I could object. I was uncomfortable [...]. It seemed to be a natural experience for them and I did not want to draw any more attention to myself. The women talked as I urinated. The sound of my urine entering the bucket seemed excruciatingly loud amongst the talking voices and I was embarrassed though no one else seemed to be. When I was done I asked [...] can I have some toilet paper? At this question, the same girl who got the bucket frowned. I could not tell if it was a "now I have to go find some toilet paper" frown or an "oh no, we don't have any toilet paper" frown. Regardless of what she was thinking I was huddled over the bucket with my pants down and my knees bent and I wanted someone to give me something to clean myself so I could get out of the situation. She left the shack and came back quickly enough [...] I cleaned myself and happily pulled my pants up.[18]

Experiences like this are commonplace in post-apartheid South Africa, arguably the most unequal society in the world, where access to toilets is as important a political issue during election campaigns as access to jobs (ROBINS, 2011). Langa is less than 20 minutes away by car from some of the filthiest rich neighbourhoods in Cape Town, neighbourhoods daily served and serviced by the devalued labour of maids, domestic workers and

---

18 Crystal Powell (PhD student, Social Anthropology, University of Cape Town), Visiting the shacks. Notes from the field, Langa township, 15 August 2011.

garbage men who are shack and dormitory dwellers in Langa, Khayelitsha, Gugulethu and beyond. Few among the majority of South Africans who are trapped in such violent and bleeding poverty in the midst of plenty can afford the extravagant illusion of contemplating a life of dignity, decency or "*ordentlikheid*" (ROSS, 2010). Apartheid may have been legislated away, but its discomforts and anxieties linger on, under various privatisation and individual freedom aliases such as "free market" and "private property rights", which is perhaps what leads one of the men who phoned in to *SAfm* on Freedom Day to conclude, "We are still an unequal society, almost as we were before".

In recognition of the fact that black workers and the urban poor continue to be hugely disadvantaged by their geographical marginalisation in townships and informal settlements, Jeremy Cronin offers the following way forward in the interest of social transformation of the economy, social spaces and state:

> [...] a sober analysis of the systemic ways in which the past continues to distort our present. Business as usual, growth (even 7% growth) along the same growth path, valiant efforts at "service delivery" through top-down patronage into the same endlessly reproduced zones of desperate need – none of these will catalyse the systemic transformation required. It is not a question of simply blaming or exonerating "apartheid". Let's rather work together to appreciate the huge weight of the past on our present, and to appreciate the collective efforts required to transform our often dysfunctional reality.[19]

Land restitution and redistribution remain a sore and sensitive problem. According to President Zuma,[20] while the 1913 Land Act systematically took away 87% of the land from its black owners (see also NTSEBEZA and HALL, 2007; YANOU, 2009), 18 years after the end of apartheid, only

---

19 Cronin, J. How history haunts us, *Timeslive*, 29 April 2012. Accessed on April 2012, <http://www.timeslive.co.za/local/2012/04/29/how-history-haunts-us>.

20 See <http://www.info.gov.za/speech/DynamicAction?pageid=461&sid=24980&tid=55960>. Accessed on August 2012.

6.7 million hectares of land have been transferred back to black people, representing only 8% of the 30% target of land redistribution for 2014 that the government set itself.[21] This means that rural South Africans are not able to earn a living through access to and harnessing land and are trapped in relationships of dependence on the state and exploitation by large-scale farmers, the vast majority of whom are white. Thus while a significant number of previously disadvantaged black (African, coloured and Indian)[22] elite have graduated into varying degrees of white, middle-class suburbs as "coconuts"[23] of various shades of the rainbow nation, the rest of South Africans continue to experience prejudices informed by past and current class structures and inherited race structures.[24] Blacks and whites in South Africa, Mbembe has written, "are becoming strangers to each other in ways not witnessed even during apartheid".[25]

White South Africans may not be a unified bloc, but the edification of biological and cultural racism under apartheid made it possible for their collective interests to be privileged, regardless of class, gender, status or the resistance of some against the structures in place (STEYN, 2008). Those who harness their intellect, art, skills, effort and time to foster greater social and cultural integration with selflessness and commitment to a common humanity, and who are recognised and encouraged for doing so, point to a

---

21 It is worth recognising that the land "returned" is not necessarily arable land and some farms that were repossessed have not been managed appropriately or effectively after the hand-over, primarily as people who are not farmers took possession of the land.

22 "Black" was the all-encompassing term used for Africans, coloureds and Indians during the "struggle days".

23 "Coconut" is a derogatory term used by black South Africans to describe black people who act "white", connoting being black on the outside and white on the inside, a suggestion of bending over backwards to embrace purported "white values" to the detriment of their supposed "black values", almost as if particular values are essential to particular racial categories.

24 But, as one female coloured academic commented on an earlier version of this chapter, "living in these areas, and upward mobility, do not protect one from prejudice". The level of institutionalised racism and prejudice is so entrenched that South African people of colour are unable to avoid being the objects of prejudice.

25 Mbembe A, Culture and demagoguery: The spear that divided the nation, *Cape Times*, 5 June 2012.

future that is neither trapped in delusions of superiority nor in the celebration of victimhood. However, the failure to enforce greater integration beyond elite circles combines with ignorance and arrogance to guarantee continuation for racism and prejudices. Apartheid may have died officially, but slow socio-economic transformation and slow reconfiguration of attitudes, beliefs and relationships in favour of greater mutual recognition and accommodation have meant its continued reproduction in less obvious and more insidious ways.

PLAYING THE BLAME GAME

Some listeners who called into SAfm blamed the government squarely for this failure, arguing that South Africans cannot continue to hold apartheid accountable for its shortcomings 18 years into its new democratic dispensation. They look to social movements, NGOs, popular politics and the privately owned media to protect their rights and freedoms vis-à-vis a state perceived to be determined to keep such rights and freedoms in check with violations and excesses of various kinds (ROBINS, 2008). To them, the incompetence of the black-dominated ANC government must be exposed, decried and derided. They pointed to corruption in government and to the rise and proliferation with impunity of tenderpreneurship and the greedy pursuit of personal wealth at the expense of public service by politicians and bureaucrats. Corruption is indeed so widespread that it has attracted consistent critical media attention, as well as condemnation from opposition parties, members of the ruling Alliance and of the ANC rank and file, as well as from moral authorities such as Archbishop Desmond Tutu and public intellectuals such as Professor Njabulo Ndebele.[26] Inspired by

---

26 For Njabulo Ndebele's critical reflections on corruption, see Ndebele NS, A meditation on corruption, *City Press*, 21 January 2012. Accessed on April 2012, <http://www.citypress.co.za/Columnists/A-meditation-on-corruption-20120121>. See also Smuts Ngonyama's comment (in 2007, when he was the ANC's spokesman): "I didn't join the struggle to be poor" (see Hold your nose: The smell of corruption, *The Economist*, 3 June 2010. Accessed on May 2012, <http://www.economist.com/node/16248621>.

the sentencing of former Police Chief Jackie Selebi to serve 15 years in jail for "engaging in illegal financial transactions for personal gain", Ndebele shared the following reflection on corruption among the new "bureaucratic bourgeoisie" now presiding over the destiny of South Africa:

> Access to accumulated state wealth reduces any inclination there may ever have been to re-order society to create new conditions for new wealth. The wealth now available will be spent far more than it can be replaced or grown. In such situations, justifications to hold on to power abound. These may include messianic notions of permanent power, "until Jesus returns"; or notions that no one else can bring about the necessary social transformations – only the leaders of the group in power can. For such consecrated leadership, constitutional rule soon becomes an impediment. It imposes the requirement of effort that is often too demanding on personal and group capability. Indeed the collective capability immediately available to the group sets the standards and the norms for maintaining group cohesion. These norms and standards are then reproduced internally and become more and more distant from external realities and the pressures they may impose. The group then becomes prone to new solidarities that eventually become corruptive. Soon, group interest substitutes for constitutional rule. The once revolutionary commitment to radical social transformation is replaced by opportunisms of the moment.[27] (See also POSEL, 2010.)

On corruption, one person phoned *SAfm* to say: "I am so happy with the people of South Africa, but not so happy with the politicians". According to this caller, South Africans have been exemplary in creating and exploring ways of "getting along better" and "maintaining a democratic right to protest", while politicians are mostly drawn by the ambition to get rich quickly and to sow discord among the constituent communities of South Africa. True as this might be, as Cronin argues, The flippant dismissal of

---

27 Ndebele, A meditation on corruption.

the weight of the past on our collective present is just as unhelpful as its opposite, a simplistic evocation of that past as an alibi for our own weaknesses. Both have tended to produce shallow explanations for the deep-seated challenges we confront.[28] Few would argue with the claim that the past informs the present, but as Joy Owen argued on reading an earlier draft of this chapter, "When people continue to go hungry, their hunger screams and promises made by politicians need to be realised. Further, neo-liberal politics compels government to spend less on its people, and this is not something that government in general would like to admit to".

The fact that the Constitution allows for the state to be taken to court, and that the government has not tampered with the Constitution in this regard, is evidence that the South African state is far from being an omniscient and omnipotent state and, therefore, can hardly be blamed for all the failures of post-apartheid society. Intellectuals, the private sector, opposition leaders, media and civil society must assume their share of the blame – and indeed, of responsibility for bringing about a democratic South Africa in which everyone has an equal chance of life in comfort and dignity. On reading this section in an earlier version of this chapter, a former white, female Honours student of mine confessed: "As a twenty-five-year-old South African who started school in 1994, I don't feel that there is much integration in my social circles, especially in Cape Town – I don't really have any close black or coloured friends".

MUTUAL TOLERANCE AND ACCOMMODATION

There is need for greater tolerance and accommodation among the different communities that constitute the rainbow, a lesson that Ndebele draws following the controversy ignited by Malema's use of the term *Makula*,[29]

---

28 Cronin, How history haunts us.

29 This translates either derogatorily as "coolie" or simply as "Indian", depending on context and intention.

to refer to Indian South Africans. Recognising that South Africans under apartheid "internalised the insensitivities and brutalities of colonialism and a formally racist society over time", until these became part of their reflex behaviour, Ndebele invites fellow South Africans, instead of rushing to court to complain against utterances by one another, to "recognise the sources of potential hurt when we see them; register the outrage internally; smother the urge for instant reaction; run through the database of past experience; consider possible options of reaction; and then select an option". He adds:

> New moral power will belong to those who do not spring to reflex self-defence and self-justification. Critical introspection will help them pry out new knowledge, redefine old notions, and clear the air for new relationships. Relationships between people are never defined or redefined instantly. They evolve from a constant effort of experience, education, and calibration.[30]

Such organic processes of reconciliation call for moral leadership across the social spectrum, leadership that is measured and unassuming and that is in touch in myriad ways with those on behalf of whom they make pronouncements and commitments. Above all, they call for leadership that distinguishes itself, not through flashy consumption and sterile accumulation, but by austere lives and commitment to principles. As Trevor Manuel put it on *SAfm* on Freedom Day, "Fighting poverty doesn't mean making millions, but removing the yoke of poverty from millions". This is imperative in a context where "only 41% of adult South Africans work in either the formal or informal sector" – a situation compounded by a very poor quality of education structured, permeated and haunted by a logic of race (SOUDIEN, 2012), especially for the majority black population, among whom only 15% of those who passed matric in 2010 received an aggregate mark above

---

30 Ndebele N, Thinking of Malema on the Day of Reconciliation, City Press, 24 December 2011. Accessed on April 2012, <http://www.citypress.co.za/Columnists/Thinking-of-Malema-on-the-Day-of-Reconciliation-20111223>.

40%.[31] With the annual debacle around matric pass rates and how these are configured, South Africa could very well end up with youth that are functionally illiterate and innumerate. As it stands, one's education depends on whether one's parents have the financial and cultural capital to send one to a semi-private or private school, as government schools (depending on the province) are not always functional and, if they are functional, teachers are not necessarily equipped to teach the new curricula (JANSEN, 2011: 10-11). Beneath the rainbow façade of many a school in the post-apartheid context, "there exists an inward struggle with racial identity amongst both the staff and the student body" and transforming the classroom into a "neutral place of discussion" remains to be achieved, as students and staff enter the classroom with "inherited racial positioning" and lived realities that have little room for neutrality. Students and teachers continue to carry and are largely shaped in their perspectives and interactions by "a distinct knowledge of the past framed in their own experiences and backgrounds" (MAZANDERANI, 2011: 17-42).

Others callers to *SAfm* on that day felt that the government appears as a soft target. While just as concerned about corruption in government and high office, they believed it takes more than government officials to be corrupt. The private or business sector is equally to blame. Tenderpreneurs would hardly be successful if there were no opportunistic bidders. On mass unemployment, they were just as critical of those who blame government for everything. While they were disappointed in the way that the government has gone about instituting black economic empowerment, they blamed the private sector for its failure to show more commitment to transformation and job creation. They deplored the tendency in some critical circles to speak and act as though the only relationship possible with the state is an adversarial one.

Writing in the *Sunday Times* two days after Freedom Day about the growing feeling of profound anxiety and disillusionment among South

---

31   See Staff reporter, In search of win-win solutions, *Mail & Guardian*, 10–16 June 2011.

Africans "over the moral and spiritual wellbeing of the nation", Archbishop Desmond Tutu stressed the urgent need to rethink democracy in South Africa, challenging everyone to consider it a collective responsibility. He was concerned about the regularity of "new stories of corruption in government, of nasty competitiveness for leadership positions in the ruling party, of a crisis in education, of so-called service-delivery protests that regularly turn destructive, of the most horrendous incidents of violent crime" and particularly worried by the fact that "instead of narrowing the gap between rich and poor", South Africans "have allowed it to become a dangerously yawning chasm".[32] Far from upholding and enshrining the years of struggle and activism for social change and for common good, 18 years of democracy seem to have delivered little more than "a nation apparently preoccupied with the accumulation of personal wealth". He continued:

> In 1994, when we all voted for the first time, we hung up our activist T-shirts and ceded total responsibility for our lives to our newly elected government. Then we folded our arms and waited for the miracle of better lives to be bestowed on us, a nation of passive recipients awaiting government largesse. When it isn't forthcoming, we organise service-delivery protests.

While he recognised the need to criticise the government "where criticism is due", Tutu was rather disappointed by the failure of many critical South Africans to "look deep inside" themselves and ask what they "can contribute to creating a better society". South Africans must ask themselves: "What can we do to hold the government accountable for its spending? But also, what can we do, as an active and organised citizenry, to improve conditions ourselves?" He challenged parent bodies to get involved in the lives and well-being of the schools their children attend, not merely as armchair critics, but by contributing their skills and time to help improve the learning environment for their children. Once a year, for example, parents should

---

32   Tutu D, Each one of us must help the miracle happen.

get together "to paint and spruce up our children's schools". Similarly, "our church congregations and our community-based organisations should be sufficiently active to be able to avoid most preventable deaths of infants", just as collectively assuming responsibility could enable South Africans "to reduce our terrible road-accident rate". By the same token, Tutu continued, "If we raised our children with decent values, surely incidents such as the gang rape of the apparently mentally impaired teenage girl in Soweto 10 days ago could never have happened". South Africans can only mitigate the blame game when they collectively realise that no one is an island entire to her/himself and that however isolated one might feel, "we do not live in a vacuum", as we are all constituent parts of a greater organism, be this our immediate community, our country, our continent, or our world. This is not to minimise the fact that in addition to the deep and resilient divisions that make collective citizenship difficult to achieve:

> We are a deeply wounded people. We carry the recent scars of apartheid and the ingrained hurt of centuries of colonialism before that. Some of us feel superior to others, and some feel inferior. For generations, instead of following the universal golden rule of reciprocity, to love one another as ourselves, we have been trained to be mistrustful, to dislike – even to hate.[33]

Coming 18 years after the Truth and Reconciliation Commission, which Tutu himself chaired, this acknowledgement that South Africans are yet to reconcile themselves to one another in the spirit of the "rainbow" conviviality and interdependence reflects his personal disappointment with the slow pace of change in attitudes and relationships among South Africans. However, for Winnie Madikizela-Mandela, for black people reduced for over four decades to living as non-people, the Truth and Reconciliation Commission was an unrealistic "fairy tale-like" idea. "It opened up wounds

---

33 Tutu D, Each one of us must help the miracle happen.

that could not heal. You learned about the method and means off your loved one's death. How can you forgive or forget something like that?"[34]

His disappointment notwithstanding, Tutu is convinced that the answer to the current anxiety and sense of disillusionment lies in collective action. He called for "teamwork", informed by an understanding that the hopes and aspirations of each and every South African are tied up not just in themselves and their material well-being as individuals, but also in one another. In this regard, the rich, who – even with the growing corruption in the ANC-led government – are mostly white, have a critical redistributive role to play. Tutu felt he had been unfairly criticised in 2011 when he suggested that "the wealthy, most of whom are white, should seriously consider contributing some of their riches to improve the lives of the poor, as a magnanimous gesture". He is still perplexed as to why he was criticised: "Surely it is not outrageous to suggest that it would be in the interests of the "haves" to contribute to a more equitable, stable and sustainable society? If not in cash, then in kind".[35] However, Tutu concluded, much as the wealthy are called upon to take leadership in socio-economic transformation, the poor are equally expected to play their part. In the interest of mutual accountability, responsibility and interdependence, the poor must.

> roll up their sleeves and participate constructively for the common good. Living in filthy and unhygienic conditions is not necessarily a product of poverty. Ensuring that our children go to school every day, joining neighbourhood watches and other community initiatives, cooking a meal for an elderly neighbour, getting involved and plugging in, these are contributions that do not depend on wealth.

Collective action as South Africans requires facing the psychological shifts that are needed both by the privileged and by the disempowered and

---

34 Wounds that will not heal
35 Tutu D, Each one of us must help the miracle happen

disenfranchised. It is not enough to assume that since equality and equity are enshrined in the Constitution, every person in South Africa is aware of his or her rights; worse still, that everyone can afford those rights.

DEMOCRACY AND RAINBOW CONSTITUTION

Singled out as an unequivocal achievement worthy of celebration by the ANC government, the opposition and citizenry alike is South Africa's stability as a country. There is a commitment and dedication across the board to the enshrinement of patriotism, nation-building, stable democracy, the Bill of Rights and a culture of human rights. This stability, it is agreed, has been brought about by sustained efforts at democracy, through free and fair elections, as part of what President Zuma in his Freedom Day speech termed an aspiration towards a free, democratic, non-racial and non-sexist South Africa, working together to achieve unity, prosperity and inclusive growth.[36] The idea that South Africa belongs to all those who live in it, as articulated in the Freedom Charter and reiterated in the Constitution is presented as a core principle and aspiration, widely shared. Unity in diversity is celebrated in principle, just as is the Constitution that guarantees this, a Constitution generally perceived by South Africans to be unique, a model and the envy of many countries around the world.

However, some South Africans with less celebratory experiences are asking themselves why there is such a commitment to protecting the Constitution and such insistence on legality when socio-economic equality has failed to materialise under the Constitution and in accordance with the law over the past 18 years. Reluctance to sign the Constitution a blank cheque also seems to come from the apparent failure to design and implement laws and policies to concretise the economic and social equality and protection

---

36 See <http://www.info.gov.za/speech/DynamicAction?pageid=461&sid=26952&tid=65956>. Accessed on August 2012.

enshrined in the Constitution. On rape, for example, there is a strong perception that the law, far from working in favour of rape victims, has tended to work in favour of rape perpetrators and to make victims feel as if they are on trial for daring to attract rapists. The majority of cases are dismissed and there are very few convictions, despite the high number of complaints of rape yearly.[37] The supreme law of the land appears to lack the testicular fortitude to protect rape victims from testicles gone wild.

Is it possible that the Constitution, as an outcome of a negotiated settlement between those who benefited from apartheid and those who were disadvantaged by it, may have made far more concessions to those afraid to lose advantages conferred upon them by apartheid than needed to redress the socio-economic predicaments of the majority whom apartheid dispossessed to make such advantages possible? Could the current tensions between the ANCYL and the ANC – personal differences between President Zuma and Malema aside – be indicative of a growing concern among masses of un- and under-employed youth about compounding socio-economic inequalities, with regard to which the law and the Constitution seem rather impotent? If the burning need for "economic freedom in our life time" as an aspiration of South African youth is capable of attracting rabble-rousing opportunists like Malema, who would settle for nothing short of "living like the whites", how does one avoid conflating legitimate aspirations with opportunism?[38] The concerns of a widening economic gap and a frustrated youth, which Malema articulated in his capacity as president of the ANCYL, seem to be characteristic of many countries

---

37 See Swart H, Terrorised by perpetrators and victimised by the legal system, *Mail & Guardian*, 26 April 2012. Accessed on May 2012, <http://www.mg.co.za/article/2012-04-26-terrorised-by-perpetrators-and-victimised-the-legal-system/>. See also Judge M, Changing the language of prejudice, *Mail & Guardian*, 12 June 2012. Accessed on May 2012, <http://www. mg.co.za/article/2011-06-12-changing-the-language-of-prejudice>.

38 See Malema's declaration, "We are marching because we want to live like the whites. Everything the whites have we want in our townships. Our townships must be beautiful like Sandton". See Magome M & Hosken G, Juju quits walk, but marches on, *Daily News*, 28 October 2011. Accessed on April 2012, <http://www.iol.co.za/dailynews/news/juju-quits-walk-but-marches-on-1.1166690>.

(including the United States and Europe) at present. While South Africa certainly has particular challenges given its history of apartheid, it is also clearly entangled in the present problematics of global capitalism and, as long as these problems exist, they will need attention.

FREEDOM: ARE YOU FREE OR ARE YOU DUMB?

A popular Vodacom advertisement on South African TV, titled "Night Shift", catches my attention every time I see it broadcast.[39] Somehow, it always pushes me to reflect on freedom, why some are better able to claim it than others, even when everyone has struggled for it. It makes me think about how freedom, in principle, is cherished by South Africans, big and small, and is evidenced by how protective they are of the very idea of freedom, even if not always for the same reason. While the rich might want the protection of freedom and rights, as enshrined in the Constitution, as the best guarantee for hanging onto inherited or newly acquired wealth and privileges, the poor and impoverished are hoping for delivery of basic services and a little dignity under the same enshrined rights and freedom. Some, unable to attain delivery through the state or from compassionate rich others, turn to religion, witchcraft, magic and games of chance for miraculous solutions (COMAROFF and COMAROFF, 1999; NIEHAUS, et al., 2001; VAN WYK, 2011, 2012).[40] In this game of life and death, it is important for every person and every important institution to seek balance and a measure of fairness among competing and equally legitimate ambitions and aspirations, so some do not become fodder for the freedoms and rights of others. In order to ensure that South Africans are genuinely free and not dumb, they must remain alert to

---

39 The heading for this section is inspired by a Vocadom advertisement entitled "Night Shift", whic ends with the words: "Recharge and get 60 minutes free between 12 am and 5 am all week". An announcer beating an armpit drum asks those on a night shift whether they are "free" or "dumb".

40 See also Annual religious special: God in Africa, *Mail & Guardian*, 5–12 April 2012.

and critical of the sort of opportunism that might clad itself in the language of freedom and equality (ROBINS, 2005). Here, the current controversy around the Protection of State Information Bill is worth a closer look.

A focus on freedom and the need to protect hard-earned rights enshrined in the Constitution are goals worth pursuing and one understands the outcry across the country over the controversial Protection of State Information Bill (McDONALD, 2011). However, a focus on freedom provokes a few questions as well. What exactly is freedom? How does one identify or authenticate it? If life is a game of interests and society the uneven playing field, how do researchers and chroniclers of the social world, as academic and media players from different backgrounds and positions, represent freedom in ways that do justice to the complexities and nuances of the games in which they partake? In recognition of the enormity of the task, if one were to settle for a minimum of common denominators, what would these be? These questions are further complicated by yet others about how to provide for the backgrounds, positions and interests of the different players and also for the varying degrees of individual and institutional creativity and inventiveness that make a difference in any game. These considerations make all the more pertinent often asked questions such as: Whose freedom? Freedom from what? As opposed to what? In whose interest? (FRIEDMAN, 2011).

In this connection, the unequivocal protection of artistic freedom by the Constitution has raised questions about the limits of freedom without responsibility. Drawing on controversial portrayals of President Zuma by artists such as Zapiro (penname of Jonathan Shapiro) (HAMMETT, 2010: 12-24) and Brett Murray,[41] the question arises: "How far is too far?"[42]

---

41 Zapiro attracted controversy with his cartoon, "Rape of Lady Justice", in *Sunday Times*, 7 September 2008, which portrayed President Zuma preparing to rape Lady Justice, and for subsequently portraying President Zuma with a shower head overhanging his head. Brett Murray's portrait, "The Spear", at the Goodman Gallery in Johannesburg, depicts President Zuma with his genitals exposed. See Mabandu P, The great spear debate, *City Press*, 20 May 2012 and Culture and demagoguery: The spear that divided the nation, *Cape Times*, 5 June 2012, comprising reflections by Achille Mbembe and Steven Robins.

42 See Mabandu P, Is the presidential penis sacred? *City Press*, 20 May 2012.

especially when the individual (President Zuma in this case) feels "shocked, and [...] personally offended and violated" by such controversial portraits that depict him as "a philanderer, a womaniser and one with no respect"?[43] Isn't a consensus around freedom a categorical imperative? Is it enough simply to wait until people feel aggrieved to invite them to seek justice and redress in a court of law,[44] while artists on the other hand are absolved a priori of the responsibilities that should go with claims of freedom to ensure that freedom is a collective good and not the monopoly of some? These are questions to which the answers may not always seem as straightforward as abstract and decontextualised articulations of freedom might suggest. It is far from a simple matter of choosing between freedom and dignity, both of which are provided for and protected by the Constitution in principle.[45] Rather, it is an issue of how to reconcile freedom with dignity in a society that recognises the value of both. Answering these and related questions meaningfully requires greater investment in understanding the hierarchies at play and the unequal relationships that continue to shape the possibilities and impossibilities in the lives of post-apartheid South Africans.

Given the disproportionate focus on politics and the political by the South African media, the question arises of whether politics and the political are necessarily the game in which freedom is the most threatened. What if the major predicaments were the rights of the politically disenfranchised majority – racial, cultural, geographical, class, gendered, generational, linguistic, or whatever? And what if it was evident that consideration of their predicaments was not the exclusive responsibility of government or the state (obviously impotent and subservient vis-à-vis the dominant

---

43 See Staff reporters, Zuma: It hurts, *City Press*, 20 May 2012. See also Laganparsad M & Govender S, Zuma's lash out at artist, *Sunday Times*, 20 May 2012, for a statement by Zuma's daughters, accusing the artist of racism, condemning his depiction of their father as vulgar and lacking in humanity and as seeking "to take away our father's dignity and destroy his true character and stature as a man, a father and a leader of the ANC and South African society at large".

44 President Zuma currently has a court case against Zapiro and the ANC has sought a court interdict against the display of the painting by the Goodman Gallery.

45 See Spear of the nation, *Mail & Guardian*, 25–31 May 2012, for various opinions on the matter.

interests of the local and global economic elite)? What if the logic and ethos of profit over people of the private sector and of the economic elite were fundamentally responsible for blatant and subtle inequality? How, in the light of these concerns, could claims of the press as harbinger, promoter and protector of Freedom as a democratic right and as a public good, in the utilitarian sense of the greatest good for the greatest number, be justified and substantiated empirically? A focus on press freedom is an invitation to accommodate press freedom as important – as an ideal, an aspiration, a right, an entitlement. More importantly, it is an invitation to examine the dangers of uncritically internalising and reproducing claims and beliefs about freedom. If life itself can be accommodating in its games – providing for improvisation and adaptation – why should the press and its practitioners opt for zero sum incarnations of these same games?

This would explain why, as we have seen above, in post-apartheid South Africa, there is room not only for continuities and discontinuities in elite terms, but also for continued contestations by the dispossessed and savagely impoverished bulk of the population over why a new dispensation should translate into nothing more than nominal rights, freedoms and citizenship with little meaningful content in everyday life (HENDERSON, 2011; ROBINS, 2005; ROSS, 2010). The warning here is against media and intellectual bandwagonism that breeds a tendency to uncritically reproduce the rhetoric of being on the side of freedom and the poor, even when the reality is that of serving and servicing the interests of the power (economic, social and cultural) elite. Media practitioners and scholars need to constantly challenge themselves to establish empirically a propensity to claim independence and objectivity in principle, while being good bedfellows with big business and/ or government in practice. When purportedly "private" or "independent" media are uncritically given the benefit of the doubt by media scholars, who equally uncritically question or greet with suspicion anything state or government, this begs the question of the meaning of independence or autonomy in real terms. It presupposes that the "private" or commercial, however bedevilled by contradictions, myopia and mediocrity, is invariably right or pardonable, whatever its excesses and the state or government, on the other hand, invariably devious and high-handed and to be criticised as a matter of principle. It overly simplifies the game of life by uncritically crediting some with angelic pretensions and others with demonic powers.

Such bandwagonism in the case of post-apartheid South Africa, as both Colin Sparks (2011) and Steven Friedman (2011) note, is often oblivious of the middle class and predominantly white biases of the mainstream press. It gives the impression – if Herman Wasserman's (2010) study of tabloid journalism is anything to go by – not only that the majority mostly black poor, un- and under-employed under-classes matter less or not at all, beyond the sweeping rhetoric of freedom, human rights and citizenship. For the poor to be kept at bay, tamed and subservient to the whims and caprices of the *ancien* and nouveaux riches of the "new" South Africa, the press is all too ready to feed them condescendingly with highly sensationalised, scandal-ridden, politically monotonic mass circulation tabloids that the middle classes shun. While a wealthy person can easily sue the media for misrepresentation, the poor often are in no similar position vis-à-vis media representations of themselves. This encourages misrepresentation with impunity. If the media's idea of freedom is limited to reproducing and protecting middle class values, concerns and anxieties – ensuring a "combination of elite continuity and renewal", no amount of press freedom could ever redress the inequalities of the past or "the rising tide of economic discontent" (SPARKS, 2011: 11-14). For no change is possible through a press that is critical only in rhetoric, while endorsing in practice an idea of humanity confined or unduly shackled by prejudices inspired by ideologies of race, place, class, gender, age, culture, religion or belonging, among others. The answer to these predicaments lies neither with the state nor private media in their current configurations and limitations, but in alternatives capable of drawing inspiration from and challenging both models in the interest of South Africa's myriad multiplicities and creative diversities.

Colonial and apartheid inventions of cultures and traditions meant the silencing of more indigenous consensual approaches and variants of rights and freedoms informed by prevalent philosophies of personhood and social action such as ubuntu (NKONDO, 2007; RAMOSE, 1999; THOMAS,

2008).[46] In this regard, distinction between "citizen" and "subject" and between "culture talk" and "rights talk", such as Mahmood Mamdani's (1996, 2000), are useful analytical starting points. Starting points because, if we are to remain faithful to the lives of ordinary South Africans and their infinite capacity to negotiate and navigate the various identity margins in their lives, there is little to suggest that South Africans who were hemmed into homelands and bantustans and only selectively allowed into urban spaces during apartheid (Bank, 2011; MAYER, 1971), today live their lives neatly as citizens or urbanites subjected to civic authority and the rule of law, on the one hand and as subjects or rural dwellers ruled by chiefs, traditions and culture, on the other. For most, citizenship remains confined to a constitutional provision, analogous to the biblical parable of many called but few chosen. This, however, is not to deny that sidestepped individuals have often refused to celebrate victimhood. Millions of South Africans are eking out a living by hook or by crook. There are way too many unsung heroes who just go about changing the "world" they live in quietly without fanfare. Arguing for greater sensitivity vis-à-vis their predicament is not to deny them agency, but rather to draw attention to how much more they would have achieved were structures, policy and practice much more accommodating in their regard.

The making of contemporary South Africa is the story, par excellence, of visible and invisible mobilities (KLAAREN, 2011; PEBERDY, 2009). As elsewhere, unregulated and even regulated human mobility in South Africa are presented as a threat to the economic and physical well-being and achievements of insiders. To be visible for citizenship, nationality or belonging, bounded notions of geography and culture are deployed as currency. Official and popular discourses are infused with a deep suspicion of those who move, particularly those moving to urban areas and between regions, countries and continents. The rhetoric is one of the necessity to avoid system

---

46 This, of course, is not to deny that even within "indigenous" traditions, there was a politics at play in silencing and voicing particular forms of consensus.

crashes by avoiding overloading them, giving the impression of a science of mobility where every country, region and community has a precise idea of its carrying capacity of human beings or human problems. Freedom of movement, especially by people deemed to be less endowed economically, is perceived by those who consider themselves more economically gifted, as a potential disaster, to be contained at all cost. Far from this only being the plight or fate of obvious outsiders, such as foreigners and non-citizens, the controversy caused by a Tweet by Helen Zille, leader of the Democratic Alliance party in March 2012, referring to pupils from the Eastern Cape coming to the Western Cape province (where she is premier) as "refugees", suggests that the problem of undesired mobility is not permanently resolved once the scapegoated outsider has been dispensed with.[47] It can also be argued that Zille is deliberately being misunderstood to fit the stereotypical view of the Democratic Alliance as a racially biased white party and that her intention was not aimed at "undesired mobility" but a well-justified attack on the incompetence of the Eastern Cape education department to provide satisfactory education for pupils in that province, while at the same time bragging about the quality of education in her province.

The game of policing belonging is not confined to the mobility of South Africans from rural to urban areas and between provinces. There is clamour as well, for policies to contain foreigners, mostly those from the rest of Africa, who continue to be seen as the source of HIV/AIDS, the primary cause of crime and a threat to South African jobs and cultural values (LANDAU, 2011a, 2011b). Such reaction by South Africans and their institutions do not always recognise and provide for how foreigners actually seek to belong and relate with South Africa and South Africans beyond stereotypes (OWEN, 2011; SICHONE, 2008). Yet, if listened to, foreigners from the rest of Africa and beyond are just as concerned about

---

47 Fellow South Africans questioned how South African nationals and citizens moving from one part of the country to another could be considered refugees. See The Tweet that caused a storm, *Sunday Independent*, 25 March 2012.

the state of the South African "nation" as are nationals and citizens.[48] Given human flexibility, agency and the imperative of interdependence, nothing prevents individuals and communities from embracing and eventually celebrating and aggressively defending imposed identities or "invented traditions", in the good old African tradition of bending over backwards to accommodate, even when not being accommodated (COMAROFF and COMAROFF, 2009). If the rich countries or regions within countries opened their imagined borders for the rest of the world, citizens and nationals, they could begin the process of reconciling yawning gaps between the haves and the have-nots (GRAEBER, 2004).

CONCLUSION

From the overview of 18 years of constitutional democracy and freedom in South Africa, it is evident that social transformations are not automatic, just as integration and nationhood are not attainable via declarations of intent and the assignment of labels. A multiracial, multiethnic and multicultural – "rainbow" – South Africa with a past of tense, bloody and highly unequal racialised and ethnicised relationships and a present of radical inequalities in citizenship, despite laudable constitutional freedoms, calls for provision to include intermediary groups (racial, ethnic, cultural, religious, political, associational, etc.) that mediate the relationship between the individual and the state, in providing for freedoms and rights in concrete terms. A multicultural, multiethnic and multiracial South Africa needs to protect itself not only against the selfish interests of individuals, but also against the selfish interests of racial, ethnic and cultural entities or communities and big business interests, making it clear that freedoms end where those of others begin. To play a meaningful role in this regard, articulations of

---

48 See The alternative state of the nation: Is South Africa really an African country? Are South Africans happy with themselves? What would you change about the country? Immigrants give their views, *Mail & Guardian*, 10–16 February 2012.

freedom in the media and elsewhere must reflect the interests and value systems not only of each and every South African as an individual, but also of South Africans belonging to cultural, ethnic and racial communities that shape their thinking, outlook and action.

It is hardly enough to freeze recognition at an abstract level of an assumed universality of freedoms and rights. The test of the freedom pudding should be in the practical eating. It is only in this way that the media and academia can ensure that the quest for the successful functioning of post-apartheid South Africa is not merely a ploy to continue serving and servicing the interests of a powerful and only marginally reconfigured elite few, to the disadvantage of the majority as individuals and also as interest groups. Nothing else quite makes sense in post-apartheid South Africa than to seek group restitution and reparations for those who were dispossessed and disenfranchised as a group, and not merely as individuals. The failures of black empowerment initiatives are a failure of approach and not of the idea and principle of collective restitution and reparation. The conversation towards representation for collectivities recommended here should be pursued concurrently with individual rights. The prospect of democracy being simultaneously an individual and a group right and aspiration must be taken seriously in rethinking freedoms in South Africa. Only in this way can scholars and the media resist the temptation to equate narrowly construed individual freedom with active, participatory citizenship and structural freedom needed to undo or significantly mitigate poverty in real terms for the bulk of South Africa.

Freedom, sensitive to the complex multiplicities of being South African, needs private and public institutions and scholarship capable of adaptation and improvisation to accommodate often neglected endogenous forms of sociality, conviviality and interdependence. If the voices of those on SAfm on Freedom Day, 27 April 2012 and in the related literature referenced are anything to go by, some South Africans have demonstrated a creative ability to modernise their inheritance and cultural capital and domesticate their encounters with others and the influences they bring – processes to be adequately provided for in all their complexity and not condescendingly dismissed in mainstream elite circles. Grassroots ideas of personhood and agency simply refus to be confined to the logic of dichotomies, essentialisms, markets, profitability and zero sum games. There are lessons to learn from South Africa's artists like Johnny Clegg, whose art navigates and negotiates myriad identity margins, challenging us to rise beyond the blinkers of our preconceptions and prejudices. Just as there are lessons to be learnt from the rest of Africa and, indeed, the world, on how to privilege the logic of accommodation over and above the logic of dichotomies and binary oppositions. It is our hope that the chapters in this section contribute, however modestly, to important ongoing conversations on the future of South Africa.

REFERENCES

BANK, L. (2011), *Home spaces, street styles: Contesting power and identity in a South African City*, London, Pluto.

COMAROFF, J. L. (1978), "Rules and rulers: Political processes in a Tswana chiefdom", in *Man*, 13, 1: 1-20.

COMAROFF, J., COMAROFF, J. L. (1999), "Occult economies and the violence of abstraction: Notes from the South African postcolony", in *American Ethnologist*, 26, 2: 279-303.

_____. (2009), *Ethnicity, Inc.* Scottsville, University of KwaZulu-Natal Press.

FOKWANG, J. D. (2009), *Mediating legitimacy: Chieftaincy and democratisation in two African chiefdoms*. Bamenda, Langaa.

FORDE, F. (2011), *An inconvenient youth: Julius Malema and the "new" ANC*, Johannesburg, Picador Africa.

FRIEDMAN, S. (2011), Whose freedom? South Africa's press, middle-class bias and the threat of control, in *Ecquid Novi: African Journalism Studies*, 32, 2: 106-121.

GRAEBER, D. (2004), *Fragments of an anarchist anthropologist*. Chicago, Prickly Paradigm Press.

GUNNER, L. (2009), Jacob Zuma, the social body and the unruly power of song. in *African Affairs*, 108, 430: 27-48.

HAMMETT, D. (2010), Political cartoons, post-colonialism and critical African studies. in *Critical African Studies*, 4, December, p. 1-26.

HENDERSON, P. C. (2011), *Aids, intimacy and care in rural KwaZulu-Natal: A kinship of bones*. Amsterdam, Amsterdam University Press.

JANSEN, J. (2011), *We need to talk*. Northlands, Bookstorm & Pan Macmillan.

KLAAREN, J. (2011), "Citizenship, xenophobic violence, and law's dark side", *in* L. B. Landau (ed.), *Exorcising the demons within: Xenophobia, violence and statecraft in contemporary South Africa*, Johannesburg, Wits University Press.

LANDAU, L. B. (2011a), *Exorcising the demons within: Xenophobia, violence and statecraft in contemporary South Africa*, Johannesburg, Wits University Press.

_____. (2011b), "Introduction", *in* L.B. Landau (ed.), *Exorcising the demons within: Xenophobia, violence and statecraft in contemporary South Africa*, Johannesburg, Wits University Press.

MAMDANI, M. (1996), *Citizen and subject: Contemporary Africa and the legacy of late capitalism*, Cape Town, David Philip.

_____. (ed.). (2000), *Beyond rights talk and culture talk: Comparative essays on the politics of rights and culture*, Cape Town, David Philip.

MAYER, P. (1971), *Townsmen or tribesmen: Conservatism and the process of urbanization in a South African city*, Cape Town, Oxford University Press.

MAZANDERANI, F. H. (2011), *Cracked heirlooms: Race, identity and the teaching of apartheid in four classrooms in the "new" South Africa*. Honours dissertation, University of Cape Town McDonald PC (2011). The present is another country: A comment on the 2010 media freedom debate. *Ecquid Novi: African Journalism Studies*, 32, 2: 122-134.

NAIPAUL, V. S. (2010), *The masque of Africa: Glimpses of African belief*. London, Picador.

NIEHAUS, I., Mohlala, E., Shokane, K. (2001), *Witchcraft, power and politics: Exploring the occult in the South African Lowveld*, London, Pluto Press.

NKONDO, G. M. (2007), "Ubuntu as national policy in South Africa: A conceptual framework", in *International Journal of African Renaissance Studies*, 2, 1: 88-100.

NTSEBEZA, L. (2005), *Democracy compromised: Chiefs and the politics of the land in South Africa*. Leiden, Brill.

NTSEBEZA, L., HALL, R. (2007), *The land question in South Africa: The challenge of transformation and redistribution*, Cape Town, HSRC Press.

NYAMNJOH, F. B. (2003), "Might and right: Chieftaincy and democracy in Cameroon and Botswana", *in* W. van Binsbergen (ed.), in *The dynamics of power and the rule of law: Essays on Africa and beyond*, Munster/Leiden, Lit Verlag and African Studies Centre.

OOMEN, B. (2005), *Chiefs in South Africa: Law, power & culture in the post-apartheid era*, Oxford, James Currey.

OWEN, N. J. (2011), "*On se débrouille*": Congolese migrants' search for survival and success in Muizenburg. PhD dissertation, Cape Town, Rhodes University.

PEBERDY, S. (2009), *Selecting immigrants: National identity and South Africa's immigration policies 1910-2008*, Johannesburg, Wits University Press.

POSEL, D. (2010), "Races to consume: Revisiting South Africa's history of race, consumption and the struggle for freedom". in *Ethnic and Racial Studies*, 33, 2: 157-175.

RAMOSE, M. B. (1999), *African philosophy through ubuntu*, Harare, Mond Books.

Rodrigues, E. *(Un)papering the cracks in South Africa: The role of "traditional" and "new" media in nation-negotiation around Julius Malema on the eve of the 2010 FIFA World Cup™*. MA Thesis, University of Cape Town.

ROBINS, S. (2008), *From revolution to rights in South Africa: Social movements, NGOs & popular politics after apartheid*, Oxford, James Currey.

_____. (2011), "How toilets became "political" in South Africa in 2011: Revisiting the politics of the spectacle and the ordinary after apartheid. Unpublished".

ROBINS, S. (ed.). (2005), *Limits to liberation after apartheid: Citizenship, governance & culture*, Oxford, James Currey.

ROSS, F. C. (2010), *Raw life, new hope: Decency, housing and everyday life in a post-apartheid community*, Cape Town, University of Cape Town Press.

SHAPIRO, J. (2011), *Zapiro: The Last Sushi: Cartoons from Mail & Guardian, Sunday Times and The Times*, Johannesburg, Jacana.

SICHONE, O. (2008), "Xenophobia and xenophilia in South Africa: African migrants in Cape Town", *in* P. Werbner (ed.), *Anthropology and the new cosmopolitanism: Rooted, feminist and vernacular perspectives*, Oxford, Berg Publishers.

SMITH, S. W. (2011), Making home in temporary spaces: Translating the spaces in between the frames. Honours dissertation, University of Cape Town, *in* C. Soudie (2012), *Realising the dream: Unlearning the logic of race in the South African school*, Cape Town, HSRC Press.

SPARKS, C. (2011), "South African media in comparative perspective", in *Ecquid Novi: African Journalism Studies*, 32, 2: 5-19.

STEYN, M. (2008), "Repertoires for talking white: Resistant whiteness in post-apartheid South Africa", in *Ethnic and Racial Studies*, 31, 1: 25-51.

THOMAS, C. G. (2008), "Ubuntu: The missing link in the rights discourse in post-apartheid transformation in South Africa", in *International Journal of African Renaissance Studies*, 3, 2: 39-62.

VAN WYK, I. (2011), Believing practically and trusting socially in Africa: The contrary case of the Universal Church of the Kingdom of God in Durban, South Africa, *in* H. Englund (ed.), *Christianity and public culture in Africa*, Ohio, Ohio University Press.

_____. (2012), "Tata ma chance": On contingency and the lottery in post-apartheid South Africa. *Africa*, 82, 1: 41-68.

WASSERMAN, H. (2010), *Tabloid journalism in South Africa: True story!* Bloomington, Indiana University Press.

YANOU, M. A. (2009), *Dispossession and access to land in South Africa: An African perspective*. Bamenda, Langaa.

The modern politics of recognition in BRICS' cultures and societies

A chinese case of superstition becoming intangible cultural heritage

Bingzhong Gao

Abstract   This paper is a response to Professor Gustavo Ribeiro's calling for promoting world anthropologies. Who's culture can be recognized (legitimized) as national or public culture, especially the key symbols of the nation-state? It has been a politics of culture since the very beginning of modern time in Russia, China, India and South Africa (maybe in Brazil too). As our studies in China and very limited studies in Russia and India show, cultures recognized by the folk (the majority of the people) as traditions experienced a denial by the political elites, but gained legitimization in recent years. For example, in China, the campaign of safeguarding of intangible cultural heritage recognized the items named as backward superstition before as national heritage. This paper narrates the story of a temple fair in countryside of North China becoming an official representative items of intangible cultural heritage from a peasants wrong belief.

Keywords   Politics of recognition, cultural identity, cultural revolution, temple fair.

The International Symposium "The BRICSs and Their Social, Political and Cultural Challenges on the National and International Levels" is a great event for BRICS scholars in multi-disciplines to become a new "we" group to study the BRICSs. For the purpose, anthropology should play a big role since ethnography is a good way to promote mutual understandings between different peoples and develop interdisciplinary area studies in the BRICSs as well as in the Western countries, especially based on the idea of world anthropologies (RIBEIRO and ESCOBAR, 2006).

Chinese anthropologists just launched the so called "overseas ethnography "program about ten years ago. More than 20 researchers have finished their one-year fieldworks in about 20 foreign communities. I can say we have started ethnographic studies in the BRICSs (WU, 2009; MA, 2011; ZHANG, 2013), but we are in the very beginning to develop sophisticated interdisciplinary studies of BRICS.

Since all members of the BRICSs are late comers in the world history of the modernization process, they have been forced to take early modernization in West (West Europe and US) as a model. This situation created many kinds of tensions: tensions between domestic and foreign imperatives, between local places and the greater society, between state and society, between traditional and modern, between popular beliefs and scientific knowledge, between the common people and elites. All the tensions reflect a dual structure: the formal and official institutions and the informal and folk cultures and organizations. We can see two versions of the dual structure in the BRICSs. Cultures and organizations of the majority of India, South Africa and Brazil took no place in the colonial states, then had opportunities to be recognized by the state after the independence (Brazil and India) or the end of the white apartheid government (South Africa). Another version is that the socialist revolution denied the legitimacy and destroyed most social agencies of native cultures and organizations both in Russia and China, and only some of them survived the underground before they revived and were recognized as right or/and legal.

Generally, the BRICSs have experienced a different state-society relationship relative to that West Europe and the United States. The story that happened and is going on in China can be narrated in terms of intangible cultural heritage and civil society, which is one case of the BRICSs as a kind.

China in the past century has seen many counter-intuitive things. So much has happened that we once would have found impossible to believe; so many out of the way things have become common. Temples, for example – a hundred years ago, who would have thought that all the temples in the cities and the countryside would be demolished? Only 20 years ago, when we saw in the media that somewhere people had privately restored a temple, we found it a bit ridiculous. Now, who would have thought that temples could again become such a common part of the landscape everywhere? This paper seeks to explore, through the life history of a building of this kind, how in our era this sort of impossible thing could become a reality technically by adopting two names, and get political recognition as intangible cultural heritage and a legal non-profit organization.

Fanzhuang Village in Hebei traditionally worships a Dragon Tablet. Locally the Dragon Tablet is referred to as Old Man Dragon Tablet. The Dragon Tablet in that place is a central deity, considered to be living and efficacious (*ling*). The villagers worship and make offerings to it to bring good fortune and prevent bad luck. The folk society of the faithful, mentioned above, is called the *Long Pai Hui*, and this is also the term for the organization of the temple fair held in homage to the Dragon Tablet on the second day of the second month of the lunar calendar. During the temple fair, villagers also pay homage to the images of Buddhist, Daoist and Confucian deities, as well as other figures worshipped in folk religion. The Dragon Tablet beliefs are thus part of a polytheistic folk religion.

I was invited to study the temple fair through participant-observation beginning in 1996; it has been held annually and I have participated ten times. So I can say that I have witnessed its development during this time.

According to the first folklore scholar who observed the temple fair in 1991, Liu Qiyin, the earlier Dragon Tablet was rather small, and villagers had tentatively and anxiously housed it in a cobbled-together temporary shed on the threshing ground. But by the time of the 1996 temple fair, the Dragon Tablet, which had once been small enough for one person to carry, was so large that it could only be moved by a group of men; rather than being just painted on a board, it was elaborately carved; and it had been made at a cost of 30,000 RMB. By 2003, this impressive tablet had been already installed in the main hall of a temple, for which the local county government held a ribbon-cutting. This temple hall was called Dragon Ancestral Hall, and on either side of its main entrance were these two signs: "Dragon Tablet Association, Fanzhuang, Hebei" and "Dragon Cultural Museum of Zhao Prefecture, China". One building, two names, expressing respectively two identities, at a considerable social distance from each other.

The birth of this "temple museum" or "museum temple" signifies something of great value in the attempt to understand contemporary Chinese society. In the 2003 ceremony to mark the completion of the building, I was sitting at the head table, watching officials perform on the stage and villagers perform in front of the stage; I felt that both groups – government and village – were happy to have found their proper place. How can officials who claim to be secular and oppose superstition be so in accord with superstition-loving villagers? There could be a number of reasons for this paradox, but I am most interested in the practice and cultural politics of recognition.

THE REVIVAL OF THE LONG PAI HUI

Fanzhuang is a village with 1300 families, and more than 5100 residents. Their livelihood depends on wheat growing, fruit cultivation, and the fruit-processing industry. During the last ten years, not only because the township government is based in the village, but also because of the crowds who come to the temple fair, many street-front houses have become profitable shops. So the income level of the village is on the high end for the region.

Though the Dragon Tablet is a very local and popular form of belief, the organization of the temple fair by the association is meticulous. Traditionally the Dragon Tablet Association has selected officers, and its structure has included a leading group, a dragon host, and a group of helpers. The host is chosen from among the village's respected men as one who has faithfully and sincerely served Old Man Dragon Tablet; he takes responsibility for everything related to the temple fair. Every year on the sixth day of the lunar new year he presides at an annual planning meeting, where the temple fair for the second day of the second month is discussed, and where the group of helpers to manage the temple fair is set up. The host for each year is usually chosen from the leading group, but sometimes the host is not from the leading group. Members of the leading group do, however, rotate the responsibility of housing the dragon tablet in their homes. For a long time there have been 19 families involved. The Leading Group members call themselves servants of the Dragon Tablet; they or their forebears have all received ritual approval from Old Man Dragon Tablet to join this *huitou* group (host family group). Once they have become *huitou* members, the status is passed down through their families. The helper group, on the other hand, has long consisted simply of everyone who assists during the temple fair who is not a member of the leading group. Now they are sometimes called a "preparatory committee" or "temple fair council".

Earlier, the villagers housed the Dragon Tablet both in their homes and in a temporary shed. During most of the year the tablet would be kept in the main room of a host family's house. The responsibility of this family was to offer incense each morning and night, and to host others who came to make offerings; they also looked after the incense fund and the money offerings made after petitions to the god were granted. During the temple fair each year, the Dragon Tablet would be set up in a temporary structure on the threshing ground – popularly called the "ritual shed" (*jiaopeng*) – for the convenience of those making offerings. On the first day of the second month, the villagers move the Dragon Tablet into the ritual shed using a sedan chair covered in yellow silk; the tablet remains there until noon on the fourth day of the month, when it is briefly returned to its former place in the home of the former year's huitou member. On the morning of the sixth day of the month, it is carried to its new site in the home of the next huitou member. The obligation of housing the Dragon Tablet thus revolves among huitou families, one each year.

Toward the end of the 1950s, the Dragon Tablet Association and Fair were suppressed with the formation of the People's Commune, and during the Cultural Revolution, all related activities disappeared. The Dragon Tablets were stored away by the villagers. In 1979, the villagers re-established the leading group system to house the Dragon Tablet, and the tablet itself re-emerged from underground into public view. The activities of the Temple Fair were re-started in 1983. At that time, the host family taking their turn was that of "Lao Liang" (1917-1997, a CCP member). His oldest son, "Xiao Suo," explained in our interview: "The last few years [in that period], we only worshipped at home; but the use of the ritual shed really began with my family in 1983. Liu Ying, the Eighth Army veteran, was acting as the dragon host (the big man). He and my father had a very good relationship, he discussed it with my father and they decided we should move the tablet to a ritual shed and hold the temple fair. They spoke with the then-party secretary of the village, but he wouldn't support them. They decided to move the tablet anyway. Liu Ying and father said, "if anything happens, we'll take our bedding [in case we're arrested] and go to court about it". In those days, everybody was worried, so we posted sentries to watch the roads into the village. If anyone saw the police coming, they would let us know in time".

By 1995, the villagers had gained the confidence to mount a very grand dragon tablet fair. They spent 30,000 RMB to make a new Dragon Tablet, which is the one installed there now. The entire height of the present Dragon Tablet is almost three meters, its base is 1.5 meters wide, it weighs 300 kilos, and in the middle of the tablet in gold letters on a blue ground it still says: "Spirit tablet of the true Dragon overlord of the ten directions, the three domains, and heaven and earth". Around these words there are dragons in carved relief. It looks magnificent with its imposing size, quite like the god images in other temples. Also, they have re-established the helper group, announced in a poster as the Dragon Tablet Fair Preparatory Group (it was later changed to be called "the Council"). On the Council are some members of the huitou leading group, and there are others as well, some from other villages. When asked about the standard of selection, they said, "having enthusiasm, ability, and general support". The Council head, the vice head, and the membership can be changed. Under its purview the Council has a number of teams, respectively in charge of outreach (hosting scholars doing research), publicity (posting public announcements, hanging banners, etc.), the ritual shed (assembling and disassembling it), entertainment (contacting performance troupes in nearby villages), opera (commissioning and hosting local opera companies who perform during the fair), science and technology (technical education), cooking (serving guests), and security.

The framework of the ritual shed we saw in 1996 was made of steel and wood, and covered in canvas; inside, the separate halls were divided by straw matting. The ritual shed opened to the south, and it was divided into three chambers accommodating three altars. The main altar in the front held the Dragon Tablet, and behind that were hung images of Buddha (*fozu*), Confucius (holding a book in his hand labeled "Collected Records on Doing Good"), and Laozi. In the ritual shed, apart from the Dragon Tablet, all the other deities were painted images – gods, immortals, Buddhas, sages, monsters, and demons. Altogether there were 150 painted images.[1] Outside the shed there were five images hung, including the God of Wealth, the Roads God, the God of Fire, the King of Ghosts, and the Stove God.[2] Also outside the front of the ritual shed were donations posters: they listed donors to the temple fair, volunteer drivers (trucks, vans, minibuses), people who gave vegetables to feed guests, and the names of the leading group and the Preparatory Committee.

The center of the Dragon Tablet Fair is worship of the Dragon Tablet. Before it had been presided over by a Taoist ritualist, but now it has become very simple: it's just people offering incense, kowtowing, and reciting sutras. These activities can be done by individual believers, or they might be done in groups by the members of self-organized incense societies.

---

1   36 of these 150 images were on the front altar. Most of the images were Buddhist, Confucian, and Daoist entities, along with the Eight Immortals and old female deities such as "Fertility Grandma".

2   Hung on the front of the ritual shed were nine dragon banners.

The Dragon Tablet Fair can attract more than 100,000 people. People's donations can be in the form of volunteer labor; in addition to that of the leading group and the preparatory committee, hundreds of villagers do temporary volunteer labor. There are also donations of the use of vehicles and other equipment; and food (such as vegetables and fruit), as well as, of course, cash are given.[3]

Note that at that time the Long Pai Hui as an organization was a grassroots association, and as an event it was a local temple fair. It had not strayed outside the category of a religious phenomenon and a folk faith.

A NEWLY EXPANDED PUBLIC SPHERE
AND NATION-STATE HISTORY

Throughout China, the rise and decline of folk religious activities like the Dragon Tablet Fair and Association are very closely related to the cultural management policies of the state. In the view of a ruling party with a philosophical foundation in materialism and atheism, any kind of religious belief, especially a folk religious activity that is not yet fully under centralized control, is a "feudal superstition" that must be cleared away from the road of a modernizing nation. The Cultural Revolution was the pinnacle of the "smash feudal superstition" movement. But since the 1980s, this policy has gradually been relaxed, and various folk beliefs have begun to appear in the guise of some kind of "folk culture". Because of the elevated status of "the people" in official ideology, and because of the contemporary rise of nationalism, "folk culture" in the last 10-20 years has gradually gained the government's tacit acceptance and even encouragement. The Long Pai Hui, from its re-emergence in 1983 to its growth and expansion in the mid and late 1990s, has been a product of the relaxation of these policies. But it remained the government's basic position

---

3   In our interviews, we were told that cash donations in 1992, 1993, and 1994 were relatively high, each year reaching 80,000 RMB. From 1995 on, cash donations lessened, each year being around 40,000.

to oppose and smash "superstition". The situation that the Long Pai Hui faced was like that of other temple fairs elsewhere in China: such activities could at any time be raided or canceled while being denounced as "superstition" by "superiors". Actually, according to folklorist Liu Qiyin, around 1990 there was an internal document of the County Public Security Bureau that called the Long Pai Hui a social problem, and argued that it should be canceled.

The fact that just after the Long Pai Hui re-emerged it was still an underground activity vis a vis the outside world suggests that it was really meant to be only a concern for Fanzhuang villagers. The organizers knew one thing: the Dragon Tablet was of no importance to outsiders or to their "superiors" in government or among cultural elites. When they started holding open activities inside the village, in 1983, they were adopting a stance directly opposed to the ideology and authority of those "superiors" who had absolute power over them: they knew that temple fairs were labeled as superstition and that superiors had a negative attitude toward their faith activities.

But they differed from other temple associations in that they didn't passively await punishment from above, rather they actively redefined the Long Pai Hui. If they wanted the temple fair to be safely and legitimately held in the future, they had to try to minimize and even eliminate the negative label of "superstition," converging instead with cultural categories that could be approved by "superiors". It is just as a key woman among the believers told me in a 1998 interview, "These last few years, whenever we saw a police hat coming this way, we would all get scared. Only when the Dragon Tablet was really established could we begin to hold our ground. The key was to eradicate superstition [and substitute culture in its place], so the police hats coming from above stopped being so scary".

Their methods included two aspects: (1) to define the temple fair as a public space for scientific and cultural activity, not just a field of superstitious activity. (2) to define the Long Pai Hui as part of Dragon Culture, thus making it a constitutive part of nationalist Chinese history instead of an oppositional form against the state.

During the temple fair, then, organizers turned all the space around the ritual shed into a site for large-scale cultural gatherings. Since 1996 I have watched, for example, the local opera troupes commissioned to perform in the village. They perform for 3 consecutive days, on a stage open to the public, attracting mostly older villagers and their relatives. Popular singing and dancing troupes also come to join the village fair, giving shows favored by a younger audience and performing on a stage set up inside a big shed. Folk art groups from dozens of neighboring villages, such as *yangge* dancing and drumming teams, are also invited to join processions along the local roads, as a way of both worshipping the gods and entertaining the villagers. At the same time, chess and calligraphy competitions provide village cultural elites with an opportunity to demonstrate their cultivation.

Outside the main ritual shed, organizers made a special effort to set up notice boards. In 1996, one of these gave information about agricultural science and technology, mainly on the prevention of pear tree blight, this being a pear-growing area. Another of these provided cultural knowledge of a very broad sort, ranging over areas far beyond village life. These announcements included, for example, shopping guides, "standards for the informed consumer," a "commonsense digest for life" to guide daily affairs, and moral education "urging filial gratitude". Some commentaries on lifestyle aimed at urbanites were also reproduced on these bulletin boards. For example, one sign announced the "Four After-Dinner Don'ts," as follows: Don't drink tea right away; don't eat fruit right away; don't take a walk right away; don't be in a rush to have a smoke".

In this way, these government-advocated cultural categories are prominently displayed all around the Dragon Tablet sacrifice; "superstitious" prayerful address to the Dragon Tablet is hedged around with "folk culture," "science education," and "modern civility". So, looked at as a whole, it all becomes a complex cultural public sphere. This process of defining the Dragon Tablet Fair through the efforts of local villagers and outside scholars working together has mainly resulted in what is called wholesome folk culture, even though it does retain a certain flavor of superstition.

The presentation of the Dragon Tablet Fair as a cultural public sphere by its organizers quickly received the approval of scholars. In 1996, in a symposium held during the Dragon Tablet Fair, many scholarly speakers noted (but dismissed) problems of superstition. A Professor Song,[4] for example, who works in a history museum said: "This festival is basically wholesome. There is superstition in it, but mostly it's a kind of entertainment, and it also has an educational function; it also works well to build the market and to develop the economy". This positioning of the Dragon Tablet Fair allows it to be seen as sound but with shortcomings. Superstition is seen as only one of many attributes of the whole activity, and not the most important. Mr. Dong, a leader in a folk artists' society, said, rather paradoxically, "Comrade Jiang Zemin recently pointed out that we should be politically vigilant. [Thus,] the Dragon Tablet Fair has the function of promoting Spiritual Civilization".

Moreover, the opinions of these expert scholars "visiting from above" were highly valued by villagers. The relevant articles and talks by these experts were photocopied and circulated by the Dragon Tablet Association, and in their publicity, these materials became powerful proofs of the legitimacy of the Long Pai Hui.

Some kind of rhetoric about "superstition" is in a sense just a façade. The villagers even have a brilliant move that cuts to the heart of the matter: they engage in a kind of knowledge production that places Dragon Tablet beliefs firmly within Dragon Culture. In the past, the faithful always asked, "will the dragon be powerful enough?" It was not necessary for them to answer the question, "Who is the dragon?" But after scholars started participating, the production of knowledge about "who is the dragon" became part of the villagers' strategy to actively establish connections with nationalist history.

Around 1990, after the scale of the Long Pai Hui had begun to expand, the cultural experts who participated in the Dragon Tablet Fair (both villagers and intellectuals from outside) gradually began to speak in one voice, saying that offerings to the Dragon Tablet were for the mythical figure Goulong [son of Sage Emperor Gonggong], the dragon invoked in

---

4   All the personal names and place names in this paper should not be referred to any person and place.

the catchphrase "heirs of the dragon". When organizers print brochures about the Long Pai Hui, and when they introduce the origins of the Long Pai Hui to visitors, they will always narrate this mythology; they also hung a huge banner in the ritual space: "All descendants of the sage emperors are heirs of the dragon". "The heirs of the Dragon" is a slogan meant to enhance the cohesiveness of Chinese people, and especially in recent years it has conveyed a deep political significance of patriotism. The organizers of the Long Pai Hui, through their reproduction of the Tablet's identity and significance (a process of re-interpreting and then publicizing), transformed their belief activities from something that could never be accepted by the outside world into something that was unarguably politically correct.

Actually, there's a vast difference between the state's formulation of the Dragon totem and the villagers' concept of Old Man Dragon Tablet. The contemporary phrasing of the "heirs of the Dragon" means that we are all descendants of forebears who took the dragon as their totem. Those forebears might have actually believed that the dragon was their ancestor, but we know that this expression is just a myth. Villagers, on the other hand, take the dragon on the Dragon Tablet to *be* the spirit of *their* ancestor – Old Man Dragon Tablet existed in the past and remains efficacious. So, although the Dragon totem and Old Man Dragon Tablet are basically different in their meaning, still, through narrative and interpretation, Dragon Tablet beliefs have been transformed from a local belief into a "living fossil" of a certain period in Chinese history, bearing witness to the ancient myth of Goulong, and thereby gaining the status of a museum object. The function of museums is to bear witness to history with actual examples. So the Dragon Tablet now had the capacity to connect to the museum function.

Both the superstition and the humanistic history of the Long Pai Hui are thought of as belonging to a past era. In the official model, the former is "dross" but the latter may be "essence". If "preserving the essence and discarding the dross" is taken as a solution to all contradictions, the dross (of superstition) ought to be abolished and only the essence (of the people's culture) should be salvaged and be allowed to exist today. Of course, this essence could not continue to exist in the temples, which are nests of superstition, but it can be displayed in a truly modern museum context. This is the stance of China's organic intellectuals. But the problem is, the agents are the villagers, and their actions themselves, which recuperate and redefine the Long Pai Hui, oppose the solution embodied in this neat standard formula. The Long Pai Hui (i.e., the temple association) not only expanded the meaning of the officially recognized "essence," it also retained the officially disapproved "dross" that they themselves appreciated. This combinatory art reached its greatest creativity with the doubly-named building, the "Dragon Culture Museum" and the "Dragon Ancestral Hall".

NAMES AND THINGS: THE BIRTH OF A NEW TEMPLE

Any newborn thing or person must occupy space. In China, everyone is used to the idea that even before you get pregnant you have to get a birth quota permit from the government, and before you build a house you need a building permit. This is because the state has established very strict control over space. Any new entity, before it takes up space, must exist first in government documents. That is to say, it must first have a "name" before it can become a "thing". Otherwise, if the entity were to come into being first, its existence would be in danger of being denied at any time. Regarding the birth of the new temple we want to introduce here, it was able to come into existence because it had not only one name but two. Anything envisioned should first have two names in two different symbol systems, so the reality can happen in both the government monitoring system and in concrete physical space.

To build a temple, first approval from the County Religion Bureau is needed. Then you need a site permit from the Land Management Bureau. Then the design must be approved by the Building Design Commission. According to the normal procedure, it would be simply impossible to build a Dragon Tablet temple legally. In the official classification of religious beliefs, the Long Pai Hui is classified as folk belief, it is not legally a religion, so the Religion Bureau refused to consider the application to build a temple.

But it did get built. When we went to the Dragon Tablet Fair in 2003, we saw a proper deity temple, the "Dragon Ancestral Hall". Later we heard that it cost 260,000 RMB [US$ 35,000]. A member of the leading committee showed it to us with pride, "We built it on the model of the Bai Lin Temple". Bai Lin Temple is a famous Buddhist site, a renowned pilgrim destination.

The development of the Long Pai Hui from a temporary shed to a permanent temple reflects a very complex process. Every year when the villagers put together the shed, they were in fact building a temple, it's just that it was temporary and had to be taken down afterward; they could not claim the site permanently. Nor could they get a permit to build a temple. But when they heard the language of "museums" from scholars, they came up with a solution to their desire to have a permanent building. When Beijing scholars in 1996 studied the Long Pai Hui, they held a symposium in Fanzhuang. According to my notes at the time, historical museum curator Professor Song said, "This place has a rich Chinese agricultural civilization, could we build a folklore museum on this basis?"

Organizers of the Long Pai Hui also attended this symposium and they were very happy to hear the scholars' suggestions that there should be a building. The leading group began to seriously consider this possibility, and among them Shi Zhenzhu was the most enthusiastic. By 1998, they had decided to build, and when Shi was elected as head of the Leading Group in 2000, he aggressively started to organize it. On one hand, he talked with government agencies about founding a museum; on the other hand, in order to raise money, he talked with villagers about building an Old Man Dragon Tablet temple.

In applying to build a museum, he avoided mentioning "folk belief," and in this way he bypassed the Religion Bureau and their regulations; rather, he directly defined the Long Pai Hui as a cultural organization. As noted above, in the process the relevant writings of scholars became an important basis for the application. By this time, the leaders of the Zhao County government had agreed that the Long Pai Hui had historical cultural content as Dragon Culture, so they accepted Shi's rationale for building a dragon culture museum. The County government then took the lead in organizing the relevant agencies to plan a tourism-development project. They lumped the Dragon Culture Museum together with the Zhaozhou Bridge and the Bai Lin Temple as officially recommended tourist destinations. Then, the County Planning Committee put the Dragon Culture Museum on their list, and the Land Management Board and the Building Design Commission all approved the project.

But this approved project was not supposed to receive state investment, and actually the government was not to pay even a penny toward it; it was to be a project independently brought into being by the Long Pai Hui temple association. Thus, the money needed for the building process had to be raised from the villagers. In August 2003 we were told by the head of the Leading Group, Shi Zhenzhu, that since he had taken charge three years before, the Long Pai Hui leading group members had contributed 36,000 RMB, over 50,000 had been raised from villagers, and they had been granted 20,000 by the Township and County governments. Most of the families of the current Leading Group donated money, ranging from 20 RMB to 1000 RMB. Ordinary villagers donated amounts ranging from one or two RMB to 2000 RMB. The money they raised was much less than what was actually spent on the building. But thanks to the creditability of the Long Pai Hui, the incense fees over the years were expected to be used to pay back the building cost.

Since they had applied to build a museum, since a museum was approved, and since the government had partly funded a museum, of course a museum had to be built. Since they had raised funds from villagers to build a temple, of course a temple had to be built. Under the name of museum there was approval, but there was no land or money to run it; under the name of temple, land use was approved by the villagers, and lots of donations and credit were extended, but there was no legal status. There was only one building, and it had to be both museum and temple at once.

Through the sustained efforts of the Long Pai Hui organizers, the plan to combine museum and temple received the support, understanding, and tacit approval of all parties. The most remarkable events were two ceremonies held during the temple fair in Fanzhuang in 2001 and 2003 respectively; one was the "Groundbreaking for Dragon Cultural Museum of Zhao Prefecture, China" and the other marked "The Completion of the Dragon Ancestral Hall and the Unveiling of the Nameplates of the Dragon Cultural Museum".

By the end of February 2001, construction of the building had been started on the site in Fanzhuang. From February 22-25 (around the second day of the second lunar month), the Zhao County Committee, the County Government, and the Hebei Provincial Folklore Society convened the "First Hebei Provincial Dragon Culture Expo and Colloquium". The meeting was held in the county town. On the second day of the second lunar month, the county leaders and a number of scholars, 140 altogether, went to observe the ritual procession of the Dragon Tablet, and they officiated at the groundbreaking. In the following two years, the families of the leading group, with the support of the village committee and township government, but short of money, worked very hard to build a proper temple. In the completion ceremony, also attended by the County government and scholars, the building that had had only one name at the groundbreaking, that of the museum, now had two names, having added that of Dragon Ancestral Hall. Now, the exact names of the building were "Dragon Tablet Association, Fanzhuang, Hebei" and "Dragon Cultural Museum of Zhao Prefecture, China". One building with two nameplates, two proper names. The formation of this relationship between names and things, one in two or two in one, was key to the very existence of the building. This provides a perspective on how we understand the cultural logic of contemporary Chinese society.

FULLY RECOGNIZED IN THE NAME OF INTANGIBLE CULTURAL HERITAGE

Either in real relations or in imagination, the organizers of the Dragon Tablet Fair are willing to explore all possibilities to become active members of the main-stream society and take on positive social images. In 2006, the Dragon Tablet Fair successfully obtained the title of "Hebei Province Non-Material Cultural Heritage," and during the temple fair on February 2, 2007, this honor was marked in the form of ritualistically setting up a stele in front of the Dragon Ancestor Palace. The Dragon Tablet Fair thus was included in a new category, becoming part of a new, positive value. Again we see clearly that the Dragon Tablet Fair is always looking for opportunities to assimilate into the main-stream social values and become members of the main-stream society, though originally there was an abyss between them. Between state and society whose relation can change from antagonism to smooth-sailing, it is possible for folk organizations to transform into organizations of the civil society and for the state community to become civil society. The significance of civil society is to let in rejected individuals, groups, and organizations as "normal," "common" members on the basis of universalistic principle. The wide-scale realization of this principle is a long and slow process, especially when it has to do with all kinds of issues concerning the civil rights of the peasants – we as a society have too many obstacles to overcome. Fortunately, we have seen that the process of actualizing the universalistic principle has started and been in motion for many years, with remarkable results, which the experience of the Dragon Tablet Fair as a vivid example.

In China, safeguarding of ICH is operated through social movements. The whole society is so enthusiastic about ICH that it is discussed with a rare unanimity from state leaders to peasants in remote villages, as well as catch words in media for many years. The Culture Heritage Day established in 2005 offers specific timing for ICH to draw public's attention. On that day, ICH items are exhibited among Chinese museums and universities. Since 2008, Tomb-sweeping Day, Dragon Boat Festival and Mid-autumn Day have been the legal holidays, altering the century-old state policy that traditional festivals were excluded from the official time system. Also, the folk arts were always rejected by the modern education system; however, ICH getting into campus has been on the educational policy and implemented around the country. Temple fairs, which were clamped down by governments because of the enshrinement and worship of all kinds of spirits, now have become objects of protection as the national or provincial representative ICH items. Safeguarding of ICH in China is a process with social participation, thus changing aspects of the whole society.

China has gradually adapted its economy to the international practice since its entry to the World Trade Organization (WTO) in 2002. In 2004, with the accession to the Convention for the Safeguarding of the Intangible Cultural Heritage, China introduced a set of culture discourses and they are practiced through the representative lists and reserves of cultural ecology respectively at national, provincial, municipal, and county levels. With a nation-wide social mobilization, it has brought forth a great social transformation.

Using tactics of renaming, operation of ICH in China classify those folk culture items which were negative in values into the ICH list after selection. Now these items have been cultural treasures which are protected by law and received financial aid. Anyone who hurt the inheritors before may benefit from the official system. But, time has changed. Anyone who hurt them may be punished while the inheritors are honored and rewarded. Some items can be transformed into products getting to the market. Therefore, a path of cultural identification from local to the state has been established through the mechanism for turning the items from negative to positive.

The golden touch of intangible cultural heritage (ICH) to folk culture has benefited from the tactics above from the perspective of operation and the priority shift of value judgment from the perspective of logic. Since the political correctness in modern times is made by political elites and intellectuals standing highly above the majority of the population, therefore the evaluation criteria of folk cultural items had to be the dichotomy of science and superstition, advanced and backward, essence and dross. There is no doubt that, according to modern ideology, folk cultural items are negative examples of superstition, backwardness and wasting. Against such historical fate, the concept of ICH has emerged in order to select representative items of a culture and people by their own choices. The first premise of such assessment recognizes that all communities have their own representative items. Secondly, it acknowledges their right to declare those items. What experts do is to confirm afterwards the reality and necessity of these listed items. Items enrolled in national lists are actually those accepted at the local communities as the most prominent. In short, the national lists just confirm the value of such items according to the people who value them best.

The case of Longpaihui shows how China has been trying to resolve the tensions between state and society, between elites and ordinary people, and between the traditional and the modern. This progress is a signal of China's distance to a "normal modern nation-state. Actually other members of the BRICSs have experienced the development process in the same or different ways which need more studies in the future.

REFERENCES

KROTZ, E. (1997), "Anthropologies of the South: Their Rise, Their Silencing, Their Characteristics", in *Critique of Anthropology*, 17, 3: 237-251.

MA, Q. (2011), Eluosi Xinling de Licheng: Eluosi Heituqu Shehui Shenghuo de Minzuzhi, in *The Road to "Russian Mind": An Ethnography of Social Life in the Black Soil Region of Russia*, PhD dissertation, Peking University.

RIBEIRO, G. L., Escobar, A. (eds.). (2006), "World Anthropologies: disciplinary transformations within systems of power", in *Wenner-Gren international symposium series*, Oxford and New York, Berg Publishers.

WU, X. (2009), "Shequn, Zuzhi yu Dazhong Minzhu: Yindu Kelalabang Shehui Zhengzhi de Minzuzhi", in *Groups, Organizations and Popular Democracy: An Ethnography of the Society and Politics of Kerala Pradesh, India*, Beijing, Peking University Press.

ZHANG, S. (2013), *The Financialization of Amazonia: Science and REDD+ in Brazil*, PhD dissertation, University of California at Irvine.

Zindabad! Modern contestation against the caste system in India

Pedro Lara de Arruda and Asleigh Kate Slingsby[1]

Abstract   This paper begins by considering the politicization of cast in modern India, reviewing confrontations to the caste-system which have been made since early colonization. The paper then traverses the evolution of the legal framework against casteism, highlighting the 1950 Indian Constitution's recognition of Scheduled Castes (SC), Scheduled Tribes (STs) as well as Other Backward Classes (OBCs). The latter Mandal Commission of 1978 is shown to be the most striking measure of caste empowerment by imposing a framework of structural reforms. Post-Mandal Commission ordinary laws and Constitutional Amendments are then presented as well as international legal frameworks against casteism. Disaggregating underprivileged classes and castes into SCs, STs and OBCs is then explored in detail. Insight into the interception of caste and gender is also provided as well as the perspective of differently-abled persons with respect to caste. The paper ultimately exposes how caste based discrimination persists in

---

1   This is a shorter version of the article presented at the 37th Annual Meeting of the ANPOCS, September 2013. Demographic data from this article may be updated as per the recently released Twelfth Five Year Plan of India, which was not officially available when the article was written.

India. Combatting casteism demands a highly inclusive definition of the term in order to achieve justice and equality for those discriminated against for the substantive transformation of Indian society.

Keywords India; Caste System; Social Inclusion.

INTRODUCTION

Caste as a practice and a concept has endured a turbulent and deeply impactful socio-historical evolution in India. The politicization of caste in modern India ushered in decades of widespread activism, championed by many now internationally acclaimed revolutionaries such as Mahatma Gandhi. Independent India and a new Constitution saw a legal framework against caste-based discrimination emerge, progressively recognizing the rights, as well as attempting to afford justice to, a historically subjugated, discriminated and marginalized portion of Indian society. As substantial as such achievements indeed were, they failed to eliminate caste based practices, resulting in the political reemergence of caste in the late 1970's. This saw the landmark institution of the Mandal Commission, propelling further legal advances right up to the 2000's. Such progress facilitated the disaggregation of caste as a category, in an effort to confront the internal power dynamics of this otherwise conflated category. This paper explores this historical trajectory of caste in Indian society. It then goes on to provide insight into caste as a category as well as broader categories of discrimination that exist in India today, including that of tribal, gender and differently-abled discrimination.

THE POLITICIZATION OF CASTE IN MODERN INDIA

Systematic confrontations of the caste-system have been recorded since early colonization times and, most sharply, since the middle XIX Century

(GALANTER, 1984). In Maharashtra, Mr Jotiba Phule (1827-1890) and his wife were precursors of movements to liberate *Unotuchables* (*Dalits*) and *Shudras* from oppression. They launched the first modern school for girls of India and several other social institutions wherein people would participate on a non-casteist basis of equality and mutual-respect. In Kerala, *Shri* Narayana Guru (1856-1928) was also an important social reformer who criticized casteism not so much on the basis of a secular discourse, but from the perspective of the very Hindu traditions that had no such reference to caste as a valid category. In the 1920's *Sri* Narayana Guru and *Mahatma* Gandhi (1869-1948) both had important roles in the event of the *Vaikom Satyagraha* (1924-1925). Later on, *Mahatma* Gandhi would again engage in anti-casteist movements in Kerala and give it an all-India dimension during the *Guruvayur Satyagraha* (1931-1932). As Eleanor Zelliot (2007) points out, from the 1920's on, Gandhi raised anti-casteist protests to another level; prompting the agenda to become an organic part of the nationalist movement.

In the late 1920's Dr. B. R. Ambdkar, himself of a lower caste, emerged as a representative in anti-casteist movements at Maharastra. He launched most of the secularist critiques of the caste system that remain prominent today. Taking lower caste dissent to an extreme, Dr. Ambedkar went on to burn the *Manu Smriti* as a protest against the casteist institutions touted in the book (GALANTER, 1984; KSHIRSAGAR, 1994).

Triggered by Gandhi's 1932 fast and the political achievements of Dr. Ambedkar, the British Administration agreed to take measures to protect "Depressed Castes" (as Scheduled Castes were officially referred to at the time). At first there was disagreement. Gandhi opposed measures of positive discrimination insisting that Hindus had to reach homogeneity by denying caste distinctions. Dr. Ambedkar took a more realist position, accepting caste would not disappear in a day-to-night legal act and, therefore, proposing that certain castes were given some reservation quotas in provincial legislatures. Even so, in the same year the two social leaders managed to agree on the approval of the *Poona Pact*, which reserved some seats for "Depressed Castes" in the provincial legislatures. However the Pact was based on a flawed definition of castes (KSHIRSAGAR, 1994).

As India gained independence, Mr. Jagjivan Ram, himself a *Dalit*, emerged as a representative of *Dalits* at a national level, being elected by the Bihar Legislative Assembly and serving as member of the Constituent Assembly of Independent India, as well as securing a position as Minister of Defense during Jawaharlal Nehru`s government (GALANTER, 1984; KSHIRSAGAR, 1994).

THE LEGAL FRAMEWORK AGAINST CASTEISM IN INDIA

In light of the progressive anti-casteist momentum, which was crucial to the Independence of India, the Indian Constitution of 1950 recognized the fragile situation of not only Dalits or *untouchables* (thereafter named Scheduled Castes – SC), but also of certain tribes (thereafter named Scheduled Tribes – STs) and other underprivileged castes and fragile groups (thereupon named Other Backward Classes – OBCs). The constitutional strategy was of both, criminalizing casteist practices and of providing for positive discrimination policies aimed at overcoming the historical structures preventing such fragile groups from enjoying full citizenship (MOHANTY, et al., 2011). As Thorat and Senapati notice:

> Article 15(4) and 16(4) of the Constitution enabled both the state and Central Governments to reserve seats in public services for the members of the SC and ST, thereby, enshrining equality of opportunity in matters of public employment [...]. The Constitution prohibits discrimination (Article 15) of any citizen on grounds of religion, race, caste, etc.; unotuchability (Article 17); and forced labour (Article 23). It provides for specific representation through reservation of seats for the SCs and the STs in the Parliament (Article 330) and in the State Legislative Assemblies (Article 332), as well as, in Government and public sector jobs, in both the federal and state Governments (Articles 14(4), 330(4) and 335). (THORAT & SENAPATI, 2006).

In addition to this, article 46 also adds that it is the state's responsibility to "promote with special care the education and economic interests of the weaker sections of the people, in particular, of Scheduled Castes and Scheduled Tribes, and shall protect them from social injustice and all forms of exploitation" (Government of India, 1950). Article 244(1) and (2) provides for special care regarding the Administration and Control of Scheduled Areas and certain Scheduled Tribes. Article 29(2) provides for unrestricted access to education, and Article 30 explicitly prohibits backward classes being prevented from access to education (MOHANTY, et al., 2011).

With Independence and a new Constitution in place, an overall feeling of unity and homogeneity emerged in India, a marker of Indian political culture until the 1970s. The mainstream view was that the modern and secular institutions upon which the Indian Constitution was based would be enough to ensure equality and prevent discrimination based on caste (HARDGRAVE and KOCHANEK, 2008). However, this period saw reduced political participation by SCs, STs and OBCs because of the merging of the caste-agenda with nationalist politics. Nationalist politics dominated in the 1950's, 1960's, and early 1970's to prevent the fragmentation and "balcanization" of India (especially in light of the secession of Pakistan – 1947; the three first Indo-Pakistani Wars – 1947, 1965, 1971; the Sino-Indian War – 1962; and the still pending dispute over Kashmir) (MENON and NIGAM, 2007).

Whatever the reasons behind the "Nehruvian Consensus" (as this period is known) and the low-profile of identity-politics from 1947 to 1976 (e.g.: either overall contentment or successful marginalization of dissent), the fact is that a decade after Jawaharlal Nehru's death India would once again have the caste debate at the centre of its political architecture. Confronted with the scarce impact of the Constitutional Provisions as well as restrained discourse by the state in relation to vulnerable groups since Independence, the 1970s ushered in a new era of anti-casteist politics. This saw the emergence of anti-casteist Ordinary Laws and overall political changes to accommodate "the recalcitrance of caste" (MENON and NIGAM, 2007). In 1976 two landmark laws to protect vulnerable castes and tribes were approved: The *Protection of Civil Rights Act* (1976), which enacted for implementation of civil rights accrued from article 17 abolishing *untouchability*; and the *Bonded Labour System Act* (1976) which provided for the abolition of bonded labour system and provided for punitive measures against such practices (MOHANTY, et al., 2011).

THE MANDAL COMMISSION (1978)

The most striking measure to empower vulnerable castes and groups, however, would come in 1978, during an unstable political moment wherein the Congress Party lost the power for the first time and the left-wing Janata Dal managed to approve the Mandal Commission. More than simply a list of SCs, STs and OBCs to be targeted through policies of seat reservation and social protection; this document was in fact a framework of structural reforms to be pursued in various alternate areas. The aim was to overcome identity-based discrimination and the related economic means by which these practices operate (MENON and NIGAM, 2007).

At the same time, a *National Commission for SC & ST* was created to seek inclusive policies benefitting these groups and also to work towards the implementation of the rights of these categories. After many transformations, the *89ᵗʰ Constitutional Amendment* (2003) created two distinguished National Commissions: one for SCs and other for STs (that provision was actually implemented in 2004). Until 1993 the OBCs were only included with similar bodies at a state level. However in 1993, the Indian Government launched the *National Commission on Backward Classes*, an achievement which civil-society granted after a favourable decision by the *Supreme Court* on the issue. Parallel to these national bodies, many other state-level Commissions were established performing similar functions on the behalf of SCs, STs and OBCs (MOHANTY, et al., 2011).

Even though concrete measures to fulfil the Mandal Commission provisions only started taking place in 1990, with the gradual reservation of up to 27% of seats in public service to OBCs and up to 22,5% to SCs and STs, the 1978 provisions were indirectly responsible for the flood of progressive and protective anti-casteist Ordinary Laws and Constitutional Amendments that followed.[2] Among other reasons, the influence was mostly due to the role the Mandal Commission played in identifying specific forms of discrimination experienced by each vulnerable group and the corresponding quota designed to overcome such realities. Concerning the 1990 provisions more specifically, it can also be argued that the Mandal Commission's reservation-quotas were based upon a strong and comprehensive system aimed at the most vulnerable among each category. So much so that people from targeted groups who obtained admission scores higher than those needed to compete under reservation would be assigned universal seats as opposed to reservation seats (leaving more reserved seats to the least privileged among the scheduled groups). More so, reservation quotas were provided not only for joining public institutions, but also for pursuing promotions and other related benefits once in a public position (MOHANTY, et al., 2011). Interesting to note is that the 2008 provision expanding these quotas of reservations to higher education institutions would also reproduce such measures of strength and comprehensiveness (MOHANTY, et al., 2011).

It is important to note however that many direct provisions of the Mandal Commission are still neglected, such as: the implementation of progressive land reforms; the provision of special educational facilities; the institution of vocational training; the establishment of separate coaching facilities for students aspiring to enter technical and professional institutions; the creation of adequate facilities for improving the skills of village artisans; the availability of subsidised loans for setting up small-scale industries; and the setting up of a separate chain of financial and technical bodies to assist OBC entrepreneurs (GILL, 2006). Not to mention that most reservation quotas in public jobs fall short of the 1990 provision for SCs, STs and OBCs – especially when looking

---

2 Also of juridical importance were the several verdicts of high Courts in India which settled important jurisprudences against casteism. This dimension of the juridical protection of vulnerable groups is not covered in this article. For a further analysis and record of landscape jurisprudences see (MOHANTY, et al., 2011).

at higher positions within public institutions (THORAT and SENAPATI, 2006; DESHPANDE, 2002; THORAT, et al., 2009).

POST-MANDAL COMMISSION ORDINARY LAWS AND CONSTITUTIONAL AMENDMENTS AGAINST CASTEISM IN INDIA

Among the many anti-casteist provisions that took the floor following the approval of the Mandal Commission, it is important to note the key role of the *Legal Aid Services Authorities Act* (1987), which expanded access to law in India by holding the state responsible for providing free and competent legal services to the weaker sections of society. This included SCs/STs, victims of human trafficking, women or children, the mentally ill, victims of mass disasters, industrial workmen, etc. It also created provisions for the implementation of Article 39(A) of the Constitution, calling for supplementary forums for the litigants for conciliatory settlement of disputes (the *Lok Adalats*) (MOHANTY, et al., 2011).

In 1989 the *SCs and STs Prevention of Atrocities Act* was approved, rendering offences against SCs and STs as non-bailable offences. *The Protection of Human Rights Act* was approved in 1993, buttressing the constitution of the *National Human Rights Commission* (NHRC), the *State Human Rights Commissions* (SHRCs) and the *Human Rights Courts* for the better protection of human rights. In the same year the *National Commission for Backward Classes Act* was approved, creating a government-body of binding decisions to examine requests for inclusion of any class of citizens as a backward class in the *Central List of Backward Classes*. The Commission also served to evaluate imbalances in reservation quotas catering to specific groups. Topping the progressive anti-casteist policies of 1993, was the confrontation of a traditional casteist practice; that of making *Dalits* work as manual scavengers for the removal of human excreta. It was rendered a punishable offence under the *Employment of Manual Scavengers and Construction of Dry Latrines Act* (MOHANTY, et al., 2011).

In 1996 the *Panchayats (Extension to Scheduled Areas) Act* was approved for the benefit of tribal people as it provided for adequate representation of tribes in Scheduled Areas. Complementary to that, in 2006 the *ST & Other Traditional Forest Dwellers Act* was approved, conferring the right of habitation for STs and other traditional forest dwellers. This Act is also designed to be understood in terms of the framework of the many laws assuring environmental protection of which STs and other vulnerable groups tend to be so dependent upon. Previous relevant laws in this vein include: The *Wildlife (Protection) Act* (1972); the *Forest Conservation Act* (1980) and its *Amendment* (1988); the state-level *Prevention of Land Alienation Regulations* (approved at different dates in different states); and the *Biological Diversity Act* (2002) (MOHANTY, et al., 2011).

Between 1992 and 1993 there were also some Constitutional Amendments that paved the way for policies directly aimed at providing policy and employment reservations to backward castes, tribes and other vulnerable social groups. This included the *73rd* and *74th Constitutional Amendments* which provided for representation of SCs and STs in local administrative bodies, proportionate to their population. In 2000, the *81st Constitutional Amendment* provided for the fulfilment of unfilled vacancies meant for SCs and STs by treating them as backlog. In the same year the *82nd Constitutional Amendment* was approved providing for the relaxation of qualifying marks for SCs and the STs. Re-validating the rule of seniority for SCs and STs candidates in reserved government posts, the *85th Constitutional Amendment* was approved in 2002 (MOHANTY, et al., 2011).

Interestingly, it was only in 2002, with the *86th Constitutional Amendment*, concerning education for children in the age-group 6-14, was granted as a fundamental right (this was supposed to be implemented within ten years of the inauguration of the Constitution). In 2009 the *Right of Children to Free and Compulsory Education Act* (2009) would provide a number of enabling conditions for school education for the age-group 6-14. A direct consequence of these advances in the education of OBCs was the *Central Educational Institutions Act* of 2006, which provided for the full implementation of the 27% reservation for OBCs in educational institutions run by the Central government until the 2008 deadline (thereby strengthening the dispositions of the Mandal Comission provisions made in 1990) (MOHANTY, et al., 2011).

INTERNATIONAL LEGAL FRAMEWORKS
AGAINST CASTEISM IN INDIA

Anti-casteist efforts rely extensively on international legal frameworks, India's voluntary commitment to anti-discriminatory agreements, and the activism of backward classes pushing for international measures against the lenience of the state regarding certain casteist practices.[3] The massive mobilization of civil society, NGO's and several *Dalits* and backward classes organizations at the 2001 *World Conference Against Racism*, held in Durban, were majorly impactful (2001) (PINTO, 2001; THORAT and UMAKANT, 2004). Despite the fact that most previous international frameworks were quite oblivious to the specificity of casteism as a kind of discrimination (the issue was usually treated by the UN as related to other more explicitly-mentioned forms of discrimination, such as racism), the anti-casteist representatives at Durban emphasized some more recent statements of the UN where caste in the Indian context was given prime attention.

Other South Asian countries affected by casteism, as well as Japanese and Nigerian organizations fighting against their own kind of casteisms (respectively, the *Burakumins* and the *Osus* underprivileged castes), were present at the Durban event. Indian activists reminded participants of the firm position India held during its sanctions on Apartheid South Africa. They asked for equally hard measures to be placed on India by the international community (PINTO, 2001; THORAT and UMAKANT, 2004). At the time, under the Bharatiya Janata Party (BJP) government of Atal Bihari Vajpayee, India reacted strongly against such recommendations, stating that the issue of casteism was a purely domestic one, not appropriate for discussion on the international stage. The Indian government went on to state that caste was different from race, therefore a world conference on racism was not the appropriate forum for dealing with the issue. Finally, they rejected the position of the Indian participants at the event by professing to already

---

3   For the complete list of such international agreements see Mohanty, et al. (2011).

be tackling the issue through a vast array of social policies rendering the attention of the forum redundant (THORAT and UMAKANT, 2004).

Despite much controversy, at least two (the 1st and the 2nd) of the three arguments by the Indian government were rejected at the Conference on account of the UN endorsing the understanding that race doesn't exist as a biological category, but a cultural category thus accommodating caste. In both cases, the position of the Conference was that such cultural categories only exist through discriminatory frameworks, which therefore required eradication. Race is culturally produced by racism just like caste is produced by casteism (PINTO, 2001; THORAT and UMAKANT, 2004).

Also important to mention, was the way in which the Conference made a strong Postcolonial and Subalternist critique of the UN, which still seems very pertinent: that is that the lexicon and values upon which the UN is based are very Western-biased, therefore rendering certain non-Western forms of violence and discrimination unaccounted for (PINTO, 2001).

As for concrete results, even though there were no sanctions placed on India of any sort (the caste agenda was constantly pushed aside for the sake of other issues of more "geopolitical interest"), it is interesting to note that explicit references to caste and reports on Indian anti-casteist policies became much more common within UN organizations dealing with discrimination.

DISAGGREGATING THE DISCONTENTS OF CASTEISM: SCS, STS AND OBCS

An important step towards understanding caste based discrimination in India involves disaggregating underprivileged classes and castes into SCs, STs and OBCs. As the Indian government legal framework itself expresses (Government of India, 1950), the overall marginalization of these groups and their subalternity relative to upper castes in India is an outcome of very different discriminatory processes for each of these cases.

More than providing for policies more accessible to each of these groups (SCs, STs and OBCs) according to their specific conjunctures and needs, a disaggregated perspective sheds light onto the complex power-dynamics that even foster rivalries between underprivileged groups as a way of maintaining casteist political agendas. Menon and Nigam's (2007) analysis of the political alliances in Uttar Pradesh during the 1990's, for instance, show how the *Bahujan Samaj Party*, originally thought to be an alliance of SCs, STs and OBCs ended up being split as OBCs were the spearheads of casteist violence against Dalits, so much so, that despite the Hindu-fundamentalist campaign that marked the BJP's profile during the decade, Dalits of Uttar Pradesh ended up privileging alliances with the BJP in exchange for token support against direct sorts of violence practiced by OBCs.

OTHER BACKWARD CLASSES (OBCS)

In general terms it is important to note that OBCs encompass the majority of the Indian population taken through a caste identity-matrix. It refers to underprivileged castes severely deprived of certain basic rights: normally they encompass castes under the *Varnas* of *Vaishyas* and, mostly, the *Shudras*. Their main challenge is their bondage to particular kinds of socially-unvalued occupations and the consequence this has for their position in society. Proponents of caste practices understand OBCs to be necessary in society to perform certain low-level functions that directly serve upper castes (for instance, performing domestic work). The marginal attention paid to OBCs heavily disempowers their capacity to make claims for equality (e.g.: Medical care being prioritized to upper castes, or food distribution being primarily distributed among upper castes) (SEKHAR, 2006).

In general terms, there is a scarcity of micro–data on the overall demographic situation of underprivileged castes and tribes (SEN, 2000; THORAT and MAHAMALLICK, 2006). In the specific case of OBCs, however, it is even more complex to present a demographic framework as these groups vary. Comparative historical series and similar analysis can't provide but a wide sketch of the situation of OBCs in India. The *Eleventh*

Five-year Plan, 2007-12 (Planning Commission, 2008), acknowledged such a situation and regretted the setbacks it caused to the planning and follow up of inclusive policies:

> State-wise, OBC-wise data on population as well as vital and demographic variables are not available, which is the main hurdle in the formulation of policies and programmes for the development of the Other Backward Classes. (Planning Commission, 2008).

Thorat and Senapati (2006) in their work on reservation policies in India, prefer to deal with a more general category of underprivileged castes that are neither SCs nor STs (they call it non – SC/ST). And even while doing so, they don't provide an overall picture of the non – SC/ST but merely point out their shares of reserved seats in public institutions and on the deliverance of social programmes. An alternative source to make sense of the overall demographical distribution of OBCs can be sought in the *Eleventh Five-year Plan, 2007-12*. It talks about the welfare of SCs, STs and OBCs (Planning Commission, 2008). However it is not as extensive as report provided by Thorat and Senapati (2006). Admittedly, neither reports are fully dedicated to the issue of anti-casteism, but are nevertheless based on more recent data, from the *61ˢᵗ Round of the National Sample Survey on "Employment and Unemployment Situation among Social Groups in India (July 2004 to June 2005)"* (Ministry of Statistics and Programme Implementation, 2006). Accordingly, OBCs are estimated to account for 41% of the Indian population. Previous estimations were made by B. P. Mandal[4] and, based on data from 1931, pointing to an even bigger share of the population at the time, of around 52% (Ministry of Statistics and Programme Implementation, 2006).

---

4   The Mandal Commission was named after Mr. B. P. Mandal, who was the idealizer of the list and reservation programmes that would be approved in 1978.

SCHEDULED CASTES (SCS)

A more delicate situation is that of the Scheduled Castes, which mostly encompasses the castes under the umbrella of the non-*Varna* (the *Dalits*). As these communities are considered to be impure by the casteist logic, they are radically excluded from society; relegated to do degrading work, precluded from any sort of contact with what is valued in society (AMBEDKAR, 1987; SCOVILLE, 1996). For these reason SCs are traditionally assigned as manual scavengers for the removal of human excreta. Their allocation as domestic workers or providers of social services – such as cooks – suffers strong casteist opposition (THORAT and SABHARWAL, 2010). Besides the economic structures alienating *Dalits*, it is not unusual for healthcare givers to refuse to touch *Dalits* in medical examinations, thereby excluding them from vital social services (THORAT and SABHARWAL, 2010; GILL, 2012).

According to Thorat and Senapati's (2010) study on the demographical disposition and overall social conditions of SCs, 16,2% of the total population of India was composed of *Dalits* in 2001, amounting to a total of 166,635,700 people. Looking retrospectively, this number represents an increase of 1,5% of the SCs share of the Indian population since 1961, when their absolute numbers were of 64,4 million. In the 2001 sample analysed by Thorat and Senapati, it can also be said that 79,8% of SCs resided in rural areas and that the overall fertility rate among them was 936 females per thousand males (which is slightly higher than the national average of 933).

Considering the distribution of STs within India, Thorat and Senapati (2006) found that, for the 2001 sample (Office of the Registrar General & Census Commissioner, 2001), almost 55% of the total SC population of India resided in the states of Uttar Pradesh (21,1%), West Bengal (11,1%), Bihar (7,8%), Andhra Pradesh (7,4%), and Tamil Nadu (7,1%.). Considering the proportion of SCs within the total population of each specific state, Punjab, Himachal Pradesh and West Bengal have the biggest shares of SCs of 28,9%, 24,7% and 23% respectively. Pondicherry, Karnataka and Andhra Pradesh have SCs accounting for 16,2% of the state's population which is the same as the national percentage of SCs. In the North-eastern states of India, where most people are of tribal descent, the population of SCs was found to be negligibly small, accounting for 0,6% of Arunachal Pradesh's population, 0,5% of Meghalaya's population and a mere 272 persons in Mizoram.

Table 1   Percentage trends of the scheduled caste population

Census year	Total population (in millions)	SC population (in millions)	Percentage of the SC population to the total population
1961	439.2	64.4	14.7
1971	547.9	80.0	14.6
1981*	665.3	104.8	15.7
1991**	838.6	138.2	16.5
2001***	1028.6	166.6	16.2

Note: * Excludes Assam in 1981, ** Excludes Jammu and Kashmir in 1991, and *** Excludes the Mao-Maram, Paomata, and Purul sub-divisions of Senapati district in Manipur.
Source: Thorat and Senapati, 2006); Office of the Registrar General & Census Commissioner, 2001.

SCHEDULED TRIBES (STS)

The situation for Scheduled Tribes is different from that of SCs and OBCs as tribes people don't really fit into the historical social imagination of the caste system. Referring mostly to tribes and forest people historically living in South Asia, the STs have a strong dependency on communal and preserved land and forests. This renders the imposition of private property a severe challenge. Far from an impartial or fair process of privatization of common lands, the construction of modern India is marked by the insertion of these tribes into the caste-system as a way of legitimizing the transfer of common rights to private groups (most notably, from tribes' collective control to upper caste private control) (BOSE, 1941; BIJOY, 2003). In a sense the tribes "inserted" into the caste-system suffer similar violence to that experienced by OBCs, with the additional fact that they experience even greater discrimination among casteist society as they are perceived as "outsiders". Furthermore, many STs still perform cultural and religious practices that subject them to religious hate from most casteist Hindus (SINGH, 1993). From a more logistical point of view, the fact that most tribes live in isolated areas (and in many cases speak only their own languages) makes it all the more difficult for social services to reach them (e.g.: Domiciliary health care hardly reach STs homes, and food distribution centres are scarcely established in forest areas where STs live) (THORAT and SABHARWAL, 2010; GILL, 2012).

The study of Thorat and Senapati (2006) on the demographical distribution of SCs reveals that, in 2001, STs represented 8,2% of the Indian population, accounting for 84,326,240 persons (Table 2) out of which 91,7% resided in rural areas with an overall sex ratio of 978 woman per thousand men. The four states/territories with the biggest share of STs were located in either tiny states of the Northeast – like Mizoran (94,5%), Nagaland (89,1%) and Meghalaya (85,9%) – or the even tinier island of Lakshadweep (94,5%). The largest share of STs within a state's population were found in Chhattisgarh (31,8%), Jharkhand (26,6%) and Orissa (22,1%). It was also noted that seven states with minor percentages of STs accounted for 68% of the total ST population of India: Madhya Pradesh (14,5%), Marahastra (10,2%), Orissa (9,7%), Gujarat (8,9%), Rajasthan (8,4%), Jarkhand (8,4%) and Chattisgarh (7,8%). Therefore, despite the existence of states with a majority ST population, issues exist of not only federalist divides in terms of tribal and non-tribal states, but also in terms of promoting the inclusion of a persistent minority of STs that is dispersed throughout the country. The demographic disposition of STs also calls for special concern for states where the ST population is extremely small as a percentage of the overall population, as is the case of Uttar Pradesh (0,1%), Bihar (0,9%), Tamil Nadu (1%) and Kerala (1,1%).

Table 2   Percentage trends of the Scheduled Tribe population

Census year	Total population (in millions)	SC population (in millions)	Percentage of the SC population to the total population
1961	439.2	30.1	6.9
1971	547.9	38.0	6.9
1981*	665.3	51.6	7.8
1991**	838.6	67.8	8.1
2001***	1028.6	84.3	8.2

Note: * Excludes Assam in 1981, ** Excludes Jammu and Kashmir in 1991, and *** Excludes the Mao-Maram, Paomata, and Purul sub-divisions of Senapati district in Manipur.
Source: Thorat and Senapati, 2006; Office of the Registrar General & Census Commissioner, 2001.

CASTE AND GENDER: A NECESSARY CROSSOVER

An important stream of criticism against anti-casteist policies in India submits that reservation policies based on caste criteria, despite playing an essential role in uplifting certain underprivileged groups out of poverty traps, it is nevertheless an unbalanced strategy that overshadows other equally fragile identities' and their claims to empowerment. Traditionally one such argument is often made in relation to the *Women's Reservation Bill*, which is a historical struggle allocating 33% of reservations to women at the local and national Parliament: a proposal usually opposed by backward castes and tribes as evidence shows that women reservations tends to strengthen casteist structures as upper caste women are normally the only empowered women (DIETRICH, 1994; MENON and NIGAM, 2007).

While evaluating the so-called exclusivist aspect of caste-based identity politics, one may be lead to believe that the stringent classifications embodied in the anti-casteist agenda often overshadow other fragile identities. However this is an unfounded argument as the struggle against casteism has proven to be more efficient in accommodating such fragile identities, rendering them constituents of caste in a broader sense (ARRUDA, 2013). Studies such as Thorat and Lee's (2006) on casteism and food programmes revealed less exclusion and distortion when the People Distribution System (PDS) and Mid-Day Meal Scheme (MMS) depended on the support of grassroots feminist movements, such as the Development of Women and Children in Rural Areas (DWACRA) in Andra Pradesh, to plan, implement and review such programmes. In this particular case, much bigger take-up rates for backward castes SCs, STs and OBCs was observed along with fewer incidences of meso-unruly casteist practices despite Andra Pradesh being a state with a strong casteist culture and not having the financial strength of other states analysed in the study.

Similarly, Das Gupta and Thorat's (2009) study on the prospect of achieveming the *Millennium Development Goals* (MDGs) for SCs, STs and OBCs in India reveals that sometimes the very recognition of other identity-based inequalities demands a caste-based framework. In the case of MDGs 2 and 3 (Addressing Educational Gender Equality and Women Empowerment), for instance, the data explicitly show that gender inequality among SCs, STs and OBCs is way more extreme than the aggregated national picture. This is, nevertheless, a trend noticeable to a lesser extent among almost all the other MDGs.

As Menon and Nigam (2007) points out, one such comprehension of caste is as a historical opportunity to reveal other identity-based forms of exclusion and discrimination. This changes the contemporary feminist discourses of India from a zero-sum framework, which opposes anti-casteism, toward the "quotas within quotas" position. This involves the inclusion of criteria for reservation that cut across different identities that lead to poverty-traps and social exclusion. For example, reserving a share for women and for differently-abled persons[5] within the share reserved dedicated to SCs, STs and OBCs.

---

5   The term differently-abled person stands for a more inclusive way of referring to people with certain physical or mental conditions traditionally understood as disabilities. As the UNTERM defines it: "The term **differently abled** is sometimes proposed as a substitute for disabled or

FRAMING SOCIALLY EXCLUDED GROUPS IN INDIA THROUGH THE PERSPECTIVE OF DIFFERENTLY-ABLED PERSONS[6]

Another fragile condition that cuts across casteism and leads to people being marginalized in India is that of differently-abled persons. As the 2007 World Bank Report on people with disability in India has pointed out, differently-abled persons are among the most excluded in India, suffering from widespread illiteracy, limited involvement with social activities and strong social stigma (World Bank, 2007). As Gopinda C. Pal (2010) adds; this situation is much worse for women, outcastes and underprivileged castes and tribes, not only due to the contempt with which these persons are treated, but also due to the extreme poverty these people face rendering them particularly vulnerable to physical and mental disabilities.

Disaggregating differently-abled persons of India in terms of their caste or tribe and in terms of the causes of their conditions, as per the *UN Enable's World Programme of Action Concerning Disabled Persons,* reveals that the highest percentage of disability is caused by anaemia (18,5%), followed by pneumonia (16,6%), malnutrition (10,2%), defective gene mutation (9,2%), congenial defects (7,8%), stunting (3,1%) and low levels of nutrition (3%) (PAL, 2010).

Pal (2010) estimates that 1,8% of the Indian population is challenged by some mental or physical condition, whereas the percentage of differently-abled persons out of the total SC[7] population amounts to 2,4%. In the overall Indian sample, the incidence of disabilities among males is bigger than that among

---

handicapped. Differently abled emphasizes the fact that many people with disabilities are quite capable of accomplishing a particular task or performing a particular function, only in a different manner or taking more time or effort than people without the disability in question. It can also be taken to mean that a person who is incapable of one act may nevertheless be capable of many or even most others" (UNTERM, 2013).

6   Ibid.

7   In Mr. Pal's study he actually refers to Dalits and not to SCs. The choice of the more specific category of Dalits, as listed on the central list, as opposed to SCs more broadly, may lead to some minor divergences in terms of the micro-data and the inferences presented.

females. However when looking at a specific sample of SCs and STs the gender gap is relatively lower, suggesting equal vulnerability irrespective of gender.

Table 3   Causes of disability across social groups

Major causes	Dalits	ST	OBC	Others	Total
Moderate or severe Anaemia	18.3	15.5	20.8	16.1	18.5
Pneumonia	16.8	11.7	15.5	18.9	16.6
Malnutrition	9.5	13.0	10.9	9.2	10.2
Defective gene mutation	9.5	10.8	9.3	8.5	9.2
Congenial defects	7.3	7.0	7.6	8.7	7.8
Depicting impact of heredity	3.8	3.3	3.3	3.6	3.5
Stunted	2.7	2.4	2.8	3.8	3.1
Low level of nutrition	3.4	3.0	2.9	2.8	3.0
Inappropriate services at the time of delivery	3.0	2.8	2.8	3.2	3.0

Source: Pal, 2010.

Dalal (2000) submits that the incidence of disability among age-groups in India follows an opposite trend to that of developed countries, where most differently-abled persons are elders. As Pal (2010) established, 21% of the differently-abled population in India is below the age of 9 years-old and another 22% is between 10 and 19 years-old, whereas only 11% of them are above 60 years-old. This may be because people with disabilities rarely live beyond 60 years-old in India. Disaggregating this age-group distribution into SCs, STs and OBCs also reveals that the proportion of young differently-abled persons is relatively higher among SCs and STs than among upper caste groups.

Table 4   Age-wise distribution of persons with
disabilities across social groups

Age range	Dalits	ST	OBC	Others	Total
0–4	10.4	10.1	10.0	8.8	9.7
5–9	13.0	12.5	12.0	10.2	11.7
10–14	12.4	12.6	12.1	11.3	12.0
15–19	9.9	10.2	10.1	10.2	10.1
20–29	15.0	15.1	15.5	16.8	15.8
30–39	13.1	12.8	12.7	13.0	12.8
40–49	10.4	10.0	9.9	10.6	10.2
50–59	7.3	6.9	7.0	7.3	7.1
60>	8.5	9.9	10.7	11.7	10.7

Source: Pal, 2010.

It is also worth noting that a disaggregated analysis of differently-abled persons according to the degree and extent of the disability reveals no noticeable differences in terms of castes and/or tribes, except in the more specific cases of hearing and visual disabilities – in which more severe disabilities are concentrated within SCs and STs (PAL, 2010).

Overall, data shows that SCs, STs and OBCs with disabilities enjoy even smaller access to education, to a stable labour-market, to social programmes and to socially valued institutions like marriage, than upper caste differently-abled persons – and that marginalization tends to be intensified for women (PAL, 2010). Interestingly, it is also suggested that similar patterns of caste and gender bias apply to non-governmental aid-programmes addressed to differently-abled persons (though it must be pointed out that many such organizations are government funded) (PAL, 2010).

Confronted with the striking social marginalization of differently-abled SCs, STs and OBCs, and with the extent to which such caste and gender bias reproduces itself even within programmes intended to be inclusive, Pal (2010) addressed various flagship programmes targeting differently-abled people. He suggests that including women and backward groups depends on diversifying the design of programmes so that doubly, triply or multiply disadvantaged groups can receive the special attention they need in the deliverance of services. *Community Based Rehabilitation* programmes are believed to be a crucial path for promoting the inclusion of differently-abled persons from backward castes and tribes. Nevertheless, a huge effort must also be made to include such vulnerable groups in the labour-market at a stable pace. Promoting the fulfilment of at least 3% of jobs being legally reserved for differently-abled persons may facilitate such inclusion. Family-centred approaches are also very relevant to compensate for the *Conversion Handicap*[8] (SEN, 2000), especially as most differently-abled persons in India tend to live with their families even if married (PAL, 2010). Quantitatively, the state must increase its aid investments as Pal (2010) estimates that one third of the differently-abled population has to pay for wheelchairs and similar appliances – and that such investments tend to be unfeasible for SCs and STs who tend to come from poor economic situations.

---

8   The term *Conversion Handicap* was proposed by Amartya Sen (2000) to designate "the cost of converting income into a good living", which he claims to be in average much higher for differently-abled persons as they tend to face additional challenges in both, costs of living and finding ways to raise income.

Figure 1   Means of acquiring Aids/appliances by social groups

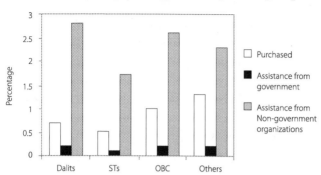

Source: Pal, 2010.

CONCLUSIONS

Despite considerable progress being achieved by the anti-casteist political movement, discrimination based on caste remains a persistent mechanism of discrimination in India, with *Dalits* baring the brunt of this injustice, relegated to the periphery of society. The issue of caste also encompasses India's tribes who similarly endure discrimination. Likewise, gender as a category of discrimination competes for recognition and representation, reflecting the complex and often contradictory nature of sociocultural policy redress in contemporary India. However, it has been submitted that caste, understood in terms of a broader definition, provides an overarching platform for discriminated groups to seek redress. More so, it has been found that individuals facing casteist discrimination are more likely to endure various other forms of identity discrimination, including gender. Furthermore, differently-abled persons in India endure some of the most severe discrimination, demanding accommodation within broader policies. Most pressingly, one has to acknowledge that poverty is the most impactful consequence and relentless perpetuator of discrimination in India. Therefore, increasing access to social programmes, labour markets, health care, education and other public services for all categories of discriminated people, most crucially those who endure extreme poverty, should serve as the guiding ambition for policies in India today.

REFERENCES

AMBEDKAR, B. R. (1987), "The Hindu Social Order: Its Essential Features", *in* B. R. Ambedkar, *Writing and Speeches*, vol. 3, Delhi, Vasant Moon.

ARRUDA, P. (2013), "Reservation and Anti-Casteist Practices as Instruments of Social Protection in India?". To be published as *IPC-IG One Pager*. Brasilia, International Policy Center for Inclusive Growth.

BIJOY, C. R. (2003), "The Adivasis of India: A History of Discrimination, Conflict and Resistance", in *People's Union for Civil Liberties Bulletin*, February, 2003. Delhi, People's Union for Civil Liberties.

BOSE, N. K. (1941), "The Hindu Method of Tribal Absorption", *in Science and Culture*, vol. 8, Kolkata.

DALAL, A. K. (2000), "Poverty, Development and Disability", *in* A. K. Mohanty, & G. Mishra (eds.), in *Psychology of Poverty and Disadvantage*, Delhi, Concept Publishing Company.

DAS GUPTA, P., THORAT, S. (2009), "Will India's Attainment of MDGs be an Inclusive Process", in *IIDS Working Paper Series*, vol. III, n. 2, 2009, Delhi, Indian Institute of Dalit Studies.

DESHPANDE, S. (2002), *Contemporary India: A Sociological View*, Delhi, Penguin Books.

DIETRICH, G. (1994), "Women and Religious Identity in India After Ayodhya", in Menon, B. R., Khan, N. S. (eds.), in *Against all odds: Essays on women, religion and development from India and Pakistan*, Delhi, Kali for Women.

GALANTER, M. (1984), *Competing Equalities: Law and the Backward Classes in India*, Oakland, University of California Press.

GILL, K. (2012), "Promoting Inclusiveness: a Framework for Assessing India's Flagship Social Welfare Programmes", in *IIDS and UNICEF Working Paper Series*, vol. I, Number 01, 2012.

GILL, S. S. (2006), "What the Mandal Commission Wanted", in *Indian Express* website, <http://www.indianexpress.com/news/what-the-mandal-commission-wanted/2343/>. Accessed on April, 25, 2013.

Government of India – GoI. (1950), *The Constitution of India*, website with the English version of the Indian Constitution of 1950, <http://lawmin.nic.in/olwing/coi/coi-english/coi-indexenglish.htm>. Accessed on April, 25, 2013.

KSHIRSAGAR, R. K. (1994), *Dalit Movement in India and its Leaders, 1857-1956,* Delhi, M D House.

MENON, N., Nigam, A. (2007), *Power and Contestation. India After 1989,* London, Zed Books.

Ministry of Statistics and Programme Implementation – GoI. (2006a). *Employment and Unempployment Situation Among Social Groups in India. 2005-5.* website, <http://mospi. gov.in/national_data_bank/pdf/516_final.pdf>. Accessed on April, 23, 2013.

MOHANTY, M., et al. (2011), *Weapon of the Oppressed,* Delhi, Counsil for Social Development. Nandy, A. (2002). *Time Warps: Silent and Evasive Pasts in Indian Politics and Religion,* 2nd ed., Delhi, Permanent Black.

Office of the Registrar General & Census Commissioner – GoI. (2001), *Census Data 2001,* website, <http://www.censusindia.gov.in/2011-common/census_data_2001. html>. Accessed on April, 20, 2013.

PAL, G. C. (2010), "Dalits with Disabilities: The Neglected Dimension of Social Exclusion", Working Paper Series, Indian Institute of Dalit Studies, New Delhi.

PINTO, A. (2001), "UN Conference against racism: Is caste race?", in *Economic and Political Weekly,* vol. XXXVI, n. 30, July 28, 2001.

Planning Commission – GoI. (2008), *Eleventh Five Year Plan 2007-2012,* vols. I, II, III, website, <http://planningcommission.nic.in/plans/planrel/fiveyr/welcome.html>. Accessed on April, 24, 2013.

SCOVILLE, J. (1996), "Labour Market Underpinnings of a Caste Economy Failing the Caste Theorem", in *The American Journal of Economics and Sociology,* 55(4).

SEKHAR, V. C. (2006), *Other Backward Classes in India: Recognition and Reservation,* Delhi, Raj Publications.

SEN, A. (2000), "Social Exclusion: Concept, Application and Scrutinity", in *Social Development Paper,* n. 1, June, Bangkok, Asian Development Bank.

SINGH, K. S. (1993), "Hinduism and Tribal Religion: An Anthropological Perspective", in *Man in India,* LXXIII, i, Delhi. Serials Publications.

THORAT, S., et al. (2009), "Urban Labour Market Discrimination", in *IIDS Working Paper Series,* vol. III, n. 1, 2009, Delhi, Indian Institute of Dalit Studies.

THORAT, S., LEE, J. (2006), "Dalits and the Right to Food – Discrimination and Exclusion in Food-related Government Programmes", in *IIDS Working Paper Series,* vol. I, n. 3, 2006, Delhi, Indian Institute of Dalit Studies.

THORAT, S., MAHAMALLICK, M. (2006), "Caste, Labour and Occupation Discrimination in Rural Area", in *IIDS Study.*

THORAT, S., SABHARWAL, N. S. (2010), "Caste and Social Exclusion: Issues Related to Concept, Indicators and Measurement", in *IIDS and UNICEF Working Paper Series,* vol. 02, n. 1, 2010, Delhi, Indian Institute of Dalit Studies and UNICEF.

THORAT, S., SENAPATI, B. M. (2006), "Reservation Policy in India – Dimensions and Issues", in *IIDS Working Paper Series,* vol. I, n. 2, 2006, Delhi, Indian Institute of Dalit Studies.

THORAT, S., UMAKANT, M. (2004), "Caste, Race and Discrimination: Discourses" in *The International Context,* Jaipur, Rawat and IIDS.

UN Commission on Human Rights. (2000), "Resolution of the Sub-Commission on the Promotion and Protection of Human Rights – E/CN4/Sub2/2000/L14", 52nd Session, August 9, 2000.

UN Committee on Civil and Political Rights. (1997), "Consideration of the Government of India Report to the Human Right Committee – CCPR/C/79/Add 81", August 4, 1997.

UN Committee on the Elimination of Discrimination Against Women. (2000), "Conideration of Country Report – CEDAW/C/2000/1/CRP/3/Add Dt.", April 31, 2000.

UN General Assembly – UNGA. (2000). *United Nations Millenium Declaration,* New York.

UNTERM. (2013), *Differently Abled persons,* website, <http://unterm.un.org/dgaacs/ unterm.nsf/8fa942046ff7601c85256983007ca4d8/b3c7f84839cd0fa08525739a0067 6b77?OpenDocument>. Accessed on April, 27, 2013.

World Bank. (2007), "People with Disability in India: From Commitments to Outcomes", Delhi, Human Development Unit, South Asian Region, The World Bank Report.

ZELLIOT, E. (2007), "Gandhi and Ambedkar – A Study in Leadership" and "Bibliography on Untouchability" in Banerjee-Dube, I. (ed.), *Caste in History: Themes in Indian History,* Delhi, Oxford University Press.

Socio-economic inclusion and justice

A comparative study of BRICS countries with a focus on India

Praveen Jha and Amit Chakraborty

Abstract   Brazil, Russia, India, China and South Africa who form the BRICS are some of the fast growing "emerging economies" that are being talked about as the new drivers of the global economy, an era in which the US and Europe are in the midst of a serious economic crisis. Though the recent "currency shocks" and comparatively lower growth rates have made most of these countries worried, it is undeniable that the rise of the countries that constitute BRICS is a significant event in the contemporary global economic and geo-political arena.

Celebrating the relatively high growth for a sustained period witnessed in BRICS nations needs to be tempered by the fact that these economies are riddled with large regional disparities, growing inequalities, substantial unemployment and significant levels of poverty. Contrary to popular perception, this paper argues that neoliberal growth is not the solution to these problems; rather, the very nature of accumulation in these economies aggravates the fundamental economic problems. The current obsession with growth distorts the priorities that these developing countries should focus on essentially, greater autonomy and coordinated efforts to defend the well-being of their citizens. A growth process driven by a neoliberal policy regime is also inherently fragile, short-sighted and exclusionary.

Keywords Emerging Economies, New Economic Architecture, Human Development, Inclusive Growth, Neoliberal economic policy.

INTRODUCTION

In the last three decades, the overall macro-economic policy regime and associated development agenda in the global economy has seen a significant shift. There has been a shift of productive base to the large developing countries for new markets and cheap labour. The developing countries with a keen interest to place their economies in the higher value-adding work in the global production network, have joined the competition to attract private foreign capital, and the erstwhile *dirigiste* regime has been broken down in many of them. The dominant prescription has been to rely on free market forces, with an increasing reorientation of the role of the state in economic affairs. The expectation associated to it is that the private capital will raise the economic activity and help generate employment and contribute to development as a whole via a "trickle down" process, and the State whose economic control and intervention crowds out the private players can now concentrate in providing better infrastructure for business and deliver social justice enabled by the money coming as a result of the higher growth rate.

In this context, the BRICS nations – Brazil, Russia, India, China and South Africa (which became member of the group in 2011) – drew global attention as the new drivers of growth, especially after showing signs of early recovery in the aftermath of the global financial crisis in 2007-2008. The acronym was originally coined as BRICs by Jim O'Neill of Goldman and Sachs in 2001.[1] This was followed by a defining report from the same

---

1 Jim O'Neill 2001, "Building Better Global Economic BRICs", Global Economics Paper n. 66, Goldman Sachs, 30 November, <http://www.goldmansachs.com/our-thinking/topics/brics/brics-reports-pdfs/build-better-brics.pdf>.

organisation which argued that large emerging economies such as Brazil, Russia, India and China have a growth potential that can replace the traditional European economy in terms of market size, and that China would replace the US as the leader of the global economy by 2050.[2]

Yet, there were skeptics, at the time the first BRICs summit was staged in 2009. Apart from the fast growing economy and large population, the regional alliance shared no significant regional, cultural or political basis for an alliance. But the perception that these countries had been able to bear the economic shocks helped the idea of BRICs to gain acceptance. In 2011, South Africa joined the group and it came to be known as BRICS. Recently the "currency crisis" and the falling growth rates have raised serious questions regarding the fundamentals of apparent economic success of many of these countries, including India.

This paper argues that the neoliberal growth strategy followed by these countries is not the solution to the problems of unemployment, poverty, regional disparity and inequality. Rather, the nature of accumulation in these economies tends to put pressure on a whole range of basic well-being indicators of the masses, like mean years of schooling, life expectancy, inequality index, hunger index, poverty and malnutrition, etc. In other words, obsession for growth and market fundamentalism, i.e., "let the market operate properly and it will take care of all problems" kind of approach, has taken hold of the development agenda across developing countries, with equity, employment, and socio-economic inclusion and justice taking a backseat. And, this kind of exclusionary growth makes the base of seemingly economic success fragile.

The *first section* of this paper locates BRICS within the changing global economic and geo-political context, with a survey of their current economic performance and importance in the global economy, particularly after the economic crisis and we provide a sketch of their respective development paths in a historical perspective and their present strategies, as in how they

---

2 Wilson and Purushothaman, 2003

confront their constraints and possibilities. The *second and third section* lay focus on the basic priorities that BRICS, and in particular India, should address. It is argued that the present growth strategy taken by these countries cannot respond to these priorities. In the *final section* we assess the ability of the BRICS together with developing countries within the G-20 major economies to defend an alternative development strategy against the global hegemonic order, in order to secure the greater well-being of the masses. They themselves could be co-opted in the hegemonic order, otherwise.

The paper largely draws on secondary literature and data sources. All the tables are put in the appendix.

BRICS IN THE CONTEMPORARY GLOBAL ECONOMY

At least 43% of the world's population lives in the five BRICS nations.[3] They also account for 17% of global trade and about 25% of global GDP computed on the basis of purchasing power parity (that takes the costs of living into account when computing GDP).[4] At this rate, they currently generate almost half of the growth of the world economy and accounts for more than one third of global foreign reserve.[5]

The BRICS have undergone major institutional transitions and changes in their economic structure since the Second World War. The governments in most of these countries entered this period with fresh waves of social revolution or national independence and a very clear awareness of a need to catch up. Post-war policies involved state-led growth fuelled by ambitious multi-year industrialisation plans with varying degrees of success. All development plans were centrally planned with the economic approach decidedly inward in

---

3 BBC NEWS Business, 26 March, 2013, <http://www.bbc.co.uk/news/business-21923874>.

4 Ibid.

5 Foreign Policy, November 2012, <http://www.foreignpolicy.com/articles/2012/10/8/think_again_the_brics>.

orientation. State intervention was considerable up till the 1980s in Brazil and China and the 1990s in Russia and India. All have now moved in favour of freeing market actors and reducing the role of the state.

Let us take a look at the respective economies under BRICS. Brazil has one of the most advanced industrial sectors in Latin America. The country's diverse industries which include automobiles and parts, machinery and equipment, textiles, shoes, cement, computers, aircraft, and consumer durables account for roughly one-third of its GDP. Brazil is also a major world supplier of commodities and natural resources. Russia, far away across the Atlantic Ocean and at the further end of Europe, is rebuilding its economy after almost a decade of turbulence since the collapse of the Soviet Union in 1991. This is on the back of significant natural resources, a pool of skilled labour, and other important prerequisites to sustain its economic growth. To come home to India: the country has sustained a high and accelerating rate of growth over the past 25 years. According to official figures, real GDP growth has accelerated from around 3.5% per annum in the 1960s and 1970s to average annual rates of 5.4% in the 1980s, 6.3% in the decade starting 1992-1993 and around 9% since 2003 up to 2007-2008. The global economic crisis affected India but the growth rate was maintained at 6.7% in 2008-2009, 8.4% in 2009-2010 and came down to 6.5% in 2010-2011.[6] China became the second largest economy in the world in 2010 overtaking Japan. By maintaining the Yuan at a low exchange rate the country attracted impressive foreign investment(171 bill. USD in 2008, 131 bill. USD in 2009, 243 bill. USD in 2010, 223 bill. USD in 2011)[7] and maintained impressive economic growth rates – 13% in 2007; 9% in 2009; 10.5% in 2010 – challenging the economic crisis.[8] Since China's growth is primarily export-led, the global slowdown and reduction in demand in the US economy, has forced a rethinking of its growth strategy. South Africa, in the period of 2003-2008, has experienced

---

6   <http://data.worldbank.org/country/india>.

7   <http://data.worldbank.org/indicator/BX.KLT.DINV.CD.WD>.

8   <http://data.worldbank.org/country/china>.

consistent growth (3.5% in 2004, 4.9% in 2005, 5% in 2006, 5.1% in 2007, 3.1% in 2008)[9] and its increasing economic and geo-political significance in the African region brought it in the ambit of BRICS.

In contrast to China and Russia, which experience a current account surplus due to high exports of commodities and natural resources respectively, India's economic growth has been supported by strong capital imports. Consequently, India currently shows a current account deficit – a clear sign of total imports having exceeded exports. With such capital inflows, which mainly consist of portfolio investments, there is always the risk that investors may suddenly withdraw their capital. For this reason economic development which is mainly based on foreign capital inflow is considered as risky in the long run.

Besides India, Brazil and South Africa have also shown long periods of current account deficits. In Brazil, the booming domestic demand is the main reason for strong imports. In South Africa, current account deficits are also a result of regional integration contracts, which force countries like Namibia to invest a considerable part of their own current account surplus – and thus their domestic savings in the neighbouring country.[10]

All these countries accelerated their growth rate by taking advantage of the rising global demand before the global economic crisis. Even so, in a scenario when global demand is stunted, the desirable path for the countries following a development strategy based on external demand – particularly China and Russia – would be to make a transition to a growth path based on domestic income growth and consumption through diversification of markets and production.[11] In other words, it would be correct to continue the transformation from export-led to domestic demand-led growth in economies.

Significantly, there has been growing co-operation within the BRICS itself, and with other developing countries. Though the $ 230 billion

---

9   <http://www.indexmundi.com/g/g.aspx?c=sf&v=66>.

10 Schrooten, 2011

11 Kregel, 2009.

trade that the BRICS now have among themselves is still a small fraction of their overall trade, the amount is growing fast, at the rate of 28% in 2011,[12] which is more than the rate of growth of world trade. For some of these countries neither the United States nor the European Union is their largest trading partners any longer.

The prevalent growth patterns among BRICS are also becoming interdependent. China is responsible both for the reduction of prices on labour-intensive manufactured goods which affect producers in other developing nations including the other BRICS nations. The country's growth has also fuelled increased commodity demand. It has been responsible for the rise of relative prices of many commodities that stimulate the demand for raw materials and energy in other parts of the developing world. India's growth, as well, has had a major influence on the price increase for specific commodities, especially petroleum. For instance, the relative strength achieved in the last few years of the Brazilian trade balance is almost totally explained by the effects of the Chinese demand for such commodities. The complex interdependences of a globalized economy make the multilateral trading system even more important. South Africa, with its membership of BRICS is now the gateway to the African continent for China and India.

THE COLLECTIVE POSSIBILITIES AND CHALLENGES IN FRONT OF BRICS TO ADDRESS ISSUES OF SOCIO-ECONOMIC DEVELOPMENT:

In the last decade, as developing countries have grown in influence on the global stage, a number of alliances have come up within themselves. This is reflected in terms of growing South-South trade, technology transfer and increased bargaining power of the developing countries in global platforms on climate change, food security and agricultural trade. Yet, apart from

---

12 <http://www.southafrica.info/global/brics/ndp-250313.htm>.

exchanging information, discovering common needs and interests and collective bargaining in international platforms, concrete outcomes of these alliances have been limited. With the global economic crisis allowing the emerging economies to gain leverage internationally, the BRICS emerges as an alliance which has potential. After the global financial meltdown there is now scope for these countries to push for a new financial architecture. The first BRICs summit, with Brazil, Russia, India, China as participants, took place on 16 June 2009, in the midst of the global economic crisis, in Yekaterinburg, Russia. The second BRICs summit was held on 15 April 2010 in Brasilia, Brazil. The third summit took place in Sanya in Hainan island, China on 14 April 2011 where South Africa joined the group. The fourth summit was held in New Delhi, India on 28 March 2012. The last one took place in Durban, South Africa on 27 March 2013.

The latest summits indicate the continued promise and possibilities of the BRICS grouping. In the last summit in Durban, South Africa, the idea of a $ 100 billion reserve Development Bank to provide a safety net to BRICS nations was developed. In the fourth summit, trade in local currencies, which was current between China and Brazil as also China and Russia, was widened to include all the countries constituting BRICS. At New Delhi, two agreements on financial cooperation were signed: a master agreement on extending credit facilities in the local currencies of the five members, and a BRICS multilateral letter of credit confirmation facility agreement.[13] The stage for BRICS cooperation had been set at the third BRICS summit. The "Sanya Declaration" section 15 states, "the governing structure of the international financial institutions should reflect the changes in the world economy, increasing the voice and representation of emerging economies and developing countries". During the New Delhi summit, this position was reiterated. The slow pace of quota and governance reforms at the International Monetary Fund (IMF) was noted and the BRICS called for the candidature of the World Bank's President's post from developing countries.

---

13   <http://www.bricsindia.in/delhi-declaration.html>.

The group also decided to explore the possibility of establishing a Development Bank "for mobilising resources for infrastructure and sustainable development projects in BRICS and other emerging economies and developing countries, to supplement the existing efforts of multilateral and regional financial institutions for global growth and development", with China expected to take a lead. If these initiatives are carried forward, then the monetary and financial architecture can facilitate a mechanism to finance imports to other developing countries including low-income countries (LICs) and deliver a market for them. This will also provide an alternative to the harsh conditions of structural adjustment to get money from the dominant financial institutions.

The BRICS has an important role to play on agricultural issues and food security. At the Delhi summit in 2012 they reiterated their task ahead "for the successful conclusion of the Doha Round, based on the progress made and in keeping with its mandate". The Doha Round, which began in 2001 under the aegis of the World Trade Organisation aims to lower trade barriers around the world, which will facilitate the increase of global Earlier, at a meeting on 26 March 2010, agriculture ministers of BRICS countries agreed to cooperate on food security, to set up a database on demand and consumption of food, to share experience in management and distribution of food stocks to vulnerable populations, to set up climate change adaptation regimes and to develop technological innovation for agriculture.[14] In a Joint Declaration of the Second Meeting of BRICS Ministers of Agriculture and Agrarian Development in Chengdu, China, 30 October 2011, they adopted a plan to set up the "BRICS Strategic Alliance for Agricultural Research and Technology Cooperation" to take joint initiative for technological innovation in agriculture, and work on an "Action Plan 2012-2016" for Agricultural Cooperation of BRICS countries, which identified five priority areas and direction of cooperation. Each area would be coordinated by a BRICS member. At

---

14 Dubochet, 2011.

the Delhi summit, food security of Africa's low-income countries was also discussed. This indicates an important focus for the future, greater cooperation with the African continent. Other important areas have also been taken up in the various summits: climate change, "green economy" and "sustainable agriculture".

The BRICS can gain most as a group by addressing internal challenges of public policy such as poverty and inequality and the agrarian crisis, by strengthening social infrastructure, and balancing regional disparities while they all try to maintain growth and stability.

Though Brazil still has quite a high gini coefficient – an index of inequality of income and wealth – its efforts to reduce inequality and emphasis on social infrastructure has been an important lesson for other BRICS countries facing similar problems. Similarly, India's experience in poverty reduction has been claimed as positive. In the case of China, the legal right of people in villages of "access to land" has been an important social security factor. The stability of the Chinese economy during the global financial meltdown has been of influence. The experience of Development Banks in China or Brazil also provides important lessons for other countries.

Still there are criticisms that BRICS needs to address. As discussed earlier the growth strategy needs to shift from an export-led mechanism to a domestic consumption-based system. On another count, trade among these countries is essentially corporate-driven and it gradually seems to be replicating the same problems that North-South trade had for the well-being of the masses in the developing bloc.

It becomes important how these countries define "development" for themselves. Merely splitting the agenda of "growth" and "development", depending on corporate-led growth in the capitalist segment or a "bubble" like real-estate boom or IT boom, and "managing" the crisis elsewhere in the economy cannot be a proper foundation of a pro-poor growth agenda. The much-discussed issues of "sustainable agriculture", "green economy" or renewable energy remain sub-ordinate to the priority on "growth".

It also becomes important how these countries look at extraction and use of global natural resources and the resulting ecological constraints. A report by The Worldwatch Institute (2006) highlights that if China and India, to say nothing about Russia and Brazil, were to consume resources and produce pollution at the current US per capita level, it would require two planet Earths just to sustain their two economies.[15] The solution, therefore, is not for emerging economies to try to copy the lifestyles of advanced capitalism, but rather for advanced capitalist countries to reduce their own levels of consumption and waste generation.

VARIOUS HUMAN DEVELOPMENT INDICATORS AND THE BRICS: A SNAPSHOT

All countries constituting BRICS seek to present themselves as powerful players in front of the global community. China spent 40 billion dollars in 2008 to organize the Olympics. Russia plans to spend 51 billion dollars for the Winter Olympics in 2014. Brazil is preparing for a similar show for the Football World Cup in 2014 and the Olympics in 2016. India and South Africa also spent huge for Commonwealth Games and the Football World Cup respectively in the recent past. The number of billionaires coming from BRICS has soared in the last decade. According to a report published by Wealth-X in February 2013, there are 49 billionaires (the figure was 18 in 2010 according to the Forbes list) from Brazil (globally 9th position) with a total wealth of 300 billion dollars. 97 billionaires (compared to 62 in 2010) come from Russia (6th position) with a total wealth of 380 billion dollars. India provides 109 billionaires (5th position) with a total wealth of 190 billion dollars. The number was 49 in 2010 as per the Forbes list. China occupies the 2nd position with 147 billionaires (the figure was 64 in 2010) with a total wealth of 380 billion dollars.[16]

---

15 Singh, Pritam. (2008).

16 The World Ultra Wealth Report 2012-2013

On the other hand, all BRICS economies have low per-capita incomes (except Russia), economic backwardness, a large informal sector, unemployment, inequality, and poverty even as the growth process is unable to respond positively to these problems. This is mirrored by the position of these countries in terms of the human development index (HDI) and similar development indicators. For example, the HDI rank has progressively fallen between 1991 and 2011 for all countries. In spite of economic growth, the mass of the population in the five countries have low purchasing power and suffer from poverty, illiteracy, low life expectancy (Tables 4, 5, 6, 7 and 8 in the Appendix).

India is estimated to have a third of world's poor, and hunger is a serious issue. The GHI (Global Hunger Index) for India in 2011, on a scale of 100 is calculated at 23.7, considered alarming. The figures for China have seen a better progression though the GHI index of 5.5 in 2011 indicates that hunger has not been eradicated (Table 8).

Poverty has been a serious concern for both these countries. An official estimate for China shows that nearly 16% of the total population was below the poverty line (less than $ 1.25 per day), and in 2009 almost 36% of total population earned less than $ 2 per day. Though the official data show a decline in poverty, as in 2012 according to the rural poverty line of annual per capita net income below 2300 yuan (2010 constant prices) the population in poverty in rural areas numbered 99.98 million, or 23.39 million less than that in the end of 2011,[17] the methodology is debated, as the declining per capita consumption of food grains raises concern. Still, the rural-urban divide is in increase; according to China's National Bureau of Statistics, the urban per capita annual income in 2009 (US$ 2,525) was approximately three times that of rural per capita annual income, being the widest income gap recorded since 1978. In the case of India on the basis of new methodology to estimate poverty proposed by Tendulkar Committee

---

17   National Bureau of Statistics of China, <http://www.stats.gov.cn/english/newsandcomingevents/ t20130222_402874607.htm>.

Report in 2009, nearly 37.2% of the population can be said to be below the poverty line by the criterion of consumption.[18]

In Brazil, though there has been a decline in inequality, the overall level does remain high. Though in recent years the official data have shown a decline in inequality, it still has a high GINI coefficient (0.543 in 2009 compared with 0.596 in 2001. Due to an expansion of export-driven agriculture and consequently a high land ownership concentration and high rural-urban divide, income disparity has been a longstanding problem. According to the 2010 census, 25% of the population still lives on an average per capita monthly income of up to R$ 188 (about $ 95), and half the population of up to R$ 375 (about $ 190), compared to the minimum wage of R$ 510 (about $ 258) in 2010.[19]

In China, India and South Africa, the per capita income in urban areas rose higher in comparison to rural counterparts (Brazil is the only exception here).[20] In China, the spatial inequality in terms of resources and services grew rapidly because of the differences within provinces. The rural-urban inequality index, as measured by Kanbur and Zhang, increases from 65.1 in 1994 to 66.9 in 1998 to 72.0 in 2004; the inland coastal inequality index increases from 5.9 in 1994 to 9.4 in 1998 to 11.6 in 2004.[21] The unequal access to health and education for urban migrants and rural population reinforced the process of unequal distribution of wealth. The so-called hukou system targeted mainly the urban permanent population. In the recent past, the social security in rural areas seems to have improved. In India, the fruits of growth are mainly concentrated in the richer states and urban centres, while the poorest and most populous states have increasingly lagged behind, reinforcing spatial inequality. In

---

18   The Indian Express, 9 December 2009, <http:www.indianexpress.com/news/37.2-of-india-is-in-poverty-by-criterion-of-consumption/551849/>.

19   Daily Maverick, 15 August 2012, <http://www.dailymaverick.co.za/article/2012-08-15-brazil-and-south-africa-united-in-inequality>.

20   OECD (2011):"Divided We Stand: Why Inequality Keeps Rising".

21   Gajwani, Kanbur and Zhang (2006).

terms of per capita nominal GDP in the financial year 2011-2012, it was Rs 1,75,812 for Delhi, Rs 108,859 for Haryana, Rs 101,314 for Maharashtra, and Rs 23,435 for Bihar, Rs 30,051 for Uttar Pradesh, Rs 35,652 for Jharkhand, whereas average per capita income in India was Rs 61,564.[22] In South Africa, the inequality in a way also reflects the inequality between races – Africans, Coloureds, Asians and the Whites. The national survey data from 1993, 2000 and 2008 show that South Africa's high aggregate level of income inequality increased between 1993 and 2008 and the same is true of inequality within each of South Africa's four major racial groups.[23] South Africa in spite of decent growth rate has a very high gini coefficient of 0.631 in 2012, or almost one-fourth of its population as unemployed.[24] In terms of widespread informal economic relation, India is ahead of all these countries, followed by Brazil, South Africa and then China, Russia.[25] Russia also has regional disparities, which has increased since transition started in 1990s. Western regions have urban concentrations, Eastern regions have de-population and the rural regions faraway from urban centres are starved of resources.[26]

The present growth trajectory has led to an economy split between the beneficiaries, the "emerging middle class", and the losers, the latter outnumbering the former. How has this come about?

Over the last few decades, the global economy has changed significantly –finance capital has come to dominate over the real economy, global production has travelled to places with cheap labour, with the reduction of the bargaining power of labour vis-a-vis capital, primitive accumulation through a resource grab having become a major tendency in the accumulation of capital. Development under neo-liberal capitalism is characterised by

---

22 Released by Planning Commission, Government of India for the year 2011-2012.

23 Leibbrandt, M., et al. (2010).

24 <http://www.housingfinanceafrica.org/country/south-africa>.

25 OECD (2011):"Divided We Stand: Why Inequality Keeps Rising".

26 Benini and Czyzewski (2007).

dominating market forces as the prime mover of generating growth with the state taking the position of a spectator.

How has this come about? To draw investment, to present itself as a lucrative destination of capital or to remain "competitive" in the export market, the economies have heavily depended on their cheap labour, which has whittled down the bargaining power of labour against capital. The informalisation and contractualisation of the labour markets have become dominant phenomena in production. The reservoir of unemployed labour and the huge informal sector has put pressure on the wage rate in the formal sector and helped keep the real wage low.

In a scenario where resources are the last frontier of growth, there is a continuous flow of resources from the non-capitalist segment of the economy to the wheels of capitalist production for keeping the return to capital high. Thus impoverishes the huge non-capitalist segment of its natural resources like water, minerals, etc. In parallel, food production globally being limited as food also becomes increasingly a commodity traded on the international market, to feed the "first world" the per capita food grain consumption falls, and this lower demand is ensured by the fall of purchasing power due to deflationary measures. The cumulative effect: regional disparity, inequality, unemployment and thus a site of poverty in these economies.

For pro-poor growth, sufficient emphasis should be laid upon a different set of sectoral issues, where incremental improvement impacts the well being of the people significantly, generates employment and thus plays a crucial role to address poverty or inequality, which is not possible in spite of high growth in real estate or advanced manufacturing. The role of the state in terms of priority lending, public infrastructure in agriculture, strengthening of development banks to boost the purchasing power of a large mass of the people are some of the important measures in this respect.

SOCIAL JUSTICE AND INCLUSION: CHALLENGES AND PRIORITIES FOR INDIA

The boom in the Indian economy since the turn of the Millennium has been fundamentally dependent upon greater global integration which has also made the growth process more uneven and vulnerable to internal and external crises. As Chandrasekhar and Ghosh (2007, 2009) argue, recent growth was the result of financial deregulation that sparked off a retail credit boom combined with fiscal concessions to spur consumption among the richest quintile of the population and the rise in private corporate investment. This led to rapid increases in aggregate GDP growth, even as deflationary fiscal policies, poor employment generation and persistent agrarian crisis reduced wage shares in national income and kept mass consumption demand low. The pre-reforms emphasis on public spending as the principal stimulus for growth was thus substituted in the 1990s with debt-financed housing investment and private consumption of the elite and "new" middle classes, and the private corporate investment. The Indian growth story in its essentials was therefore not unlike the story of speculative bubble-led expansion that marked the experience of several other developed and developing countries in the same period.

During the reform period, the tertiary (or service) sector has seen rapid expansion, but growth of commodity producing sectors, in particular, agriculture and large segments of small-scale manufacturing has seen a sharp dip. Total capital formation in agriculture continues to suffer since sharply reducing public investment is not being compensated by rising private investment. There is no economic rationale for believing that "public investment crowds out private investment", which is the common deflationist argument for reducing the state's role in rural development. Precisely the contrary has been shown to hold for certain types of investment essential for an irrigation-dependent agriculture like India's.[27] The growth process

---

27 Patnaik, Utsa,2007

is periodically coming under pressure on account of inflation, fed largely by supply bottlenecks from this sector.

Another major problem for Indian economy: there has been no effective generation of employment in the capital-intensive formal sector manufacturing. As agriculture shows signs of stagnation in absorbing labour, the surplus population is joining the informal sector economy. The growth of the formal sector has failed to generate employment and absorb labour from the informal sector. Unemployment, under-employment or self-employment of a huge mass of people has been a site of poverty and malnutrition.

During the period of economic reforms there has been a marked increase in the share of informal employment in Indian economy.[28] India is ranked just 134 in the HDI. Due to gradual retreat of the state from health or education, these sectors are in bad shape[29] (Table 9 in the appendix shows the share of health and education in the GDP of India, and compares it to other BRICS nations, and India fares poorest in this respect). As mentioned earlier, the GHI or proportion of undernourished in the population remains alarming for India throughout the last two decades. 43% of Indian Children under five are underweight, compared to only 4% in China and 2% in Brazil. Half of the Indian household lack lavatories, compared to 1% in China. As we discussed earlier, in terms of absolute poverty reduction, India is in a sorry state, whereas in recent past China and Brazil have taken significant steps forward in this direction.

In terms of per capita food grain consumption, India faces a precarious situation. In the year 2012, food grain output touched a record 252 million tons. The economic survey in 2012 shows that per capita food grain availability rose from 468.7 grams per day (GPD) in 1961 to 510.1 GPD in 1991 and then fell to 438.6 GPD in 2011. Pulses availability has also come down from 69.0 GPD in 1961 to 31.6 GPD in 2011. The decline

---

28 NCEUS report: "The Challenge of Employment in India – An Informal Economy Perspective", vol. 1 (April, 2009).

29 See Jha and Negre (2007) to have a detailed discussion on indicators of development deficits for India related to these two sectors for the reform period.

in food grain availability is confirmed by another data source – the food grain intake data from consumption surveys of NSSO, which show that per capita, per month consumption of cereals in rural areas declined from 13.4 kg per month in 1993–1994 to 11.35 kg per month in 2009–2010 and from 10.60 kg per month in 1993–1994 to 9.37 kg per month in 2009–2010 in urban areas. Pulses consumption declined from 0.84 kg per month in 1999–2000 to 0.65 kg per month in 2009–2010 in rural areas and from 1 kg per month in 1999–2000 to 0.79 kg per month in 2009–2010 in urban areas. Calorie intake figures from the same consumption surveys corroborate these findings and point to the secular decline over the years.

But what comes out from the recent data is the extent of decline in calorie intake during 2005–2010, the highest in any five–year period. Per capita calorie intake in rural areas was 2,266 in 1972–1973, 2,149 in 1999–2000, 2,047 in 2004–2005 and 1,929 in 2009–2010 on comparable basis. Calorie intake in urban areas was 2,107 in 1972–1973, 2,156 in 1999–2000, 2,020 in 2004–2005 and 1,908 in 2009–2010. That is, while calorie intake declined by 117 calories per capita between 1972–1973 and 1999–2000 in rural areas, it fell by 220 calories per capita in the last 10 years. In urban areas calorie intake rose by 49 calories in the first 27 years, and fell by 248 calories in the last 10 years. The trend in protein intake was similar with protein intake in rural areas declining from 60.2 GPD in 1993–1994 to 55.0 GPD in 2009–2010 and declining in urban areas from 57.2 GPD in 1993–1994 to 53.5 GPD in 2009–2010.[30] This alarming situation is often avoided by the Indian policymakers attributing to various reasons like diversification of consumption, etc., while Table 8 in the Appendix shows the extent of hunger prevalent in India compared to other countries.

If we compare the tax–GDP ratio of the various countries constituting BRICS, India is in the worst position with 15.5% in 2013. Even among the G-20 nations, India has the third lowest tax base, after Mexico and

---

30 <http://www.livemint.com/Opinion/Xm4DKDFTlHGrk5roPIsgVI/A-consumption-puzzle-in-India.html>.

Indonesia. Even the major share of it is indirect tax. The 37.7% share of direct taxes to India's total taxes was lower and regressive compared to developing countries such as South Africa (57.5%) and Russia (41.3%). The tax–GDP ratio for Brazil is now 36% and it had a steady growth since the past three decades (in 1994 it was 28.4%, in 2000 it was 31.9%, in 2005 it was 34.1%).[31] It has enabled the Brazilian Government to implement various social development schemes even within the compulsions of a neo-liberal framework. The annual growth rate of Brazilian minimum wage has been above the annual inflation rate since 2000. The minimum wage increased by 238% from BRL 151 in 2000 to BRL 510 in 2010, in 2012 it was BRL 622 and in 2013 it became BRL 674.96.[32] In the case of India, the real wage has stagnated for the last few decades. Even the conditions which should be considered while deciding minimum wage are not addressed by the government. The declared criteria according to the Minimum Wages Act, 1948 were:

1. The total expenditure of the worker and three dependants on him/her.
2. 2700 Kcal food for each everyday.
3. 72 gauge garment in a year.
4. Average room rent in that area or state.
5. 20% of the minimum wage for fuel, electricity, etc.
6. 25% of the minimum wage for education, health, recreation, old age expenditure, etc.

According to these criteria, the minimum wage required to live a life turns out to be around Rs 10,000–12,000 a month. But the actual

---

31 "The Political Economy of Tax: Class Coalitions and political institutions in Brazil", Aaron Schneider, 2013

32 <http://blog.securities.com/2011/06/brazil%E2%80%99s-minimum-wage-increased-twice-first-five-months-2011/>.
<http://riotimesonline.com/brazil-news/rio-politics/brazil-to-increase-2013-minimum-wage/#>.

minimum wage in India is around Rs 5000-7000 a month at present. At a time when the major employment generation in even the formal sector is of informal nature with a salary around minimum wages, and the expanding informal sector can hardly provide money more than that, the large working masses do not get any fruit of growth "trickled down" to them and are bound to suffer from poverty, malnutrition, lack of health facilities, education, social and job securities. And, they are evidently excluded in the process of growth and development. In recent times, as the growth rate of India has come down around 5% and the economy faces a sharp fall of value of Rupee vis-à-vis Dollar amounting to higher import prices for petroleum and other imports leading to higher inflation, the government, with low tax-GDP ratio resulting in huge fiscal deficit, and such a lesser share of spending for the health or education sector, can provide even a lesser amount of its income for human development, inclusion or social justice.

In this context, to give a narrow focus on growth is deeply problematic. The situation calls for larger responsibility of the state to take a proactive role to invest in agricultural infrastructure, to ensure universal food security and access to health and education, to generate real employment, etc., in order to increase the purchasing power of the people and to regenerate growth on internal demand when the effects of the global crisis are far from over. In recent times, to address the crisis the Indian Government has announced a number of social security schemes like MNREGA (Mahatma Gandhi National Rural Employment Guarantee Act 2005, to provide 100 days of work a year to combat rural unemployment, generated as a result of the crisis in Indian agriculture), RTE (Right to Education Act 2009, to expand the scope of child literacy), NRHM (National Rural Health Mission, 2005) and this year Food Security Bill to provide food and nutritional security by providing food items at cheap rates to two-third of population of India. But in almost all cases the government failed to have an infrastructural support and will to implement these on the ground level. The universal PDS system, which could have played a key role to provide food and nutritional security, is in a process of withdrawal.

CONCLUSION

As this paper argues, the growth strategy currently pursued cannot respond well to the problems of poverty, inequality, unemployment or regional backwardness of these large economies. The global economic crisis has exposed the myth of market fundamentalism quite sharply and has also brought back the role of the state in the economic discourse. The global slowdown also has created the condition for these countries to focus on their internal market, to increase the purchasing power of the masses, to create a foundation for a sustainable growth and development embracing the society as a whole.

Towards this end, the BRICS countries need to have a constructive engagement with other developing countries in G-20, so as to push for an alternative development agenda against the hitherto hegemonic global order. Their interventions on issues like the Doha Round negotiations or world peace in the context of Libya have been positive in this direction. On a whole set of other policy issues such as opposition to FTT (Financial Transaction Tax) or Tobin Tax, the resistance to total capital account convertibility, the role of BRICS in defense of the interests of the developing countries has become important. This is not just in the short run but aimed at the global financial architecture and economic order and larger development issues in the future. The difference of BRICS from other erstwhile formations like IBSA is, BRICS is a market-driven formation and not bound by any treaty. IBSA took up the issues of development fund to address issues of poverty, development and participation. But for BRICS there is a danger of becoming the elite G-5 of the global South.

However, the simultaneous Indian and Chinese expansionism in Africa to capture land and resources, the continuing anti-labour policies of the ruling elite of these countries in collaboration with global capital raises fears that they may get co-opted in the hegemonic order as the junior partners. Thus, for some people the prominence of BRICS may ultimately lead to a situation where the interest of the ruling elites dominates over the broader interest of developing countries. However, many others positively believe that in the present context when the global economic and geopolitical order seems to be in a transition, the role of the BRICS countries has been more important to ensure the well being of the distressed masses of their own country and to defend the interest of the developing countries against the hegemony to a decisive extent and the growth of the BRICS economies can be beneficial for the growth and development of global south, including Sub-Saharan African countries.

APPENDIX

Table 1   Different indicators of BRICS in the period 2000–2010

	Brazil	Russia	India	China	South Africa
GDP in PPP in Billions US$					
2010	2172	2223	4060	10090	524
2000	1130	1120	2200	4500	369
GDP per capita in PPP in US$					
2010	10800	15900	3500	7600	10700
2000	7400	7700	2200	3600	8500
GDP growth rate in real terms (%)					
2010	7.5	4.0	7.5	10.4	2.8
2000	4.2	3.2	6.0	8.0	3.0

Source: <http://www.indexmundi.com>.

Table 2   Real GDP of BRICS as a percentage of
           global GDP at various time points

	1990	2000	2010
Brazil	1.98	1.94	2.15
Russia	2.79	1.43	1.78
India	1.15	1.49	2.44
China	1.74	3.58	7.55
South Africa	0.57	0.52	0.57
BRICS total	8.23	9.96	14.49

Source: United States Department of Agriculture (USDA), 2012.

Table 3   Export and Share in Global Export for
           BRICS (in thousand million US$)

	Export in 2000	Share in global export in 2000	Export in 2010	Share in global export in 2010
India	44	0.69%	331	2.1%
China	213	3.3%	1274	8.4%
Brazil	57	0.89%	185	1.2%
Russia	42	0.65%	225	1.5%
South Africa	27	0.42%	87	0.57%
BRICS Total	383	5.95%	2102	13.77%

Source: UNCTAD STAT.

Table 4 Some Indicators of BRICS countries at various time points

	Human development index (HDI)	Life expectancy at birth	Mean years of schooling	Expected years of schooling	MMR	Under five (< 5) mortality (per 1000 live births)	National poverty line (%)	Gross national income (GNI) per capita (constant 2005PPP \$)	Per zapita GDP (PPP \$)
1990									
Brazil	0.600		4						4078 (1995 US\$)
China	0.490		5.9						349 (1995 US\$)
India	0.410		4.1						331 (1995 US\$)
Russia	NA		NA						3668 (1995 US\$)
South Africa	0.616		5.4						4113 (1995 US\$)

	Human development index (HDI)	Life expectancy at birth	Mean years of schooling	Expected years of schooling	MMR	Under five (< 5) mortality (per 1000 live births)	National poverty line (%)	Gross national income (GNI) per capita (constant 2005PPP $)	Per zapita GDP (PPP $)
2000									
Brazil	0.665	67.7	4.9			38	17.4 (1987–2000)		7625
China	0.588	70.5	6.4			40			3976
India	0.461	63.3	NA			96			2358
Russia	0.691	66.1	5.1			22			8,377
South Africa	0.615	52.1	6.1			70			9401

Recent values of indicators(in 2010)

	Human development index (HDI)	Life expectancy at birth	Mean years of schooling	Expected years of schooling	MMR	Under five (< 5) mortality (per 1000 live births)	National poverty line (%)	Gross national income (GNI) per capita (constant 2005PPP $)	Per zapita GDP (PPP $)
Brazil	0.718	73.5	7.2	13.8	58 (in 2008)	21 (in 2009)	21.4 (2000–2009)	10,162	10367 (2009)
China	0.687	73.5	7.5	11.6	38 (in 2008)	19 (in 2009)	2.8 (2000–2009)	7,476	6828 (2009)
India	0.547	65.4	4.4	10.3	230 (in 2008)	66 (in 2009)	27.5 (2000–2009)	3,468	3296 (2009)
Russia	0.755	68.8	9.8	14.1	39 (in 2008)	12 (in 2009)	11.1 (2000–2009)	14,561	18932 (2009)
South Africa	0.619	52.8	8.5	13.1	410 (in 2008)	62 (in 2009)	23.0 (2000–2009)	9,469	10278 (2009)

Source: Human Development Reports, UNDP, different year.

Table 5   Different human development indicators for BRICS, year 1991

	Brazil	Russia	India	China	South Africa
HDI	0.759	0.908	0.308	0.614	0.766
HDI rank	60	31	123	82	57
Life expectancy at birth	65.6	70.6	59.1	70.1	61.7
Adult literacy rate(%)	78.5	99	44.1	68.2	85
GDP per capita in PPP (US$ 1985-1988)	4620	6270	870	2470	5480
Mean year of schooling	3.3	7.6	2.2	4.8	3.7

Source: Human Development Report, 1991.

Table 6   Different human development indicators for BRICS, year 2002

	Brazil	Russia	India	China	South Africa
HDI	0.757	–	0.577	0.726	0.695
HDI rank	73	60	124	96	107
Life Expectancy at birth	67.7	66.1	63.3	70.5	52.1
Education index	0.83	0.92	0.57	0.80	0.88
GDP per capita in PPP (US$ 2000)	7625	8377	2358	3976	9401

Source: Human Development Report, 2002.

Table 7   Different human development indicators for BRICS, year 2011

	Brazil	Russia	India	China	South Africa
HDI rank	84 (85 in 2012)	66 (55 in 2012)	134 (136 in 2012)	101 (101 in 2012)	123 (121 in 2012)
Life expectancy at birth	73.5	68.8	65.4	73.5	52.8
Education index	0.663	0.784	0.450	0.623	0.705
Inequality adjusted HDI	0.519	0.67	0.392	0.534	–
Multidimensional poverty index	0.011	0.005	0.283	0.056	0.057
Gender inequality index	0.449 (0.447 in 2012, rank 85)	0.338 (0.312 in 2012, rank 51)	0.617 (0.610 in 2012, rank 132)	0.209 (0.213 in 2012, rank 35)	0.490 (0.462 in 2012, rank 90)

Source: Human Development Report, 2011– 2012.

Table 8   Global hunger index

	1990	1996	2001	2011	2012
Brazil	7.6	6.2	5.3	<5	<5
Russia	–	<5	<5	<5	<5
India	30.4	22.9	24.1	23.7	22.9
China	11.7	9.1	6.8	5.5	5.1
South Africa	7.0	6.5	7.4	6.4	5.8

Source: Global Hunger Index 2011, IFPRI, Welt Hunger Hilfe and Concern Worldwide.

The Index combines three equally weighted indicators into one score: the proportion of people who are undernourished, the proportion of children under five who are underweight, and the under-five child mortality rate. An increase in a country's GHI score indicates that the hunger situation is worsening, while a decrease in the score indicates an improvement in the country's hunger situation.

Table 9   Proportion of undernourished people in the population (%)
(average value of three consecutive years
has been taken as each entry)

	1990–1992	1995–1997	2000–2002	2005–2007
Brazil	11	10	9	6
Russia	–	4	3	1
India	20	17	19	21
China	18	12	10	10
South Africa	5	5	4	4

Source: Global Hunger Index 2011, IFPRI, Welt Hunger Hilfe and Concern Worldwide.

Table-10   GDP and its shares in different sectors

Countries	GDP in 2011 (2005 ppp $ billion)	GDP per capita in 2011 (2005 ppp $)	Spending on health (% of GDP)	Spending on education (% of GDP)	Spending on military (% of GDP)
Brazil	2021.3	10,278	2.9 (2000) 4.2 (2010)	4.0 ('00) 5.7 ('10)	1.8 ('00) 1.6 ('10)
Russia	2101.8	14,808	3.2(2000), 3.2 (2010)	2.9 ('00) 4.1 ('10)	3.7 ('00) 3.9 ('10)

Countries	GDP in 2011 (2005 ppp $ billion)	GDP per capita in 2011 (2005 ppp $)	Spending on health (% of GDP)	Spending on education (% of GDP)	Spending on military (% of GDP)
India	3976	3203	1.3 ('00) 1.2 ('10)	4.4 ('00) 3.1 ('10)	3.1 ('00) 2.7 ('10)
China	9970.6	7418	1.8 ('00) 2.7 ('10)	... ...	1.9 ('00) 2.1 ('10)
South Africa	489.6	9678	3.4 ('00) 3.9 ('10)	5.6 ('00) 6.0 ('10)	1.5 ('00) 1.3 ('10)

Source: Global Hunger Index 2013, IFPRI, Welt Hunger Hilfe and Concern Worldwide.

REFERENCES

BARACYHY, B. (2012), "The Geopolitics of Mutilateralism: The WTO Doha Round Deadlock, the BRICs, and the Challenges of Institutionalized Power Transition", in *CRP Working Paper*, n. 4.

BENINI, R., CZYZEWSKI, A. (2007), *Regional Disparities and Economic Growth in Russia: New Growth Patterns and Catching Up*. Springer.

BRICS Joint Statistical Publication. (2011).

EPW. (2011), "Defending Mutual Interests: The Sanya Declaration Shows That BRICS is Slowly Getting its Act Together to Defend Mutual Interests", in *Economic and Political Weekly Editorial*, April 30, 2011.

FERRARI-FILHO, F., Spanakos, A. (2009), "Why Economic Performance Has Differed Between Brazil and China: A Comparative Analysis of Brazilian and Chinese Macroeconomic Policy", in *Revista Venezolana de Analisis de Coyuntura*.

GADY, C. G., Ickes, B. W. (2010), "Russia after the Global Financial Crisis", in *Eurasian Geography and Economics*, 51(3).

GAJWANI, K., Kanbur, R. and Zhang, X. (2006), "Comparing the Evolution of Spatial Inequality in China and India: A Fifty Year Perspective", in *DSGD Discussion Paper*, n. 44, IFPRI.

GHOSH, J. (2012), "Using the Potential of BRICS Financial Co-operation", in *Frontline*, 7th, April 2012.

GHOSH, J., CHANDRASEKHAR, C. P. (2007), "Recent Employment Trends in India and China: An Unfortunate Convergence?", in *ICSSR-IHD-CASS Seminar Paper*.

_____. (2009), "The Costs of 'Coupling': The Global Crisis and the Indian Economy", in *Cambridge Journal of Economics*.

GHOSH, J., MAVLIK, P., et al. (2009), "Models of BRIC's Economic Development and Challenges for EU Competitiveness", in *WIIW Research Reports*, n. 359. <http://www.bricsindia.in>.

JHA, P. S. (2012), "Delhi Could Be A Turning Point", in *The Hindu*, 10 April 2012.

JHA, P., NEGRE, M. (2007), *Indian Economy at Sixty: Prospects and the Key Challenges at the Current Juncture*, <http://www.macroscan.org>.

KREGEL, J. (2009), "The Global Crisis and the Implications for the Developing Countries and the BRICs: Is the B Really Justified?", in *The Levy Economics Institute of Bard College, Public Policy Brief*.

KUBONIWA, M. (2011), "Impact of Trading Gains on Economic Growth in BRICs for 1995-2010: Some Lessons from BRICs", in *RRC Working Paper*, Series n. 31.

KUMAR, R. (2012), "BRICS can provide a fall-back option", in *Asia Weekly*, 6-12 April 2012.

LEIBBRANDT, M., et al. (2010), "Trends in South African Income Distribution and Poverty since the Fall of Apertheid", in *OECD Social, Employment and Migration Working Papers*, n. 101, OECD Publishing.

MAY, P. H. (2008), "Overcoming Contradictions Between Growth and Sustainability: Institutional Innovation in the BRICS", in *EN Working Paper*.

OECD. (2011), "Divided We Stand: Why Inequality Keeps Rising", in *OECD Publication*, December 2011.

_____. (2012), "Looking to 2060: A Global Vision of Long-term Growth", in *OECD Economics Department Policy Notes*, n. 15, November 2012.

PATNAIK, P. (2011), "Economic Growth and Employment", in *Economic and Political Weekly*, June 25, 2011.

PATNAIK, U. (2007), "Neoliberalism and Rural Poverty in India", in *Economic and Political Weekly*, July 28, 2007.

PATNAIK, U., Natarajanm, S. (2000), "Output and Employment in Rural China: Some Post-reform Problems", in *Economic and Political Weekly*, September 16, 2000.

PRABHAKAR, A. C. (2011), "An Overview of the New Emerging Balance of Forces – The BRICS, G20 and G7: Response to the Global Financial Crisis", in *Asian Economic and Financial Review*, 1(2), p. 67-82.

SCHROOTEN, M. (2011), "Brazil, Russia, India, China and South Africa: Strong Economic Growth – Major Challenges", in *DIW Economic Bulletin*, 4, 2011.

SEKINE, E. (2011), "The Impact of the 3rd BRICS Summit", in *Nomura Journal of Capital Markets*, 3(1).

SHAW, T. M., et al. (2007), "Global and/or Regional Development at the Start of the 21st Century? China, India and (South) Africa", in *Third World Quarterly*, 28(7).

SINGH, P. (2008), "Contemporary Global Capitalism: Multi-pronged Crises", in *Economic and Political Weekly*, October 11, 2008.

The Worldwatch Institute, Annual Report. (2006), <http://www.worldwatch.org>.

WILSON, D., PURUSHOTHAMAN, R. (2003), "Dreaming with BRICs: The Path to 2050", in *Emerging Economies and Transformation of International Business, (2006) edited by Subhash C. Jain, Edward Elgar Publishing Limited.*

Income security systems in comparative perspective

Brazil and South Africa

Maria Paula Gomes dos Santos

Abstract   Despite the similarities between Brazil and South Africa, in respect to economic development and social investment by the State, among others, each of these countries has had different achievements regarding poverty and inequality reduction in the last 15 years. While Brazil succeeded in reducing poverty by 44%, and inequality by 0,059 points of Gini, between 1995 and 2009, South Africa's reduction rates for both indicators have been less expressive: poverty ratios were reduced by 14,8%, while inequality increased by 0,03 points of Gini, between 1993 and 2008 (LEIBBRANDT, et al., 2009: 20, 23). In view of that, this study investigates possible determinants of such disparities.

Based on secondary data, and on other authors´ findings about the effects of social protection on poverty and inequality in both countries, the paper examines the hypothesis that the differences observed between them has to do with the absence in South Africa of a mandatory, broad and public social security system, which might protect active workers from the risk of not being able to work for a wage.

The paper initially presents a review of South African and Brazilian social protection history, followed by a summarized description of each income security system´s framework. Some comparative findings are presented in the last section, leading to the conclusion that, more important than the existence (or not) of wide social security schemes, the distinctive results of these countries, regarding poverty and inequality reduction, are related to the differences in their labour markets performance.

Keywords Social protection, Social security, compared social policies.

SECTION I: INTRODUCTION: BUILDING THE STUDY HYPOTHESIS:

In spite of the many similarities that can be found between Brazil and South Africa – including the presence in both countries of huge social assistance systems – each of these countries has had different achievements regarding poverty and inequality reduction in the last 15 years. While Brazil succeeded in reducing poverty by 44%, and inequality by 0,059 points of Gini, between 1995 and 2009,[1] South Africa's reduction rates for both indicators have been less expressive. Between 1993 and 2008, while poverty ratios were reduced by 14,8%, inequality increased by 0,03 points of Gini (LEIBBRANT, et al., 2009: 20,23).

The importance of social grants for poverty reduction is indisputable in the two cases. In Brazil, according to Soares (2013), if all government transfers were removed from their recipients overnight, 27,7% of the country's population (about 30 million people) would fall beneath the poverty line of PPPD$ 1,25 per day. Applying the same exercise for South Africa, Woolard, et al., (2010) argue that *"grant income does not change the* (poverty) *headcount measure (p0) substantially. However, when the depth (p1) and severity (p2) of poverty measures are used, then poverty is seen to improve markedly due to government grants"*.[2]

---

1   Considering a poverty line of PPP$ 1,25 per day.

2   Woolard, et al., 2010, p. 28.

In view of that, it becomes relevant to investigate what are the differences between these two countries that account for such disparities. This paper is an attempt to explore possible explanations.

Similarities between Brazil and South Africa appear, among other things, in the pace of their recent growth cycle; in the value of their respective GDPs per capita; in their exclusionary development history; and in the great amount of public resources they both spend in social protection since the mid 90's (Table 1). On that decade, South Africa and Brazil underwent political transitions to democracy, which involved national commitments with social transformations towards more inclusive societies. To pursue that, expansion of Social Protection systems has been strategic in both cases, particularly when it comes to income security benefits.

Table 1   South Africa and Brazil: some similarities

Year	As of	South Africa	Brazil
Population (min)	2011	51,2	194,93
GPD per capita, PPP	2012	11.375	11.875
Average growth rate (1994–2010)		3,49%	3,51
Social Assistance Expenditure (PPP)	2009/2010	13.859.315	14.057.824
Social assistance beneficiaries	2010	13.859.770	66.900.00(*)
% pop		27%	34,00%
Social Assistance Expenditure (% GPD)	2010	3,50%	1,00%

(*) The Bolsa Familia Program benefited 12,7 million families in 2010. Here, an estimate of total beneficiaries is shown, considering 5 persons per family on average.
Source: Quandl dataset, available at <http://www.quandl.com>.

In this paper, *income security benefits* are those which protect people's income either when they cannot work, or when their income is not enough to keep them out of extreme poverty. These benefits can be contributory, such as unemployment insurance and retirement pensions; or non-contributory, like social assistance grants. As mentioned before, income security provisions were importantly extended in both countries since the mid 90´s, and have played significant roles against poverty, although results have been far less spectacular for South Africa than for Brazil.

What, then, makes for this distinction between the two countries?

When looking at each of their income security systems, some differences appear, beyond their commonalities. Table 2 presents the benefits' baskets offered in Brazil and South Africa – contributory and noncontributory – as well as the amount of benefits paid as a share of total population in 2010. Some distinctive features can then be noticed, such as the share of benefited persons of noncontributory benefits in the total population; the extension of population covered by private pension schemes; but especially, the absence, in South Africa, of a statutory national security arrangement.

According to different studies about Brazil,[3] Social Security benefits has been pointed at as one of the most significant variable in determining poverty reduction, in the last growth cycle (2004-2010). By decomposing the effects of all kinds of cash benefits of the Brazilian income security system on poverty, Soares (2013) found that the country´s 27,7% poverty rate is reduced to 17,3% when Social Security benefits are added, while the addition of the non-contributory Social Assistance grants (Old Age and Disability Grant, altogether with the Family Grant/Bolsa Familia), would make an additional reduction of only 2,8%. According to this author,

> [...] the effect of Social Insurance on poverty reduction of those (at) 60 or more is much greater than the effect of any other transfer for any other age group. It brings poverty rates from over 60% to less than 5%".[4]

---

3   Soares, 2013; IPEA, 2009 – Comunicado 63; IPEA 2012, Comunicado 155.

4   Soares (2013).

Table 2 Brazil and South Africa: income security systems and benefits paid as a share of total population

| | Brazil | | South Africa | |
| | Contributory | | | |
Item	% pop.	Item	% pop.	
Unemployment Insurance (public) Job loss; Workers rescued from slave labour	3,8 (2010)	UIF – Unemployment Insurance Fund (public) Job loss; Illness; Maternity;	0,40 (2009/2010)	
		Compensation Fund – workers injured at work (public) Work accidents Occupational diseases Dependent's pension	0,45 (2009/2010)	
Social Security (Public) Retirement pension (old age, invalidity, occupational diseases) Dependent's pension	70 (insured) 12,5 (received benefits in decem/2010)			
Aids (Illness, Maternity, Work accidents, Occupational diseases, Imprisonment)				

	Brazil	South Africa
Contributory		
Social Security (Private)	1,66	Social Security (Private Pensions and provident funds) — 11,7
Retirement pension	(2010)	Retirement pensions
Dependent's pension		Dependent's pension — (2007/2008)

	Brazil	South Africa
Non-contributory	% pop.	% pop.
Old Age Pension	0,83	4,86
Disability Grant	0,91	2,54
Child Support grant		18,32
Family grant (Bolsa Familia)(*)	32,58	
Foster care grant		1,35
Other (RMV)	0,15%	
Total	**34,48**	**27,07**

Sources: Republic of South Africa: *Budget Review*, 2012.
Brazil: For Social Security benefits, MPS – Social Security's Estatistical Bulletin 2010 (BEPS); For Social Assistance Benefits, MDS – Ministry of Social Development; For Unemployment Insurance Benefits, IPEA. For Private Pensions (Brazil and South Africa):Towers Watson & Co., 2012
★ Data about Bolsa Familia recipients were estimated considering official data of 12,7 million families, multiplied by 5 members.

Soares (op cit) also shows that Social Security benefits reduce poverty of other age groups than the elders, especially of youngest living in households with retired people.[5] In turn, the Brazilian non contributory grant for elders and people with disabilities[6] – the brazilian Old age and Disability Grant – is totally irrelevant for all but their direct beneficiaries; Bolsa Família (the Family Grant), in turn, reduces poverty by 3% to 4%, mostly among children and those at the ages of 25 to 40 (their parents, presumably).

With these information in mind, the main hypothesis of this study was set, which is:

In developing countries undergoing economic growth, poverty and inequalities can be faster and more significantly reduced if these countries count on broad, public and mandatory social security arrangements in their social protection system.

To test the adherence of this hypothesis, the paper brings in secondary information from recent studies about Brazil and South Africa,[7] which focus on each country's income security system, and their effects on poverty and inequality reduction. The comparison follows the strategy named by Przeworsky and Teune (1982/1970) as *Most similar systems,* which starts from the similarities between countries to explore their differences. To do that, the paper will develop through more three main sections. Sections II and III will sketch relevant information about South Africa (II) and Brazil (III) development history and their respective income security systems. Each of these sections ends with a review of different author's analysis about the system's impacts on poverty and inequality. Section IV compares the two countries and ends with final remarks.

---

5   Poverty defined by household per capita income.

6   Granted to those below the poverty line of ¼ of the minimum wage per month per capita, a value close to the poverty line of less than PPP$ 1,25 per day.

7   Leibbrandt, Woolard, et al., (2009); Leibbrandt, Finn, Argent and Woolard (2010a); Leibbrandt, Woolard, et al., (2010b), Woolard and Leibbrandt (2010); van der Berg, Burger, Burger, Louw and Yu (2005).

SECTION II: SOUTH AFRICA

While boasting its continent's most affluent economy, South Africa has historically been characterized by high levels of poverty and social inequality, thanks to the peculiarities of its colonization process and to the apartheid regime that marked its history. It was only when the African National Congress (ANC) took office in 1994 that South Africa would truly deinstitutionalize the traditional ethnic and racial cleavages that had long prevailed in the country. Notwithstanding, South Africa would herald the arrival of the twenty-first century with an enormous social debt, particularly in relation to those that represent its original inhabitants – the black Africans.

To pay this debt, the country has undertaken significant efforts since the end of the *apartheid*, particularly through income security devices made of non-contributory monetary transfers, focused on the poorer and more vulnerable segments of the population. In 2010, around 30% of the South-African people (14 million) received some kind of cash transfer, especially children, people with disabilities and elderly in poverty.[8] The effects of these transfers have been positively evaluated by observers. Nevertheless, poverty and inequality have persisted, especially within the African population.[9] In fact, income inequality, as measured by the Gini coefficient, has increased since the beginning of the ANC government, rising from 0.67 to 0.70 between 1993 and 2008, while poverty rates were only slightly reduced (Table 3).

---

8   People living with less than US$ 1,25 per day – the World Bank poverty line.

9   During the apartheid regime, South African population was classified under different racial groups: white, coloured, Asian, Indian and African (black). Despite this classification is no more used for civil purposes, it is still adopted in demographic analysis

Table 3   South Africa: inequality and poverty evolution

Year	Gini coefficient	Poverty (*)
1993	0,67	20,7
2000	0,67	16,8
2005	0,72	16,8
2008	0,70	17,7
1993-2008 Mean variation	3,1	-14,8

(*) % of the population subsisting on US$ 1,25 per day.
Source: Leibbrandt, et al., (2009), p. 19. With data from the PSLSD (1993); IES (2000, 2005) and NIDS (2008).

Evolution of social protection in South Africa

Non-contributory grants were first used in South Africa in the period between the 1st and 2nd World Wars, because of economic recession that affected this country. In 1928, social pensions were given to those elderly in poverty that were not covered by private contributory social security pensions. Following the racial divide then imposed to society,[10] these pensions were unequally distributed among racial groups, so that Africans were only entitled if they were blind.

In 1992, on the eve of the apartheid's collapse, the "Social Assistance Act" ended all pre-existing racial discrimination in social grants. Therefore, all social aid and subsidies were gradually expanded to all South Africans, on more egalitarian criteria. According to Lund (1993),

---

10 The apartheid regime had classified the country's population according to racial criteria, being them: whites, coloured, asian, indian and africans, the letter meaning the black people, who could be both the original south african inhabitants and immigrants from other African countries. For most of the apartheid era, Africans were the less entitled population.

> This made the South African system an example of a system with extraordinarily ample coverage, when compared to those systems found in other developing countries (LUND, 1993: 22).

During the political transition, other benefits were added to expand coverage to different vulnerable groups. Among these, the Disability Grant stands out as the only one intended for adults in active age. This grant was focused on disabled people and those with chronic diseases, between 18 and 60 years of age.[11] At the end of the 90s, the number of disabled beneficiaries had increased significantly. Beyond that, benefits' values were equaled for all racial groups (WOOLARD, et al., 2010: 8).

The transition government also instituted three other benefits: the *Foster Care Grant*, for children adopted by court order; the *Care Dependency Grant*, conceded to children with serious disabilities, as to require full-time care; and the *State Maintenance Grant*, given either to the father, the mother, or the tutor of children under 18, who fulfilled any of the following conditions: if their father/mother/tutor were single, widowed or separated; if one of the parents were abandoned by the other for more than six months; if the children caregiver received some kind of social grant; or if one of the parents were imprisoned or interred for drug rehabilitation for more than six months. Another condition for the children's single parent to take up the grant was to prove his/her effort to get money from the other parent. Besides that, children under the care of adults who weren't their biological parents, or who were born out of a wedlock, were not entitled to the benefit. These restrictions prevented many African children from having access to the grant.

After taking office in 1994, the ANC recognized that the widespread access to the State Maintenance Grant would lead to increasing fiscal cost. On the other hand, the grant seemed inadequate for South Africa, since it took for granted that the only children in need were those that lived without one of their parents – and this did not the country's reality. Therefore, in

---

11   Those at 60 and older were eligible for an Old Age pension.

1995, the government appointed the Lund Committee in order to evaluate the State Maintenance Grant and to propose reforms.

The committee recommended the substitution of the State Maintenance Grant for another benefit to be given to every child in poverty, between 0 and 7 years old, regardless of his/her family arrangement. The new benefit would have a smaller value, but in turn it would reach a greater population. Thus appeared the Child Support Grant (CSG), which was introduced on April of 1998, paying around R100 (One hundred South African Rands, approximately 37 dollars PPP) per month to every child aged 7 or less.

As a condition to receive the aid, applicants had to pass through a means test, besides demonstrating efforts to obtain the desired income from other sources. However, the rigorous enforcement of these conditions prevented many children to be eligible by then. One year after its inception, the CSG has been taken by only 20.000 children, a small number when compared to the estimated eligible population (at over 5 million). Therefore, the government changed the calculus´ formula of the applicant's income, while removing some conditions to the families – such as immunization requirements and participation in development programs – after recognizing the latter a further discrimination against children who lived in places with poor public services.[12]

Around the year 2000, the Child Support Grant (CSG) was extended to children up to 14 years of age, doubling its coverage. By 2003, 2.6 million children received the grant, and by 2010, all children born after 1996, eligible by income, were entitled to the CSG until the age of 18.

In 2000, as the Taylor Committee was appointed to propose new improvements in the South African social protection system, a conclusion was reached that, despite the substantial range of both the Old Age and the Child Support Grants, the gap in social protection for the active-aged population was clearly growing. After showing that all the grants

---

12 It's worth noting that public health services in South Africa are considered to be low quality, and their coverage, especially in rural areas, is very limited.

taken up did not cover more than 60% of the poor population, the Taylor Committee recommended the creation of the **Basic Income Grant (BIG)**, conceived to be universal, in order to guarantee a safety net to all South Africans. Estimates indicated that this new grant would be help to take 6.3 million people out of poverty. The government, however, didn't accept the recommendation, due to its estimated fiscal costs.[13]

The South-African income security system's structure

When evaluated on the basis of its public expenditure, the South African income security system is quite wide in scope. It comprehends contributory and non-contributory benefits, but the latter predominate. This section will present all the monetary benefits that have been offered in the country. The first subsection addresses the contributory benefits, while the second addresses non-contributory income security devices.

Contributory benefits

The South African State offers two types of statutory benefits attached to formal employment: the Unemployment Insurance Fund (UIF) and the Compensation Fund. Both are contributory and backed by their own funds. The Unemployment Insurance Fund (UIF) offers short-term protection for workers in the formal sector, covering unemployment, illness, maternity, child adoption and the death of the insured person (paying aids to his/hers dependents). Benefits are paid for a maximum of 238 days, and only in the period immediately after the loss of the job. The UI Fund is financed by contributions coming from workers and employers, amounting 1% of both the workers' wages and the employers' payroll. Domestic workers were added to the program in 2003.

---

13 According to Triegaardt (2008), ILO research (Research Review on Social Security Reform and the Basic Income Grant) had shown that the grant would be financially viable, in addition to promoting poverty reduction, economic increase and greater job offer (SAMSON, 2002: 32). Differently, Van der Berg & Bredenkamp (2002: 40) had the opinion that benefits wide range like the BIG would certainly face fiscal and administrative restrictions (see TRIEGAARDT, 2008).

The Compensation Fund is aimed at occupational health, and provides medical assistance and monetary benefits in face of work-related accidents and occupational diseases. This fund is also financed by workers and employers, and its coverage is restricted to formal workers.

As mentioned, the country has no statutory social security arrangement for retirement or survivals. Workers may contribute to private pension plans, which can be sponsored by the employing companies, with bipartite funding (employers and employees). Most of these funds offer defined contribution plans. However, companies are not statutorily obliged to support pension funds to their workforce, although they must include all their workers, once they decide to do so. Workers not covered by company's retirement pension plans can purchase them individually in the market place.

As estimated, South African private pensions industry is one of the greatest in the world, when assets are concerned Its assets represented 64% of the country's GDP in 2012.[14] Membership is estimated in 6 million people, although the number of purchased plans amounts to 9,4 million.[15] Anyway, total coverage is significant, having reached almost 12% of the population at that year.

Analysts have pointed many pitfalls in theses retirement protection schemes, however.[16] The gap between the number of employed workers and those who effectively contribute to pensions schemes is very high: according to estimates, it can be around 5.4 million people. As a result, the majority of retired workers depend on social assistance. On the other hand, while very substantial contributions are made to the funds, the final amount of benefits to be withdrawn tends to be low, due to high administration costs, and most of the pensions do not replace the wage earnings properly, despite the subsidies received by pension funds. Finally,

---

14   Towers Watson. Assets estimated as of 31/12/2012 and include only assets from closed entities.

15   The number of purchased plans are bigger because some members contribute to more than one plan, leading to double counting. *Republic of South Africa, 2010 Budget Review.*

16   See "Pension Funds On Line". Available at: <http://www.pensionfundsonline.co.uk/country-profiles/south-africa/98>. And *Republic of South Africa, Department of Social Development – Reform of Retirement Provisions Discussion Document, 2007*

many workers withdraw their savings long before retirement because of long term unemployment.[17]

In view of that, South African government has been discussing, since 2007, the creation of a mandatory, public and state-owned National Social Security Fund, financed by contributions levied on workers' payrolls.[18] The system's framework should be *"anchored around three pillars, being, first, a non-contributory system of social assistance, providing a safety net for the most vulnerable; second, a mandatory contributory system of social insurance covering all income earners and, third, a voluntary scheme in terms of which all are free to purchase additional cover"*.[19] This reform, however, has not been decided until 2013, when this study was completed. Table 4 synthesizes the South African income security contributory benefits, also showing the total number of beneficiaries.

The impressive short coverage of both the Unemployment Insurance and the Compensation Fund is mostly explained by the country's low employment rates, since only workers in formal jobs are entitled to these benefits. Unemployment in South Africa has been very high for a long time. It reached 29% of the active population in 2003 (narrow definition[20]) and still affected 25,5% in 2010,[21] much of it being long-term unemployment. As

---

17 Republic of South Africa. Department of Social Development/Reform of Retirement Provisions Discussion Document, 2007.

18 In order to create a single institution that offered retirement and risk benefits, the Taylor Committee had suggested the creation of this fund in 2002, foreseen the consolidation of the various guaranteed income funds – the Unemployment Insurance Fund, the Compensation Fund (for work-related accidents) and the Road Accident Fund.

19 Idem, op. cit., p. 5. Note that the system described follows the prescriptions of the World Bank, as put in the documents *Averting the old age crisis: policies to protect the old and promote growth* (1994) and *Coverage, The Scope of Protection in Retirement Income Systems*, World Bank Pension Reform Primer, 2005.

20 Narrow (Official) – Number of people who were without work in the week preceding the interview have taken active steps to look for work and were available for work. Broad (unofficial) – Number of people who were without work in the week preceding the interview and were available for work

21 If the broad definition is adopted, unemployment rates reach 39% in 2003 and 36% in 2010. Rep. of South Africa, Performance Indicators, 2012

a matter of fact, overall labour force participation rates in South Africa are low (55%) by international standards. As stated by Leibbrandt, et al., (2009), even informal jobs are unable to absorb the labour force supply. In 2008, only 26,2% of the workforce was engaged in these jobs. (LEIBBRANDT, et al., 2009: 9).

Table 4   South Africa: South Africa – contributory statutory benefits

Benefits	As for	Beneficiaries
Unemployment Insurance Fund	2009/2010	
Recipients/month		207.967
Compensation Fund	2009/2010	
Claims registered		234.266
Pension and Provident Funds	2007/2008	**9.412.169**
Active members		7.273.897
Pensioners		2.138.272

Source: Republic of South Africa: *Budget Review*, 2010.

When racial divides are considered, it becomes clear that unemployment, informal occupation and low wages are more prevalent among the African population than for any other group. According to Leibbrandt, et al., (2009), this is a legacy of the apartheid regime, when African workforce was segregated and *"confined to tribal homelands" and urban townships* (op. cit., p. 10). In addition, the quality of education for African communities had been much inferior than that offered to other groups, especially to the white population.

Figure 1   South Africa: unemployment rates: 2002–2010

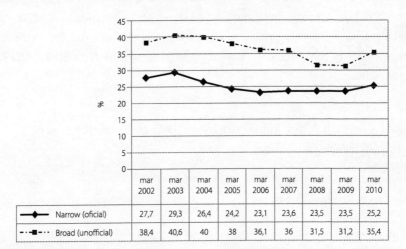

	mar 2002	mar 2003	mar 2004	mar 2005	mar 2006	mar 2007	mar 2008	mar 2009	mar 2010
◆ Narrow (oficial)	27,7	29,3	26,4	24,2	23,1	23,6	23,5	23,5	25,2
■ Broad (unofficial)	38,4	40,6	40	38	36,1	36	31,5	31,2	35,4

Source: Statistics of South Africa. Quarterly Labour Force Surveys.
Definitions: Narrow (official) – Number of people who were without work in the week preceding the interview have taken active steps to look for work and were available for work.
Broad (unofficial) – Number of people who were without work in the week preceding the interview and were available for work.

Non-contributory benefits

The non-contributory income security subsystem in South Africa is much bigger than its contributory counterpart, considering both coverage and expenditure. Benefits are administered by the South African Social Security Agency (SASSA), and are given mainly to children, elders and people with disabilities.

Financial support for children involves three different grants. The Child Support Grant is given to children up to 18 years of age who live with guardians subsisting with low incomes; the Foster Care Grant (FCG) addresses children adopted by court order; and the Care Dependency Grant (CDG) is provided to those who intensively take care of disabled children up to 18 years of age.

The State Old Age Pension (SOAP) is paid to the low-income elderly over 60; and the Disability Grant (DG) is offered to persons with disabilities at the age of 18 or older, be them temporarily or permanently unable to work. In 2009/2010, 14 million people (out of a population of 50 million) were receiving social grants in South Africa.

Table 5   South Africa Social grants: 2009-2010

Grant type	Beneficiaries N	Spending ($ PPP)
Old age pension	2.490.000	5.243.182
Disability grant	1.299.000	2.946.329
Child	9.381.000	4.768.007
Other	689.770	1.002.797
Total	13.859.770	13.960.315

Source: Republic of South Africal, National Treassury, 2012.
Conversion to PPP$ by the author.

The Child Support Grant's main objective is to guarantee income for children in poverty; therefore its provision is based on a means test. Concerning the sheer number of beneficiaries, this aid represents South Africa's largest unconditional income transfer program. Despite being the lowest valued of all state transfers, it makes for 40% of the income of the poorest families, on average; and for around 5% of the whole population's income (see UNICEF, 2008a).

The Foster Care Grant (FCG) is paid to children up to 18, who are not taken care by their biological parents, and then live with foster families, by judiciary decision. This criteria includes orphans, as well as children that have been abused, and those that have problems with the law. The benefit wasn't conceived to fight poverty, and therefore doesn't require any means test, except when the concerned child has an independent income. The benefit has a value many times greater than that of the CSG. Finally, the Care Dependency Grant is given to children from 1 to 18 who suffer from serious functional disabilities, and then require intensive full-time care.

The State also offers the State Old Age Pension for the poor elders that don't count on retirement pensions. So, eligibility to this grant also depends on a means test. Its value is the same of the Disability Grant, both being the highest valued among all the social assistance benefits, and capable of reducing poverty substantially. Beneficiaries of the Disability Grant also have to go through a means test, which assesses family income, as well as the applicant's inability to generate his/her own income. Permanently disabled people are eligible to receive permanent benefits, while those who are expected to recover from transitory diseases receive temporary benefits during a short period.

Impacts of the South-African income security system on poverty and inequality

Research on the evolution of poverty and income inequality in South Africa has shown controversial results, especially when income measures are used (LEIBBRANDT, et al., 2010). Essential issues in this particular debate are indicated in the literature, which will be presented below.

Income inequality, as measured by the Gini coefficient, has always been high in South Africa by international standards. According to different studies, inequality has even increased since the end of the apartheid regime, being associated with the rise of **intra**-racial inequality, which has dominated the previous **inter**racial inequality. As shown in Table 6, income inequalities among the whites were the lowest between 1993 and 2008, while the largest rates were found among the African population.

According to Leibbrandt, et al., (2010), the decrease in intra-racial inequality can be partly explained by the significant rise in the Gini coefficient of the Africans that occurred after 1994. Somehow, the Black Economic Empowerment program – introduced in 2003 to allow the upward mobility of the Africans – has contributed for this increase. On the other hand, the African population has grown faster than other groups. Between 1970 and 2001, the share of Africans in the total population rose from 70% to 80%, while the percentage of whites fell from 17% to 9%. According to Van der Berg and Louw (2004):

The increase in the black population's per capita income over the last three decades, along with the decrease in the interracial income difference during the same period, increased inequality within the black population and seems to have impeded any significant decline in the country's total inequality.[22]

To Leibbrandt, et al., (2010), this dynamic wasn't unexpected, and it was not even undesired, since it was a result of South Africa's democratization. However, the "reconciliation" pact that commanded the democratic transition in South Africa made it difficult to alter the initial asset distribution among racial groups let by the apartheid regime, what prevented, for instance, a better distribution of land among racial groups.

Table 6   South Africa: Gini of the aggregate per capita income, by racial group

Year	Aggregate	Africans	Coloured	Indians/Asians	Whites
1993	0,67	0,55	0,43	0,46	0,42
2001	0,67	0,61	0,53	0,50	0,47
2005	0,72	0,62	0,60	0,58	0,51
2008	0,70	0,62	0,54	0,61	0,50

Source: PSLSD (1993); IES (2000, 2005); NIDS (2008) apud Leibbrandt, Woolard, et al., 2009, p. 19.

The determinants of South Africa's income inequality have been investigated by some studies[23] which decomposed income sources into four categories:

---

22   Van der Berg and Louw, 2004, p. 568-569. Free translation.

23   Shorrocks (1984), Leibbrandt, et al., 2000, Bhorat, et al., 2000, Leibbrandt, et al., 2009.

work income (including those which originate from self-employment); social welfare income (the country's many grants); remittances[24] and capital income (such as dividends, interest, rental incomes, income generated by not having to pay rent, private retirement pension plans). These studies indicate that work income is by far the most dominant category among household incomes, counting for 78.8% of all incomes earned by South African families in 2008, and for 85% of the total income Gini (Table 7). These figures evince the great concentration of work income, which is confirmed by the comparison between its concentration coefficient (0,7) and the total income Gini index (0,65).

The high correlation between work incomes and total family income (correlation rate of over 0.9) indicates that, among households, the insertion of a family into a certain income distribution class (quintiles or deciles) is strongly determined by its insertion into the work income distribution. Therefore, this income source is the main determinant of total income inequality. On the other hand, social assistance transfers, which make for 8% of the total household income, and contributes with 0,27% for the income Gini, prove to be highly progressive, with its concentration coefficient of 0,02 being quite lower than the total income Gini index of 0,65. From the different studies one can conclude that, whatever data sources are used, income inequalities increased in South Africa, from the 1990's to the 2000's. However, it can also be argued that social assistance transfers have had an important role not only in fighting poverty, but in softening income inequality in the country.

In order to better understand inequality among family's per capita income, Leibbrandt, et al., (2009), tested the influence of three factors: the composition of the family (the number of people at working age); access to jobs; and wage inequality. The study showed that this kind of inequality is mostly caused by differences in both access to jobs and

---

24 Generally sent by migrant workers to their families, who still reside in the workers' places of origin.

access to good earnings, but not by the number of working members in the family.[25] The expressive contribution of the work income to the aggregate income Gini is explained not only by high income differentials among workers, but also by the differences between those who have a job, and those who don't.

Table 7   South Africa: decomposition of income by sources and their contribution to inequality, 2008

Income source	% Share in total income	Gini for income source for all households receiving such income	Gini correlation with total income rankings	Concentration coeficient	Contribution to Gini	% Share in ocerall Gini
Labour market	78,8	0,74	0,95	0,70	0,55	84,90
State transfers	7,9	0,73	0,003	0,02	0,00	0,27
Capital income	7,9	0,97	0,83	0,81	0,006	9,75
Remittances	5,4	0,96	0,64	0,61	0,03	5,08
Total	100	0,65			0,65	100

Source: Data from the National Income D Survey, South Africa, 2008.
Elaboration: Leonardo Rangel (IPEA), adapted from Leibbrandt, et al., 2010, p. 35.

On the other hand, impacts of state transfers on income inequality have been practically negligible, even though these transfers account for

---

25 Op. cit.

8% of the country's total income. This is due to the transfer's low Gini coefficients, and also to their strict application range among the income distribution classes. As seen on Table 8, the highest valued grants (the Old Age Pension and the Disability Grant) are mainly concentrated in the 2nd and 3rd quintiles, which shows that they alone are able to move benefited families out of the 1st quintile. However, the children grants (especially the broad-scoped Child Support Grant) don't have this power, because of their low values. Many families who receive the CSG remain in the 1st quintile.

Table 8   Percentile of beneficiaries´ households, by type of grant and quintile, 2008

Quintile	% of grants for children	% of disability grants	% of old age pensions
1	55.8%	5.7%	9.8%
2	57.9%	10.9%	27.1%
3	45.4%	14.7%	23.5%
4	26.5%	9.9%	17.7%
5	9.0%	2.8%	5.0%
All	33.6%	8.2%	15.3%

Source: National Income Dynamics Study, 2008. Apud Leibbrandt, et al., 2010.

Taking into account what has been seen so far, one can come to the conclusion that the high (and still rising) income inequality among South Africans derives primarily from the differences in work incomes. These predominate over other interracial inequalities, even though the African population is still the group mostly affected by unemployment and low wages. In face of this, it seems that social assistance benefits have not been capable of changing radically the legacy of South African inequalities.

Evolution of poverty rates in South Africa is even more controversial than inequality (LEIBBRANDT, et al., 2010). Some studies found evidence of poverty increase in the period between 1994 and 2000.[26] Others[27] indicate decrease or stabilization of poverty after 2000. To Van der Berg, et al., (2007), the incidence of poverty rose between 1993 and 2000, and then underwent a sharp decrease between 2000 and 2004. These authors repeated the same exercise in 2008, finding similar trends. Poverty rates found in the latter were: 50.1% in 1993; 51.7% in 1995; 50.8% in 2000 and 46.5% in 2004. On the other hand, per capita income among individuals in the two poorest quintiles of the income distribution rose more than 30% between 2000 and 2004.[28]

Studies also point that poverty incidence among racial groups has remained unaltered. According to Leibbrandt, et al., (2010), for any given poverty line, the Africans show the largest share of poor individuals (95%). They are followed by the coloured (around 4%) and other groups (whites and Asian/Indians), with 1% or less. Nevertheless, the *per capita* income of the Africans has grown significantly from 42% of the whites' income in 1993, to 60% of the whites' income in 2008, Table 9). Leibbrandt, et al., (2010: 13), argue that even though the magnitude of income increases may be debatable, poverty rates decreased between 2000 and 2004, due to social grants.

Woolard, et al., (2010), have investigated the impact of social grants on poverty looking at the evolution of these grants distribution among household income quintiles, between 1997 and 2008 (Table 9).

As shown by Table 9, in 1997 the largest concentration of grants' beneficiaries was in the 2nd quintile, in view of the higher values of the Old Age Pension and the Disability Grant. As already mentioned, these

---

26 Hoogeveen & Ozler (2006), *apud* Leibbrandt, M., et al., (2010).

27 See UNDP (2004), Van der Berg & Louw (2004) and Van der Berg, et al., (2006).

28 Adopting a poverty line of R250 per capita per month, which amounts to around PPP$ 36/ per month.

grants' value is enough to take most of the benefited households from the first quintile (except for large families). Since 2002, the share of benefited families in the 1st quintile rose, because of the rapid implementation of the Child Support Grant (started in 2000). Since its value is low, it does not allow for a drastic reduction of poverty of its beneficiaries. However, it is worth noting that during this whole period, the percentile of granted households in the lower quintile rose from 16% to 64%.

Table 9   South Africa: households receiving social grants, by income quintiles, 1997-2008

Quintile	1997	2002	2003	2004	2005	2006	2008
1	15.9	32.0	31.7	40.2	47.7	69.4	63.7
2	54.0	55.8	50.9	71.2	73.3	69.9	73.7
3	46.7	51.6	53.2	67.1	69.1	69.4	66.8
4	33.8	33.2	34.8	35.8	40.1	45.4	47.6
5	14.0	11.3	7.9 8.	8	10.0	12.0	12.4
Total	32.9	36.8	32.0	38.6	45.5	55.2	52.2

Sources: October Household Survey(1997); General Household survey (2002, 2003, 2004, 2005 and 2006); National.

Reductions in the poverty gap (p1) and in the severity of poverty (p2), are much less controversial in the literature about South Africa. Using a poverty line of R515,[29] Leibbrandt, et al., (2010), found the figures shown in Table 10. Through a counterfactual test – that is, adopting the improbable

---

29   five hundred fifteen Rands, or PPP$ 3,3 per day in (ANO).

hypothesis that all social grants were suddenly removed from one month to the next – the authors conclude that the grants do matter when it comes to fighting poverty, since they significantly reduce both p1 and p2, as shown in Table 10 (LEIBBRANDT, et al., 2010, op. cit., p. 46) (Table 10).

Table 10 South Africa: Poverty, with and without SOCIAL grants

	Poverty (p0)		Poverty gap (p1)		Severity of poverty (p2)	
	With	Without	With	Without	With	Without
1993	0,56	0,60	0,32	0,40	0,22	0,32
2000	0,54	0,57	0,29	0,37	0,29	0,29
2008	0,54	0,60	0,28	0,44	0,28	0,37

Sources: Saldru (1993), IES (2000) and NIDS (2008); elaborated by the authors (LEIBBRANDT, et al., (2010, p. 46).

This data has allowed for some consensus among analysts concerning the positive role of post-apartheid income security benefits in poverty reduction, even though there are still divergences about the levels and precise moments where this reduction has taken place.

SECTION III: BRAZIL

Historical evolution of the Brazilian income security system

As many Latin-American countries, Brazil had first instituted a Bismarkian model of social security, along with the country's industrialization and urbanization. During the 20's, a collection of private pension schemes were set to cover a few categories of urban workers, under a bipartite contribution arrangement (contributions from employers and employees). This system was expanded and nationalized in the 1930´s, though yet restricted to the urban labor force.

But contributory social security coverage grew continuously throughout the 20th century. In the 1970´s, while the country experienced an "economic miracle",[30] employment rates escalated, and other workers were added to the system, such as domestic, autonomous and rural workers. However, contributions from, and benefits to these groups were differentiated. Rural workers, for instance, were exempted from contributions, while their pensions represented one half of the minimum wage paid to urban workers. By 1974, a social assistance grant was created to protect not insured poor elders at 75 or older, with an equal value of ½ of the minimum wage.

It was only after the enactment of the 1988 Constitution[31] that more people became entitled to noncontributory grants. Elders and persons with disabilities, who have no social security pensions, and who live with less than ¼ of the minimum wage per month, were then entitled to a grant of one minimum wage. This benefit – the Old Age and Disability Grant (Benefício de Prestação Continuada – BPC) was first paid in 1996. In 2010 it already reached 3,4 million people. The Constitution also entitled peasants, fisherman and collectors to the same contributory social security benefits that were given to urban workers. By that time, unemployment insurance was completely reframed, allowing for the growth of this benefit's take up rates.[32]

Of great importance for the effectiveness of these benefits in fighting poverty was their indexation to the minimum wage, as commanded by the 1988 Constitution.[33] Between 2003 and 2010, in face of the GDP growth

---

30 Under the rule of a military dictatorship, that endured from 1964 tom 1988.

31 Which put and end to the military regime.

32 Unemployment insurance was first created in 1986, but needed a new funding strategy, which was established in 1991. See next sub-section for more details.

33 Indexation applies for the unemployment insurance benefits, for the social security floor and for the OA&DG.

of 4,4% (on average), the State to determined continued increases in the minimum wage value, which came to be even higher since 2007. At that year, an agreement between the national government and trade unions convened that the minimum wage would be adjusted in line with the inflation plus the GDP growth rate of the preceding two years.[34] As a result, the minimum wage rose 50% in the period (Figure 6), leading to spectacular improvement in both labour and social protection incomes (such as social security, unemployment insurance and the Old Age and Disability Grant).

Figure 2   Minimum Wage growth, 1985 jan/2011

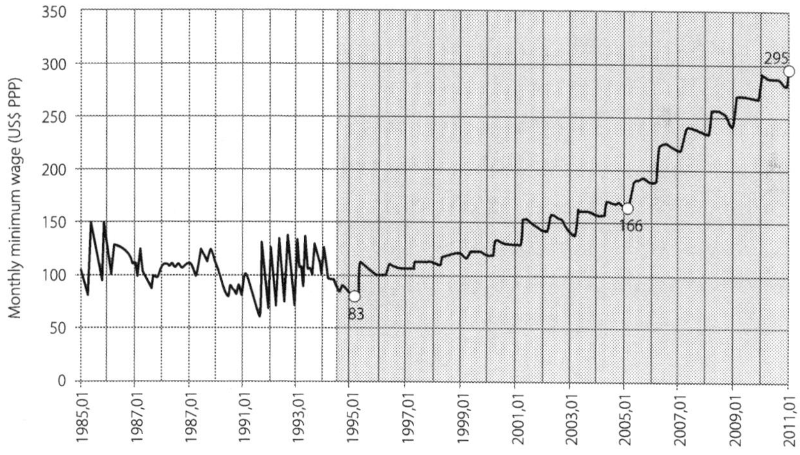

Source: IPEA, 2011.

Programs of conditioned cash transfers had been first initiated in Brazil at the end of the 90's and beginning at the 2000's, by some member states and municipalities. But soon the national government created similar grants,

---

34   This rule is still in place.

that were implemented by different ministries and agencies.[35] The various grants were unified in 2003, giving birth to the *Bolsa Familia Program*. Since then, its coverage has been expanded, having reached 12,8 million families since 2010. Bolsa Família benefits are calculated according to the family poverty level[36] and depending on the number of pregnant women in the family, as well as children and their ages.[37] The average monthly benefit value in 2013 (July) was R$ 152 (one hundred fifty two reais), which correspond to approximately US$ 76.

However, the grant is not a constitutional right yet, like the Old Age & Disability Grant, and its value is not indexed to the minimum wage.[38] Besides, the poverty line applied in the Bolsa Familia program is below the line used in the case of constitutional benefits. For the time being, it's value is R$ 70 (seventy Reais), which is close to the World Bank poverty line of PPP$ 1,25 per day per capita.

As seen, the Brazilian income security system today is made of different benefits, ranging from contributory social security to family allowances. Each kind of benefit protects different needs, and are complementary to one another. While non contributory benefits work for poverty alleviation – an *ex-post* support – contributory benefits protect those who take part in

---

35 The grants that preceded Bolsa Familia were: the Gas Assistance Program, the Bolsa Escola (Schooling Allowance), the Food Allowance and Food Card. See Soares and Satyro, 2009.

36 Families without children are entitled only if they live under the extreme poverty line of approximately US$ 1,25 per day per capita.

37 The program has four types of benefits: the basics, the variable, the variable linked to teen and extraordinarily variable. The Basic Benefit of R$ 70 is paid to families considered extremely poor, with monthly per capita income of up to R$ 70, even if they have no children. A Variable Benefit of R$ 32 is paid to poor families with monthly income of up to R$ 140 per person, if they have children and adolescents up to 15 years, pregnant and/or breastfeeding women. Each family can receive up to five variable benefits, or to R$ 160. There's also the Variable Benefit Linked to Teen (BVJ), of R$ 38, which is paid to all families in the program who have teenagers of 16 and 17 years attending school. Each family can receive up to two variable benefits related to adolescents, or up to R $ 76. The Extraordinary Variable Benefit (BVCE) is paid to families to whom the migration from previous CCT programs caused financial losses.

38 It pays different values to different families, according to the number of children in the family and their age. See annex 1.

the formal labor market, preventing them from falling into poverty, when their work capacity is impaired. In the following section, a description of each benefit will be provided.

The Brazilian income security system's structure

In 2010, more than ½ of the Brazilian population was granted with monetary benefits from the country's social protection system. These transfers, of both contributory and non contributory nature, represented an investment of more than 300 billion Reais (or US$ 150 billion) of the public fund (Table 11). Each of these benefits meets different risks and circumstances that go from job loss to insufficient family income. In the following lines, a brief description of the existing monetary benefits of the Brazilian income security system will be given.

Table 11 Brazilian Income Security System (2010)

Type	Benefits claimed/month (million)	Expenditure (% GDP)
Contributory		
Social Security (*)	24,4	3,36
Unemployment Insurance	7,8	0,5
Non-contributory		
Old Age and Disability Grant	3,7	0,6
Bolsa Família/Family Grant	12,8	0,4

Source: MPS/Social Security Statistical Bulletin (2010) (BEPS); IPEA (2010b).
* The figure considers the amount funded by the National Treasury to both social security regimes (private and public sector employees).

Contributory benefits: social security (pensions and Aids)

After 90 years, this is certainly the strongest and most traditional instrument for income protection in the country. In spite of not achieving the total working population, social security mobilizes the greatest share of the federal social spending. Its institutional configuration is given by a two pillars system: the first is public and mandatory, totally managed by the State (through the Social Security National Institute); while the second is represented by the complementary pillar, of voluntary adhesion and run by private agents.

The mandatory pillar is organized in a pay–as–you–go model. It is mostly funded by contributions of employers and employees, though the State is supposed to cover any deficits derived from a mismatch between payments and revenues. This pillar comprises two branches: the so called "General Regime" (RGPS), which applies to workers in the private sector of the economy; and the branch of the "Special Regimes" (RPPS), which cover public servants in all government levels. Both assure a variety of benefits, such as pensions for retirees and survivors; and temporary aids that assist insured workers in case of sickness, maternity/paternity, accidents, and imprisonment (paid to the family of the insured sentenced person).

The complementary pillar, in turn, consists of pension schemes provided by private firms, and can be organized through two different arrangements: pension funds and pension insurances. Pension funds are mutual schemes, sponsored by employers and employees of public and private organizations. Pension insurance is purchased on an individual basis, by banks and insurance companies. Both of these work in addition to the first pillar, either the general or the special regime.

As defined by the 1988 Constitution, social security benefits from the General have a minimum value that equals to the minimum wage, while their maximum value is periodically established by the parliament (Today, it amounts to almost R$ 4.000,00 – four thousand reais, approximately US$ 2.000,00 – two thousand US dollars). All workers in the formal labor market are compulsorily affiliated to the system, and pay contributions that amount up to 11% of their wages, while employers pay 22% of their total pay roll.

In spite of the system's Bismarkian principle, rural workers (peasants) as well as fisherman and collectors, are entitled to a special contributory regime. Instead of paying a share of their salaries (in many cases, non existing), their contributions are paid by the buyers of their tradable goods, as a share of their values. Indeed, workers this group was the mostly benefited by the changes made by the 1988 Constitution, since they were entitled to the same rights held by urban workers. Their benefits values were raised from 50% to 100% of the minimum wage. Additionally, until the enactment of the Constitution, it was not possible for a single rural household to apply for more than one pension benefit, no matter how many individuals worked in it. Since then, benefits granting was no more based on household production unit, but on individual workers. All of those working in household production, among peasants, fisherman and collectors, at the age of 16 or above, were then included as "special insured" workers, and not only the head of the family. This led to a great expansion of social protection over workers in this group, in just two years. From 1990 to 1992, the number of special insured workers jumped from 2,5 million to about 8 million. This number had felt though in the following years, to about 6,5 million thanks to a decrease in the rural population (IPEA, 2009 – BPS 17).

For insured workers whose benefits values rank above the minimum wage, and who retire after the full contributory period (30 years if woman, 35 years if man), a deflator rate is applied to their pensions according to their age. It is the "pension factor", which happens to reduce pension values for the youngest retirees.

Among the current beneficiaries of this regime, no less than two thirds receive benefits worth up to one minimum wage (US$ 311,00, at 2012 current prices). The system covers around 65% of the country's active population (data from 2010), which is not enough, but still a good number in comparison with those presented in the years between 1992 and 2002, when economic activity was depressed, formal job vacancies shrank and social security coverage fell to its lowest historical levels. (Figure 3).

Since 1996, but more intensively after 2006, a number of policy initiatives have been implemented in order to improve coverage of informal urban workers. These initiatives focus on workers with low contributory capacity, who work in individual jobs or small firms, and consist of reductions in contributions to a very basic level (in some cases, to 5% of the minimum salary), while ensuring access to all kinds of benefits, except for retirement before the age of 60/65.

Figure 3 BRAZIL: Evolution of Social Security Coverage, 1994-2009

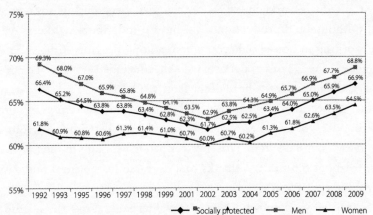

Green: men; Yellow: women; Black: total number of workers protected by social security system.

Source: BRASIL, Minister of Social Security, 2010, with data from IBGE/PNAD, 2009.

Special regimes for public servants

Regarding the public servants´ regimes, new legal rules were provided in 2012. For new servants, pension benefits will be limited to the same value of those in the general regime (R$ 4.000,00). Benefits can be complemented by financial resources accumulated by civil servants in a pension fund, with individual accounts and defined contribution. This arrangement has just started to be implemented and is not mandatory. It affects only workers who entered the civil service since 2013. Those who entered before are entitled to pension benefits whose values are equal to 80% of their best wages,[39] according to the old rule.

Unemployment insurance

First created in 1986, unemployment insurance has had a short coverage until 1990, due to inexistence of specific funding sources, as well as to very restrictive access criteria. The 1988 Constitution included it among the workers' rights and set a new funding mechanism, no more linked to revenues of the public budget, but supported by a specific capitalized fund. This allows for rising disbursements in times of extensive unemployment. The fund joins resources from specific contributions from enterprises to the national treasury.

At present, the benefit's value corresponds to the average of the wages received by the worker in the last three months before his/her dismissal. This value cannot be lower than one minimum wage. Figure 2 shows the evolution of the number of benefits paid from 2000 to 2009, as well as the total amount expended in the period.

Figure 4 Unemployment Insurance: number of benefits claimed (2008-2012)

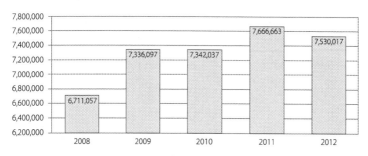

Source: Ministry of Labor. Consolidation: IPEA/Disoc, 2013.

---

39 Before 2004, benefits to civil servants amounted to 100% of their last wages. Reforms have been promoted since the end of the 1990's, in order to equalize the entitlements of civil servants to those of private sector workers.

Non contributory benefits

Until the mid 1990´s, social assistance cash benefits values in Brazil were inexpressive, while its distribution was made under unclear criteria. Payments were often discontinued, the number of beneficiaries was very low, and funding resources were scarce. As mentioned before, the 1988 Constitution commanded the integration of Social Assistance to the national social security framework, discontinuing the tradition of contributory based social protection. Two kinds of noncontributory benefits compound the Brazilian income security system: the Old Age and Disability Grant (Benefício de Prestação Continuada – BPC) and the Family Grant (Bolsa Família – PBF).

The Old Age and Disability Grant
(Benefício de Prestação Continuada – BPC)

The Old Age and Disability Grant provides a monthly income to elderly citizens aged 65 or more; and to disabled people of any age, with no conditions to work or to make an independent living. In both cases, applicants must be considered in "extreme poverty", which means living with a family per capita income up to ¼ of the minimum wage (approximately US$ 77, 5). Given the indexation of this benefit to the minimum wage, its poverty line suffers automatic correction when the minimum wage increases. In turn, this can generate automatic increases in the amount of eligible beneficiaries.

The benefit is means tested and its value equals to one minimum wage. 3.500.000 people received the benefit every month in 2010, being 1.600.000 persons with disabilities and 1.400.000 elders.

Altogether with contributory social security pensions (especially that applying to rural workers, peasants, fisherman and collectors[40]), the Old Age and Disability Grant has been of great importance for fighting poverty among elders in the country. In 2008, there were less than 8% of people aged 65 or more living with less than ½ of the minimum age.

---

40 Who are granted with special contributory rules, as mentioned before.

Due to the significant coverage of the rural elders by the contributory social security, the Old Age and Disability Grant is mostly an urban benefit, which has been extremely valuable to those segments of urban workers with no social security due to precarious employment history or to low wages.

Table 12 Brazil: Old Age population (65 +) x per capita income
(in N of Minimum Wage) (2008)

Age	0-½	½-1	1-2	2-3	3-5	> 5	Total
65-69	8,6	24,3	41,9	11,2	7,4	6,6	100
70-74	6,4	23,9	43,8	11,8	7,4	6,7	100
75-79	6.8	22,3	44,7	12,6	7,1	6,5	100
> 80	6,6	22,3	44,3	11,1	8	7,6	100
Total	7,3	23,4	43,4	11.6	7,5	6,8	100

Source: IBGE/PNAD (Yearly Household Survey), 2008.

Figure 5 BRAZIL: Old Age and Disability Grants: number
of Old Age benefits paid (1996-2011)

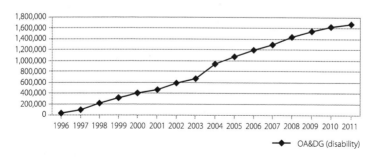

Source: IPEA, 2011.

Figure 6   BRAZIL: Old Age and Disability Grants: number
of Disability benefits paid (1996-2011)

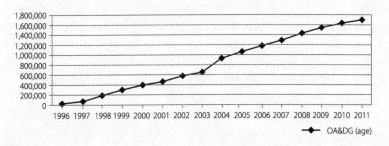

Source: IPEA, 2011.

The Bolsa Família Program (Family Grant Program)

Bolsa Familia ensures a monthly cash transfer to families in poverty and extreme poverty. Therefore two poverty lines are considered, though both of them are different from the one used for the Old Age and Disability Grant. The first one corresponds to a monthly per capita income up to U$ 35 (extreme poverty); and the second, a monthly per capita income between U$ 35.01 and U$ 70 (poverty).[41]

Being a conditional cash transfer program, there are some elements that condition the reception of benefits by families, such as: (1) Education: School attendance of at least 85% of the annual school days, for children and adolescents aged 6 to 15 years; and a minimum of 75% for adolescents aged 16 to 17 years; (2) Health: compliance with the national immunization schedule for children, as well as submission to state's monitoring of their growth and development, through the national health system (SUS). Pregnant women and nursing mothers aged 14-44 years have also to undergo official monitoring.

The program is coordinated and funded by the Federal Government, with the partnership of Municipalities. Some states and municipalities have their

---

41   The US$ 70 poverty line corresponds to the USD 1,25 dollars per day poverty line.

own cash transfer programs and, in these cases, agreements are convened with the federal government, which enable integration of benefits. When Bolsa Familia was first launched, in 2003, it covered initially 3,6 million families, but very soon in 2004 it already reached 9 million households. In 2010 there were 12,7 million families receiving its benefits.

Figure 7 BRAZIL – Evolution of Bolsa Familia benefits granted (2004-2011)

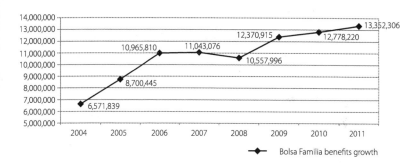

Source: IPEA and Ministry of Social Development.

Since 2011, extreme poverty eradication became a government priority. Despite the significant reductions in poverty and inequality in the preceding 7 years,[42] data from the 2010´s national census showed 16 million people still living in extreme poverty. A number of initiatives were then taken to find out these people and to include them in the Bolsa Familia Program and an extra benefit has been paid to extreme poor families with children from 0 to 6. Due to this action, 3,5 million people have been lifted from beneath the extreme poverty line so far.

---

42 According to data from the Ministry for Social Development, 28 million people have left extreme poverty in the last 8 years, considering a extreme poverty line of R$ 70 per capita, per month.

Impacts of the Brazillian income security system on poverty and Inequality

There is consistent convergence among students that the Brazilian income security system has led to significant positive outcomes in poverty and inequality reduction, in the last 10 years.[43] From 1995 to 2011, the Gini Index fell from 0.598 to 0.527, and the percentage of poor people (household per capita income less or equal to US$ 2 a day[44]) dropped from 24,5% in 2001, to 10.2% in 2011.

Table 13 Brazil: Poverty and inequality indicators – 1995 to 2011

Year	Gini (household per capita income)	% pop with per capita income beneath US$ 2
1995	0,598	24,1
2001	0,594	24,5
2007	0,552	13,0
2009	0,539	12,4
2011	0,527	10,2

Source: IPEA, 2012.

As mentioned before, decomposition of the effects of social benefits (contributory and non contributory) on poverty has shown the major importance of social security contributory benefits in this regard. Notwithstanding, if all income sources are considered, it becomes clear that labour income has

43 Soares, 2013; IPEA 2012; IPEA 2010.

44 ODM poverty line

been the main source to contribute relatively to the increase of the country's average income, as well as to inequality reduction, between 2001 and 2011.

Table 14   Brazil: Income source's relative contribution to average income increase, and to inequality reduction (2001-2011)

Income sources	Income increase	Inequality reduction
Labour	76%	58%
Social Security	21%	19%
Old Age and Disability Grant	2%	4%
Bolsa Familia	3%	13%
Other (rents, interests)	−3%	6%

Source: IPEA, 2012a.

These figures show the great capacity of the Brazilian labour market to absorb labour supply, as well as to pay satisfactory wages, in both formal and informal jobs, since 2004.[45] According to IPEA (2012a), the reduction of poverty rates by 14,1% between 2001 and 2011 has to do half to the total income increase (6,8 p.p.), half to the decrease of income inequality (7,3 p.p.), since the income of the poorer rose faster than that of other groups, due to government transfers. Bolsa Familia has had particular importance in inequality reduction since its inception in 2003, for it is granted to families in the lowest end of the income distribution.

---

45   In fact, the growth of employment rates and wages has not ceased after 2010, despite the sharp decrease in GDP growth rates from 2010 to 2012. According to recent data from household surveys (PNAD, 2012) employment and wages has continued to grow between these years.

Table 15 shows the effects of transfers in household per capita income and the growth of these effects from 1998 to 2008. Based household surveys, it points out the number of persons in each income span, with and without transfers from Social Security and Social Assistance (Old Age and Disability Grant, and Bolsa Familia) as a counterfactual exercise.

Table 15 Number of persons by income span, with and without
social security and social assistance transfers (1998-2008)
(in million people)

Minimum wage (2008)	1998			2008		
	Without (a)	With (b)	(b-a)	Without (a)	With (b)	(b-a)
< 1/4	44,5	30,4	14,2	40,5	18,7	21,7
≥ 1/4 e < 1/2	32,2	33,6		33,9	32,4	
≥ 1/2 e < 1	33,4	38		44,7	49,7	
≥ 1 e < 2	22,8	26,8		34,9	45,8	
≥ 2 e < 3	7,6	9,2		11	14,3	
≥ 3 e < 5	5,9	7,2		7,9	10,1	
≥ 5 e < 10	3,4	4,2		4,4	5,6	
≥ 10	1,3	1,6		1,5	2	
Total	151	151		178,7	178,7	

Source: IPEA, 2009 with data from IBGE/PNAD 1998, 2008.

Notwithstanding the great contribution of the labour market to inequality and poverty falls, the Table above makes evident the importance of the income security benefits in this matter. Still, it is important to say that this system owes most of its positive responses to the funding arrangement that underpins it. Besides the fact that the State bears the costs of non-contributory benefits – with funds from taxes – it also subsidizes part of the contributory social insurance system, for some categories of workers with low contributory capacity, such as rural workers in domestic production, and all workers, whose amounts of contributions are not sufficient to guarantee lifelong benefits of at least a minimum wage. This means that Brazilian social insurance system is based not only on solidarity between generations, but also between risk categories.

SECTION IV: BRAZIL AND SOUTH AFRICA: A COMPARISON

Considering the similarities between Brazil and South Africa, regarding their growth pace, GDP per capita and social protection expenditure, in the last 15 years, this essay tries to investigate the hypothesis that the main factor to account for the different outcomes found in these countries, regarding poverty and inequality reduction, is the absence, in South Africa, of a comprehensive, mandatory and distributive social security system, that protect active workers against wage income loss.

As shown before, social security benefits have played an important role in the case of Brazil, where public and mandatory social security has shown increasing coverage, and basic benefits are indexed to the minimum wage – which value, in turn, has been steadily improved in the last two decades. South Africa, instead, shows an important protection gap, especially with regard to active workers. In spite of their reasonable coverage by private pension funds (12% of the population), pensions values are low, when compared to lifelong contributions, and, as seen, many workers with contributory capacity don't have any pension plan (about 5 million). In this sense, social security is definitely a missing link in the South African income security matrix.

However, when it comes to poverty and inequalities reduction, it is plausible that labour markets performance may be a more determinant variable. As shown by the studies about South Africa reviewed in the previous pages, employment shortage and low labour incomes (or the lack of it) stand out as the main factor to keep unaltered the South African poverty levels, as well as to increase inequalities among the country's population.

On the other hand, it became clear that in Brazil, during the main growth cycle of the 2000's years, growth of employment and earnings was decisive in compressing distances among income strata, as well as in taking people out of poverty.

As a matter of fact, social security has traditionally been a dependent variable of labour markets performance. Its emergency, back in the 19th century, was due to the need to protect salaried workers and capitalists from risks and contingencies that impeded workers to work and industries to profit. In this sense, its contributory arrangement represents a "pact" between capital and workforce to keep production on. Despite the expansion, since the mid 1900's, of income security devices not related to employment, social security schemes have persisted as the most robust "safety net" mechanism in capitalist economies, precisely because of its intrinsic links to labour. Therefore, as labour markets become unable to absorb labour, the protective potential of social security schemes js weakened.

The evidence reviewed in this paper does not disqualify entirely the initial hypothesis – that public, broad and redistributive social security schemes play an important role in reducing poverty and inequality; but it certainly brings an important condition to it, related to the labor market performance.

REFERENCES

BRITTO, T., SOARES, F. (2011), *Conditional Cash Transfers and the Basic Income Grant in Brazil: Will They Ever Merge?* IPC One pager, n. 124. Brazil: International Policy Centre for Inclusive Growth. Available at: <http://www.ipc-undp.org/pub/IPCOnePager124.pdf>.

CARDOSO JR., J. C., JACCOUD, L. (2003), "Políticas Sociais No Brasil: Organização, Abrangência e Tensões da Ação Estatal", in *Questão Social e Políticas Sociais no Brasil Contemporâneo*. Brasília, IPEA.

COTTA, T. C., PAIVA, L. H. (2010), "O Programa Bolsa Família e a Proteção Social no Brasil", in *Bolsa Família 2003-2010: Avanços e Desafios*, vol. 1, p. 57-101, Brasília, IPEA.

ENSOR, L. (2003), "Civil society bodies call for income grant", in *Business Day*. 10/6: 4.

IPEA. (2009a), "Politicas Sociais: acompanhamento e análise", n. 17, in *Vinte Anos da Constituição Federal*, ch 2, Brasilia, IPEA.

_____. (2009b), "Politicas Sociais: acompanhamento e análise", n 17, in *Vinte Anos da Constituição Federal*, ch. 4, Brasilia, IPEA.

_____. (2010a), *Comunicado*, 63, October.

_____. (2010b), "Perspectivas para o sistema de garantia de renda no Brasil", in *Perspectivas da política Social no Brasil*, livro 8, cap. IX, p. 345-414.

_____. (2011), "15 Anos de Gasto Sociqal Federal: Notas Sobre O Periodo de 1995 a 2009", in *Comunicado IPEA*, n. 98 Available at <http://www.ipea.gov.br/portal/images/stories/PDFs/comunicado/110708_comunicadoipea98.pdf>.

_____. (2011a), *Politicas Sociais: Acompanhamento e analise*, Brasilia, IPEA.

_____. (2011b), "15 anos de gasto social federal – Notas sobre o periodo de 1995 a 2009", in *Comunicados do Ipea*, 98, Brasilia, IPEA.

_____. (2012), *Comunicado*, 155, September.

JACCOUD, L., HADJAB, P., CHAIBUB, J. (2010), "The Consolidation of Social Assistance in Brazil and its Challenges, 1988-2008", in IPEA, Working Paper, n. 76, December.

KERSTENETZSKY, C. L. (2009), *DADOS – Revista de Ciências Sociais*, Rio de Janeiro, 52(1), 2009: 53-83.

LAVINAS, L. (2007), "Gasto social no Brasil: Programas de transferência de renda *versus* investmento", in *Ciência e Saúde Coletiva*, 12, 6: 1463-1476.

LEIBBRANDT, M.V., FINN, A., ARGENT, J., WOOLARD, I. D. (2010a), "Changes in income poverty over the post-apartheid period: an analysis based on data from the 1993 Project for Statistics on Living Standards and Development and the 2008 base wave of the National Income Dynamics Study", in *Journal for Studies in Economics and Econometrics*, 34, 3: 25-43.

LEIBBRANDT, M., WOOLARD, I., et al. (2009), *Employment and Inequality Outcomes in South Africa: What Role for Labour Market and Social Policies?* Cape Town, Southern Africa Labour and Development Research Unit.

LEIBBRANDT, M., WOOLARD, I., et al. (2010b), "Trends in South African Income Distribution and Poverty since the Fall of Apartheid", in *OECD Social*, Employment and Migration Working Papers. Geneva, OECD.

LUND, F. (1993), "State Social Benefits in South Africa", in *International Social Security Review*, 46, 1: 5-25. Paper 5572, NBER, Cambridge, MA. Africa, 14, 4: 481-503.

_____. (2009), "Welfare, Development and Growth: Lessons from South Africa" in *Building Decent Societies* (Peter Townsend ed.). ILO/Palgrave – Macmillan. p. 290-309.

MIDGLEY, J., PIACHAUD, D. (eds.). (2013), *Social Protection, Economic Growth and Social Change Goals – Issues and Trajectories in China, India, Brazil and South Africa*, London, Edward Elgar.

National Planning Commission. (2011), *National Development Plan: Vision for 2030*. Available at: <http://www.npconline.co.za/medialib/downloads/home/NPC%20 National%20Development%20Plan%20Vision%202030%20-lo-res.pdf>.

OLIVEIRA, J., TEIXEIRA, S. F. (1986), *Previdência Social: 60 anos de história da Previdência no Brasil*, Rio de Janeiro, Vozes.

PAUW, K., MNCUBE, L. (2007), "Expanding the social security net in South Africa: opportunities, challenges and constraints", in *International Poverty Centre: Country Studies of the Cash Transfer Research Programme*.

PRZEWORSKY, A., TEUNE, H. (1982/1970), *The Logic of Comparative Social Inquiry*, Malabar, Florida, Krieger Pub. Co.

Quandl dataset. (2013), available at <http://www.quandl.com>.

Republic of South Africa/Department of Social Development. (2007), *Reform of Retirement Provisions Discussion Document*.

Republic of South Africa/National Treasury. (2010), *2010 Budget Review*, Pretoria.

_____. (2012), 2012 Budget Review.

Republic of South Africa/The Presidency/Department of Performance monitoring and evaluation. Available at: <www.thepresedency-dpme.gov.za>.

SOARES, F.V., et al. (2006), "Cash transfer programmes in Brazil: Impacts on poverty and inequality", in *IPC-IG Working Paper*, n. 21, Brasilia, UNDP/IPC.

SOARES, S. (2006), "Análise de Bem-Estar e Decomposição por Fatores na Queda da Desigualdade entre 1995 e 2004", in *Econômica*, Rio de Janeiro, UFF, vol. 8, n. 1, p. 83-115.

_____. (2013), "The efficiency and effectiveness of Brazilian Social Protection System", in *Midgley and Piachaud*, op cit., 2013.

SOARES, S., RIBAS, R. P., SOARES, F.V. (2010), "Targeting and Coverage of the Bolsa Família Programme: Why Knowing What You Measure Is Important In Choosing the Numbers" (IPC Working Paper n. 71), in *Brazil: IPC*. Available at: <http://www.ipc-undp.org/pub/IPCWorkingPaper71.pdf>.

SOARES, S., SATYRO, N. (2009), "O Programa Bolsa Família: Desenho Institucional, Impactose Possibilidades Futuras", in *IPEA Discussion Text Series*, n. 1424. Brazilia: IPEA. Available at: <http://www.ipea.gov.br/sites/000/2/publicacoes/tds/td_1424.pdf>.

SOARES, S., SOUZA, P. H. G. F., OSÓRIO, R. G., SILVEIRA, F. G. (2007), "Os Impactos do Benefício do Programa Bolsa Família Sobre a Desigualdade e Pobreza", *in* J. A. de

Castro & L. Modesto (eds.), *Bolsa Família 2003-2010: Avanços e Desafios*, vol. 2, p. 27-52. Brazil, IPEA.

SOUZA, P. H. G. (2012), "Poverty, inequality and social policies in Brazil, 1995-2009", in *IPC-IG Working Paper*, n. 87, Brasília, UNDP/IPC.

Taylor Committee. (2002), *Transforming the Present – Protecting the Future: Report of the Committee of Inquiry into a Comprehensive System of Social Security for South Africa*, Pretoria, Department of Social Development.

Towers Watson & Co. (2013), Available at <http://www.towerswatson.com/en/Insights/IC-Types/Survey-Research-Results/2012/01/Global-Pensions-Asset-Study-2012>.

TRIEGAARDT, J. D. (2008), "Accomplishments and challenges for partnerships in development in the transformation of social security in South Africa", in *DBSA*. Available at <http://www.dbsa.org/Research/Documents/>.

VAN DER BERG, S. (1997), "South African social security under apartheid and beyond", in *Development South Africa*. 14: 4, 481-503.

VAN DER BERG, S., BREDENKAMP, C. (2002), "Devising Social Security Interventions for Maximum Poverty Impact", in *Social Dynamics*. 28: 39-68.

WOOLARD, I., LEIBBRANDT, M. (2010), "The Evolution and Impact of Unconditional Cash Transfers in South Africa", in *SALDRU*, Working Paper, n. 51, Cape Town, School of Economics, University of Cape Town.

World Bank. (1994), *Averting the old age crisis: policies to protect the old and promote growth*, Washington, D.C., Oxford University Press.

_____. (2005), *Coverage, The Scope of Protection in Retirement Income Systems*, World Bank Pension Reform Primer.

Part three

EMERGENT POWERS AND TRANSFORMATIONS IN THE INTERNATIONAL SYSTEM

The BRICS in the international system

Very relevant countries, but a group of limited importance

Eduardo Viola

When we talk about BRICS it is fundamental to remember that the original abbreviation, BRIC, was made in 2002 by Goldman Sachs Bank of Investments, and it represents a group of four countries – Brazil, Russia, India, and China – whose potentialities for future economic growth were enormous, and that was why the managers of investment and pension funds should increase the share of their financial resource in those countries. In the beginning of 2000´s, the BRIC were emergent countries that were huge in terms of territory, population and natural resources, but very heterogeneous and socially unequal, all of them with high rates of poverty. Due to these features, the four countries were pointed out to have a big economic potential. Very quickly many economy and international relations analysts started to consider those countries as part of a broader process of transition to a multipolar world in which there would be seven major economy poles: EUA, European Union, Japan and BRIC.

During the 2000´s, China and India could keep a gross domestic product (GDP) growth rate respectively at about 11% and 8% per year, and Brazil and Russia also increased their GDP rate, but in a more modest way: respectively 5% and 3,5% per year. In 2009 with the great recession unfolding Brazil and Russia lead the creation of the BRIC as a political group whose presidents would meet once a year to try to stand by the same position in the international organizations: International Monetary Fund (IMF), World Bank, World Trade Organization (WTO), United Nations Human Rights Council (UNHRC), and United Nations Security Council. In 2010, Brazil, Russia, India and China achieved high rates of economic growth significantly exceeding the rest of the world and especially exceeding developed countries which were still trapped in their economic crises. The BRIC reached their peak of recognition as an important group of countries.

Due to China pressure, in 2011 the BRIC became the BRICS with the addition of South Africa, which was very important to Chinese expansion ambitions. That change made the economic consistency weaker when compared to its first composition. If the criteria to add new countries was to be a big emergent market or a future pole of the world economy, it would be more correct to have added Indonesia, Turkey and Mexico. All of them fulfilled all those criteria, though in a smaller scale than the BRIC. Also they have relatively big territory, population and natural resources. In addition all those three countries can potentially increase their economy growth rates. South Africa is far beyond those criteria and features.

Finally in 2011 and 2012 the economic fate of BRICS started to change: China kept its enormous economic growth in the world economy with a GPD growth higher than 10%, meanwhile India had a GPD growth rate about 4% a year. Brazil, Russia and South Africa rated 2% per year. United States of America (USA) and Japan economies also started to recovery (in 2013) from the 2008 crisis. This entire situation creates a doubtful scenario about the BRICS representativeness as an alternative pole to the western economic powers. At the Johannesburg summit in March 2013, Brazil, Russia, India, China and South Africa could not achieve an agreement about creating a Development Bank. The discussion about this matter was postponed to the forthcoming Fortaleza summit which will take place in 2014. However, there are still a lot of doubts concerning the Bank viability due to differences related to its objectives, relative power and *modus operandi*. The number of skeptical economy and international relations analysts who think that BRICS may not have the capacities to be a significant actor within the international system have been increasing since 2013.

To consistently analyze the BRICS problematic within the international system it is necessary to separate two questions: firstly the importance of each country alone within the international system; secondly the importance of BRICS as a group – collectively.

In 2011 China's population was about 1.35 billion, a $ 9.6 trillion GDP, a $ 8.400 GDP per capita, fertility rate around 1.6 (child per adult woman), life expectancy rate about 74 years, Human Development Index (HDI) at 0.687 and Gini index at 0.415. India's population was about 1.2 billion, a $ 4.5 trillion GDP, a $ 3.700 GDP per capita, fertility rate around 2.7 (child per adult woman), life expectancy rate about 65 years, Human Development Index (HDI) at 0.547 and Gini index at 0.368. Russia's population was about 142 million, a $ 2.4 trillion GDP, a $ 16.800 GDP per capita, fertility rate around 1.4 (child per adult woman), life expectancy rate about 68 years, Human Development Index (HDI) at 0.755 and Gini index at 0.423. Brazil's population was about 195 million, a $ 2.3 trillion GDP, a $ 11.800 GDP per capita, fertility rate around 1.9 (child per adult woman), life expectancy rate about 74 years, Human Development Index (HDI) at 0.718 and Gini index at 0.550. South Africa's population was about 50,6 million, a $ 555 billion GDP, a $ 11.000 GDP per capita, fertility rate around 2.6 (child per adult woman), life expectancy rate about 53 years, Human Development Index (HDI) at 0.619 and Gini index at 0.578.[1]

China spends 1.54% of its GDP on research and development (P&D), and its budget for national defense is $ 120 billion which represents 7.5% of the total world spending. India spends 0.8% of its GDP on research and development (P&D), and its budget for national defense is $ 41 billion which represents 2.6% of the total world spending. Russia spends 1.05% of its GDP on research and development (P&D), and its budget for national

---

1   These entire comparative data are from The Economist, World Bank Data, International Monetary Fund, World Resources Institute, Climate Analysis Indicator Tool and United Nations Human Development Report.

defense is $ 58 billion which represents 3.7% of the total world spending. Brazil spends 1.1% of its GDP on research and development (P&D), and its budget for national defense is $ 33 billion which represents 2.1% of the total world spending. South Africa spends 0.93% of its GDP on research and development (R&D), and its budget for national defense is $ 4.5 billion which represents 0.3% of the total world spending.

In 2011 China emitted 11 billion tons of carbon, which corresponds to 21% of the total world emission; Chinese emissions per capita were about 8 tons, and this represents an intensity of 0.96 tons of carbon per $ 1.000 of GDP, and 87% of Chinese energy consumption comes from fossil fuels. India emitted 3.6 billion tons of carbon, which corresponds to 7% of the total world emission; Indian emissions per capita were about 3 tons, and this represents an intensity of 0.81 tons of carbon per $ 1.000 of GDP, and 73% of India energy consumption comes from fossil fuels. Russia emitted 2.8 billion tons of carbon, which corresponds to 5.5% of the total world emission; Russian emissions per capita were about 20 tons, and this represents an intensity of 1.20 tons of carbon per $ 1.000 of GDP, and 90% of Russian energy consumption comes from fossil fuels. Brazil emitted 1.5 billion tons of carbon, which corresponds to 3% of the total world emission; Brazilian emissions per capita were about 8 tons, and this represents an intensity of 0.7 tons of carbon per $ 1.000 of GDP, and 51% of Brazilian energy consumption comes from fossil fuels. South Africa emitted 0.6 billion tons of carbon, which corresponds to 1.3% of the total world emission; South-African emissions per capita were about 12 tons, and this represents an intensity of 1.1 tons of carbon per $ 1.000 of GDP, and 71% of South-African energy consumption comes from fossil fuels.

We also have to compare those 4 countries in a different level: the civilizing dynamic. China, India, Russia and South Africa are non-western societies; meanwhile Brazil is in many ways a western society. It is necessary to define a western society nowadays: an economic system based on the market which is regulated by the State, and incorporates the environmental sustainability dimension; a society based on the rule of law, on equality of all individuals before the laws; a Republic with a substantive equality of opportunities achieved through an education system free to all citizens; a society in which the individuals can pursue his or her interests and develop freely his or her skills, even though these might be contradictory with the needs of the community, but it is important to maintain this tense balance; a political system based on representative democracy and accountability; a low level of corruption, violence and criminality; a culture that values science and humanism as one of its mains vectors; and finally a foreign policy which aims to build up global governance in economy, in security, in human and environmental rights.

USA and Europe are in the center of the western civilization. However, this is a heterogeneous centrality. The Nordic countries like Germany, United Kingdom, France and Holland are the center core, because in these countries the western societies' characteristics of the 21th century are better developed and improved. USA however has its own limitations in many dimensions: an increasingly dysfunctional democracy; a radical individualism which promotes conflicts with collective interests; an important part of USA society gives more importance to religion than to science and denies the scientific evidences about the evolution theory and climate change, and USA foreign policy is not t guided towards the buildup of global governance. Some parts of Europe also have their own limitations in the characteristics we defined to a western society.

Since 1980's, Brazil is progressively becoming a part of the western civilization: an economy based on markets instead of centered on the State; environmental sustainability is becoming stronger among citizens and the political elite; democracy has established itself and is now a consolidated political regime even though with low quality and high levels of corruption; the principle of equality before the law is gradually advancing although it is far from becoming fulfilled due to the judicial procedures that allow infinite appeals to superior courts, and this is only possible for those who can afford lawyers for a long period; the development of science has advanced recently. In other dimensions Brazil is still stagnant. There is no equality of opportunities because of the precarious primary education and high school public systems. In consequence, the majority of the population is still functionally illiterate or has low levels of education. The criminality rates increase extraordinarily in all Brazilian cities. The foreign policy is still ambiguous concerning the construction of global governance: it continues with a discourse strongly based on sovereignty; supports the principle of non-intervention in other countries' internal affairs even in situations of extreme human rights violations; and argues that Brazil must be treated as the others big countries, but curiously at the same time considers itself as a kind of representative of developing countries.

In terms of relative power, the BRICS countries are situated on three levels in the international system. In a first order of magnitude, China can be compared to USA (largest world economy) and to the European Union (second largest one) by its leading position in the international system (the third largest economy in the world). In a second order of magnitude there are India (fifth largest economy in the world), Russia (sixth largest) and Brazil (seventh largest world's economy). South Africa is situated in a third order of magnitude, with a quite smaller economy than the other countries. Brazil, India and South Africa are low quality democracies, Russia is a hybrid authoritarian regime and China definitely is an authoritarian regime. China, Russia and India are nuclear powers and the first two have very well developed military power. Brazil and South Africa on the other hand have limited military power.

China is the largest global emitter of greenhouse gases, and India is rapidly growing its share in global emissions. Russia and Brazil have relevant emissions, and South Africa's ones are limited. China, India, Russia and South Africa rely heavily on fossil fuels in its energy matrix. Brazil already has half of its energy sources classified as non-fossils. Russia, Brazil, China and South Africa are countries that have a middle per capita income. India is a low-income country. China, India and Russia are very unequal countries; meanwhile Brazil and South Africa are extremely unequal. China, Brazil and Russia have relatively high life expectancy, while India and South Africa life expectancies are low. Regarding carbon emissions per capita Russia is one of the world's biggest polluters. China, Brazil and South Africa have their emissions around world's average and Indian emissions are low. However, this scenario is likely to change significantly because during this decade India might reach an average emission per capita and China may increase its emissions too, approaching high standards. We also have to consider the fertility rates when analyzing emission per capita. In the 21st century fertility, rates above 2 children per woman are irresponsible and contribute to global climate change. China, Russia and Brazil have responsible fertility rates, but India and South Africa have extremely irresponsible ones.

The BRICS group cannot have a consistent performance as a group on most issues of the international system due to their extreme heterogeneity and divergence of interests. The five countries agree only in two matters: the increasing share contributions and power inside the International Monetary Fund and the World Bank. Meanwhile, in the economic dimension and especially regarding negotiations for greater trade liberalization in the WTO: India and Russia have more protectionist positions than China, Brazil and South Africa. For instance, to Brazil more open agricultural markets are essential, which is opposed to China's and India's interests (particularly the latter). China is very inclined to a full manufactures market opening, which is opposed to India's, Brazil's and Russia's interests. India stands alone in the defense of the opening of the market in information services.

Regarding international security: China and India have a strong geopolitical rivalry and extremely conflictive borders. China and Russia also have strong geopolitical rivalry, even when mitigated by the fact of both being undemocratic regimes that tend to ally against Western democracies on many issues. China and Russia are not in favor of the UN Security Council reform, which is a very important issue to India, Brazil and South Africa.

With respect to international defense of human rights the five countries have recently found a common ground: defending positions of non-intervention in the internal affairs of other countries even when there are massive violations of human rights. Russia and China have led the BRICS on these issues, and Brazil, India and South Africa have had lower performances on these matters. This happens even though Brazil and South Africa have strong domestic political opposition standing for the defense of international human rights. In international climate change negotiations,

Russia and India are generally extremely conservative countries and tend to block the attempts to restrict greenhouse gas emission. Brazil, China and South Africa have more favorable positions to decarbonize the global economy. The BASIC group – made up of China, India, South Africa and Brazil – represents well the first three countries as all of them are strongly dependent on fossil fuels, but Brazil has a relatively clean energy matrix.

Summarizing, China, India, Russia and Brazil are very relevant countries in the international system, but South Africa doesn't have that relevance. The four countries, taken individually, would likely continue being very relevant for the dynamic of the international system. However, the BRICS as a group, because of their very different interests in many dimensions, will not have the capacity of shaping the dynamic of the international system.

Is the BRICS a harbinger of a new matrix of global governance in trade, energy and climate change?

Alexander Zhebit

Abstract   The impressive "hard" data concerning the BRICS should not hide the unimpressive "soft" side of the BRICS frailties, as finance and currency, trade asymmetries, energy dependence and a debt on the climate change issues. The group as an alternative to the existing governance institutions will emerge as a result of its concerted action to face and overcome challenges to its purpose and its substance. Thus, testing the BRICS ability to perform as a meaningful body of governance and not just a group of giant powers with diversified or even conflicting policy outlooks, is a means to know if the BRICS is capable to harness and lead global politics. What these challenges are and where and how they should be met depends on the issues and the policies through which the BRICS will position itself in the world politics today.

Keywords   trade, finance, energy, climate change, BRICS, global governance, European agenda, African agenda.

The impressive facts about the BRICS' countries GDPs, territories, populations and rates of growth during the last decade or so have been publicized and awed throughout the world community. The so-called emerging giant countries would become leading world economies by 2050 or most probably much earlier than that. What truly must be said is that a huge part of this success is owed to the People's Republic of China growth and economic, technological and commercial advance, though some uneven success in growth was also remarkable in India, Russia, Brazil and South Africa through all these years. Since the beginning of the first decade of this century these giant emerging economies were observed as separate entities with some comparable macroindicators that showed their quite sustainable perspective progress towards economic growth and eventual prosperity in some near future. Their transformation into a cohesive group of purpose-oriented powers in 2009 (First BRIC Group Summit in Yekaterinburg) changed the perception of giant emerging powers acting on their own. A new body of alternative world governance came to the scene of world politics to challenge the more than half a century old structures of power and decision making, first, in financial and monetary issues and, later on, in global and regional governance initiatives. The BRICS started to be viewed as a politically motivated group of countries, whose policies should be coordinated in a meaningful and duly oriented manner, according the group's declared purposes and principles.[1]

---

1 "12. We underline our support for a more democratic and just multi-polar world order based on the rule of international law, equality, mutual respect, cooperation, coordinated action and collective decision-making of all states [...] 15. [...] The dialogue and cooperation of the BRIC countries is conducive not only to serving common interests of emerging market economies and developing countries, but also to building a harmonious world of lasting peace and common prosperity". (Joint Statement of the BRIC Countries' Leaders. June 16, 2009, Yekaterinburg) Available at: <http://archive.kremlin.ru/eng/text/docs/2009/06/217963.shtml>. Accessed on September, 15, 2013. "2. We underline our support for a multipolar, equitable and democratic world order, based on international law, equality, mutual respect, cooperation, coordinated action and collective decision-making of all States. 4. [...] we reaffirm the need for a comprehensive reform of the UN, with a view to making it more effective, efficient and representative, so that it can deal with today's global challenges more effectively". (2nd BRIC Summit of Heads of State and Government Joint Statement Brasília, April 15, 2010) Available at: <http://www.brics.utoronto.ca/docs/100415-leaders.html>. Accessed on September, 15, 2013. "7. We share the view that the world is undergoing far-reaching, complex and profound

Before the influence of the BRICS as a transgovernmental network of global governance (ZHEBIT, 2010, 17-18) can be estimated, some interesting and defiant facts which show the BRICS' well known frailties must be put in evidence so that a more realistic glimpse should be thrown on what is a "soft" vulnerability of the group in the issues under discussion: trade, finance, energy, climate change, respectively.

According to the Standard Bank Group, the **intra-BRICS trade** reached in 2012 USD 310 billion, up eleven-fold since 2002. Today, intra-BRICS trade accounts for almost one-fifth of BRICS total trade with emerging markets, up from just 13% in 2008. China accounts for about 85% of intra-BRICS trade flows and 55% of total BRICS GDP. For each of the BRICS, China

---

changes, marked by the strengthening of multipolarity, economic globalization and increasing interdependence. While facing the evolving global environment and a multitude of global threats and challenges, the international community should join hands to strengthen cooperation for common development. Based on universally recognized norms of international law and in a spirit of mutual respect and collective decision making, global economic governance should be strengthened, democracy in international relations should be promoted, and the voice of emerging and developing countries in international affairs should be enhanced". (Full text of Sanya Declaration of the BRICS Leaders Meeting) Available at: <http://news.xinhuanet. com/english2010/chin a/2011-04/14/c_13829453_2.htm>. Accessed on September, 15, 2013. "3. BRICS is a platform for dialogue and cooperation amongst countries that represent 43% of the world's population, for the promotion of peace, security and development in a multi-polar, inter-dependent and increasingly complex, globalizing world. Coming, as we do, from Asia, Africa, Europe and Latin America, the transcontinental dimension of our interaction adds to its value and significance. 4. We envision a future marked by global peace, economic and social progress and enlightened scientific temper. We stand ready to work with others, developed and developing countries together, on the basis of universally recognized norms of international law and multilateral decision making, to deal with the challenges and the opportunities before the world today. Strengthened representation of emerging and developing countries in the institutions of global governance will enhance their effectiveness in achieving this objective". (Fourth BRICS Summit – Delhi Declaration) Available at: <http://pmindia.nic.in/press-details.php?nodeid=1404>. Accessed on September, 15, 2013. "1. [...] Our discussions reflected our growing intra-BRICS solidarity as well as our shared goal to contribute positively to global peace, stability, development and cooperation. We also considered our role in the international system as based on an inclusive approach of shared solidarity and cooperation towards all nations and peoples. 2. [...] We aim at progressively developing BRICS into a full-fledged mechanism of current and long-term coordination on a wide range of key issues of the world economy and politics" (5th BRICS Summit – eThekwini Declaration and Action Plan). Available at: <http://www.mea.gov.in/bilateral-documents. htm?dtl/21482>. Accessed on September, 15, 2013.

ranks as a top three export destination (STEVENS, 2013). Only Chinese foreign trade is ten times bigger than the intra-BRICS trade, not to mention Russian, Indian and Brazilian foreign trade. Nevertheless, all the intra-BRICS trade accounts for less than 0,7% of the global merchandise trade and trade in commercial services put together (International, 2013). That means that the BRICS have traded much more with the outer world than amongst themselves and their common share of global trade is quite insignificant.

Financial and monetary problems of the BRICS are more acute than they may appear. All the huge trade in merchandise and services that the BRICS maintain with their partners or even among themselves is made on the basis of hard currencies, in spite of the efforts of the BRICS to rely upon the mechanisms of SDR and special EXIM banks loans. According to the eThekwini Declaration, "the unconventional monetary policy actions which have increased global liquidity" lead to "the unintended consequences of these actions in the form of increased volatility of capital flows, currencies and commodity prices, which may have negative growth effects on other economies, in particular developing countries"(5th BRICS, 2013). The creation of a Contingent Reserve Arrangement (CRA) amongst BRICS countries worth USD 100 billion as an initial value is still a project due to have a positive result, notwithstanding the modest size of the investment. The statutes of the new development bank planned by the BRICS group of five emerging powers could be ready in 2014, to be approved at the next BRICS Group Summit in Brazil. But at their last summit in Durban, leaders of the BRICS – Brazil, Russia, India, China and South Africa – failed to launch the much-anticipated bank. Instead of a $ 50 billion fund, the leaders agreed only that the initial capital contribution would be substantial and sufficient for the bank to be effective (Brazil, 2013). Also the 2010 agreement on the International Monetary Fund (IMF) Governance and Quota has not been completed and must be achieved only by January 2014. The BRICS leaders' meeting held on the margins of the G20 leaders' summit, St Petersburg, Russia, confirmed this concern (Brazil: 2013).

What is really clear is China's reluctance to create a new international reserve currency based on a basket of key international currencies (US dollar, euro, pound, yen, renminbi, real, ruble, gold). A devalued renminbi is much better for China in terms of trade than a revalued and difficult to maintain renminbi as a reserve currency. "Is China prepared to make the renminbi a currency with a global reach? Is it willing to make its exchange rate considerably more flexible and permit it to appreciate at a much faster pace – if that is what the market determines? Apparently, not yet", says a macro – economic desk chief and senior editor of influential Chinese Caixin Media Zhu Changzheng (Brasil-China: 2013, 133).

According to the Recommendation to Euro-BRICS leaders by LEAP/E2020 (Laboratoire Européen d'Anticipation Politique), "Of course, the BRICS have an interest to see a new international currency put in place, but they also have other options available to them, those related to the logics of blocks [...] even by combining their five influences, they still lack weight for a real rebalancing of powers"(Recommendations, 2013). What the authors of the Recommendations suggest is that the BRICS join some strong currencies, as euro and gold reserves and start working together with European currency zone for a new reserve currency.

The BRICS dependence on the main world currencies is reflected in a sharp increase of borrowings from the developed countries in 2012 – beginning of 2013. While cross-borders credits to developed countries experienced contractions in 2012 – first quarter of 2013, claims on borrowers in emerging markets economies expanded strongly. So, higher lending to borrowers in Brazil, China and Russia accounted for 85% of the growth, whose total value amounted to US$ 267 billion. Cross-border credit to borrowers in China increased by $ 160 billion (31%) and accounted for 81% of the increase in cross-border claims on Asia-Pacific. Lending to Latin America and the Caribbean in the first quarter of 2013 expanded most strongly in Brazil ($ 39 billion or 14%), especially to banks ($ 34 billion or 27%). The expansion was also driven by strong cross-border credit to borrowers in Russia (up $ 29 billion or 18%). Claims on South Africa increased by $ 2.8 billion or 7.7% (BIS: 2013).

The economic behavior of the BRICS depends much on the strength of their national energy sectors. As the economies of the BRIC nations continue to grow, their energy demands are also increasing. According to the news forecasts, much of the growth in energy consumption occurs and will occur in countries outside the Organization for Economic Cooperation and Development (OECD), known as non-OECD, where demand is driven by strong, long-term economic growth. Energy use in 2040 in non-OECD countries will increase by 90%; in OECD countries, the increase will be 17%, while mostly the economic growth of China and India will drive world energy consumption. China and India continue to lead both world economic growth and energy demand growth. Since 1990, energy consumption in both countries as a share of total world energy use has increased significantly; together, they accounted for about 10% of total world energy consumption in 1990 and nearly 24% in 2010. From 2010 to 2040, their combined energy use will more than double and they will account for 34% of the projected total world energy consumption in 2040. China, which recently became the world's largest energy consumer, is projected to consume more than twice as much energy as the United States in 2040, says the International Energy Outlook 2013 Report, released by the US Energy Information Administration (EIA)(IEO, 2013, 159). As Charles K. Ebinger and Govinda Avasarala write in a opinion column of the Indian Express, some members of the BRICS group are better endowed in energy than others. Brazil and Russia are energy-secure nations in renewable and fossil resources likewise. China and India are much more vulnerable, but superior infrastructure and a centralized government leave China in a better position to meet its rising energy demand, while India has the most unstable energy situation among the BRICS, and possibly the most uncertain energy future of all (EBINGER, et al., 2013).

This will push India and China to look for energy supplies elsewhere (in Sakhalin, Arctic region, pre-salt coastal shelf of Brazil, North Sea or Africa). This last region is already under the scrutiny of Chinese and Indian explorers, which causes a natural concern by African politicians: "The issue of growing project aid from the BRICs also requires some careful consideration by African policymakers. While such aid is helping Africa narrow the infrastructure gap, it is important that this aid not be used as a way to endow monopoly rights for the BRICs in the exploitation of Africa's natural resources or to hold African countries hostage to future contracts related to new projects and maintenance" (The BRICS, 2011).

According to Alex Vines from The London School of Economics, "Having first become a net importer of oil in 1993, in 2003 China became the world's second largest consumer of petroleum products behind the United States, and the third largest importer. Although some 55% of African oil and gas went to Europe and the US in recent years and only 16% went to China this is changing. China is projected to surpass the US in 2015. China currently receives around 33% of its imported crude oil from Africa. [...] Nine out of ten of China's top trading partners in Africa in 2008 were oil producing states, the exception being South Africa. The competition for African oil is heating up and not just by Western and Chinese companies. India and South Korea are prominent among other G20 members trying to get footholds. India produces oil only in Sudan but Nigeria was its third largest source of imported oil in 2008, representing over 11%. India is seeking deals across the continent, and in 2010 its Oil and Natural Gas Corporation (ONGC) signed a memorandum with Angola" (VINES, et al., 2009).

The last but not the least of the "soft" data BRICS frailties has to do with the climate change and most significantly with carbon dioxide emissions, especially so because energy consumption is an important component of the global climate change. If new global policies to limit greenhouse gas emissions are not adopted, the International Energy Outlook July 2013 Projections trace references of world energy-related carbon dioxide emissions up to 2040. According to the document, the lack of relevant global and national measures to limit and decrease the emissions will result in its increase from 31.2 billion metric tons in 2010 to 36.4 billion metric tons in 2020 and 45.5 billion metric tons in 2040. Much of the growth in emissions is attributed to the developing non-OECD nations that continue to rely heavily on fossil fuels to meet fast-paced growth in energy demand. Non-OECD carbon dioxide emissions will total 31.6 billion metric tons in 2040, or 69% of the world total. In comparison, OECD emissions will total 13.9 billion metric tons in 2040 – 31% of the world total. World energy-related carbon dioxide emissions will increase at an average annual rate of 1.3% from 2010 to 2040, with much of the overall increase occurring in the non-OECD nations. OECD emissions will increase by 0.2% per year on average, while non-OECD emissions will increase by an average of 1.9% per year. In the OECD regions, the United States will continue to be the largest source of energy-related carbon dioxide emissions through 2040, followed by OECD Europe and Japan. Carbon dioxide emissions in the United States and OECD Europe will grow only slightly, and in Japan they will decline over the long term. Thus, total emissions from the three largest OECD emitters will increase by only 91 million metric tons over the 30-year period. For the other OECD countries combined, carbon dioxide emissions will increase by a total of 727 million metric tons from 2010 to 2040. The fastest rate of increase in carbon dioxide emissions in the OECD region will be for Mexico/Chile, at 2.1% per year on average from 2010 to 2040, followed by South Korea at 0.8% per year (IEO, 2013, 159).

By contrast, the non-OECD countries together will account for 94% of the total increase in world carbon dioxide emissions from 2010 to 2040, and non-OECD Asia alone will account for 71% of the total increase. China's emissions will grow by an average of 2.1% per year and will account for 69% of the increase for non-OECD Asia and 49% of the total world increase in carbon dioxide emissions. India's emissions will increase by 2.3% per year, and emissions in the rest of non-OECD Asia will increase by an average of 1.9% per year. The increases in non-OECD Asia, particularly China, are led by coal-related carbon dioxide emissions, and emissions from natural gas and liquid fuels use will also increase substantially. (IEO, 2013, 160-161).

If we look at how the BRICS tries to manage the problems of trade, finance, energy and greenhouse emissions, we will see that it is most successful in monetary and financial issues, as an entity, because in this area there is a reasonable and sufficiently well coordinated common policy within the group, related to the idea of reforming the old Bretton Woods bodies. As to the WTO and the continuation of the Doha round which could open doors to a more equitable world trade structure, there are more wishfull thinking and declarative positions than real business. What may be said is that the BRICS have more durable and solid partnership agreements and trade relations with the European Union than among themselves, and are engaged in talks to expand these relations even more (The EU's, 2013). The energy policies of the BRICS are very much apart, so that in relations between them and with other energy providers they look much more like competitors than allies. And if the climate change issue unites them, it occurs more verbally than factually. So when policies are not coordinated they lead to mixed results which produce a governance without common purpose and goals.

What the BRICS really lacks coordinated activities and their common results in those issues show their vulnerability as a group of global governance. But also the weight of the existing governance structures. The BRICS relations with the G-20 and the UN are as recent as the proper BRICS, while the first of the other two governance bodies is as new as the BRICS themselves and the second one is as old as the end of the World War II and carries the fullest bondage of the post-War world order. As a new instrument of the governance reform, the BRICS paves its way along an evolutionary path of international political action and is quite successful at the beginning of its efforts to influence world politics, though its influence is still of little significance. It happens mostly because the biggest challenge to the world governance reform – an admission of Brazil, India and South Africa to the UNSC as permanent members – is hampered either by the unwillingness of the current holders of permanents seats at the SC to share power, or because the reform at the UN system itself is very slow and inconclusive. Moreover, the South-South appeals of the BRICS converge with the development efforts of the UN system itself.

In order to be more influential and politically more effective the BRICS should use its huge natural endowment among the established international governance bodies, as the World Bank, OMC, OECD, as well as among the developed and developing countries institutions, like the European Union, free trade agreements, UNCTAD and others. Some successful entries into the ten most influential members of the IMF and into the G-20 are already important breakthroughs, but more needs to be done for the BRICS to be *system-influencing states* or *system-affecting states* (KEOHANE, 1969, 295-296).

The first measure that should be taken by the BRICS to strengthen its influencing capability on world governance is to start a process of building a Euro-BRICS partnership deals with a mutual acceptance and an issue overlapping between the consolidated and mature international institutions, such as the European Union, and the newly born and innovative networks, such as the BRICS, with the purpose of adaptation to a changing world governance.

The European Union is a natural and an active partner for the BRICS in trade and in global diplomacy. Formed in 1992, the European Union is a post-Cold War construction built as an alternative governance structure for Europe facing globalization. It fits very well *la grandeur* of the BRICS, in terms of population, economy, trade, minus rapid growth rates, even if we concede that the BRICS growth rates have been going down.

The foreign policy of the European Union was and has been based on a different set of principles than those of the post-World War II global institutions. Its policies have anti- and post-colonial presumptions, bordering with the BRICS' South-South paradigm, as the European Union faced the problem of transitional economies of the Central and Eastern Europe.

The European Union is nowadays an important partner in solving global and regional problems. Without it, no solutions to developmental challenges, no conflict resolution, no trade promotion, no finance reform or a climate change recovery and many other global issues are attainable, no matter what the degree of financial crisis it has been undergoing. Crisis or no crisis, the European Union is a major economic, financial, technological and commercial player in the world politics.

That is why alternative trans-governmental networks combine very well with the European Union, which is, speaking very broadly, an intergovernmental network of national states. Under these circumstances, its strategic partnership with the BRICS should be seen as a transnational neo-functionalism and should be faced as a challenge for the BRICS in its venue to gain more weight and authority in world governance.

It should be stressed that the inter-structural partnership construction has to be based on and driven by the existing diplomatic and political framework and through the use of particular political instruments, such as the European strategic relationships.

One should observe that the existing partnerships of the European Union with the BRICS countries and other emerging countries have already formed a significant grid of bilateral negotiating platforms in international relations. If they are smart grids or talking shops, it does not matter. They were invented for good purposes, so they must be used. Among the ten strategic partnership agreements of the European Union (with Brazil, Canada, China, India, Japan, Mexico, Russia, South Africa, South Korea, United States), five are with the BRICS countries.

Second, the South-South potential of the intra-BRICS should be fully used on those concrete projects that have already paved the way for the IBSA countries and have been so artfully presented at the Durban BRICS summit and a Retreat together with African leaders under the theme "Unlocking Africa's potential: BRICS and Africa Cooperation on Infrastructure". Why Africa?

Africa will defy the global economic slowdown in 2013, with most countries predicted to show much stronger growth than the global average, according to the UN economic annual report, World Economic Situation and Prospects (WESP) 2013.

Despite the global slowdown, Africa's economic growth rate (excluding Libya) will see a visible rebound to 4.5% in 2013 compared to 3.4% in 2012. The upward trend is expected to continue in 2014, with growth reaching 5.0%.

The report said the key factors underpinning Africa's strong growth prospects include:

a) solid growth in oil-exporting countries supported by increased oil production and continued high prices;
b) increased fiscal expenditure, especially on infrastructure.

WESP says Africa's increasing trade and investment ties with emerging and developing economies are likely to mitigate the impact of negative shocks emanating from the recession in Europe (World, 2013).

Increasing diversification into services, telecommunication, construction and other non-primary commodity sectors, including manufacturing, will also contribute to Africa's positive growth outlook in the medium term.

The African population is rapidly growing. More than in any other continent. By the beginning of the XXII century it will increase by 2,5 billion people, while in Asia the increase will be only by 432 millions, in Northern America, by 182 millions, in Latin America, by 97 millions and there will be a decrease of population in Europe, by 63 millions.[2]

The European Union and the BRICS may have cross activities in Africa because of the existing EU programs for Africa.

The Joint Africa-EU Strategy (JAES) strategic orientations, adopted in the Lisbon Summit on December 2007, are being implemented on a day to day basis through Action Plans which have reinforced the intercontinental dialogue and led to concrete action in key areas of common concern. The two successive action plans are structured around eight thematic areas:

1. Peace and Security.
2. Democratic Governance and Human Rights.
3. Regional Economic Integration, Trade and Infrastructure.
4. Millennium Development Goals.
5. Climate Change.
6. Energy.
7. Migration, Mobility and Employment.
8. Science, Information Society and Space.

Its Action Plan 2011-2013 for Energy may serve as a building block for Euro BRICS cooperation and not rivalry in Africa:

---

2   Source: United Nations, Department of Economic and Social Affairs, Population Division (2011): World Population Prospects: The 2010 Revision. New York.

- Increased access to modern and sustainable energy services in Africa, focusing on sustainable models: to provide energy for basic services (health, education, water, communication); to power productive activities; and to provide safe and sustainable energy services to households.
- Increased use of natural gas in Africa, as well as African gas exports to Europe, by building natural gas infrastructure, notably to bring currently flared gas to market.
- Increased use of renewable energy in Africa: by building new and/ or rehabilitating existing hydro-power, wind power and solar energy facilities and other renewable facilities, such as geothermal and modern biomass.
- Improved energy efficiency in Africa in all sectors, starting with the electricity sector, in support of Africa's continental, regional and sectoral targets (Joint, 2013).

The BRICS cooperation with Africa is very extensive too, serving to transform the African agenda into a real business for the BRICS.

- Forum on China-Africa Cooperation (FOCAC), 2000.
- Fórum para a Cooperação Econômica e Comercial entre a China e os Países de Língua Portuguesa (Fórum de Macau), 2003.
- India-Brazil-South Africa Dialogue Forum (IBSA), 2003.
- New Asian-African Strategic Partnership, 2005.
- Africa-South America Strategic Partnership (ASA), 2006.
- Índia-Africa Forum, 2008.

A cooperation for the sake of development is burgeoning topic of intra-BRICS studies (BRICS, 2013).

The New Partnership for Africa's Development (NEPAD), an African Union strategic framework for pan-African socio-economic development has its own program of development which should be supported by the BRICS.

Priority areas for NEPAD's energy program include energy infrastructure development in Africa up to 2040 known as PIDA, bio energy development for energy and food security, energy accessibility through renewable energy solutions, development of the continent nuclear power resources, energy efficiency, regional energy market and capacity development at national and regional levels. The program also supports development of power generation from natural gases, coal bed methane and geothermal power in the Rift Valley. The program promotes the development of regional and continental energy policy frameworks and strategies, development of energy regulatory systems and realistic tariff that attracts private investment in the energy sector (BRICS, 2013).

There is a Program for Infrastructure Development in Africa (PIDA), designed to develop a vision and strategic framework for the development of regional and continental infrastructure (Energy, Transport, Information and Communication Technologies (ICT) and Trans-boundary Water Resources)(PIDA, 2013).

According to the final document of 4th Euro-BRICS Seminar «Towards a renovated global governance – Peace, Energy, Currencies, Trade: the Euro-BRICS partnership, a condition to a non – conflictive cooperation between world blocks», "[...] the participants agreed on the need for a EU-BRICS cooperation platform. Other than competitors for resources, a joint initiative would prove to be the path to sustainability, stability and democratic progress. The Durban Declaration following the BRICS summit in April of 2013 has pushed for an Africanization of the BRICS Agenda. The participants urged the EU to support this initiative, as the commodities super-cycle reaches its end (shale-gas revolution?) it will be vital to support African nations with foreign direct investment (development) rather than overseas development assistance (aid). This change in rationale would truly recognize Africa not as a pumping station for resources but as a partner in the world of the 21st century"(EURO-BRICS, 2013, 6).

On a new model of global governance, the document says the following: "These few practical steps allow one to see that the Euro-BRICS partnership can provide a space for combined decision-making freedom in a huge area for truly effective action for the construction of a new framework of global governance. The Euro-BRICS aren't the whole world but they make up a not-insignificant part by their demographic numbers, their close fit with each other, their diversity, their common interests and destiny, the areas for exchange and the flows they represent – it's not the BRICS alone and even less so the Eurozone alone. The Euro-BRICS can therefore be the laboratory of a new global governance, quickly transforming decisions into action which the institutions of the 20th century are no longer capable of doing-establishing themselves solely by the effectiveness of their solutions in contrast to the do-nothing attitude prevailing elsewhere. A matrix of this type is able to lead the world towards a model of modern governance, supple, capable of integrating the vast diversity of national and supranational entities which have covered the world these last few decades, a decentralized model running on the basis of all these entities being connected with each other ad hoc via simple secretariats or agile authorities coordinating a particular subject, a multi-faceted networking of all of the new pillars of today's world" (EURO-BRICS, 2013, 8).

Answering my initial question "Is the BRICS a harbinger of a new matrix of global governance in trade, energy and climate change?", I must say that it is not the fact yet. Though real challenges, among which a Euro-BRICS agenda and an African agenda, as most challenging and practical ones, will lead the BRICS to transform itself into a real alternative world governance body, as it happened to declare itself when it was born.

The paper completed on September, 17, 2013

REFERENCES

BIS Quarterly Review, September 2013. Highlights of the BIS international statistics. Available at: <http://www.bis.org/publ/qtrpdf/r_qt1309.htm>. Accessed on September, 16, 2013.

BRAZIL: BRICS Bank Pillars Could be Ready Next Year, by Naharnet Newsdesk. Available at: <http://www.naharnet.com/stories/en/92567-brazil-brics-bank-pillars-could-be-ready-next-year>. Accessed on August, 4, 2013.

BRICS Summit, (5ᵗʰ) – eThekwini Declaration and Action Plan. Available at: <http://www.mea.gov.in/bilateral-documents.htm?dtl/21482>. Accessed on September, 15, 2013.

EBINGER, C. K., AVASARALA, G. (2012), "The Energy-Poor BRIC", in *The Indian Express*. Opinion. October 19, 2012

(The) EU's free trade agreements – where are we? European Commission Memo. Brussels, 18 June 2013 Available at: <http://europa.eu/rapid/press-release_MEMO-13-576_en.htm>. Accessed on September, 17, 2013.

EURO-BRICS PROCESS 4ᵗʰ Euro-BRICS Seminar "Towards a renovated global governance – Peace, Energy, Currencies, Trade: the Euro-BRICS partnership, a condition to a non-conflictual cooperation between world blocks", Moscow (MGIMO), May 23-24, 2013, p. 6. Available at: <http://www.europe2020.org/IMG/pdf/Report_4ᵗʰ_Euro-BRICS_seminar_Moscow_May_2013_EN.pdf>. Accessed on September, 16, 2013.

IEO. (2013), *International Energy Outlook*, p. 10. Available at: <http://www.eia.gov/forecasts/ieo/>. Accessed on September, 16, 2013.

International Trade and Market Access Data. World Trade Organisation. Available at: <http://www.wto.org/english/res_e/statis_e/statis_bis_e.htm?solution=WTO&path=/Dashboards/MAPS&file=Map.wcdf&bookmarkState={%22impl%22:%22client%22,%22params%22:{%22langParam%22:%22en%22}}>. Accessed on September, 14, 2013.

Joint Africa EU Strategy Action Plan 2011-2013. Available at: <http://europafrica.net/jointstrategy/>. Accessed on September, 17, 2013.

KEOHANE, R. (1969), "Review: Lilliputians' Dilemmas: Small States in International Politics", in *International Organization*, vol. 23, n. 2 (1969), p. 295-296.

KIMENYI, M. S., LEWIS, Z. A. (2013), "The BRICS and the New Scramble for Africa", in *Foresight Africa: The Continent's Greatest Challenges and Opportunities for 2011*. Report. January 11, 2011. The Brookings Institution: Africa Growth Initiative. Available at: <http://www.brookings.edu/research/reports/2011/01/africa-economy-agi>. Accessed on May, 18, 2013.

NEPAD Energy Program Available at: <http://www.nepad.org/regionalintegrationandinfrastructure/energy>. Accessed on September, 17, 2013.

PIDA (Program Infrastructure Development for Africa). Available at: <http://pages.au.int/infosoc/pages/program-infrastructure-development-africa-pida>. Accessed on September, 17, 2013.

Recommendation to Euro-BRICS leaders. December 17ᵗʰ, 2012 GEAB (GlobalEurope Anticipation Bulletin). Available at: <http://www.leap2020.eu/15-01-2013-A-recommendation-to-Euro-BRICS-leaders-Organize-a-mini-Euro-BRICS-Summit-ahead-of-the-St-Petersburg-G20-in_a13116.html>. Accessed on September, 15, 2013.

STEVENS, J. (Standard Bank). (2013), BRIC and Africa – BRICS trade is flourishing, and Africa remains a pivot. Available at: <https://m.research.standardbank.com/

Research?view=1671-5e15d65cf1904d22850b65e04864fc94-1>. Accessed on September, 14, 2013.

VINES, A., WONG, L., WEIMER, M., CAMPOS, I. "Thirst for African Oil: Asian National Oil Companies in Nigeria and Angola" in *Chatham House Report*, August 2009. Available at: <http://www2.lse.ac.uk/IDEAS/publications/reports/pdf/SU004/vines.pdf>. Accessed on May, 9, 2013.

World Economic Situation and Prospects. (2013). *UN report: Africa's economy rebounding despite global downturn.* Available at: <http://www.un.org/en/development/desa/policy/wesp/index.shtml>. Accessed on January, 11, 2013.

ZHEBIT, A. (2010), "BRIC: Uma emergência global das novas potências", in *V Conferência Nacional de Política Externa e Política Internacional – CNPEPI, "O Brasil no mundo que vem aí".* Textos Acadêmicos. Palácio Itamaraty, Rio de Janeiro, 28 e 29 de outubro de 2010, Brasília, FUNAG.

ZHEBIT, A. (org.). (2013), *Brasil-China: construindo o BRICS,* Rio de Janeiro, Editora UFRJ.

South Africa in the international politics of climate and energy

Kathryn Hochstetler

Abstract   South Africa has become an important player in international climate politics. Beyond its role as host of the COP17 in Durban, it has joined with the BASIC coalition (Brazil, China, India) in climate negotiations since 2009. The BASIC countries have raised important questions about the changing role of a small subset of emerging powers; while they continue to negotiate as part of the G77, their economic and political weight sets them partially outside the traditional North-South dynamic. For South Africa, this is even clearer in the closely related topic of energy. South Africa is the dominant economic power of its region and its "national" energy planning will have important consequences for both energy production and consumption across the region.

Keywords   BASIC, energy, climate.

INTRODUCTION

As this book makes clear, the emerging powers of Brazil, China, India, Russia, and South Africa (BRICS) have many reasons to develop international alliances with each other and many similarities and differences that affect the vitality of those alliances. In the closely related areas of climate and the environment, the key alliance is among just four of the five. Russia's classification in global climate politics has placed it for more than a decade in the so-called "Annex 1" of developed and transitional states that have formal obligations in the 1997 Kyoto Protocol to the United Nations Framework Convention on Climate Change (UNFCCC, opened for signing in 1992). While it has not made a second round of Kyoto commitments, it continues to stand apart from the other BRICS. The remaining four countries, known as BASIC in the climate regime, were classified as developing countries without formal international obligations under the Kyoto Protocol. They began to work closely together in 2009, however, as questions of their role in a post-Kyoto agreement rose to the top of the international climate negotiations.

Climate change cannot be stopped or ameliorated without significant changes in the energy sector, and not without decreased use of fossil fuels in particular. The energy theme significantly rearranges the positioning of the BRICS countries, as the political divide that separates Russia from the others in the climate regime disappears. The energy issue has no global regime, but the 28 industrialized countries of the International Energy Agency (IEA) have provided much of its governance from the perspective of consumer countries while OPEC has for producers (HUGHES and LIPSCY, 2013). The five BRICS countries, with Mexico and Indonesia, have been added to the IEA as key "Partner Countries," with initial meetings beginning in 2010 (HUSAR and BEST, 2013). One of the most relevant lines of differentiation among the BRICS countries divides Brazil, with its non-fossil-fuel based energy matrix, from the other four, which are heavily dependent on petroleum, gas, and coal – although Brazil's offshore oil reserves, found in 2006, may bring it closer to the others. The other relevant line of differentiation divides those with substantial needs to import energy – China, India, and South Africa – from Brazil and Russia, which are at near self-sufficiency or an exporter, respectively.

This chapter discusses South Africa's position in both of these contexts. An initial section examines the ways its participation in BASIC significantly raised its visibility in the climate negotiations, with its role peaking at the 17th Conference of Parties to the UNFCCC, which it hosted in Durban. The following section outlines South Africa's energy profile, both before and after President Jacob Zuma committed the country to substantial greenhouse gas (GHG) emissions reductions in 2009 at the Copenhagen negotiations. The concluding section asks what impact the participation of the BRICS countries in these two critical international issue areas has for larger questions of global order and organization.

Throughout the chapter, I pay attention not only to South Africa's relationships with the other BRICS countries, but also to the African region. More than the other BRICS, South Africa's emerging power status is tied to its regional leadership ambitions and achievements, especially in the economic realm (ADEDEJI and LANDSBERG, 2007). South Africa's international strategy thus reflects a multi-level game of global, regional, and BRICS-level initiatives that do not always find an easy resolution among them.

SOUTH AFRICA IN INTERNATIONAL CLIMATE POLITICS: AN EMERGING, BUT AFRICAN, LEADER[1]

South Africa had a low profile in the climate debates until it joined with the BASIC countries in 2009. The Kyoto Protocol negotiations came just after the end of apartheid, and accompanied a battle with the United States and Europe over whether it should be classified as a developing country in

---

1   This section draws from Hochstetler (2012). It is also based on observation of the 2009 Conference of Parties to the UNFCCC in Copenhagen and the 2011 Conference of Parties to the UNFCCC in Durban.

the GATT system, a position the new regime strongly defended (HENTZ, 2008). Similarly, post-apartheid South Africa chose to not opt for the Annex 1 listing in the Kyoto Protocol.[2] In its early reports to the UNFCCC, South Africa stressed that it should not be obliged to act and listed a series of other national priorities for why it was only in an exploratory phase in mitigation strategies: "poverty alleviation, providing basic facilities and health issues, as well as financial and technological imitations" (South Africa, 2000: xi). In 1998, it tabled several documents stressing the need for technology transfer for adaptation to climate change "whilst optimally developing" (UNFCCC, 1998: 9). South Africa spoke multiple times in the early documents on technology transfer about what "Africa" needs, clearly positioning itself as a leading member of this grouping.

In climate position, South Africa does stand far apart from other African countries, however. Its much higher levels of industrial development give it a different greenhouse gas emissions profile from the rest of the continent. South Africa is not just more developed industrially, but also has an industrial structure with unusually high emissions intensity (emissions per unit of GDP) (WINKLER, 2009). Energy-intense industries like mining and minerals processing depend on low quality coal-based electricity, making a "minerals-energy complex" that dominates its economy (FINE and RUSTOMJEE, 1996). With electricity prices among the world's cheapest until 2008, there were few incentives for energy efficiency. For all these reasons, South Africa's greenhouse gas emissions per unit of GDP are higher than those of many European countries. Thus while South Africa was originally left out of such economic groupings as the BRIC countries and has a smaller economy than other emerging powers, it was included with them whenever rising climate emissions were raised.

Like Brazil, China, and India, then, South Africa also sought allies against international pressure for climate action in the months preceding the

---

2   These positions were in contrast to those of the apartheid government, which often stressed South Africa's status as an industrialized country.

2009 Copenhagen climate negotiations, which were intended to introduce the first new climate obligations beyond those of the Kyoto Protocol. The four countries together, known as BASIC, met to coordinate their positions right before Kyoto, as well as announcing national climate actions (HALLDING, et al., 2013). Brazil (HOCHSTETLER and VIOLA, 2012), China (CONRAD, 2012), and India (VIHMA, 2011) all had national climate actions that were well-advanced before the meeting and had at least some sectors of national support.

In contrast, when President Zuma announced that South Africa would reduce its emissions by 34% below business-as-usual levels by 2020 and further in the future, he surprised even members of his own delegation. By the time of the Copenhagen conference, South Africa had signaled some willingness to reduce its emissions as part of an international agreement and had initiated its initial national climate planning in the form of modeling some long-term strategies and timetables for reducing emissions (Scenario Building Team, 2007). Even so, the ambitious targets Zuma announced during the conference were hastily put together and reflected his desire to make an attention-grabbing announcement.[3] The announcement was apparently driven more by a desire to keep up with BASIC partners than by an existing national consensus and the next section on South African energy politics makes it clear that there is still no strong consensus for climate action in South Africa.

Beyond the quantitative ambitions, South Africa has also acknowledged its dual role in climate politics, as a perpetrator as well as victim of climate change, "given that it has an energy-intensive, fossil-fuel powered economy and is also highly vulnerable to the impacts of climate variability and change" (Department of Environmental Affairs, 2010: 4). The Media Statement from the Office of the Presidency that announced South's Africa's new emissions goals consequently emphasized the need for an "outcome that will be inclusive, fair and effective; that has a balance between adaptation and

---

3 Interview, Anton Eberhard, Cape Town, 7 August 2013. Two past members of the national delegation confirmed the claim.

mitigation; and a balance between development and climate imperatives". The document stressed South Africa's intention to be a "responsible global citizen" and committed South Africa to an ambitious level of mitigation that was meant to be South Africa's final, rather than first, offer. But it also asked for an equally ambitious financing package for adaptation and mitigation and conditioned South Africa's action on the monies available for it.[4]

A notable feature of these and other South African climate documents is that the documents continue to include multiple statements on behalf of the African region, and South Africa clearly has negotiated as part of and for that region in a way that the other emerging powers did not for their regions. South Africa is a regional power in Africa, and has moved to extend its political and economic leadership there since the end of the apartheid regime (ALDEN and SOKO, 2005; GELDENHUYS, 2011; KAYUNI and TAMBULASI, 2012; QOBO, 2010). African unity in the negotiations is under threat, however, in part from South Africa's complex dual positioning (MASTERS, 2011). Some African countries saw South Africa as betraying the region by allying with the BASIC countries, with the Sudanese G-77 Chair accusing South Africa in particular of "undermining the negotiating position of developing countries" (MASTERS, 2011: 265). The tensions between South Africa's identities as an emerging power with the BASIC countries and its African roots were exacerbated in 2011 when South Africa hosted the 17th Conference of Parties (COP-17) in Durban.

Being the host of COP-17, with its associated responsibility to act as a bridge-builder between the developed and developing world, doubtless contributed to South Africa's stance as an emerging power willing to take on more responsibility in the climate regime.[5] Any conference host has a vested interest in reaching an agreement, which is related to its reputation of possessing skilled and professional conveners. Second, being in an exposed

---

4   "President Jacob Zuma to Attend Climate Change Talks in Copenhagen" 2009. South Africa. Office of the President. Press Release. December 6.

5   This discussion of the Durban conference is based on work being developed with Manjana Milkoreit.

procedural position while seeking to manage high African expectations, South Africa was compelled to act in the interest of the most vulnerable countries, and to demonstrate leadership on the African continent. Third, South Africa's mediator identity was coupled with a self-perception as a hybrid between a developed and a developing country, and as having an innate conflict-resolution skill, based on its history of peacefully ending apartheid (GELDENHUYS, 2011). In addition South Africa has come to consider climate change and the need to transition to a low-carbon economy as an opportunity rather than threat. Identifying green technologies as a potential source of economic growth, South Africa hopes to maximize the benefits such a transition offers and has already begun adjusting its domestic policies, in particular its industrial policies, towards that goal (Republic of South Africa, 2011). As a responsible global stakeholder, bridge-builder, and hybrid economy with a clearly identifiable economic interest in global climate action, South Africa was ready to lead in Durban.

As other BRICS have found, being ready to lead does not mean easily finding followers (MALAMUD, 2011; VIEIRA and ALDEN, 2011), and this also proved true in Durban. South Africa's fellow BASIC members were among the most challenging participants. China and especially India were hesitant to move towards a new agreement that would give them international climate mitigation obligations even as Brazil and South Africa signaled their readiness to sign on. India tabled a proposal to add three contentious items to the already crowded COP-17 agenda, which placed South Africa in a difficult position as both the conference chair and BASIC member. Developing countries, including many in Africa, pleaded for action and financial assistance, pressuring South Africa strongly from the other side. After an exhausting set of negotiations that extended well beyond the initial time frame, an early morning huddle on the negotiating floor among BASIC countries, the US, and the EU found enough common language to write a Durban statement that all could accept (HOCHSTETLER and VIOLA, 2012: 766-767) – although India felt that it "was in the end left isolated, and fighting its own corner" (Hurrell and Sengupta 2012: 472. The Durban Platform for Enhanced Action is mostly a commitment that international negotiations will go on, and subsequent meetings have shown that consensus beyond that is still very hard to reach.

SOUTH AFRICAN ENERGY POLITICS

At the level of international climate negotiations, South Africa has been a constructive and even eager participant. Translating its climate commitments into energy policy at home is a more protracted affair, although South Africa has taken steps that seemed unlikely just a few years ago. In this section, I briefly sketch South Africa's existing energy framework in both physical and political terms. I then discuss the initial steps toward diversification of its energy sources to ones with less climate emissions. Most of this story is a domestic one. As South Africa seeks to go further toward both enhancing its energy security and reducing its climate emissions, its options take on a more international, and especially regional, cast.

The foundation of the basic story of the South African energy framework is coal: the country has had abundant, easily mined, coal; lower quality coal fueled emissions-intense industrial development at home, while higher quality coal is an important export sector, including to other BASIC countries (EBERHARD, 2007; WINKLER, 2009). Like much else in South African politics, the apartheid government left a legacy with at least three important effects for South African energy (TSIKATI and SEBITOSI, 2010). One is the dependence on coal itself. As the apartheid state became more and more of a pariah state subject to international exclusion, South Africa relied more heavily on its locally available fuel, coal, even developing new strategies to turn coal into liquid fuel in what is said to be one of the facilities with the highest point source of GHG emissions in the world, Sasol. Second, the apartheid state, paranoid about energy security, significantly overbuilt electricity generation capacity for its distribution capacity in the 1970s and 1980s, so that South Africa went through several decades with minimal construction of new plants and ever-lower prices. Third, the apartheid state had significant over-capacity in good part because it built a racially distinguished distribution system that had brought only about one third of the consumer population – the non-black African – onto the national grid as of the early 1990s (McDONALD, 2011: 72).

Politically, control over the South African electricity system is unusually concentrated in just a few actors. There is a single national electricity grid. Until very recently, a single state-owned actor, Eskom, held a near-monopoly (about 95%) on generation and transmission for it, although distribution is done by a larger number of actors at lower levels. Political control of this system passed from the monopoly white government to the African National Congress' (ANC) dominant party administrations.

The first ANC policy document on energy was published in 1998 (Republic of South Africa, 1998) and already called for diversification of energy sources, attention to climate change, and a new build program so that South Africa could meet the increased demand that would come from expanding the national grid to all South Africans. Of all of these ambitions, the only one that was approached was expansion of grid coverage. By 2011, almost 85% of South Africans had access to grid electricity, although many of them were too poor to pay for more than the minimal share of monthly free electricity each received (National Planning Commission, 2011). The other two aims still require substantial effort.

After scattered blackouts starting in 2006, South Africa developed severe electricity shortages in 2008, which Eskom managed with scheduled rolling downtimes. The supply shock jolted the country into an accelerated build plan, including two more of the world's largest coal-fired power plants, Medupi and Kusile (RAKY and SOVACOOL, 2011). With pricing policies requiring cost recovery, electricity rates skyrocketed just as many gained access to the grid. Long-term contracts with aluminum smelters that require Eskom to provide 9% of its output at prices well below generation costs complete a picture of an electricity sector that has made a series of costly, short-sighted decisions.[6] At the same time, a number of indicators suggest

---

6   "Eskom puts R11.5bn tag on Billiton Power Deal," *Business Day* 12 August 2013, p. 1. This figure for potential lost revenue is USD 1.17 billion.

that South Africa is now moving towards some of its long-ago ambitions. The renewable energy sector, in particular, shows signs of life that were not visible when Zuma offered his big emissions reductions promises in 2009, but were arguably spurred by those promises – along with the new urgency that the shortages brought to electricity planning.

Eskom had been asked to develop renewable energy programs as early as 2002, but studies as recent as 2010 concluded that its monopoly on all aspects of electricity stifled energy innovation decisively (TSIKATI and SEBITOSI, 2010). Three different initiatives from different parts of the government filled the vacuum Eskom left, developing in parallel for a time before the Department of Energy – created as a separate department only after the shortages – was able to decisively create a renewable energy program.

The South African Renewables Initative (SARI) was one of the earliest and most interesting in conception, but quickly sidelined. SARI brought together a coalition that was interested in trying to attract new international climate funds (known as "Fast Start" climate finance) to South Africa with individuals in the Departments of Public Enterprises and Trade and Industry. The latter saw the possibility of a coordinated industrial policy that could make South Africa a producer rather than consumer in the "third industrial revolution" of clean energy. SARI was launched during the Durban negotiations with European representatives who promised new climate finance, but the coalition had not built ties early enough with the Department of Energy, and the funds have gone undeveloped.[7]

Meanwhile, the electricity regulator NERSA had also decided to use one of the tools in its portfolio to push renewable energy forward. NERSA controls rates/tariffs, and set up a feed-in tariff system known as REFIT in 2009 to promote renewable energy production in the private sector. NERSA published some original tariffs and then revised them after public

7   The "third industrial revolution" language is from the speech of Minister of Trade and Industry Rob Davies, observed at the SARI launch in Durban, December xx, 2011. The rest of the analysis is based on an interview with SARI participant Saliem Fakir, Head, Living Planet Unit, WWF, Cape Town, 12 August 2013.

consultation (Pegels, n.d.). The process served the purpose of drawing private investors to South Africa to put together proposed projects. It was stymied by Eskom, which continued to resist signing agreements that would give the firms access to the grid.[8]

At this point, the Department of Energy stepped in, with a plan developed with the National Treasury that would involve regular auctions where companies would place tenders to supply electricity to the national grid under long-term contracts. Only nine countries operated this kind of auction as recently as 2009, but the number had jumped to 44 countries by 2013 (IRENA, 2013: 9-10). While the auctions have faced numerous obstacles and delays in South Africa, the initial round in 2011 resulted in contracts for 1416 megawatts installed (MW) from 28 preferred bidders, mostly in wind and solar PV. Round 2 selected 19 projects to provide 1044 MW, again mostly wind and solar (IRENA, 2013: 39). A third round of tenders came in August, and the first round should begin coming online in 2014.

While renewable energy sources continue to be a small part of the South African energy matrix – the new Medupi coal plant itself is more than twice the size of these two rounds together – these are important changes that were unimagined as recently as 2009. The projects challenge not only the dominance of coal, but also of Eskom as a single state-owned generator of electricity. Both of these shake up the energy sector in South Africa in unpredictable ways.

South Africa's energy choices do not only affect it. The degree of regional electricity integration, for example, is quite high. The Southern African Power Pool (SAPP) was created in 1995, shortly after the end of apartheid, links most members of the South African Development Community (SADC) (HANCOCK, 2013: 5-7). The wider sub-Saharan region relies on Eskom to generate 60% of its electricity, with Botswana, Lesotho, Namibia, Swaziland, and Zimbabwe particularly dependent (RAKY and SOVACOOL, 2011: 1144). Eskom does a significant share of its production beyond South

---

8   Interview with Anton Eberhard.

Africa's borders as well, with electricity exports to South Africa forming a major part of the exports of much poorer neighbors like Mozambique. In South African electricity planning documents, one major source of energy diversification is a series of proposed schemes for hydroelectric plants in neighboring countries, not least of which is the Grand Inga project in the Democratic Republic of the Congo, whose giant size – perhaps 40,000 MW – is matched by the equally large logistical and political challenges of bringing it into being. It would feed the SAPP (HANCOCK, 2013: 1).

Sub-Saharan Africa is falling even further behind globally in meeting the power needs of its citizens as the rest of the world has improved generation capacity (EBERHARD and SHKARATAN, 2012). Back in 1993, Nelson Mandela warned that, "South Africa cannot escape its African destiny. If we do not devote our energies to this continent, we too could fall victim to the forces that have brought ruin to its various parts (MANDELA, 1993: 89)". Democracies, it turns out, provide electricity to their citizen residents at rates higher than equally poor authoritarian systems do (BROWN and MOBARAK, 2009). This does not mean that the converse is true, of course: providing electricity does not make a country a democracy. It does say something about the stakes of providing electricity, though, which is that this is a significant benefit for ordinary citizens of the sort that responsive governments provide. South Africa has a continuing deficit with its own citizens, and it is a regional challenge that all might be able to meet together better than alone.

CONCLUSION

As this paper shows, South Africa presents the classic BASIC profile:[9] impressive new international roles and visibility coexist with lingering

---

9 In considering the role of these countries in international affairs, I have deliberately chosen to refer to BASIC rather than BRICS. While it may be a controversial point of view in this

inequalities that leave some of their own citizens well outside of any experience of "emerging". That duality is one of the most important characteristics of the BASIC countries. In good measure, the countries themselves recognize this in their own foreign policy behavior. On the one hand, they attend meetings of the G-20 and the Major Economies Forum and increasingly wield veto power over trade and other negotiations, even if they are unable to impose their preferred solutions. Unlike an earlier generation of climbers like the Republic of Korea and Mexico, however, they have chosen to remain allied with the G77/China and politely refused moving to the OECD. They are emerging in both senses of the term: rising to power, but not fully there.

In this way, the BASIC countries are themselves claiming the status I also see for them: after a half century or more of a world whose fundamental order was conceived in part as a division of North and South, the BASIC countries – and some others – are interrupting that order. Like other shifts in organizing principles, the level of uncertainty is now higher. On the whole, however, I see this as a productive shift, especially in the ways it multiplies the trajectories and development paths that are available for countries to follow.

REFERENCES

ADEDEJI, A., LANDSBERG, C. (2007), *South Africa in Africa: The Post-Apartheid Decade*. Durban, University of KwaZulu-Natal Press.

ALDEN, C., SOHO, M. (2005), "South Africa's Economic Relations with Africa: Hegemony and its Discontents", in *Journal of Modern Africa Studies*, 43, 3: 367-392.

BROWN, D. S., MOBARAK, A. M. (2009), "The Transforming Power of Democracy: Regime Type and the Distribution of Electricity", in *American Politics Science Review*, 103, 2: 193-213.

CONRAD, B. (2012), "China in Copenhagen: Reconciling the 'Beijing Climate Revolution' and the 'Copenhagen Climate Obstinacy'", in *The China Quarterly* 210: 435-455.

---

setting, in my view Russia is following a very different trajectory and it is nearly impossible to characterize alongside the others.

Department of Environmental Affairs and Tourism, Republic of South Africa. (2010), *National Climate Change Response Green Paper 2010*, Pretoria, Ministry of Water and Environmental Affairs, Department of Environmental Affairs.

_____. (2011), *National Climate Change Response – White Paper*, Pretoria, Department of Environmental Affairs and Tourism.

DUBASH, N. K. (ed.). (2012), *Handbook of Climate Change and India: Development, Politics and Govenance*, London and New York, Earthscan.

EBERHARD, A., SHKARATAN. M. (2012), "Powering Africa: Meeting the Financing and Reform Challenges", in *Energy Policy* 42: 9-18.

FINE, B., RUSTOMJEE, Z. (1996), *The Political Economy of South Africa: From Minerals-Energy Complex to Industrialisation*, Boulder and London, Westview Press.

GELDENHUYS, D. (2011), "The Challenges of Good Global Citizenship: Ten Tenets of South Africa's Foreign Policy", in *Africa Review*, 3, 2: 179-199.

HALLDING, K., JÜRISOO, M., CARSON, M., A. (2013), "Rising Powers: The Evolving Role of BASIC Countries", in *Climate Policy*, 13, 5: 608-631.

HANCOCK, K. J. (2013), Comparative Regionalism and Natural Resources: A Focus on Africa. Presented at the annual conference of the International Studies Association, San Francisco, United States, April 2-6.

HENTZ, J.J. (2008), "South Africa and the 'Three Level Game': Globalisation, Regionalism, and Domestic Politics", in *Commonwealth and Comparative Politics*, 46, 4: 490-515.

HOCHSTETLER, K. (2012), "Climate Rights and Obligations for Emerging States: The Cases of Brazil and South Africa", in *Social Research*, 79, 4: 957-982.

HOCHSTETLER, K., VIOLA, E. (2012), "Brazil and the Politics of Climate Change: Beyond the Global Commons", in *Environmental Politics*, 21, 5: 753-771.

HUGHES, L., LIPSCY, P. Y. (2013), "The Politics of Energy", in *Annual Review of Political Science* 16: 16.1-16.21.

HURRELL, A. (2006), "Hegemony, Liberalism and Global Order: What Space for World-Be Great Powers?", in *International Affairs*, 82, 1: 1-19.

HURRELL, A., SENGUPTA, S. (2012), "Emerging Powers, North-South Relations and Global Climate Politics", in *International Affairs*, 88, 3: 463-484.

HUSAR, J., BEST, D. (2013), *Energy Investments and Technology Transfer Across Emerging Powers*. International Energy Agency.

IRENA. (2013), *Renewable Energy Auctions in Developing Countries*. IRENA.

KAYUNI, H., TAMBULASI, R. (2012), "Big Brother or Big Opportunist? South Africa's Enthusiasm for a Multifaceted Relationship with the Rest of Africa", in *Africa Review*, 4, 1: 17-32.

MALAMUD, A. (2011), "A Leader Without Followers? The Growing Divergence Between the Regional and Global Performance of Brazilian Foreign Policy", in *Latin American Politics and Society,* 53, 3: 1-24.

MANDELA, N. (1993), "South Africa's Future Foreign Policy", in *Foreign Affairs,* 72, 5: 86-97.

MASTERS, L. (2011), "Sustaining the African Common Position on Climate Change: International Organisations, Africa and COP17", in *South African Journal of International Affairs,* 18, 2: 257-269.

McDONALD, D. A. (2011), "Electricity and the Minerals-Energy Complex in South Africa", in *Africa Review,* 3, 1: 65-87.

National Planning Commission. (2011), *National Development Plan Vision for 2030,* Pretoria, Office of the Presidency.

QOBO, M. (2010), "Refocusing South Africa's Economic Diplomacy: The "African Agenda" and Emerging Powers", in *South African Journal of International Affairs,* 17(1).

RAKY, W., Sovacool, B. K. (2011), "Competing Discourses of Energy Development: The Implications of the Medupi Coal-Fired Power Plant in South Africa", *Global Environmental Change,* 21: 1141-1151.

ROBERTS, J.T. (2011), "Multipolarity and the New World (Dis)Order: US Hegemonic Decline and the Fragmentation of the Global Climate Regime", in *Global Environmental Change,* 21, 3: 776-784.

Scenario Building Team. (2007), *Long Term Mitigation Scenarios: Strategic Options for South Africa,* Pretoria, Department of Environmental Affairs and Tourism, Scenario Document, October 2007.

South Africa. (2000), *Initial National Communication under the United Nations Framework Convention on Climate Change.* Online at: <http://unfccc. int/resource/docs/natc/zafnc01.pdf>.

TSIKATI, M., SEBITOSI, A. B. (2010), "Struggling to Wean a Society Away from a Century-Old Legacy of Coal Based Power: Challenges and Possibilities for South Africa [check] Electric Supply Future", in *Energy,* 35: 1281-1288.

UNFCCC. (1998), UNFCCC Subsidiary Body for Scientific and Technological Advice, National Communications, FCCC/SBSTA/1998/MISC.3. Online at <http://unfccc. int/cop4/resource/docs/1998/sbsta/misc03.htm>.

VIEIRA, M. A., Alden, C. (2011), "India, Brazil, and South Africa (IBSA): South-South Cooperation and the Paradox of Regional Leadership", in *Global Governance,* 17: 507-528.

VIHMA, A. (2011), "India and the global climate governance: between principles and pragmatism", in *Journal of Environment and Development,* 20, 1: 69-94.

WINKLER, H. (2009), *Cleaner Energy Cooler Climate: Developing Sustainable Energy Solutions for South Africa,* Cape Town, HSRC Press.

Brazilian climate and energy policies and politics in the 21st century

Eduardo Viola and Matías Franchini

Abstract   Climate and energy policies have become central civilizational drivers of the 21st century. Within the context of a major threat of global warming, both national and international societies are faced with a central dilemma: how the reformist forces become strong enough to bypass the efforts of conservative forces to articulate a rapid and profound response to the climate crisis. This paper overviews the policies and politics of climate change – and energy in its dimensions directly related to de-carbonization – in Brazil between 2005 and 2013 considering that central civilizational dilemma, focusing on the dialectic of reformist and conservative players (economic and social forces, and the role of the government). In doing so, three periods are identified: between 2005 and 2008 reformist forces grew strongly from a weak base; in 2009-2010, as the influence of reformist forces is increasing, conservative forces are growing strong; and between 2011 and 2013 conservatives become become predominant, with strong support by the government.

Keywords   Climate Powers, Energy Policy, Low Carbon Development, Brazilian Foreign Policy, Global Governance, Reformist Contesting Conservatives.

Climate and energy policies have become central civilizational drivers of the 21st century. Within the context of a major threat of global warming, both national and international societies are faced with a central dilemma: how the reformist forces become strong enough to bypass the efforts of conservative forces to articulate a rapid and profound response to the climate crisis.

The global governance framework of climate change relies heavily on the behavior of the "climate powers" (VIOLA, FRANCHINI and RIBEIRO, 2013; DA VEIGA 2013a), states with singular capacities to alter the "climate social outcome" at the global level. The concept of climate powers comprehends a combination of diverse dimensions of power. The first two dimensions have been widely contemplated in IR tradition: military capacity and economic power. The third dimension – *climate power* – is more innovative and closely related to the climate issue. Climate power resides in: volume and trajectory of greenhouse gases (GHG) in the atmosphere; human and technological capital to generate a considerable impact on the transition to a low-carbon economy; and the relation between resources and energy culture – also called energy behavior.

There are three categories of climate powers, depending on their agency level: superpowers, the United States, the European Union and China; great powers, Brazil, India, Japan, Russia and South Korea; and several middle powers. The future of any successful response to the climate crisis depends on the logic of interaction between these agents, especially the superpowers, which are indispensable for any global agreement.

The logic of the global governance of climate change is also defined by the interaction of reformist and conservative forces (VIOLA, FRANCHINI and RIBEIRO, 2012). Reformist states are those willing to take post-soberanist measures to tackle climate change, choosing the transition to a low carbon economy. Conservative states, by contrast, are those resisting any major changes in the way business is conducted and prioritize the traditional high carbon intensity development paradigm. Within this context, both national and international societies are faced with a central dilemma: how the reformist forces become strong enough to bypass the efforts of conservative forces to articulate a rapid and profound response to the climate crisis.

Using the concept of climate commitment – the degree in which societies and political leadership assimilates and responds to the climate crisis as a civilizational challenge – as a categorizing criteria, we identified three types of climate powers: conservative, moderate conservative and reformists.

The international system is dominated by conservative forces, and that is why it has been so difficult to achieve any major breakthrough in the governance of the climate system. In another work (VIOLA, FRANCHINI and RIBEIRO, 2013), we refer to this situation as the "international system under conservative hegemony," given the system's evident incapacity to develop an adequate response to the major challenges of our time, such as global financial crises, climate change, planet boundaries, which are deeply demanding problems in terms of global governance. Climate change is the major interdependence challenge.

The traditional locus of climate governance – the United Nations Framework Convention on Climate Change (UNFCCC) – has been unable to stimulate the necessary transition of the global economy into a low carbon paradigm. After the failure of Copenhagen in 2009 (COP 15), year after year, the Parties of the UNFCCC have been only capable to agree on vague statements of principles and to declare their willingness to achieve a binding agreement at COP 21 in Paris in 2015. At COP 19, held in Warsaw in November 2013, once again were clear the huge obstacles standing in the way of an effective agreement. The 195 countries that gathered at the European city could only reach a last minute arrangement, in which they agreed to submit their plans for reducing emissions no later than the first quarter of 2015. These proposals are expected to be the basis of the new regime, which is to be established in 2015 and put into force in 2020.

The Warsaw COP also signaled the emergence of the "like-minded Developing Countries", an heterogeneous group that includes the superpower China; the great power India; medium powers like Saudi Arabia, Venezuela and Malaysia and finally; some less significant countries in terms of climate power, such as Bolivia, Nicaragua and Cuba. Despite the visible differences in terms of per capita income (from rich Saudi Arabia to poor Bolivia) climate power (from superpower China to Nicaragua) and climate commitment (from moderate China to conservative Saudi Arabia), the group promoted a single and extreme conservative position, stating that the strict division between developed and developing countries should be the center of any future agreement.

This insistence on a radical view of the principle of historical responsibilities was strongly rejected by the United States and the European Union. This dialectic of responsibilities – that has been developing for more than two decades and shows no signs of achieving a synthesis – is key to understand the lack of effectiveness of climate cooperation at the multilateral level. In this sense, we argue that advances in climate multilateral negotiations are only possible if some consensus is built between the major powers. Despite Brazil's conservative turn months before the COP – expressed in the resurrection of the doctrine of historical responsibilities – the government did not become part of the new group, which is a positive outcome for reformist forces in the country and for the general dynamics of global climate governance.

Within this framework that combines the concepts of climate power and climate commitment, we categorize Brazil as a moderate conservative great power.

Brazil is a great power because of its economic and climate dimensions, while its military assets are relatively lower than that of other great powers. Brazil's GDP in 2013 is 2.5 trillion in Purchasing Power, its territory encompasses 8.5 million Km^2 and its population in 2013 is 200 million people, with a fertility rate of 1.9 (Instituto Brasileiro de Geografia e Estatistica, 2014; International Monetary Fund Data and Statistics, 2013; The Economist, 2014). As a consequence, Brazil is the fifth country in the world in territory, the fifth in population and the seventh in GDP. Other relevant economic features are: *per capita* GDP of $ 12,500, public budget as proportion of GDP, 37%; economic growth has been an average of 3.2 a year between 2005 and 2013.

Brazil is a key country in the world in terms of the carbon cycle and natural and environmental resources because it has (SCHAEFFER, 2012; MOUTINHO, 2012; ASSAD, 2012; GOLDENBERG, 2007):

1. Annual GHG emissions in 2012 of approximately 1,7 billion tons of CO_2e – 4.5% of world emissions – 8,8 tons *per capita* and 0,72 tons for every $ 1,000 of GDP (PPP). We use here authors own estimations based on World Resource Institute Climate Analysis Indicator Tool (http://cait.wri.org/);
2. the most important carbon stock in forests in the world;
3. the largest stock of biodiversity in the world;
4. the largest reserve of agricultural land and the most competitive agribusiness in the world;
5. the third stock of fresh water in the world – after Russia and Canada;
6. the most efficient and second largest – after USA – production of ethanol in the world;
7. the largest reserve of hydropower in the world that could be easily used because it has a globally competitive industry in the field.

In terms of climate commitment, in the last five years, Brazil transitioned from the conservative side to the moderate conservative field in global climate governance. This transition had three main pillars: (a) drastic reduction in deforestation rates between 2005 and 2012 (see Figure 1 and Table 1); (b) a voluntary commitment to reduce emission trajectory in November 2009 and; (c) the sanctioning of a Climate Bill (Brazilian Law, #12.187) at the beginning of 2010.

However, after this positive impulse between 2009 and 2010, the climate agenda suffered considerable setbacks, like the expansion of the oil sector, the reform of the Brazilian Forest Code, increase in gasoline consumption, the stagnation of ethanol, and the persistent expansion of individual/private transport. Policies at the federal level have abandoned the focus on issues of low carbon, in particular, and environmental, in general: not only has the implementation of the Climate Law barely advanced, but, in early 2012, the government responded to the international crisis with a traditional carbon intensive industrial stimulus package, focused on the car manufacturing sector; resolved to eliminate a taxation on oil consumption on the same day as Rio+20 ended, in June 2012; and decided a populist reduction of electricity tariffs in December 2012.

The aim of this paper is to overview the politics of climate change in Brazil in the last decade, identifying the main actors and processes responsible for Brazilian ambivalence in terms of climate commitment, swinging between conservative and moderate conservative behavior. To achieve this aim, three periods in Brazilian climate politics are identified, in each one of them the equilibrium between reformist and conservative forces changes, having the government a central role in this irregular behavior.

CLIMATE POLITICS IN THREE MOVEMENTS: THE DYNAMIC OF REFORMIST/CONSERVATIVE FORCES.

The period between 2005 and 2013 has been intense in terms of climate politics in Brazil: the environmental movement grew stronger benefiting from the success of deforestation control, many private firms embraced the low carbon narrative and asked for changes in the government's standing towards climate change, the topic entered the legislative agenda in 2009 and the national election in 2010, some relevant cities and states made movements towards climate commitment, some establishing mitigation plans – such as the state and the city of Sao Paulo – and others demanding changes in Brazilian international standing – such as the Amazonian states (VIOLA and FRANCHINI, 2013).

However the advances – expressed in the National Policy on Climate Change (NPCC) established by National Law in 2010 and the decrease in the path of GHG emission rate since 2005 – there have been some relevant setbacks since 2011, as conservative forces grew in strength and political influence: particularly in the oil, agriculture and automotive sector. At the same time, the national government has been more sensitive to these sectors and has been operating, consequently, as a conservative force itself.

However, and before entering in each one of the periods, some brief consideration regarding those actors is needed; especially concerning the basic features of the Brazilian political system, which limits the development of any long-term policy, including climate change, and because of the high weight of Brazilian public sector in terms of GDP and investments.

In general terms, most relevant economic sectors in Brazil are mainly conservative (YOUNG, 2012; ABRAMOVAY, 2013).

1. The manufacturing sector has been traditionally inefficient in terms of energy consumption and production processes, with some exceptions, such as some sectors of the steel industry, which are replacing coal from deforestation with coal from planted forests.
2. The agribusiness tends to see the climate/environmental narrative as a threat to the expansion of the sector, since it is intensive in terms of use of freshwater, soil, chemicals and fertilizers and has been a beneficiary from illegal deforestation in the past. The generalized use of no-till farming, and some marginal experiences with low carbon and organic agriculture as well as forestation for cellulose and steel industry has not been enough to incline the sector to reformist positions (ASSAD, 2012).
3. The transportation sector is highly inefficient, heavily road-based, and carbon intensive, both in cargo and passengers (Confederação Nacional do Transporte, 2011). The area shows a very negative trend, with systematic increases in gasoline consumption and individual transportation, resulting in both growing emissions and degrading the quality of life in many Brazilian cities (traffic congestion, pollution, much time consumed in commuting). Despite the reformist forces linked to the ethanol production chain (which was responsible in 2010 for approximately 17% of the energy matrix) (Brazil Ministry of Science and Technology, 2010), the transportation sector is a conservative bunker in terms of climate mitigation. However, corporations that produce buses and trains are supporters of a shift in the system.

4. The energy sector in Brazil is more complex in term of trends and has some interesting specificities. In the 1970s Brazil was extremely vulnerable on the energy equation: ¾ of oil was imported and had no relevant coal reserves. In the last four decades, however, the country managed to develop an energy power status, building a diverse and relatively secure energy matrix, both dirty and conservative (oil) and clean and reformist (hydro, nuclear, wind, ethanol).

The electricity subsector is a unique and very important low carbon asset for Brazil, since around 90% of electricity comes from renewable sources and 80% from hydropower (SCHAEFFER, 2012). This is a divergent pattern from the rest of the world, where the electricity status quo tend to be conservative. However, the development of this low carbon asset is based on structural conditions – the huge hydropower potential of the country and the absence of coal and, in the past, oil – and not on climate or environmental considerations by political leaderships. In this case, the conservative or reformist standing of the government has little to do with the path of the sector, which has some significant space for expansion.

The other relevant sector in energy is the oil industry, which has experienced a big expansion in the period here considered – especially since the discovery of the huge pre-salt reserves off shore of Rio de Janeiro and Sao Paulo states in 2007. In most countries, the oil sector tends to be conservative, and Brazil is no exception.

In regards to the Brazilian political system, it promotes a low quality governance for many reasons (SINGER, 2012): political parties are weak, based on the particular interests of individual politicians and they are not usually drivers of political preferences aggregation according to programmatic issues; the general electorate has a very low educational level – and average of six years of formal education, which is generally very poor, particularly in mathematics and hard science – and a poor civic culture; representation in Congress is the most fragmented in the world – 23 parties represented in the House of Representatives and 15 parties in the Senate in 2012 – and no party has ever more than 20% of the seats in Congress; corporations and unions are powerful in financing electoral campaigns and most Congress elected members have a political debt with them during their tenures; and the executive power has 30,000 officers – middle and high level – appointed according to political criteria – generally poor in technical expertise – fact that promotes high levels of corruption (MAINWARING, 1999).

All the Presidents since the re-establishing of the democratic system in 1985 have depended on a wide and very heterogeneous Parliamentarian coalition, oscillating from three parties in 1985-1990 to 11 parties in 2012. Many parties among the governing coalition – and even inside the parties – have contrasting positions in many issues. Most laws have executive initiative, but for passing each one it is necessary to build up a specific coalition, in both the House and the Senate, with bargain advantages for a wide range of political parties and regional networks of politicians.

There are currently 39 ministries in the federal government, ten among them involved, directly or indirectly, in climate and energy policies. The Ministry of Environment has been historically occupied by people emerging from the environmental community or very friendly to the environment and climate agenda. On the contrary, the Ministry of Foreign Affairs – usually hold by a top career diplomat – has always been conservative in relation to climate policy for three reasons: priority given to the G77 and the alliance with China, India and South Africa (BASIC Group); concerns about the Brazilian capacity to control deforestation in the Amazon and its expression in vetoing any global framework to regulate forest carbon for fears of losing national sovereignty in the Amazon; and, a radical climate doctrine of historical responsibilities according to which emissions should be counted cumulatively since 1850 and consequently giving Brazil and all emerging economies a large space for carbon emissions increase during decades (VIOLA, FRANCHINI and RIBEIRO, 2013).

The department of climate of the Ministry of Science and Technology has been strongly colonized and influenced by the Ministry of Foreign Affairs since its creation in the middle 1990's. For that reason it has developed a position that is progressively inconsistent with the consensus of the national scientific community until 2010. It changed significantly since 2011.

Political parties that privileged fast economic growth over environmental considerations have occupied the Ministries of Agriculture and Industry. Contrasting forces shape the Ministry of Mines and Energy: pro-climate coming from hydropower and ethanol interests and pro-fossil fuels coming from the powerful state oil corporation – Petrobras.

There is however, an important reformist force in the political system: the Federal Public Ministry, a body of independent public prosecutors, which has been supporting the environmental agenda since the early 1990s, and has been increasing its influence over the political system since then. The institution is committed to the defense of long-term constitutional precepts, where environmental ones are central.

Within this framework of fragmented governance, where most actors are focused on short-term egoistic considerations, the construction of long-term public goods in Brazilian society is extremely difficult. That is why, in other works (VIOLA and FRANCHINI, 2012a), we have categorized Brazil as an underachiever environmental power, a society where the huge physical environmental capital is sterilized by the lack of social environmental assets. That is the main reason behind the absolute priority of economic growth in the Brazilian notion of development, which is shared by the government and most part of society and the private sector. The social pillar of sustainable development comes in second, while environmental concerns are placed last.

2005-2008: THE RISE OF THE REFORMISTS

This period is characterized by the growth of reformist forces within Brazilian society, fueled by relevant movements in areas such as deforestation control, ethanol and hydropower. Also, the environmental movement, as part of the Lula Da Silva (PT: Labour Party) administration since 2003, managed to gain some political influence over the government, forcing the abandonment of conservative alliances, such as illegal deforestation sectors.

The main movement of the period was the success of deforestation control policies, which led the annual rates of deforestation in the Amazon from an annual average of almost 21,000 km² in 2000-2004 to a record low of 4,656 km²/year in 2012 (Figure 1). Data from the government shows a significant increase (around 30%) in deforestation rates in 2013.

Figure 1 **Annual rates of deforestation in the Amazon Region, 1988-2013 in km²**

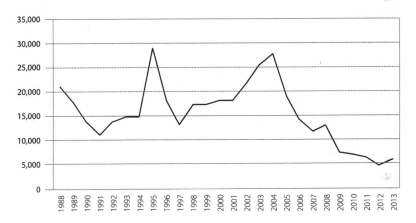

Source: PRODES-IMPE, <http://www.obt.inpe.br/prodes/prodes_1988_2013.htm>.

That remarkable fall in deforestation, which caused a unique decrease in the world process of GHG emission reduction, approximately 25 to 30% between 2005 and 2009, had several causes (DA VEIGA, 2013b): an improved institutional capacity and a more effective law enforcement system at the federal level; the creation of extensive protected areas; the role of big national and international NGOs in promoting public awareness; a gradual process of cooperation between Amazonian state authorities and the federal government and periods of decline in soybean and meat prices, even though the positive correlation that existed between those prices and deforestation was broken since 2007, when a major escalation in soybean and and meat prices had no effect on the deforestation rate in the Amazon.

However, central for this final positive outcome was the new approach developed by the Ministry of the Environment (MMA), chaired by Marina Silva – a major historic symbol of Brazilian environmental movement – between 2003 and 2008. Marina Silva was able to lead the formation of a vast but loose anti deforestation coalition, and convinced President Lula of deactivate the tacit alliance the government had with the illegal deforestation sector (VIOLA and FRANCHINI, 2012b).

As a consequence, the MMA increased the influence over the core of the federal government, especially in forest related policies, but also in other areas. This influence had even impacts over Brazilian international foreign policy: at the 12th COP in Nairobi, December 2006, Brazil started to change its historical position regarding forests in the climate regime, proposing the creation of a global fund for slowing down deforestation (CARVALHO, 2010). This was a victory for reformist forces over the traditional ones, historically limited by sovereignty concerns in the Amazon Region.

The strategy to openly attack illegal deforestation was also stimulated by the fact that in those years it became clear that that kind of practice was an aggression to a public good (the Amazon ecosystems) was inconsistent with a middle-income society, and had no impact over economic growth. At the end, deforestation control policies proved to be almost cost-free, both in economic and political terms. In 2008, Marina Silva was replaced by Carlos Minc, also a famous environmentalist, who managed to maintain, and even increase the influence of the MMA in Brazilian policies.

The success of deforestation control policies in this period led to a sharp decrease in Brazilian GHG emissions, from 2.03 billion Co2e to 1,25 billion in 2010 (Table 1). However, it is necessary to highlight that these figures are estimations made by the Brazilian government, more rigorous data will only be available within the next three or four years. In this sense, some analysts (FEKETE, et al., 2013) – including the authors of this paper – have considered these figures to some extent inaccurate, especially regarding the year 2010, which underestimates the level of emissions for two reasons: first, in 2010 Brazilian GDF grew 7.5% with high levels of gasoline consumption, and second, because it probably overestimates the level of carbon sequestration in forests. Even more, since it is in the interest of the Brazilian government to show decreasing numbers in GHG emissions, there could have been some distortion based on political concerns. From the information we have gathered from specialists and observing the trajectory of Brazilian main emitting sectors, the level of GHG emissions in 2010 should have been around 1.6/1.7 billion ton of CO2e. However, this situation does not change the fact that between 2005-2012 Brazil reduced emissions sharply in absolute terms and changed its emission profile.

The process of deforestation control also led to a major change in the emission profile of the Brazilian economy: in 2005 the major emitting sector was LULUFC (57%), followed by agriculture (20%) and energy (16%), in 2010 agriculture became the major emitting sector (35%), followed by energy (32%) and LULUFC (22%) (Brazil, Ministry of Science and Technology, 2013).

Table 1 Brazilian CO2eq, emissions 2000-2010, in billon tons

2000	2005	2010
2.08	2.03	1.25

Source: Brazil, Ministry of Science and Technology, 2013.

Table 2 Carbon intensity of Brazilian GDP (exchange rate), 2000-2010, in tonsCo2e/US$ 1,000

2000	2005	2010
3,2	2,3	1,1

Source: Brazil, Ministry of Science and Technology, 2013; World Bank, 2012.

Other relevant movement for reformist forces was the decision to reintroduce hydroelectric power plants in 2006, which were blocked since the mid-1980s by the fiscal collapse of the Brazilian state and by the pressure of environmental and social movements. Even when this sector operates as a reformist force, it is worth noting that the hydropower come back was – and still is – heavily resisted by other reformist forces, such as important sectors of the environmental movement, and it can be consider as a victory of the conservative forces, especially those sectors focused in traditional economic growth. This represents an interesting paradox, because the expansion of these projects in the Amazon – which have a positive impact in terms of reducing GHG emissions – was resisted by sectors that are usually constituencies for mitigation policies. On the other hand, they were supported by governmental and economic sectors that are not usually concerned with environmental issues, but they were seduced by the relative low price of hydro energy. The paradox had also another dimension; the environmental movement was strong enough to prevent the construction of big reservoirs for the new power-plants, thus reducing their capacity to produce clean and cheap energy, as shown in following pages. In this case, the environmental agenda and the climate one were fairly non-convergent.

This period is also characterized by the comeback of ethanol as a relevant quota of the Brazilian energy matrix (HIRA and OLIVEIRA, 2009). After two decades of expansion the sector suffered a period of decadence during the 1990s. It was only rescued in 2003-2004 by the massive incorporation of flex-fuel technology, which allows consumers to alternate between ethanol and fossil gas. Within this context, President Lula launched in 2005 the so-called "Ethanol Diplomacy", aiming to constitute a global economy of bio-fuels for Brazil. This strategy, that was advanced in terms of the national interest, but was in-congruent with the alliance with China, India and Indonesia in the UN climate negotiations, had a main evolvement in March 2007, when an agreement with the USA to develop the market was announced.

Finally, it is important to say that in 2007 is was announced the discovery of the Pre-salt, vast deep water off shore oil reserves. This event proved to have profound consequences in Brazilian climate politics over the next two periods.

2009-2010: REFORMIST VICTORIES, CONSERVATIVES GROWING

This is a very paradoxical period: at the same time that Brazilian climate constituencies begin to have sensitive impacts over national policies, strong conservative forces are growing, especially the oil industry. The environmental movement continues gaining ground inside Lula's administration and the government is sensitive to climate commitment demands coming from society, sub-national actors and the private sector, even when the main frame still is the priority of economic growth (VIOLA, FRANCHINI and RIBEIRO, 2013).

In 2009 there was a strong increase in public attention on the climate agenda: media coverage, public events, scientific conferences, NGOs mobilization, and corporate meetings. In this line, governments from Amazon states – under the leadership of Amazon and Mato Grosso – created the Amazon Forum in July 2009 and claimed for a change in the Brazilian international position in relation to forests. They wanted Brazil to accept the inclusion of Reducing Emissions from Deforestation and Forest Degradation (REDD+) into the Clean Development Mechanism (CDM) or any other market mechanism. Also, three corporation coalitions launched documents in September 2009 asking the political authorities to modify the Brazilian climate – domestic and international – standing (VIOLA and FRANCHINI, 2012b).

In October 2009 the Minister of the Environment Minc increased his pressure in order to change the Brazilian position in COP15 in Copenhagen. Finally, after heavy resistance coming from Foreign Affairs and Science and Technology, the new position was announced. Brazil made a voluntary commitment to reduce GHG emissions between 36% and 39% having as baseline the year 2005 and having as future reference the projected emissions for the year 2020 within a BAU scenario (Brazil, Ministry of the Environment, 2009).

By the time the announcement was made, another relevant development took place: the strong presence of the climate issue in the early presidential electoral campaign. The already settled presidential candidature of Marina Silva changed the whole scenario, enhancing the importance of topics such as sustainability and the transition to a low carbon economy. That fact forced President Lula and his candidate Dilma Rousseff to pay much more attention to climate issues on the national public debate and had an immediate impact in the changing of the Brazilian climate policy for the Copenhagen Conference. Ultimately, in the first round of the presidential elections – 3 october 2010 – Green's Party candidate Marina Silva had 19% of the total valid vote, in an event of historic proportions in Brazil (VIOLA and FRANCHINI, 2012b).

In October 2009, the House of Representatives passed the climate change bill, after significant efforts by the trans-party environmental block. Under the influence of the new pro-climate public atmosphere the Senate debated and approved the bill in December 2009. In January 2010 the climate bill was sanctioned by President Lula. The climate law (12,187) institutes the National Policy of Climate Change (NPCC), adopts the 2009 voluntary commitment of emission path reduction, and mandates that specific adaptation and mitigation sector plans will be establish by the Executive Power, pursuing the transition to a low carbon economy.

With the climate law and the voluntary commitment, the reformist forces were at the peak of political influence, fueled by Marina Silva presidential nomination, the strong presence of Carlos Minc in Lula's cabinet, and the positive international environment for climate reformist standings stimulated by the Copenhagen COP. However, that momentum did not last: at that very same time conservative forces were gaining space.

The oil sector has been significantly growing since the discovery of the pre-salt depositions in the coastal seas in 2007, but in this period the path was accelerated, including the US$ 120 billion mega capitalization of Petrobras in 2010. These oil findings are probably the main obstacle in Brazilian policy makers choosing a transition to a low carbon economy. In this sense, some negative effects have already been felt: growing GHG emissions from oil refining and petrochemical industry and the relative decline of ethanol as transport fuel. Ethanol's decline involves both the stagnation of the production of this biofuel since 2009 (Unica, 2013) (fact that forced Brazil to import ethanol from the USA) and the abandonment of the ethanol diplomacy. In fact, the only area in the energy sector with some progress regarding the climate agenda was the unexpected growth of wind power, having several projects approved with competitive prices in 2009 and 2010 energy auctions. Behind this development are strong and traditional political forces – such as the family of former Brazilian President José Sarney – and relevant economic groups – such as Siemens and Odebretch. In mid-2013 Brazil had 117 wind power stations with an installed capacity of 2.753,2 MW/h (Associaçao Brasileira de Energia Eolica, 2013) (around 0.5% of the national electric matrix).

Another conservative trend came as a result of the process of reform of the new Forestry Code, which began in 2010 and ended in 2012. The anti-deforestation coalition, which grew stronger until 2009 (further stimulated by the soy moratoria in 2006 and the meat moratoria in 2009 – a series of agreements between private firms, NGOs and the government that banned the commercialization of soy and meat coming from illegal deforested areas) began to lose terrain against the agriculture sector, as shown in the following pages.

Yet, other setbacks for the reformist forces in this period were:

a) The substitution of Carlos Minc as Minister of the Environment in March 2010, his successor, Izabella Texeira, lacks the political weight of her predecessor; as a consequence the MMA began to lose influence in the federal government. Traditionally, the Ministry of the Environment has been a reformist force within the fragmented Brazilian government, resisting non-sustainable policies and pressuring for a green agenda. However, since 2011 it has been operating in convergence with the conservative view of President Rousseff, supporting, for instance, the reform of the forestry code, which was heavily resisted by the environmentalist movement. As shown in following pages, this behavior led to an ending of the alliance between the environmentalist forces and the Workers Party in 2012.

The delay in the construction of the huge hydropower plants of Jirau and Santo Antonio due to environmentalist resistance and bureaucratic inefficiency and corruption.

b) The capacity of the automotive sector (a powerful alliance between the firms and labor unions with strong link to the Worker's Party administrations) to gain governmental support during the crisis, with no conditionality regarding energy efficiency or CO2 emissions.

c) The continuity of private transportation and gasoline consumption growth, and the chaotic situation of the public transportation sector. This is an area of increasing importance in the Brazilian public agenda, given the changes in the country's GHG emission profile – where emissions coming from modern sectors of the economy are increasingly important – and given its potential as a driver for social unrest. In fact, large demonstrations in favor of the quality of public transportation erupted all of a sudden in most major cities in June 2013. However, the sector operates as a conservative bunker, where the obstacles for major chances are high: heavy investments, the need for long term planning and, the power of lobbies.

The role of government was ambivalent in those years, fueling the paradox of the period. On one side, Lula had a reformist reaction in the face of the Copenhagen COP, embracing the voluntary commitment and the climate law, but at the same time supported the oil expansion, subsidized the automotive sector and other traditional manufactures during the crisis, and made no major effort in the critical area of transportation. In this sense, it was a mixture of opportunistic and conservative standings.

2011-2013: CONSERVATIVE HEGEMONY

In this period there is a clear predominance of the conservative forces, expressed in the further expansion of the oil industry, the privileges of the manufacture industry, the growing subsidies to energy (gasoline, diesel and electricity), the final result of the forest code reform and the lack of advance of the implementation of the NPCC. The Dilma Rousseff administration (PT), beginning in January 2011, has been clearly inclined to support the conservative forces, giving absolute priority to economic growth (REZENDE, 2013). As a consequence, the environmental movement migrated to the opposition and the role of the MMA was reduced. The lack of climate and environmental sensitivity by the federal government, however, has not generated political costs, probably because of the absence of a political force able to aggregate the reformist constituencies.

Regarding the implementation of the sectorial plans of NPCC, only one of them has had actual results – reduction of deforestation in Amazonia – but it was already working before the law was formalized. The energy plan is not yet being implemented and there are some doubts regarding the rationality of the new hydroelectric power plants in the Amazon region, due to fact that they were planned with little reservoirs, which make them highly vulnerable to dry conditions and consequentially reduces their potential. The low carbon agriculture plan has offered financing for sustainable practices and finally the farmers started to take those loans in 2013.

Other sector plans in vital areas – such as transportation, health care, construction, mining and chemical, paper and cellulose, and manufacturing industry – have been delayed and many uncertainties exist regarding their future, since they are very difficult to negotiate with the sectors, involve many difficulties and there are no major political or social forces pressuring for immediate regulation. That is why the forecast of an actual low carbon path in Brazil is negative. Despite of the fact that there is a significant number of corporations committed to the transition, most private sector actors are conservative and almost all the political leadership has been opportunistic – supporting the climate agenda when it was helpful in electoral terms – and conservative – lacking a clear low carbon agenda.

The ethanol industry is still stagnated both in terms of production and investment, even when it has a big potential for development. In fact, five years ago no analyst anticipated such a crisis. Two main reasons explain this situation: the systematic discourse of the government favoring the oil sector and the structure of relative prices that favors gasoline, subsidized by the government to mitigate inflation pressures. This is a clear example of the conservative behavior of Dilma´s administration based on short term concerns, as developed in following pages. Yet, other elements that prevent further expansion of ethanol are the prevailing *flexfuel* engine when a clear incentive would be the introduction for pure ethanol engines; the transportation matrix based on diesel trucks and heavily road-based.

In 2012 reformist forces had a major defeat with the reform of the forest code. The process and outcome of the reform process have been negative for the future of deforestation control for three reasons: first, it actually lowers the level of forest protection in Brazilian law; second, since it exempted many producers from previous obligation to recover deforested areas, the new version of the Code could operate as an incentive to deforestation and; third, it showed how powerful the conservative agriculture (also known as "ruralistas") sector is. In this sense, is has been a major political shift: in 2009 reformist forces gained support in Congress and the executive branch to pass the climate law; in 2012, the Congress overwhelmingly supported the agriculture movement and Dilma's administration, which tried to make a deal between the two sectors, ended closer to the ruralistas.

In terms of the government, there is a growing inconsistency between the political discourse, which broadly embraces the need for climate action, and the actual policies, which are focused on short-term carbon – intensive economic growth. In 2012, the Dilma administration took several short term economic measures oriented to increase consumption, such as the new automobile policy law promoting the production of parts in Brazil with no reference to carbon intensity, and the tax reduction for fossil fuels. In December, a populist reduction of electricity tariffs (promoted particularly by the manufacturing sector) was also decided and has had serious negative consequences on the firms of the sector: the market capitalization of the electricity corporations – state and private owned, generators and distributers – fell dramatically and investment stopped. Because of huge miss-calculations in the electricity policy during 2013 electricity prices to consumers were lower than production cost. During the whole year the government has given huge subsidies to the consumer and the same is expected to happen in 2014. Another major mistake in government policy in the last years has been a regulation of the national greed that doesn't match technological innovation and diminish the reliability of the whole system.

In this sense, one of the main assets of low carbon in Brazil is seriously hit by a measure inspired in short-term considerations. The focus of the government is to avoid the deindustrialization of Brazil in the hands of Chinese manufactures and to grow the economy as much as possible, even with artificial means (VELOSO, et al., 2012). There is no room for low carbon concerns in this definition of development and in the end, the obsession with the short-term and immediate outcomes results in higher carbon intensity and conservative behavior.

This vision was clearly shown in the Rio+20 Summit, held in Rio de Janeiro in June 2012 (VIOLA and FRANCHINI, 2012a). From the starters Brazilian official position was to exclude climate change as a main topic for the Summit, and trough official documents it made clear that the economic and social pillars of sustainable development are the main priority, being peripheral the environmental one. In this, sense, the Brazilian document is in the opposite direction of the climate law.

However, the Dilma administration is not paying major political costs for neglecting the reformist path. Her government is supported by a vast coalition of forces, with a weak and divided opposition in Congress, and the network of socio economic forces committed to the low carbon agenda do not have a significant political expression in Congress and among the political parties. The sharp fall in President Rousseff's approval ratings in June 2013 had more to do with issues of urban mobility and overall dysfunctions of the Brazilian political system than on issues of sustainability. In this sense, there has been, at least temporarily, a dramatic undermining of the reformist pole that existed in 2009-2010.

In that period, the "threat" of Marina Silva presidential nomination had a strong impact. However, the green agenda heavily depended on that one person, and once the election was over, the reformist constituencies were unable to build a more organic and institutionalized force. At the end, that experiment was another expression of the power of Personalism in Brazilian politics: in fact, even when Marina Silva had almost 19% of the national vote as Presidential nominee, the Green Party only had two percent of the total vote for the House of Representatives. The reformist gain momentum when an specific person, Marina Silva, was perceived as a threat by another relevant figure, President Lula, who feared the impact of a charismatic and former ally political leadership over his own leadership.

According to international polls (Pew Research, 2010) Brazilian society is highly concerned about the climate crisis, with 85% saying that is a very serious problem. However, in terms of public choices, things are different if we consider the vote on Marina Silva in the 2010 election as a proxy for climate commitment: she had only 19% of the votes, and many of them were related to non-sustainable issues, such as corruption, abortion and gender (JACOB, et al., 2011). This vote also shows some strong regional divisions in terms of climate concerns, Marina had a better performance in the rich South-East states (São Paulo, Minas Gerais, Espirito Santo and Rio de Janeiro) the also rich Federal District of Brasilia and the poor Northern region; the lower performance was in the poor Nor-eastern states and the richer South. She was also more popular between the more educated populations.

Given the conservative features of Rousseff's administration, the environmental movement abandoned the nine-year alliance with the Workers Party government in early 2012. This migration to the opposition was expressed in a highly acute document (Instituto Socioambiental, et al., 2012) signed by the most relevant environmental organizations where several aggressions to the green agenda were denounced. The Ministry of the Environment was a main target of criticism, accused of conniving to those aggressions and being insensitive to the public opinion. The fact is that since Izabella Teixeira's tenure, the influence of MMA in Brazilian politics has been dramatically reduced.

In October 2013 a political coalition was formed between two parties – the Brazilian Socialist Party and the Sustainability Network (lead by Marina Silva). This has implied a shift in Brazilian politics since the leader of the Socialist Party (a social-democratic party that belonged to Dilma's coalition until the middle of 2013), Eduardo Campos, could be a competitive presidential candidate, particularly with the support of Marina Silva as vice-presidential candidate.

CONCLUSION

Brazil has been a great paradox in terms of climate change between 2005 and 2013. At first glance, if the trajectory of GHG is considered – with a dramatic fall between 2004 and 2009 – it looks as if there was a low carbon revolution in the economy. However, what happened was that Brazil was able to control in the 21th century a 19th century problem: illegal deforestation, whose rate was extremely high for a consolidated middle-income democracy. Ultimately, the task was relatively easy, and did not result in economic or political costs. With deforestation under control, GHG emission in Brazil fell radically, creating a fiction of a low carbon revolution, used frequently by the government propaganda, however, if other major emission sectors are considered – energy, transportation, agriculture and industry – the situation changes: emissions are growing fast.

The situation is also paradoxical in terms of climate politics: when the reformist forces were having their major victories – the voluntary commitment and the climate law – conservative forces were gaining enough strength to eventually reverse the Brazilian transition to a more reformist position in the governance of climate change. After a first period (2005-2008) of sensitive gains, such as deforestation control, the ethanol and hydropower came back; the reformist forces were able to impose part of their low carbon agenda in a second period (2009-2010). The stronger position of the Ministry of the Environment within the core of the government, the climate-sensitive scenario stimulated by the COP 15, and especially, the gathering of the climate/environmental constituencies around the presidential nomination of Marina Silva, are the main vectors of that progress.

However, once those two elements were gone, the government was able to pursue an environmentally insensitive agenda with no major political costs in the third period (2011-2013). The growth of the conservative forces in the second period – specially oil, some manufacturing sectors and agriculture – was openly supported by the new federal administration, which took several short-term measures in order to guarantee economic growth that ended hurting the most important low carbon assets of Brazil

– electricity and ethanol. Between those measures are subsidies to gasoline prices, electricity tariffs and the car industry and other manufactures, as well as tax reductions for fossil fuels.

As a consequence, the situation at the beginning of 2014 is the stagnation of the implementation of climate law, except in relation to deforestation in the Amazon and low carbon agriculture loans; the oil industry raised its economic, political and cultural power, and there has been a dramatic increase of the power of agribusiness. In transportation and urban mobility there has not been any effort to avoid the current non-sustainable path. The ethanol industry is stagnated and no major gains in energy efficiency have been made. In the Rousseff´s cabinet there is no minister with power and will to rise the low carbon agenda, while the environmental movement has migrated to the opposition in early 2012, after a decade old alliance with the Worker's Party governments. On the positive side, hydropower is slowly developing because it is the cheapest energy but not because of a commitment to climate change.

As a balance of the whole period is can be stated that is has been more continuity than change in terms of climate politics and policies. Even when the climate law is a mark for a low carbon revolution, it is not being implemented, because of the hegemony of conservative forces. In 2009-2010 an opportunistic administration had a reformist reaction to the international scenario created by the Copenhagen Summit fueled by the political threat of Marina Silva´s Presidential nomination. But Lula´s successor, Dilma Rousseff, went back to a fully conservative position, in part due to personal factors. Different from Lula, who was more a pragmatic leader, Dilma has a more rigid vision on development, nationalistic and even likely climate skeptic; and in part due to the lack of a political force able to aggregate the reformist constituencies.

In this sense, the climate law of 2010 is more advanced than the average climate commitment of Brazilian society, where the implicit alliance between the cynical (those who support the climate agenda in the discourse but not in practice) and the deniers (usually opposed to climate action based on nationalistic development concerns) is stronger than the climate believers – both realistic and utopic. The problem is that the climate/reformist political pole was not able to consolidate, in part because of the structural features of the Brazilian political system, which limits the rise of political leaderships outside the status quo.

As stated before, the main characteristics of Brazilian politics – the extreme focus on short term considerations and the predominance of fragmented interests – are the central obstacles for the full development of Brazil as reformist agent in the climate governance. As an underachiever environmental power, Brazil has been unable to complement its huge physical environmental capital, with an advanced social environmental capital.

The giant popular demonstrations of protest against the quality of public transportation, education and public health, the overspending in the stadiums for the FIFA Football World Cup and pervasive corruption – in June 2013 – seemed to mean a tectonic shift in Brazilian society and politics that had re-invigorated the reformist coalition, expressed in the new alliance between the Socialist Party and the Sustainability Network. The general elections of October 2014 will be crucial to assess how far Brazil could be transforming.

REFERENCES

ABRAMOVAY, R. (2013), *Muito além da economia verde*. Editora Abril, São Paulo, 2013.

ASSAD, D. E., MARTINS, S., PINTO, H. (2012), Sustentabilidade no agronegócio brasileiro. *FBDS* <http://fbds.org.br/fbds/IMG/pdf/doc-553.pdf>. Accessed on July, 7, 2012.

Associação Brasileira de Energia Eólica. (2013), <http://www.abeeolica.org.br/>. Accessed on May, 11, 2013.

Brazil. Ministry of the Environment. (2009), *Cenários para Oferta Brasileira de Mitigação de Emissões*. <http://www.forumclima.pr.gov.br/arquivos/File/CenariosparaOfertaBrasileiradeMitiga. pdf>. Accessed on March, 7, 2011.

_____. Ministry of Science and Technology. (2010), *Segunda Comunicação Nacional à Convenção-Quadro das Nações Unidas sobre Mudança do Clima*. <http://www.mct.gov. br/index.php/content/view/326988.html>. Accessed on November, 2, 2010.

_____. Ministry of Science and Technology. (2013), *Estimativas anuais de emissões de gases de efeito estufa no Brasil*. <http://www.mct.gov.br/upd_blob/0226/226578.pdf>. Accessed on June, 20, 2013.

CARVALHO, F. (2010), *Posição brasileira nas negociações internacionais sobre florestas e clima (1997-2010). Do Veto à Proposição.* Tese submetida ao Programa de Pós-Graduação em Relações Internacionais da Universidade de Brasília.

Confederação Nacional do Transporte. (2011), *Plano CNT de transporte e logística.* <http://www.cnt.org.br/Paginas/Plano-CNT-de-Log%C3%ADstica.aspx>. Accessed on September, 23, 2011.

DA VEIGA, J. E. (2013a), *A desgovernança mundial da sustentabilidade.* Editora 34, São Paulo, 2013.

_____. (2013b), *Os estertores do código florestal.* Armazem do Ipê, Campinas. 2013.

FEKETE, H., HÖHNE, N., HAGEMANN, M., WEHNERT, T., MERSMANN, F., WEHNERT, T., MERSMANN, F. (2013), "Emerging economies – potentials, pledges and fair shares of greenhouse gas reductions", in *Federal Environment Agency* (Umweltbundesamt), <http://www.uba.de/uba-info-medien-e/4483.html>. Accessed on July, 3, 2013.

GOLDEMBERG, J. (2007), "Ethanol for a sustainable energy future", in *Science*, 2007, 315: 808-810.

HIRA, A., DE OLIVEIRA, L. (2009), "No substitute for oil? How Brazil developed its ethanol industry", in *Energy Policy*, vol. 37, issue 6: 2450-2456.

Instituto Brasileiro de Geografia e Estatistica. (2014), Bancos de Dados <http://www.ibge.gov.br/home/>.

Instituto Socioambiental, et al. *Retrocessos do governo Dilma na agenda socioambiental.* (2012), <http://www.socioambiental.org/banco_imagens/pdfs/SOBRE_OS_RETROCESSOS_DO_GOVERNO_DILMA_final_6mar2012.pdf>. Accessed on November, 11, 2012.

International Monetary Found. *Data and Statistics.* (2013), <http://www.imf.org/external/data.htm>.

JACOB, C. R., HEES, D. R., WANIEZ, P., BRUSTLEIN, V. (2011), "A eleição presidencial de 2010 no Brasil: continuidade política e estabilidade na geografia eleitoral", *Revista de Comunicação, Cultura e Política*, vol. 12, n. 23: 189-229.

LARA REZENDE, A. (2013), *Os limites do possível – A economia além da conjuntura.* Companhia das Letras, São Paulo.

MAINWARING, S. (1999), *Rethinking Party System in the Third Wave of Democratization, the Case of Brazil.* Stanford University Press, Palo Alto.

MOUTINHO, P. (2012), "Redução de emissões por desmatamento e degradação florestal (REDD+): construindo os alicerces da economia verde no Brasil", in *FBDS*, 2012. <http://fbds.org.br/fbds/IMG/pdf/doc-547.pdfr>. Accessed on June, 10, 2012.

Pew Research. *Global Attitudes Project.* (2010), <http://www.pewglobal.org/2010/09/22/brazilians-upbeat-about-their-country-despite-its-problems>. Accessed on April, 11, 2013.

SCHAEFFER, R., et al. (2012), "Energia e economia verde: cenários futuros e políticas públicas", in *FBDS*, 2012. <http://fbds.org.br/fbds/IMG/pdf/doc-545.pdf>. Accessed on June, 18, 2012.

SINGER, A. (2012), *Os sentidos do lulismo, reforma gradual e pacto conservador*, São Paulo, Companhia das Letras.

Unica. *Dados*. (2013), <http://www.unica.com.br/dadosCotacao/estatistica/>. Accessed on March, 27, 2013.

VELOSO, F., FERREIRA, P., GIAMBIAGI, F., PESSOA, S. (2012), *Desenvolvimento Econômico: Uma Perspectiva Brasileira*. Campus, São Paulo.

VIOLA, E., FRANCHINI, M. (2012a), "Os limiares planetários, a Rio+20 e o papel do Brasil", in *Cadernos EBAPE*, 2012, vol. 10, n. 3: 470-491.

_____. (2012b), "Climate Policy in Brazil. Public awareness, social transformations and emission reductions" *in* I. Bailey & H. Compston (eds.), *Feeling the Heat: The Politics of Climate Policy in Rapidly Industrialising Countries*, Hampshire, Palgrave.

VIOLA, E., FRANCHINI, M. (2013), "Brasil na Governança Global do Clima, 2005-2012: A Luta entre Conservadores e Reformistas", in *Contexto Internacional*, vol. 35, n. 1, jan/jun 2013, Rio de Janeiro, PUC, Instituto de Relações Internacionais.

VIOLA, E., FRANCHINI, M., RIBEIRO, T. (2012), "Climate governance in an international system under conservative hegemony: the role of major powers", in *Revista Brasileira de Política Internacional*, 2012, 55: 9-29.

VIOLA, E., FRANCHINI, M., RIBEIRO, T. (2013), *Sistema Internacional de Hegemonia Conservadora: governança global e democracia na era da crise climática*. Annablume, São Paulo.

World Bank. *Datos*. <http://datos.bancomundial.org/indicador/NY.GDP.MKTP.CD?page=2>. Accessed on December, 15, 2012.

YOUNG, C. E. (2012), "Setor financeiro: suporte fundamental de transição para a economia verde", in *FBDS*, <http://fbds.org.br/fbds/IMG/pdf/doc-561.pdf>. Accessed on June, 20, 2012.

Resource rents, resource nationalism and innovation policy

Perspectives on Africa and the BRICS

Michael Kahn

Abstract   This paper explores the politico-economic implications of the BRICS vis a vis Africa; the phenomenon of resource nationalism in the context of the developmental state; the nature of African innovation systems; and the possibilities to leverage financial resources toward economic diversification and innovation system development and consolidation. The rise of the BRICS (Brazil, Russia, India, China and South Africa) has triggered a second 'Scramble for Africa'. This time around the capture is not overtly violent, being advanced in the form of multinational corporations, both private and state-owned. As a response to the new modes of exploitation, and in the attempt to advance their development, resource nationalism has emerged as a powerful force along with a return to the promotion of the developmental state, an idea that was pushed aside during the triumphalist phase of the neo-liberalism of the last decades of the twentieth century. These dynamics hold for the possibility that resource rents may be deployed to modernize and regenerate institutions, to deepen industrialization and to grow country innovation systems. A specific issue that faces the BRICS nations is the way that their scientific expertise is to be shared among themselves and with the African continent. Co-publication analysis serves to inform these possibilities.

Keywords Scramble for Africa; resource nationalism; developmental state; innovation systems; innovation policy; co-publication.

INTRODUCTION

As China and India resume their prior status as the world's largest economies the shift in economic power from West to East informs a new dynamic in the development dialogue. Both countries have a vast appetite for natural resources, and to satisfy these needs Africa is once again a contested terrain. This exploitation generates considerable resource rents, has elicited resource nationalism, and offers the hope that African states may now deal with the triple burdens of poverty, employment, and inequality. Underlying these burdens is the dynamic tension between consumption and long-term investment in the form of infrastructure, communications, health, education, and even support for innovation.

Various drivers are propelling the shift in economic power: differences in the cost of labour and capital; the ongoing ICT revolution; reductions in transport costs; changes in the terms of trade. Hence the BRICs: China the factory of the world, Russia the gas station of Europe, Brazil source of foodstuffs and minerals, and India global back office. In 2011 South Africa became the fifth member of the BRICS club even though it is a small player. But this misses the point: South Africa's financial market sophistication, its position within the Southern African Development Community, large trade with the BRICs and geopolitical role as "the Gateway to Africa" underscore its claim to membership.

The rise of the BRICS has triggered a second "Scramble for Africa". Unlike the Scramble for Africa of the late 19th century, the second Scramble does not call for the capture of assets through extra-territorial force. Instead capture occurs through the role of multinational corporations, both private and state-owned, almost as a throwback to the days of the quasi-sovereign trading companies. The terms of engagement of African states with the new interlopers are often as unequal as those of yesteryear since they are based on weak institutions – political, administrative, health, education and communications.

The Second Scramble is coincident with the dawn of the 21st century. For Africa this marked the point when the decolonization agenda of the Organization of African Unity was complete. At that point President Mbeki of South Africa announced the African Renaissance looking to "the African Century", and together with the heads of state of Nigeria, Algeria, Egypt and Senegal founded the New Partnership for African Development (NEPAD). This organ sought a new path for sustainable development, with reduction of poverty, inequality, and gender discrimination (CILLIERS, 2002; HERBERT and GRUZD, 2008). The Organization of African Unity duly transformed itself into the African Union that in turn adopted NEPAD as the means to achieve its strategic goals of "policy reforms and increased investments in the areas of agriculture and food security, science and technology, environment, trade and market access, governance, infrastructure (energy, transport and water sanitation, and information and communication technologies), gender and capacity development" (NEPAD, 2012).

According to *The Economist* (2011) this period witnessed a clutch of African economics becoming amongst the fastest growing in the world. However this growth has been insufficient to meet employment demands (ADB, 2011) and conflict over the distribution of resource rents witnesses rising populist forces and a resurgence of resource nationalism (JOHNSON, 2007; Africa Initiative, 2013). Properly managed resource nationalism holds out the prospect for considerable revenues to devolve to the state. This quest is linked to the idea of the developmental state that was pushed aside by the neo-liberalism of the last decades of the twentieth century. The nature and behaviour of the state is thus pivotal in determining whether resource rents will be invested for the future, or deviated to consumption by elites. In particular one should consider the possibilities of resource rents being used to deepen industrialization and build associated innovation systems.

THE COLD WAR: LOST YEARS FOR AFRICA

Africa was the last continent to shrug off colonialism and regain its sovereignty. In the dubious tradition of European Great Power diplomacy the 1884-1885 Berlin *Kongokonferenz* demarcated spheres of influence and the boundaries of Africa's states. While nationalism had played a strong role in the struggle for liberation, the very arbitrariness of state boundaries often hindered nation building. The centrifugal forces at work in Congo, Ethiopia, Sudan, Libya, Nigeria, Mali and Somalia attest to this claim.

In response to the crisis of nation building, and inspired, if not induced by the central planning formalisms of Comecon, the Peoples' Republic of China, and those of Western development economists, African governments conceived statist models that offered the semblance of nationhood, holding out the promise of future economic growth. These statist interventions were accompanied by a rhetoric of modernity. In particular the Lagos Plan of Action (OAU, 1980) gave prominence to the role of science and technology in national development, advocating the goal of spending 1% of GDP on "S&T" within the decade. The "neutrality" of S&T stood above ideological contestation. The Lagos Plan envisioned a well-functioning state that would have the capability to promote import substitution, identify national demands, and mobilize the necessary resources to address these.

What happened to its good intention? The answer is painful. Africa became host to numerous dictatorships, civil wars and failed states, and to large measure the post independence period became "lost years" as instability, poor governance and mismanagement limited growth with consequent decline in the quality of life (MEREDITH, 2011). Over the period 1980-2000 average GDP/capita in Sub-Saharan Africa fell from $US 1750 down to $US 1450 twelve years later (Figure 1).

The widespread mismanagement included the neglect of the emergent innovation systems created under the colonial period. These institutions had been associated with export commodities and public health and included subsidiaries of premier scientific institutions of the metropoles alongside local research organizations paid for out of user levies. In general the higher education sector remained neglected through to the 1990s (Bloom, Canning and Chan, 2006), and with the exception of South Africa, no African state reached the goal of spending 1% of GDP on R&D (DNE, 1993).

Figure 1   GDP/capita in Sub-Saharan Africa, 1980-2010 (current $US)

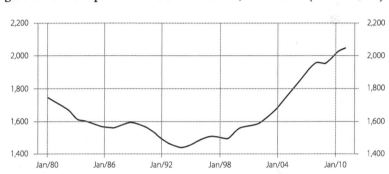

Source: <http://www.tradingeconomics.com/sub-saharan-africa/gdp-per-capita-ppp-constant-2005-international-dollar-wb-data.html>.

The ending of the Cold War, the collapse of the Soviet Union, and rise of the BRICs then opened up new possibilities for Africa's states.

Resource nationalism and the developmental state

The simplest way of describing resource nationalism is that it represents the attempt of governments to assert control over the natural resources lying within their sovereign territory. To quote Conseição, et al., (2011: 1): "At a minimum, it is important to capture the rents and to manage the macro-economic impacts of the large and volatile inflows of foreign exchange that emanate from the sales of the extracted resources".

Resource nationalism is a stance adopted in both advanced and developing countries according to circumstance. So in 2012 the Australian government sought a tax on mining company windfall profits; a much earlier position was Mexico's 1938 famous declaration: "the oil is ours".

Ward (2009) distinguishes three types of resource nationalism: producer, consumer and investor. Our concern is with the first, that of the producers. Effective and transparent control of natural resources raises the issue of the possibility of extracting resource rents limited by scarcity and barriers to entry (KAPLINSKY, 2005). The politics of resource nationalism elides into the role of the state in economic development, and in particular the quest to build and operate a "developmental state". This may include the promotion of state capitalism (RADEK, 2012).

In *Africa 2011* the United Nations Economic Commission for Africa and African Union laid out the case for state intervention: "engagement of the state, producers and consumers will enable African countries to take full part in shaping norms for environmentally sound agricultural and industrial goods and services" (UNECA, 2011: 5). To enable this transformation the authors advocate a developmental state "that authoritatively, credibly, legitimately and in a binding manner" is able to formulate and implement its policies and programmes (UNECA, 2011: 95).

By this definition, in an earlier epoch Korea, Taiwan, apartheid South Africa, and China would have qualified to be termed (authoritarian) developmental states. In Africa enlightened authoritarian leadership has been the exception rather than the rule, with Kagame (Rwanda), Museveni (Uganda), Zenawi (Ethiopia) representing a modernizing authoritarian approach. Among the fast growing states, Botswana has since independence in 1966 enjoyed the modernizing and relatively tolerant authority of founding president Seretse Khama and his successors.

The four original BRICs still practise various forms of developmentalist intervention especially through their state-owned enterprises and restrictions on foreign penetration. South Africa, the BRICS latecomer, having abandoned statism in the early 1980s, has recently adopted a National Development Plan (Presidency, 2012) that promotes the idea of the developmental state.

According to the Freedom House appraisal, over 1990 to 2005 the number of "democracies" in SSA increased from 3 to 29. Using stronger criteria, the Economist Intelligence Unit (*Economist*, 2012) labels Mauritius as fully democratic, with Tunisia, Senegal, Ghana, Cape Verde, Benin,

Rwanda, South Africa, Zambia, Namibia, Botswana, Lesotho and Sao Tome listed as partially so. The remaining states are a mix of hybrid and authoritarian regimes in which state economic involvement is highly directed. Many actions typical of developmental states are thus to be found across Africa; the missing element is popular legitimacy. But there are signs of improvement with no less than ten African countries in the list of thirty most improved nations measured in the World Bank's *Doing Business 2011* survey.

Politics aside, the demand for commodities and the desire to engage politically has seen a steady rise of foreign direct investment and overseas development aid to Africa (Figure 2). The major Sub-Saharan African (SSA) countries benefiting from recent FDI flows are Ghana, Nigeria, Congo, the Democratic Republic of Congo, Equatorial Guinea, Madagascar, Angola, South Africa and Zambia (UNCTAD 2011; CIA Factbook, 2012). The data provide a sense of the scale and relative importance of FDI in economies – without FDI Congo would not grow at all; South Africa could continue without FDI. The sharp rise in China's FDI to Africa to follow its 2002 decision to "go global" (OECD, 2008).

It is useful to place FDI in context (Figure 2). At peak (2008), the inward flow to SSA was $ US 70 billion; in that year the flow to all developing economies was seven times greater. It is thus clear that African countries have yet to experience the full impact of FDI, as in the prior cases of Malaysia and China. The fact is that even though China is often portrayed as the investment colossus in Africa, its record is modest and varied, with FDI having peaked at around $US 6 billion in 2008 and declining thereafter (Kobylinski, 2012). By contrast, in the same year Chinese FDI in its neighbouring countries was seven times higher.

While FDI to Africa rose seven-fold to USD 70 billions, ODA to Africa tripled in value to around $ 52 billion revealing ongoing dependence on donor funding for the bulk of development programmes, a situation roundly criticized by new Chairperson Nkosazana Dlamini-Zuma upon her accession to the role of African Union Chairperson in November 2012. Even so, this level of aid falls short of the G-20 Gleneagles Agreement of 2005.

Figure 2 ODA and FDI inflows to Africa (current $ US)

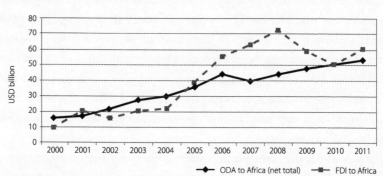

Source: <http://www.tradingeconomics.com/sub-saharan-africa/gdp-per-capita-ppp-constant-2005-international-dollar-wb-data.html>.

The result of this ODA flow is that in many states higher education and research are essentially captive to the agendas of international donors. FDI flows may be accompanied by equipment purchases and technology transfer that contribute to innovation and learning (PETROBELLI and RABELLOTTI, 2009) but thus far there is little evidence of this occurring. Bloom, Canning and Chan (2006) note various initiatives to boost higher education enrolments, especially in technical fields and for women, but with the SSA average participation rate hovering around 6% in 2009 (UIS, 2012), it is clear that there is still a very long way to go. SSA had a gross enrolment of 5 million higher education students in 2009; this needs to increase fivefold by 2025 to make a serious dent in the skills deficit. It is encouraging to note a general increase in the HDI for SSA, with average gains of 23% over 2000 to 2010.

Even so, China is now the largest source of FDI to Africa, and is also a significant provider of ODA. Unlike Western donors, China does not insist on governance conditionalities, making "a clear distinction between economics and politics [...] (that) [...] has led China to support undemocratic regimes, raising concerns about its contribution to the development of governance in African countries. Africa cannot expect assistance from China to improve governance, which can only result from internal choices and consultations between the State and its citizens" (RENARD, 2011: 30). An example of China's hands-off stance is provided in the AERC (2011: 32) study of FDI in Sudan: "the open door policies upstream and downstream, the need for resources, the historic relations, and China's stance on non-interference smooth the progress of its companies in Sudan".

In the quest to gain economic sovereignty various African governments have experimented with a range of means to pressurize the private sector: "indigenization" (Zimbabwe); "black economic empowerment" (South Africa); "local partnership" (Mozambique). Others have resorted to the pillage of resource revenues as in Mobutu's Zaire (MEREDITH, 2011), or questionable business practices as in Nigeria that reputably lost \$ 400 billion in oil revenues over the last half century (The Guardian, 2012). The mood has now changed, with the realization that the resource super cycle has temporarily shifted the balance in favour of the owners of natural resources. A means is thus needed to defeat the resource curse and set aside rents for the future. In the phrase of Ramdoo (2012) Africa must engineer the shift "from curse to purse".

While the notion of the developmental state had not completely disappeared from the agenda, it now enjoys renewed standing through the rise of the BRICs and the 2008 global financial meltdown. The rise of the BRICs, reaction against the Washington Consensus and the failure of the global financial system are of course intimately linked, creating an element of *schadenfreude* in the dialogues of the non-aligned nations. The meltdown, accompanied by ideological backtracking of the Bretton Woods institutions, has seen the pendulum swing toward state-driven development. Lee and Mathews (2010) provide a counterpoint for 21st century latecomers with the idea of the "BeST Consensus" based on the interventionist models of Beijing-Seoul-Tokyo.

In summary therefore: the first decade of the 21st century has seen high rates of growth across Africa; there has been some deepening of democracy with signs of a commitment toward responsible corporate governance; FDI and ODA have increased; education has seen some gains. This raises the next question: how have the continent's innovation systems performed?

AFRICA'S INNOVATION SYSTEMS

The importance of innovation systems lies in their role as the locus of technological learning, product and process improvement. In so doing innovation systems enable technology absorption and the generation by firms of entirely new products and processes. The innovation systems approach has an extensive literature (LUNDVALL, 1985; FREEMAN, 1987; KLINE and ROSENBERG, 1986; NELSON and WINTER, 2002; FAGERBERG, 2004), and a measurement toolbox (GAULT, 2010). This literature has gone a long way toward explaining the relationship between innovation and growth in advanced economies. Its extension to emerging and developing economies is a work in progress (LUNDVALL, et al., 2009).

Development economics focuses on improvement in the wellbeing of households and individuals through interventions by sovereign, bilateral, multilateral and philanthropic actors (LEWIS, 1975; SINGER, et al., 1970; SHAH, 2009). Development economics has its own measurement toolbox (BANERJEE and DUFLO, 2011).

With their quite different foci innovation systems and development economics tend to function within their own silos. In recognition of this communication failure the multilateral organizations and major donors have recently entered into a development dialogue (OECD, 2012). Well functioning, adept, and intelligent innovation system players must surely play a central role in this dialogue: "The real policy challenge is not to existing industry, but to potential industry. And, what implications does this have for the growth of dynamic capabilities, learning externalities and structural transformation?" (KAPLINSKY, McCORMICK and MORRIS, 2007: 36).

Writing on Latin American experience with China and India, Lederman, Olorranga and Perry (2006: 1) claim that this has created new production possibilities in sectors "that rely on natural resources and scientific knowledge, which not only benefit from the growing internal markets of the two Asian economies and their effect on commodity prices, but also from complementarities in third markets through production networks, cheaper inputs and capital, and innovation spillovers" that call for improvement in education, innovation, and natural resource management (see also IIZUKA and SOETE, 2011). While Brazilian manufacturing has reeled under the impact of cheaper Chinese imports, Brazil is now also an important player in Africa as revealed by its six-fold increase in trade over the last decade. Ninety percent of its imports from Africa are oil and other commodities; its exports include processed foods, machinery, and services in health and agricultural R&D. However Brazil's political-economic agenda may overshadow the importance of mere access to resources, with its desire to internationalize and gain recognition as a world power (STOLTE, 2012). The similarities in tropical diseases (22 country bilateral agreements in health), geology, climate and vegetation, give Brazilian technologies comparative advantage against advanced economies. Brazil has proactively forged its influence in Africa: it was the second country to recognize the 1975 MPLA government in Luanda (KAHN, 2011); agricultural research agency Embrapa opened an office in Ghana in 2008; Brazil is now the second most important destination for Mozambicans studying abroad; it is sharing synthetic fuel know-how with Angola, the Democratic Republic of the Congo, Ghana, Kenya, Mozambique, Nigeria, Senegal, Sudan, Uganda and Zambia. Stolte (2012) maintains that in the long-term Brazil is less interested in Africa's natural resources; more in its consumer market potential. South African companies are active in resource exploitation and infrastructure development, and are highly visible in the services sector, providing banking, insurance, retail, wholesale, logistics, transport, leisure, scientific and technical services, telecommunications and energy supply. As noted earlier China is a major source of infrastructure development, and the source of cheap consumer goods.

Faced with such competition, African countries must diversify their industrial base and develop their innovation systems to engage, compete and prosper. Technological deepening will be vital to counter the effects of the present wave of deindustrialization (with urbanization) that is sweeping across Africa.

It is all very well to talk up the youth dividend that Africa may enjoy a generation hence, but that youth must be well-educated if it is to enjoy fruitful and decent work opportunities. Designing smartphone apps is a niche activity that serves those who can afford a smartphone; it is not a substitute for broad employment. As UNCTAD (2012: 4) notes: "if African countries want to achieve high and sustained economic growth, they have to go through the process of structural transformation involving an increase in the share of high productivity manufacturing and modern services in output, accompanied by an increase in agricultural productivity and output".

The starting point for discussion of recent attempts to build and revitalize their innovation systems must be the S&T Consolidated Plan of Action (CPA) of the African Ministers Council (AMCOST, 2005). The CPA sets out to establish a number of S&T flagship projects (biosciences, mathematical sciences, energy, water and environment, material science, post-harvest technologies, laser sciences, ICT and space science) and to strengthen innovation policy capacity through the African Science, Technology and Innovation Indicators Initiative (ASTII) project. These flagship projects have seen varying degrees of implementation with laser science, space science, mathematical sciences and ASTII having made most progress. It is no coincidence that South Africa has played a strong role in these four. "Neutral" scientific activity appears to have trumped the more technologically inclined activities.

The CPA has conceptual resonance with the Lagos Plan of 1980 but is being implemented in a quite different environment. Most important is its advocacy of the innovation systems approach. This builds on a growing consensus – for example the Southern African Development Community (SADC) Protocol on S&T formulation of the national innovation system. This articulation is identical to that found in South Africa's White Paper on S&T (DACST, 1996 20) that is hardly surprising given South Africa's strong role in promoting S&T in the SADC, and in supporting the NEPAD S&T Secretariat from inception to its absorption into the African Union in 2011.

It is against this background that ASTII set out to quantify the continent's innovation systems. The first product of its work is the *African Innovation Outlook* (AU, 2010) that provides R&D and innovation activity data for thirteen countries.

The R&D Survey data reveal four outlier cases, namely Gabon and South Africa for GERD/capita, and Malawi and Uganda for GERD/ GDP. However the Gabon data are based on desk estimates, and South Africa is only a relative outlier as its GERD is so large. On the other hand Malawi and Uganda record high levels of GERD in relation to low GDP that necessarily produces a large quotient, begging the question as to the source of funds. In both Malawi and Uganda the bulk of GERD is foreign – funded infectious diseases clinical trials. This clinical trial activity has weak linkage to the industrial base. In terms of innovation activities South Africa really is the exception, producing upwards of twenty five percent of the continent's scientific publications, fifty percent of its US patent awards, and seventy percent of registered plant cultivars. Second in line is Tunisia (WEF, 2010) that also displays a well-functioning innovation system. Other countries host sectoral systems of innovation (e.g. sugar in Mauritius; agriculture in Kenya).

A final matter for consideration is the role of the BRICS as scientific partners for African states. To shed more light on this issue one turns to the bibliometric evidence of co-publication that serves as a proxy for scientific collaboration (Table 1).

Table 1   Article counts and co-publication, 2012

	Brazil	Russia	India	China	South Africa
Brazil	**36111**	533 (2.0)	373 (0.8)	623 (0.3)	266 (2.9)
Russia	533 (1.5)	**27303**	393 (0.8)	898 (0.5)	237 (2.6)
India	373(1.0)	393 (1.4)	**46348**	699 (0.4)	262 (2.8)
China	623 (1.7)	898 (3.3)	699 (1.5)	**183760**	325 (3.5)
South Africa	266 (0.7)	237 (0.9)	262 (0.6)	325 (0.2)	**9217**

Source: Author extract from Web of Science SCI-E, SSCI and A&HCI.

The diagonal (boldface) gives the country article count and the columns the country pair co-publication counts and the ratio of this count to the country total. These ratios show that South Africa, the smallest of the BRICS has the highest intensity of country pair collaborations.

The next step (Table 2) is to inquire into Africa-foreign collaboration of the most scientifically active nations on the continent, namely Egypt, Nigeria, Tunisia, Morocco, and Kenya, in that order. (Only Kenya and South Africa provided data for the *African Innovation Outlook*). Production of 1000 articles per year is used as the cut off point for "scientifically active". Country publication totals are shown at the top of each column. For completeness South Africa is included, along with the major global players.

Table 2   Scientific articles and co-publication, selected countries, 2012

	Egypt 7158	Tunisia 2825	Nigeria 1896	Morocco 1525	Kenya 1245	South Africa 9217
Brazil	131	12	25	140	17	266
Russia	110	6	3	136	3	237
India	151	17	44	24	37	262
China	203	19	46	152	44	325
South Africa	35	7	163	140	135	–
England	347	34	121	174	282	1080
United States	723	89	204	204	502	1709
France	213	866	23	544	63	628

Source: Author extract from Web of Science, SCI-E, SSCI and A&HCI.

Colonial history, language of publication, and the opportunities for postgraduate study all play their part in determining the level of co-publication. It is clear that the role of the BRICS as co-publication partners remains much lower than that of England, France, and the United States with Egypt serving as a prime example. Once again South Africa is the outlier. Collaboration levels are generally low. The implication is that there remains a very long way to go for Africa's research systems to blossom.

So the challenges are very clear: to build demand-led country innovation systems; to strengthen standards, metrology, testing and quality control institutions; to learn from others; to share expertise and experience; in short to realize the CPA. Availability of financial resources must underpin this realization.

INVESTING FOR THE FUTURE

Implicitly following Hartwick's Rule of "invest resource rents" (HARTWICK, 1977) a number of resource-rich countries have been able to develop and implement policies to capture resource rents and invest these for the future. Recent outstanding examples are Norway and Brazil with South Africa presenting a somewhat unusual case. Botswana serves as an example of a state that seems to know what must be done but is unable to effect this in practice.

Norway, a leading social democracy, draws rents from state-owned oil and gas major Statoil, and boasts one of world's largest sovereign wealth funds. Yet Norway has lagged below the OECD research and innovation average, so much so that analysts refer to the "Norwegian puzzle". Some speculate (see e.g. HUGHES and KREYLING, 2010) that this indicates that constituencies seeking to ensure the continuation of the Norwegian welfare state have prevailed over those that would divert funding to blue-sky research and risky innovation activities. It is feared that without significant innovation activity, long-term Norwegian prosperity will be unsustainable (SCORDATO, 2011).

Next is Brazil with its strong tradition of statism, best exemplified in the ongoing role of state development bank, BNDES. From 1999 onward the Brazilian government introduced legislation to tax firms active in natural resource exploitation and to divert these taxes toward Sectoral Funds that would serve to promote innovation in respective industry sectors[1] (CRESO, 2005). Araujo, et al., (2010) evaluated the impact of the Brazilian Sectoral Funds over the period 2001 to 2006 and found that firms that accessed the Sectoral Funds showed an increase in R&D inputs but there was no appreciable increase in high technology exports. Brazil is investing heavily in R&D, but like Norway the benefit does not appear to show in high technology exports or patenting activity.

We turn next to Botswana where enlightened leadership and strong government institutions, coupled with shrewd political calculation on the part of De Beers laid the basis for a 50:50 equity agreement with the state. The Botswana government-De Beers example has been available for others to study, and the African Development Forum now recognizes its unique lessons (AU/UNECA/ADB, 2012). Come 2010 the Botswana government used the fact of being the source of seventy percent of global gem diamond production to "persuade" De Beers to re-locate its sorting, valuing and sales operations from London to Gaborone, and allow Botswana to sell 10% of its diamonds. This is a perfect example of enhanced rent capture where scarcity prevails. As part of the realization of the Botswana Excellence Strategy, the first phase of constructing a Botswana Innovation Hub is out to tender. The Strategy looks ahead to the eventual depletion of diamonds, and the vulnerability of dependence on a single export. The underlying approach is to use the lock-in of De Beers to deepen the emergent innovation system as the basis for industrialization.

These three countries enjoy "inclusive political and economic systems" (ACEMOGLU and ROBINSON, 2011). Norway appears to show some reluctance to divert the resource rents toward R&D, while

---

1   <http://www.access4.eu/brazil/330.php>.

Brazil has been more than generous. In the case of Botswana it is simply too soon to tell. Despite well-developed universities and public research institutions (Norway and Brazil) these countries have been unable to broaden their portfolio of industrial exports and thereby reduce their dependence on resources.

The South African case is more complex. Up to 1990 restrictions on capital outflows explain the emergence of a world class financial services sector, now ranked third after Hong Kong and Singapore, as well as expertise in retail, insurance, logistics, communications, pulp and paper, brewing, and communications. Today the South African industrial goods market is uncompetitive as China, with its opaque finance system, and access to huge domestic and world markets, is able to compete on price for almost any steel-based item. Hence the present call in South Africa to "re-nationalize" steel to recreate comparative advantage. Alongside implementation of this variant of state capitalism are attempts to grow the South African innovation system and develop technologies based on natural resource endowments of titanium, platinum, manganese and fluorine.

In other countries attempts are underway to renegotiate resource-based royalties. In cases where MNCs were induced to develop resources in exchange for low or no taxation and modest royalty payments (Tanzania, Mozambique) or enjoyed subsidized input costs as in South Africa's provision of cheap coal-fired electricity, pressure has emerged to renegotiate better terms of engagement. After all, history shows that Botswana, hailed as a paragon of democracy, in 1977 renegotiated its original fifteen percent equity share in De Beers Botswana up to fifty percent once the wealth of the planned Jwaneng diamond mine was determined. This experience underpins the African Union African Mining Vision of 2009 that seeks to promote "transparent, equitable and optimal exploitation of mineral resources to underpin broad based sustainable growth and socio-economic development" (ADF, 2012: 3).

The commodity super-cycle and global financial disorders provide an opportunity for resource-rich African states to re-evaluate their development paths, international relations, and their relationships with investors. An underlying weakness is that outside North Africa and South Africa, there has been insufficient investment in higher education. Innovation systems are at best emergent, and in most cases disarticulated.

Turning the resource rent capture into growth and societal well being is predicated on gaining a fair share of the benefits of resource extraction, and ensuring that resource rents are not dissipated in elite circles. Brazil and South Africa have both moved some way toward using resource rents to provide a social safety net, though both countries also demonstrate the power of bureaucracies to divert resources toward their own advantage. Broadening and deepening scientific collaboration with the BRICS is an important counterpart to establishing industry R&D labs no matter how modest these may be. The precise areas for collaboration are critical: will these be "blue sky" or needs driven? Detailed case studies of resource rent capture, the functioning of "sectoral funds" and the way that horizontal and vertical value chains may be developed around resource exploitation will be of value further to inform the discussions on resource nationalism, sustainability and growth with equality.

REFERENCES

ACEMOGLU, D., ROBINSON, J. (2012), *How Nations Fail*, London, Profile Books.

ADF. (2012), Eighth African Development Forum (ADF-VIII) 23-25 October 2013. "Governing and Harnessing Natural Resources for Africa's Development", in *Document ECA/ADF/8/2*. Addis Ababa, African Union.

AERC. (2010), "China-Africa Investment Relations: A Case Study of Nigeria", in *Final Report*.

Africa Initiative. (2013), *Resource Nationalism Threatens Africa's Mining Boom*. <http://www.africaportal.org/>. Articles/2013/02/14/resource-nationalism-threatens-africa's-mining-boom.

DA MOTTA, E., ALBUQUERQUE, E. (2003), *Immature systems of innovation: Introductory notes about a comparison between South Africa, India, Mexico and Brazil based on Science and Technology statistics*. Working Paper, n. 221, Belo Horizonte, UFMG/Cedeplar.

AMCOST (2005), *Africa's Science and Technology Consolidated Plan of Action*. Addis Abab, African Union.

ARAÚJO, B. C., PIANTO, D., DE NEGRI, F., CAVALCANTE, L. R., ARBER, P.A. (2010), *Impacts of the Brazilian science and technology sectoral funds on the industrial firms' R&D inputs and outputs*, Brasília, Institute for Applied Economic Research.

AU/UNECA/ADB. (2012), "Mineral Resources for Africa's Development: Anchoring a New Vision", in *Eighth African Development Forum (ADF-VIII)*. Addis Ababa, African Union, United Nations Economic Commission for Africa, African Development Bank.

BANERJEE, A., DUFLO, E. (2011), *Poor Economics: A Radical Rethinking of the Way to Fight Global Poverty*. New York, Public Affairs.

BLOOM, D., CANNING, D., CHAN, K. (2006), *Higher Education and Economic Development in Africa*. Washington, World Bank.

CILLIERS, J. (2002), "NEPAD's Peer Review Mechanism", in *ISS Paper*, 64, Johannesburg, Institute for Strategic Studies.

CONCEIÇÃO, P., FUENTES, R. LEVINE, S. (2011), *Managing Natural Resources for Human Development in Low-Income Countries*. Geneva, United Nations Development Programme.

CRESO, S.A. (2005), "Research policy in emerging economies: Brazil's Sector Funds", in *Minerva*, 43: 245-263.

DACST. (1996), *White Paper on Science and Technology*, Pretoria, Department of Arts, Culture, Science and Technology.

Economist. (2011), *The Lion Kings*, p 66, 8 January.

_____. (2012), <http://www.economist.com/topics/economist-intelligence-unit>.

FAGERBERG, J. (2004), "Innovation: A guide to the literature", in J. Fagerberg & D. Mowery (eds.), *Oxford Handbook of Innovation*, Oxford, Oxford University Press.

FREEMAN, C. (1987), *Technology Policy and Economic Performance, Lessons From Japan*, London and New York, Pinter Publishers.

FREEMAN, C., SOETE, L. (2007), "Developing science, technology and innovation indicators: what we can learn from the past", in *MERIT*, Working Paper #2007/001.

GAULT, F. (2010), *Innovation Strategies for a Global Economy, Development, Implementation, Measurement and Management*, Edward Elgar, Cheltenham, UK and Northampton, MA.

HARTWICK, J. M. (1977), "Intergenerational Equity and the Investment of Rents from Exhaustible Resources", in *American Economic Review*, 67 (December) 972-74.

HERBERT, R., Gruzd, S. (2008), *The African Peer Review Mechanism. Lessons form the Pioneers*. Joahnnesburg, South African Institute of International Affairs. <http://econpapers.repec.org/article/blaapacel/v_3a24_3ay_3a2010_3ai_3a1_3ap_3a86-103.htm>.

HUGHES, L., Kreyling, S. L. (2010), "Understanding resource nationalism in the 21st century", in *Journal of Energy Security*. July 2010.

IIZUKA, M., SOETE, L. (2011), "Catching up in the 21st century: Globalization, knowledge & capabilities in Latin America, a case for natural resource based activities", in *MERIT*, Working Paper 2011: 071.

JOHNSON, S. (2007), *The Return of Resource Nationalism*. Washington, Council on Foreign Relations.

KAHN, M. J. (2011), "The BRICS and South Africa as the gateway to Africa", in *SA Institute of Mining and Metallurgy*, 111, 7: 493-496.

KAPLINSKY, R., McCORMICK, D., MORRIS, M. (2007), *The Impact of China on Sub-Saharan Africa*. Working Paper, n. 261. Lewes, Institute of Development Studies.

KLINE, S. J., ROSENBERG, N. (1986), "An Overview of Innovation", in Landau R & N Rosenberg (eds.), *The Positive Sum Strategy: Technology for Economic Growth*, National Academy Press, Washington, Wagner C. Kobylinski, 2012.

LEE, K., MATHEWS, J. A. (2010), "From Washington Consensus to BeST Consensus for world development", in *Asian-Pacific Economic Literature*, vol. 24, issue 1, p. 86-103.

LEWIS, W.A. (1977), "The evolution of the international economic order", in *Discussion*, Paper 74. New Jersey, Woodrow Wilson Centre, Princeton University.

LUNDVALL, B.-A. (1985), *Product Innovation and User-Producer Interaction*. Aalborg, Aalborg University Press.

MEREDITH, M. (2011), *The State of Africa. A history of the continent since independence*. Lomdon, Free Press.

NELSON, R., WINTER, S. (2002), "Evolutionary Theorizing in Economics, Journal of Economic Perspectives", in *American Economic Association*, 16, 2: 23-46.

NEPAD. (2012), <http://www.au.int/en/NEPAD>. Accessed on December, 29, 2012.

OAU. (1980), *Lagos Plan of action for the Economic Development of Africa*. Addis Abab, UN Economic Commission for Africa.

OECD. (2008), <http://www.oecd.org/investment/investmentpolicy/40283257.pdf>.

_____. (2012), *Innovation for Development*. Paris, Organization for Economic Cooperation and Development.

PIETROBELLI, C., RABELLOTTI, R. (2009), "The global dimension of innovation systems: linking innovation systems and global value chains", *in* B. A. Lundvall, K. J. Joseph, C. Chaminade & J.Vang (eds.)", in *Handbook on innovation systems and developing countries: building domestic capabilities in a domestic setting*, Cheltenham, Edward Elgar Press, 214-238.

RADEK, M. (2012), *The Roots of Resource Nationalism*. Washington, Washington, Council on Foreign Relations.

RAMDOO, I. (2012), "From Curse to Purse Making Extractive Resources Work for Development", in *Discussion Paper*, n. 136. Maastricht, European Centre for Development Policy Management.

RENARD, M.-F. (2011), "China's trade and FDI in Africa", in *Working Paper*, n. 126. Tunis, African Development Bank.

SADC. (2008), *SADC Protocol on Science and Technology*. Gaborone, Southern African Development Community.

SHAH, E. (2009), "Manifesting Utopia: History and Philosophy of UN Debates on Science and Technology for Sustainable Development", in *STEPS Working Paper*, Brighton, University of Sussex, Institute of Development Studies.

SINGER, H., Cooper, C., Desai, R. C., Freeman, C., Gish, O., Hill, S., Oldham, G. (1970), *Draft introductory statement for the world plan of action for the application of science and technology to development, prepared by the "Sussex Group"*, Annex II in "Science and Technology for Development: Proposals for the Second Development Decade", United Nations, Department of Economic and Social Affairs, New York, Document ST/ECA/133.

SCORDATO, L. (2011), *Mini Country Report Norway*. Brussels, DG Enterprise and Industry.

STOLTE, C. (2012), "Brazil in Africa: Just Another BRICS Country Seeking Resources?", in *Briefing Paper*, AFP/AMP BP 2012/01, London, Chatham House.

The Guardian. (2012), <http://www.ngrguardiannews.com/index.php?option=com_content&id=103315%3Anigeria-lost-n16tr-to-scams-in-oil-gas-sector-says-report&Itemid=559>. Accessed on January, 5, 2013.

UIS. (2012), *Global Education Digest 2011*, Montreal, United Nations Institute for Statistics.

UNCTAD. (2012), *Economic Development in Africa Report 2012. Structural transformation and sustainable development in Africa*. Geneva: United Nations Conference on Trade and Development.

WARD, H. (2009), "Resource nationalism and sustainable development: a primer and key issues", in *IIED Working Paper*, London, International Institute for Environment and Development.

WEF. (2010), *Global Competitiveness Report 2010-2011*. Geneva, World Economic Forum.

Russia in G20

Lessons and opportunities for BRICS's macroeconomic policy[1]

Natalia Khmelevskaya

Abstract   The paper focuses on G20's policy coordination mechanics for understanding how much it may help Russia to fulfill its development potential facing challenges of a new world order. For this purpose B20-G20 partnership is examined to show that the narrower distance between governments and outreach groups in global dialogue the more G20 capable in translating recommendations into practice. Analysis of discrepancies between "coordinated policy" recommendations and national labour policy measures has proved that even for relatively similar in structural features BRICS policy interventions may be only tailored to country-specific circumstances to be sound and credible. Finally, the logic of research steams to review of Russia's approach to foster its recommendations from discussion to concrete G20's decisions. It became quite clear that the ground for pushing them forward is international economic institutions and therewhy for BRICS countries it may be a route to act within global agenda more promoted and coordinated.

---

1   Responsibility for this paper's contents lies exclusively with the author. To ensure accuracy and comprehensiveness I would be grateful for comments and feedback, which can be sent to Khmelevskaya@mgimo.ru. The paper is based on analisys of G20 official documents, ILO, OECD, World Bank and G20 Task Force on Employment reports for G20, etc.

Keywords G20's Policy Coordination Framework, Russia's extra impetus agenda to the G20 discussions, B20–G20 Partnership, Russian Outreach Strategy, MAP, BRICS Coordinated Policy Recommendations.

INTRODUCTION

In an era of changes brought to the international system much by coordinated actions may G20 help BRICS articulate their collective political will and/or steer their economies toward strong and balanced growth?

The paper first focuses on the genesis of G20 policy coordination for understanding how the G20 decision-making process is framed. Transforming from its members' premier forum to address global imbalances into an implementation mechanism for international economic cooperation G20 enhanced its legitimacy before countries, regional and international organizations, outreach groups, then its global dialogue formats and international institutions involvement.

So far the business community determines growth globally. The analysis of B20's and L20's recommendations translated into G20 decisions promotes vision a which macroeconomic policy areas global dialogue may be viable for the BRICS to articulate their development priorirties.

The other emphasis is put on revision of such Russia's policy priorities as quality jobs and growth through coordinated policy recommendations and BRICS's Structural Reform Commitments under MAP to accentuate G20 decisions' applicability. Finally, the logic of this research reviews Russia's approach to foster its recommendations from discussion to concrete G20's decisions.

G20'S POLICY COORDINATION FRAMEWORK

Since its first summit in November 2008 (Washington DC) G20 has significantly strengthened its international cooperation abilities gradually setting up its specific framework for coordinated policies and collective actions (further PCF for Policy Coordinated Framework). First, to transform its members' premier forum addressing persistent global imbalances in its decisions into an implementation mechanism for international economic cooperation G20 started to enhance its legitimacy standing on "consistent engagement". G20 has engaged more countries, regional and international organizations, and outreach groups in a working process through participation in selected working groups, workshops, conferences, etc.

Spain today is the permanent invitee. Ethiopia, Malawi, Nigeria, and Vietnam made their first G-20 summit appearances in Toronto. Kazakhstan, Ethiopia, Senegal and Brunei Darussalam participated in the G20's St. Petersburg summit as member and chairs of regional organizations (the EurAsEC Custom Union and the Commonwealth of Independent States (CIS), the African Union and the New Partnership for Africa's Development, ASEAN), and Singapore – as the Chair of the IMF International Monetary and Financial Committee and the Chair of the Global Governance Group (3G).

Besides traditional meetings of officials since 2012 Troika's dialog (includes previous, current and future presidencies) with all other G20 members and non-members and other relevant organizations has been promoted to gather and tramsmit between presidencies the best practices (e.g. Australia was asked to assist with the program of outreach in the Asia-Pacific, and Mexico in the Americas).

For BRICS countries that extensive dialogue has generated divergent effects. The Russian, Brazilian and South African proposals might be more effective as transmitted within their Custom Unions by their non-members representatives, but not the Chinese or Indian. To certain extent BRICS have launched their own pre-summit meeting in 2012 aimed to "steer to consolidated vision on common problems".

The other G20 PCF's pillar comprises various global dialogue formats proclaimed as ensuring that G20 decisions "carry the consent of and have the desired impact on most actors of international society". To respond to the possibly wider scope of G20's parties interests, the approach to allow proposals from all sectors of international society to be studied, discussed and transmitted to the G20 decision-making level has been introduced in 2010 and formulated onto Outreach Strategy when it came to Russian Presidency of the G20 in 2013.[2] The underlying objective of that approach was to accumulate "cross-fora synergy" between governments and outreach groups. The largest of them, Business 20 (B20), was established during the summit in Toronto to organize dialogue with business partners and private sector groups responsible for the stability in national economies through investments and jobs. Labor 20 (L20) was established in Cannes and outreached with the Joint G20 Finance and Labour Ministers' Meeting in Moscow, July 2013. Civil 20 Summit was held in Russia for the first time.

Today Think 20, B20, L20, Civil 20 and Youth 20 put forward reports and papers for G20 leaders to feed the discussions of the G20 policy-makers and enrich final documents with growing awareness of how to translate recommendations into practice. Thus, during G20's St. Petersburg summit most of L20 recommendations prepared in collaboration with ILO and OECD were translated in the St. Petersburg Action Plan (September 6, 2013). B20 also has enhanced its engagement into G20's decision-making process through its seven Task Forces (from Investment and Infrastructure to G20-B20 Dialog Efficiency) and participating in Sherpa meetings, roundtables, working seccions and conferences.

G20's ammunition for setting out collective actions presents the next element of its PCF. Sofar it is commited to "consistent and effective engagement" with the international organizations which are informally divided into groups "historically valuable to make inputs to the G20 discussions" – the United Nations, the International Monetary Fund, the Organization of Economic Cooperation and Development, the World Bank, the World

---

2 Following the Outreach Strategy Russia has organized and held in 2013 more than 50 different "dialogue events" with outreach partners and groups including non-G20 countries and their regional associations, international organizations, private sector, labour unions, youth, think thanks and academic institutions, non-governmental organizations. Some of them led to formulating concrete proposals to the G20 (e.g. B20's White Book, G20 Task Force on Employment's recommendations).

Trade Organization; and groups of having "necessary expertise relevant to G20's agenda" – the World Food Program, the Food and Agriculture Organization, the International Labor Organization, the Financial Stability Board, the International Organization of Securities Commissions, etc.

Special focus is traditionally put on engaging the United Nation institutions as they are capabile to represent countries which otherwise cannot be involved in the G20 process, and due to its international coordination mechanisms which provide G20 with internationally approved expertise. For instance, during its Presidency Russia primarily had consultations with the UN General Assembly, ECOSOC, UN agencies and commissions for feeding in the G20 agenda, and then with other specialized organizations and regional intergovernmental organizations, including the CIS and the Organization International de la Francophonie for highlighting their specific interests.

ASSESSING G20'S DECISION-MAKING MECHANISM THROUGH B20-G20 PARTNERSHIP

For deeper understanding of how the G20 decision–making mechanism works, in this paper, first, B20 and L20 recommendations translated into G20 decisions are reviewed. The primary focus of the review is set on the way B20 and L20 recommendations are translated into G20 decisions.[3] It is guided by two criteria of how many G20 directs references to the reports of B20 and L20, and how often G20 mentions the keywords "business", "private sector" and "labor", "employment", "job". To set whether B20/L20 recommendations were addressed or not in G20's documents they have to be set or contained in concrete decisions. Thus further analysis looks at what B20 and L20 recommendations made to the G20 within Russian presidency and addressed in the G20 documents were agreed within the

3   [1] The methodology is based on Larionova M., 2012.

same presidency. For this B20's White Book and G20 Task Force on Employnment's recommendations were reviewed.

The previous B20 experience proves that since its first summit in Toronto the B20 grew awareness of how to translate recommendations into practice. The 11 B20's Toronto recommendations were not presented in a final document but reported by the chair of the B20 meeting. The number of B20 recommendations translated into G20 decisions from 16 in Seoul reached 45 in Cannes and each third in Los Cabos.

With mandate from the Russian G20 Presidency to coordinate the G20-B20 dialogue, the Russian Union of Producers and Entrepreneurs (in Russian RSPP) has made the following recommendations:

For macroeconomic stability G20 should prioritize public debt management within which corporate tax, social contribution and personal income tax hikes should be avoided, as well as cuts in public infrastructure spending which helps boost private investment.

For pro-growth regulation. New financial regulation standards and requirements should be transparent, up-to-date, predictable, and not lead to deterioration of financing conditions for industries and the real economy.

For structural reforms. G20 members should consolidate efforts to raise productivity, to increase investment in human capital and enhance citizens' participation in the labor market, improve efficiency of government expenditure, remove barriers to competition and investment, and support innovation with due regard to the countries' national circumstances.

The direct G20 references to the above mentioned B20's White Book recommendations are easily detected in both G20's final decisions – St. Petersburg Action Plan and G20's Leaders Declaration. Moreover about 40% of the total mentions of the keywords "business" and "private sector" as an integral part of B20 recommendations have been reflected in the final G20 documents as commitments and/or mandates (including Annexes).

In terms of policy areas, most of B20 recommendations were inicially oriented by G20's policy priorities – financial regulation, international monetary system reform and macroeconomic policies – insofar as they have the highest correlation with G20's policy priorities (about 64%, 19% and 10% of items in G20's agenda, respectively (LARIONOVA, RACHMAGULOV, 2012: 49)). In Seoul and Cannes new areas addressing challenges for public-private relations have been incorporated from B20 recommendations – green growth, ICT and innovation, infrastructure development, food security, anticorruption, global governance and financing for development. Most of them are in line with BRICS "consolidated global vision", but with some discrepancies stemming from diverse national policies and structural features. As a common "Achilles' heel" of BRICS economies there are infrastructure development and fight with corruption with Russia's stressing ICT and innovation, Brasil and India – food security and green growth, China – global governance. Finally, the issues of deepest concern for all the BRICS – investments and infrastructure – have been translated into G20's Agenda (4 out of 14 recommendations and 3 out of 10 recommendations respectively) in Cannes and Los Cabos. As a result of 7 meetings of B20's Task Force on Job Creation, Employment and Investment in Human Capital in 2013 the following recommendations have been presented at the G20 Summit in St. Petersburg:

1. Increasing employability through education systems that meets the needs of labour markets as well as increasing mobility of workers in labour markets. *States must follow-up their commitments and implement the training strategy.*
2. Creating an environment for enterprises and entrepreneurship that promotes start-ups, and conducive to enterprise growth. A diversity of work contracts is an essential part of this environment.
3. Mastering the demographic challenge by adjusting retirement ages in ways that stabilise the old-age dependency rate, by promoting diversification within the pension system, insurance-based private pensions systems, as well as adapting immigration policies in line with labour market needs to allow the immigration of the labour force.

Almost 76% of them have been directly referenced in St. Petersburg Action Plan and 50% in G20's Leaders Declaration. The main result is that employment became the example of the B20-G20 sound dialogue. The track record of the B20's Task Force on Job Creation, Employment and Investment in Human Capital provides evidence that the B20 is capable of identifying key challenges which G20 members face and pursuing their priorities consistently in the dialogue with the G20 to get the issues addressed by the leaders. Simultaneously I have to add that the validity for these assessments may be proved only by sound individual actions of the parties involved.

RUSSIA'S GROWTH PRIORITIES AND G20'S AGENDA: QUALITY JOBS AND GROWTH

Since G20 was etablished jobs and growth have been like "a red string" of G20's decision-making processses insofar as it backed up economic activity. In its turn economic growth has led to different employment outcomes depending on countries. Brazil and South Africa have had broadly similar GDP growth rates since 2007. In China and India the rates of employment generation have been low in spite of different growth rates (World Bank, 2013). These contrasting results stem from diverse national policies and structural features.

In response to the global financial crisis many countries has stimulated labor demand and protected income. The ILO has estimated that in G20 countries government actions created or saved 21 million jobs in 2009 and 2010 (ILO, 2010: 5). Among the countries surveyed in the ILO-World Bank policy inventory, 40% of them have implemented training programs and employment services (e.g. BRICS). Labour activation mechanisms for the vulnerable groups in BRICS countries were also commonly designed to encourage the hiring of young people even for a short-term (6 months), investments in dual training systems, self-employment and entrepreneurship support, direct job creation in the public and not-forprofit sectors. Besides most countries adopted policies to support the creation of new jobs through supporting small and medium-size enterprises (SMEs) and entrepreneurs by facilitating access to credit, giving preferential treatment in public tenders, or reducing taxes (China, Brazil). Countries also intervened to protect the incomes of workers affected by the crisis (Brazil and Russia). Brazil has implemented the program of conditional cash transfers *"Bolsa Verde"* ("Green Grant") which includes now payments of R$ 1.200 (US$ 600) per year to low-income households engaged in sustainable activities. Russia had and expanded conditional cash transfer program "Maternity (family) Capital" after the crisis hit.

But following "coordinated policy recommendations" presented on the first joint Fianance and Labor Ministers meeting in Moscow (July, 2013) a choice in favour of a labor policy instrument should be stipulated by at least two prepositions: (1) whether its main objective is to mitigate short-term fluctuations or to promote longterm growth and (2) whether it promotes/sustains labor demand or protects household income. To contain short-term impact labor policies should be countercyclical, that is, should have the ability to be scaled up in contractions and scaled down as recovery begins. For example, unemployment insurance and cash transfers refer to this type of countercyclical measures as they automatically increase when more people need them.

The labor market movements reveal various lessons for the BRICS. The experience of labor-regulation reforms in 14 Latin American countries (incl. Brazil) proved that making labor regulations more flexible would lead to increase in total employment (average net of 2.08% with data for 10,396 firms (KAPLAN, 2008)). Small firms with fewer than 20 employees would benefit twice more (net employment of 4.27%). And globally most of the newly created jobs are created in the private sector (around 9 out of 10 jobs in Brazil and South Africa (ILO, 2013)). That is countries with more regulated labor markets (China and Russia) may have larger gains in total employment which, however, would be achieved through higher rates of hiring and higher rates of termination.

An increased emphasis on creating flexible and enforceable labor market regulatory laws and institutions is also crucial for promoting labor productivity and improving the welfare of workers (DINH, 2013). Ultimatly, it was important to complement the protection offered by firms with a public safety net and mitigate restrictions in the Russian Labor Code facilitating layoffs in strategic state sectors and protecting workers in case of job or skill loss.

Besides in BRICS countries their openness to trade produces divergent effects on employment and growth. The terms of trade improvement proved to benefit both firms and workers increasing hiring. In contrast the terms-of-trade inducing wealth effects reduces the individual labour supply, increases wages, and reduces hiring (DAO, 2013). It was also found that in open economies domestic debt and banking crises produced very severe impacts on employment (the reduction in the employment growth was more than twice as strong (GAMBERONI, 2010). In China and India the expansion of financial market activity since the 1990s has been more limited where firms could obtain financing and growth (DIDIER, 2013).

In Brazil employment was revealed to respond more to growth in less productive and more labor-intensive sectors (ARIAS-VAZQUEZ, 2012). It is also susceptible to a resource course, and grows rapidly in response to manufacturing and export manufacturing growth (which is also the character of Russia). In Brazil and China the differences in sectoral growth effects on employment and wages are substantially reduced in provinces with higher measured labor mobility. Consistent with this, the growth in more labor-intensive sectors and manufacturing is important to generate employment in all the BRICS, although only manufacturing and natural resource growth show distinctive labor market effects.

Russian authorities have used different instruments to facilitate labour mobility and reduce unemployment (retraining, encouragement of self-employment, assistance in removal, etc.). Among them was a set of regional employment programmes integrated into a federal roadmap "Establishing a national system of competence and qualification" and including measures to stimulate migration from regions with oversupply of labor to labor-deficient regions, to develop separate hiring mechanisms for big investment projects and for skilled foreign employees, etc. Immigration helped to lessen the burden of ageing for the welfare states of most Western economies

(MUYSKEN, 2013). And even temporary immigration may help to alleviate the ageing problem through a positive long-term contribution to employment, wages and GDP per capita, as long as the immigrants are able to participate in the labour force in tandem with the native population. But unfavourable short-term effects should be handled through a gradual phasing in of immigration policies.

BRICS countries also have rather substantial experience of various measures to expand the coverage of basic social protection. Brazil's Brasil Sem Miséria plan combines cash transfers, employment opportunities and access to public services directed at poverty groups, especially in rural areas. China expanded both rural a pension scheme piloted in 2009 and social pension insurance for urban residents launched in 2011. India has reorganized the National Rural Employment Guarantee Scheme now reaching over 40 million households in rural areas. India also introduced additional maternity services and expanded nutrition and health care to 8.7 million girls. South Africa is piloting a new National Health Insurance which is proclaimed to give all citizens access to essential health care, regardless of their employment status and ability to pay. In November 2012 Russia has adopted an Employment Promotion Programme targeting to reduce the unemployment rate up to 5.5% in 2015 (Annex 1). But analyzing the Russian labour market policy "before and after" G20, there are any differences and/or progress.

Since 2002 Russia has actively developed the basis for its labour legislation as a new Labour Code was passed with a wide range of changes in legal framework, Federal Law "On the Bases of Mandatory Social Insurance" (2004) introducing a new consolidated insurance system, Federal Law "On Trade Unions, Their Rights and Guarantees of Unions Activities" (2005) promoting collective agremments in Russia. For the first time in Russia the Code has guaranteed the 35 hour work week and vacation time accounted on the basis of 5-day week.

All these measures have permitted reducing unemployment (during 2005-2013 its rate varied within 5.5-8.5%), and liberated a significant portion of budgetary funds that have been expended on maintenance of the employment assuring institutions (Center of macroanalysis and forecasting, 2012). Alongside with labour market reforms Russian Government tried to scale up Russian labour market outcomes and reduce poverty. Today it sets up minimum level for salaries in both public and private sectors, for unemployment compensation and targets compulsory payments in social insurance. Still the main deffience of the Russian labor market after that legal framework reforms are the unadequate labour standards regulating earnings and income inequalities (OECD, 2011). Moreover the income inequality rising over the past decade in Russia was determined, in particular, by influencing the distribution of income labour, education and tax policies (KOSKE, 2013).

Besides, rapid population ageing further contributes to the need to address the low standard of pensionable ages at which pensions become payable in Russia and the limit of access to early pensions. According to the Federal Statistics Service (Rosstat), the share of the population past the retirement age is 22%, and by 2020 it will rise to above 25%, and by 2030 it will approach 30%. According to Rosstat, 13.5 million retirees keep working and getting salaries and pensions at the same time. Recent regulation in Russia has proclaimed to eradicate poverty among pensioners, as measured by official benchmarks, but raises questions on the long-term financial sustainability of the private pensions system. The Pension Fund's of Russia's deficit in 2012 reached 1.75 trillion rubles or 3% GDP, or 14% of the federal budget spending (e.g. twice per year state pensions are indexed in line with inflation). Thus, the next determinant of the labor market situation in Brazil, Russia, India and China are demographic factors (BIAVASCHI, 2012).

In China the correlations between labour force age and production characteristics exists (LI, 2013). Moreover the household-level technical efficiency was increasing until maximum efficiency was reached when the average age of the household labor force was 45, after which efficiency declined. Thus, the aging of the rural labor force may affect efficiency and productivity in crop production and therefore agricultural policies may need to pay more attention to the aging of the agricultural labor force. In this line China has merged separate medical insurance schemes for urban and rural residents in Tianjin and 5 other provincesof China. Today around 70% of the medical spending within the basic medical insurance scheme are covered by a medical insurance fund for both urban and rural residents. As a result, completed in 2012 the increase of the basic pension for enterprise retirees increased the per capita monthly average pension by 200 RMB yuan relative to 2011. By May 2013, the number of urban and rural covered residents has reached 487 million, and 134 million senior residents receive pension benefits on a monthly basis.

So, since the summit in Cannes, Russian participation in G20 initiatives became evidently oriented to a wide discussion on labour and social policy and aimed to share good practice on increasing the effectiveness of public mechanisms for social protection and inclusion. To stress one of the key Russian initiatives to facilitate job creation, a G20's Task Force on Employment (ETF) was created during the Russian Presidency of the G20 with an agenda on such topics as job creation through sound monetary and fiscal policies, structural policies to foster innovation and promotion of smaller enterprises; labour activation for the vulnerable groups. In the report prepared by the ILO and OECD for the ETF, investments in infrastructure were proposed as "common instruments to generate employment across G20 countries" capturing back the BRICS experience. Brazil and South Africa have dedicated significant resources to infrastructure investments with high direct and intrinsic employment content through backward and forward linkages. India has commited to continue with its ambitious infrastructure programme, including the Delhi-Mumbai Industrial corridor connecting the national capital and the commercial capital with high speed rail and road links entailing nearly $ 100 billion in investment. In addition, two new major ports will be established and a new outer harbour will be developed in an existing port starting in 2013(MAP, 2013). Boosting entrepreneurship and supporting SMEs are commonly used in job creation strategies. Examples include the Russian Bank for Small and Medium Enterprises Support which was set to increase the funding to SMEs.

To conclude, first of all, "applicable" economic policy interventions may be only tailored to country-specific circumstances. Second, comprehensive policy packages accumulate "cross-sector synergy" responses because of synergy within macroeconomic policy. Third, the labor policy as implemented in response to economic stress should be quick and capable due to sound and credible institutions. In practice, many policy interventions have yielded limited returns because of weak targeting and the difficulties associated with implementing packages. For instance, during the 1998 Russian crisis while the safety net fell in shortages the fully protecting living standards helped provide protection against extreme poverty.

RUSSIA'S GROWTH PRIORITIES IN G20'S AGENDA: FROM FEEDING DISCUSSION TO SETTING UP DECISIONS

To strengthen implementation of G20's decisions Russia regularly attaches an extra impetus agenda to the G20 discussion. Officially, it comprised an extended version of Russia's position in G20, which might be characterized as reflecting Russian policy's urgent priorities "ensuring shared international objectives". Most of them have served to feed G20's discussions up to then separate and to incorporate them into G20's agendas (e.g. St. Petersburg's Global Energy Security Principles, Global Partnership Financial Inclusion (GPFI) and financing development initiatives). Following the logic for changes in the international system generated both by global actors and new market-makers, and through coordinated actions, Russia has tried to modify its strategic collaboration with G20.

Initially, to foster its extra impetus ideas Russian officials relied on an approach mainly backed by behind-the-scene activities during high level meetings. But the outreach discourse since 2011 proved to be crucial for Russia's progress in making its proposals more practically oriented and applicable. For instance, St. Petersburg's Global Energy Security Principles have been put into G20's agendas sporadically: in Pittsburg – efficiency and transparency for energy markets through JODI initiative have been discussed; in Toronto – it was only referenced; and came back in Seoul. 2012 became "the turning point" for Russian extra impetus agenda to grow into

G20 setting out coordinated decisions – by developing its "collaborative sense" and through "back-to-back dialogue". For G20's Agenda in 2013 both principal Russian extra impetus items "financing for investment" and "government borrowing and public debt sustainability" have been translated into G20's decisions.

Public debt management has been introduced to consider on G20's platform in Moscow(2013). The IMF–World Bank Guidelines for Public Debt Management were put in the center of discussion together with the Guidelines for Public Debt Management (2003) and IMF–World Bank–OECD's "Stockholm Principles" (2010) as they are universally utilized by all G20's members. That is why most of G20 decisions' on this topic are affected by international institutions as they are related to G20's mandate (IMF, World Bank, FSB, BIS, IOSCO, etc.). Looking back on evolution of their engagement into G20's decision-making process – among traditionally referenced FSF and IMF (during 2008-2010 about 24% and 20% (LARIONOVA, 2011: 63)) IOSCO, OECD and BIS appeared (Figure 1) as they are capable as international standards setting bodies.

Figure 1   International organizations in G20's decisions
in 2011-2013, as a % of those referenced

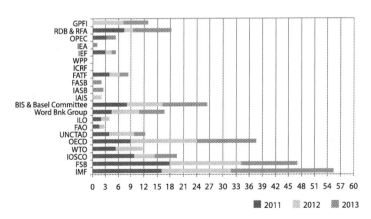

Sourse: author's calculations, 2014.

Financing for investment is a key precondition for economic growth and a principal factor for job creation. Institutional investors allocate over $ 70 trillion of assets in alternative sources of financing looking for new sources of long-term, inflation protected returns in volatile stock markets in recent years. Investments in real, productive assets, such as infrastructure could potentially provide income driving growth. However, there are also major challenges to higher allocations to such assets, from the small size of many pension funds and insurers to regulatory barriers.

The main task of the G20 was formulated as "to foster such an environment that would be more conducive to financing for investment and identify new sources for long-term investment". The study group on Financing for Investment was established at the G20 Finance Ministers Meeting in February 2013 in Moscow. In St. Peterbursg G20 Leaders endorsed the OECD's initiative aimed to encourage the flow of institutional investment towards longer-term assets, such as infrastructure and renewable energy projects. Today only 1% of the assets held by pension funds, insurers, mutual funds and sovereign wealth funds were invested in infrastructure projects, in clean energy projects. While pension funds alone managed over USD 20 trillion in assets as of the end of 2012, with a net annual inflow of savings of over $ 1 trillion (World Bank, 2013).

Together with G20's members OECD Task was working over High-Level Principles of Long-Term Investment Financing by Institutional Investors which set out the preconditions to long-term investment, such as a clear and transparent government plan for projects, public procurement and public-private partnerships investment. The principles also address specific policies, including: (1) improving incentives to mobilise higher levels of long-term savings; (2) strengthening the governance of institutional investors to provide the right incentives for the adoption of long-term perspectives and the management of often illiquid assets; (3) ensuring the tax and regulatory framework that reflects the particular risk characteristics of the investments, promotes long-term strategies and lowers barriers; (4) informing and educating consumers about the virtues of long-term saving.

Traditionally, banks have been key players in the financial system, transforming savings into long-term capital to finance private sector investment. Over time, two main changes have taken place in the structure of the financial system. First, the banking model has evolved, becoming increasingly dominated by wholesale markets and derivatives. The last lending collapse was the result of the interaction between a prior weak regulation and the rapid evolution of bank business models towards products that created excess leverage (e.g. originate-to-distribute' products) and put the entire financial system at risk.

Second, disintermediation and the growth of capital markets has led to a shift in the structure of the financial sector, with institutional investors also becoming central players as providers of long-term capital. But after the financial crisis, the traditional sources of investment financing are all facing challenges with the main blockages to investment remaining in the banking sector. UNCTAD data that private equity funds activity in cross-border infrastructure investment has risen during the first half of 2000s, reaching $ 17.5 billion.

It is also necessary to understand the extent to which institutional investors may provide alternate sources of financing for infrastructure. As highlighted in the G20/OECD Policy Note "Pension Fund Financing for Green Infrastructure Initiatives" investments in infrastructure by institutional investors are still limited due to, among other things: a lack of appropriate financing vehicles and investment and risk management expertise; regulatory disincentives; lack of quality data on infrastructure; and a clear and agreed investment benchmark and challenges specific to "green infrastructure" (e.g. regulatory and policy uncertainty and inexperience with new technologies and asset classes). These challenges should be examined for possible implications for the policy framework under which financial institutions operate.

In the St. Peterburg Summit Russia has committed to streamlining regulation and easing administrative burdens, in combination with an increase of financing for infrastructure projects aimed to achieve 25% of GDP by 2015 and 27% of GDP by 2018. At the same time the All-Russian Organization of Small and Medium Business (OPORA, from the Russian), estimates that SMEs accounts for about 25% of the jobs and generate only 17% of Russian GDP. While State budget expenses on SMEs Support Programmes 16 times in the last 5 yeas, in 2011 the Russian government spent just 600 million for SMEs.

Brazil agreed to support with tax incentives and innovative financing initiatives the $ 71 billion Logistics Investment Program in a 5 years time horizon to tackle bottlenecks, increase competitiveness, create jobs and promote growth (MAP, 2013). India has also committed itself to precede its ambitious infrastructure programme the Delhi-Mumbai Industrial corridor connecting the national capital and the commercial capital to high speed rail and road links entailing nearly $ 100 billion in investment. In addition, two new major ports were claimed to be established and a new outer harbour to be constructed in the existing port untill 2014 (MAP, 2013). China accelerates the development of the services sector, which may raise its value-added contribution to GDP by 4% by 2015, and increase spending on R&D to 2.2% of GDP (MAP, 2013). South Africa takes steps to resolve the energy constraint by starting the process to build a third coal-fired power plant and finalising the process of authorising shale gas exploration in a responsible and environmentally friendly manner.

CONCLUSION

I have examined a number of preconditions for assigning a role to G20's policy coordination to promote collective political will and steer global governance toward a coordinated and balanced policy.

It became evident that G20 Policy Coordinated Framework is equipped with three pillars to make functional its decision-making process: (1) legitimacy standing on "consistent engagement" of all actors in the international system, (2) various global dialogue formats (summits, outreach events, etc.) and (3) the collective actions capabilities of international organizations.

The case of B20-G20 partnership proved that the narrower the distance between governments and private sector groups in global dialogue (in numbers of discussions and correlation between proposed topics) the more G20 is capable of translating recommendations into practice. Of course, this is hardly a proof that G20 may stand alone to implement its decisions – countries must be committed (e.g. under MAP).

Examining the roots of discrepancies between "coordinated policy" recommendations and national labour policy measures, I found that even while relatively similar in structural features, BRICS policy interventions nust be only tailored to country-specific circumstances to be sound. G20 may be assigned an "important role": to set recommendations from which BRICS countries can pick up the most relevant to their growth models in due time.

To be responsible for the appeal of the idea that G20 may serve for international cooperation, I made a diagnostic of possibilities for countries to incorporate their ideas and concerns into G20's agenda. It is quite clear that the ground for pushing them forward lies in international economic organizations (predominantly setting standards): through this G20 may be discovered to have new virtues (e.g. global accountability for IO).

REFERENCES

ARIAS-VAZQUEZ, F. J., LEE, J. N.; NEWHOUSE, D. (2012), "The Role of Sectoral Growth Patterns in Labor Market Development", in *World Bank*, Washington, October 2012.

B20–G20 Partnership for Growth and Jobs: Recommendations From Business 20, Moscow, 2013.

B20's Task Force on Job Creation, Employment and Investment in Human Capital recommendations, 2013.

BIAVASCHI, C., EICHHORST, W., GIULIETTI, C., KENDZIA, M. J., MURAVYEV, A., PIETERS, J., RODRÍGUEZ-PLANAS, N., SCHMIDL, R., ZIMMERMANN, K. F. (2012), "Youth Unemployment and Vocational Training", in *World Bank*, Washington, D.C., October 2012.

Center for Macroanalisys and Focasting <http://www.forecast.ru/>.

DAO, M. C. (2013), "International spillovers of labour market policies", in *Oxford Economic Papers*, 65, (2).

DIDIER, T., SCHMUKLER, S. L. (2013), "The Financing and Growth of Firms in China and India: Evidence from Capital Markets", in *World Bank*, Washington. D.C., April 2013.

DINH, H. T., RAWSKI, T. G., ZAFAR, A. W. L., MAVROEIDI, E. (2013), *Tales from the Development Frontier: How China and Other Countries Harness Light*.

G20's Leaders Declaration, St. Petersburg URL: <http://en.g20russia.ru/documents/>.

GAMBERONI, E., UEXKULL, E., WEBER, S. (2010), "The Roles of Openness and Labor Market Institutions for Employment Dynamics during Economic Crises", in *World Bank*, Washington, D.C., September 2010.

ILO. (2010), *Accelerating a Job-Rich Recovery in G-20 Countries: Building on Experience*. ILO. Geneva.

Institutions for Employment Dynamics during Economic Crises, in *World Bank*, Washington, D.C., September 2010.

Interantional Organizations Research Juinal. (2011), (1), p. 41-64.

KAPLAN, D. S. (2008), "Job Creation and Labor Reform in Latin America", in *World Bank*, Washington, D.C., September 2008.

KOSKE, I., WANNER, I. (2013), "The drivers of labour income inequality – an analysis based on Bayesian Model Averaging", in *Applied Economics Letters*, 20 (2), 2013.

LARIONOVA, V. B., RACHMAGULOV, M. R. (2012), "G8 and G20 Contribution to the Development of Global and Regional Regulation", in *Interantional Organizations Research Juinal*, 2012 (2), p. 30-63.

_____. *Assessing G8 and G20 Effectiveness in Global Governance: diversification of labour – opportunities for efficiency growth*.

LI, M., SICULAR, T. (2013), "Aging of the labor force and technical efficiency in crop production: Evidence from Liaoning province, China", in *China Agricultural Economic Review*, 5 (3), 2013.

MALONEY, W. (2009), "How will Labor Markets Adjust to the Crisis? A Dynamic View", in *World Bank*, Washington, D.C., March 2009.

MAP Policy Templates URL: <https://www.g20.org/about_g20/interactive_map>.

MUYSKEN, J., ZIESEMER, T. H. W. (2013), "A permanent effect of temporary immigration on economic growth", in *Applied Economics*, 45 (28), 2013.

OECD. (2011), *Reviews of Labour Market and Social Policies: Russian Federation*, December 2011.

St. Petersburg Action Plan URL: <http://en.g20russia.ru/documents/>.

World Bank. Addressing the Jobs Challenge in G20 countries, World Bank, 2013.

_____. *Manufacturing to Create Jobs and Prosperity*. Washington. D.C., World Bank, September 2013.

ANNEX 1   RUSSIA'S STRUCTURAL
REFORM COMMITMENTS UNDER.

MAP Policy Templates, September 6, 2013.

1. Qualitative/quantitative targets for every year till 2020 (for the unemployment rate, the assessment of gaps between supply and demand for foreign labour force and a set of indicators reflecting the sanitary conditions of workplaces):
   At Los Cabos Leaders' Summit Russia declared an objective to reduce the unemployment rate to 6.3% in 2013 and to 5.6% in 2015.
   An Employment Promotion Programme sets an even lower target for 2013 – 5.9%. In 2012 unemployment already reached 5,5%.

2. Increased labour mobility and reduction of unemployment spells.

3. Increasing population's financial literacy and strengthening financial consumer protection in order to minimize debt and fraud risks; to promote more efficient and responsible participation of the population in the financial services' market; to increase the financial wellbeing of the population, and to give protection and trust to the financial system as a whole.

4. Development and implementation of educational programs, information campaigns, and the scaling up of existing financial literacy and consumer protection initiatives. Development of a National Financial Literacy Strategy by 2015 with the following targets:
   - To establish no less than 50 federal and regional financial literacy centers for preparing trainers and train not less than 20 000 of trainers in the period 2013-2016.
   - To provide free information and educational materials through financial education and information campaigns to no less than 15 mln of people in the period 2013-2016.
   - To increase the availability of the dispute resolution, complaints handling and redress mechanisms, information disclosure and sources of available information to financial consumers by 25% in the period 2013-2016. Progress with these targets can be observed through the All-Russia National Survey on Measuring the level of population's financial literacy (conducted once

every two years: 2012, 2014, 2016) and a National Panel survey on Consumer Finance/Financial Behavior of the Population (2013, 2015), WB Project monitoring as well as through sources of official data, such as Central Bank statistics and Rospotrebnadzor public reports, for independent consumer protection monitoring.

Notes on contributors

Gustavo Lins Ribeiro is president of National Association of Graduate Studies and Research in Social Sciences (ANPOCS) and Professor of Anthropology and researcher of the Americas' Research Center (Centro de Pesquisa sobre as Américas) at University of Brasilia (UnB).
gustavor@unb.br

Tom Dwyer is Professor of Sociology at University of Campinas (Unicamp/Brazil), coordinator of the Computing and Society Interdisciplinary Laboratory (Unicamp) and member of the Executive Committee of the International Sociological Association (2010-2014).
tomdwyer@terra.com.br

K. L. Sharma is currently Vice-Chancellor at Jaipur National University (India) and recently he has co-authored a book on Social Stratification and Change in BRIC Countries (2013).
klsharma@hotmail.com

P. S. Vivek is Professor at the Department of Sociology of the University of Mumbai.
psvivek@ymail.com

Naran Bilik is Distinguished Professor of Fudan University (China), Associate Dean of Fudan Institute for Advanced Study in Social Sciences, and China Ministry of Education Changjiang Chair Professor at Guizhou Normal College.
naranbilik@gmail.com

Zhou Lei is Co-Founder and Director, *Oriental Danology Institute and BRICS FUTURES Consultancy* and Researcher of *South China Sea Studies Center, Nanjing University.*
leizhou60@gmail.com

Freek Cronjé is professor of Sociology at the School of Social and Government Studies and Director of Bench Marks Centre for CSR, North-West University, South Africa.
Freek.Cronje@nwu.ac.za

Sultan Khan is Associate Professor in the Sociology Programme at the School of Social Sciences, University of KwaZulu-Natal, Durban.
khans@ukzn.ac.za

Antonádia Borges is professor at the Department of Anthropology at the University of Brasilia and coordinator of the Anthropological Theory Research and Study Group (GESTA). She is also currently member of the International Exchange Committee of ANPOCS.
antonadia@gmail.com

Francis Nyamnjoh is Professor of Social Anthropology of the School of African and Gender Studies, Anthropology and Linguistics at the University of Cape Town.
francis.nyamnjoh@uct.ac.za; nyamnjoh@gmail.com

Bingzhong Gao is Professor of Anthropology of the Institute of Sociology and Anthropology and Director of the Center for Civil Society Studies at Peking University (Beijing, China).
gaobzh@pku.edu.cn

Pedro Lara de Arruda is a Researcher at the International Policy Centre for Inclusive Growth of the United Nations Development Programme (IPC-IG/UNDP).
pedro.arruda@ipc-undp.org

Ashleigh Kate Slingsby is a Consultant at the International Policy Centre for Inclusive Growth of the United Nations Development Programme (IPC-IG/UNDP).
ashleigh.slingsby@ipc-undp.org

Praveen Jha is on the faculty of the Centre for Economic Studies and Planning, and the Chairperson of the Centre for Informal Economy and Labour Studies, Jawaharlal Nehru University (India).
praveenjha2005@gmail.com

Amit Chakraborty is a Ph.D. research scholar at the Centre for Economic Studies and Planning, Jawaharlal Nehru University (India).
amitdinhata@gmail.com

Maria Paula Gomes dos Santos is Research Technician at IPEA – Institute for Applied Economic Research (Brazil) and PhD in Political Science, IUPERJ (Brazil).
mariapaula.santos@ipea.gov.br

Eduardo Viola is Full Professor at the Institute of International Relations of the University of Brasilia, Senior Researcher at the Brazilian Council for Scientific and Technological Development and Coordinator of the Research Group on "International System in the Antropocene and Global Climate Change". He has been visiting professor in several Universities, among them Stanford, Texas, Amsterdam, Notre Dame, Colorado and San Martin. Professor Viola is member of several international scientific committees. He is the author of 8 books, 76 articles and 73 book chapters. He has 2866 citations on Google Scholar with Index H: 24 and Index H-10: 63. His main areas of research are: Globalization and Governance, the International System in the Antropocene, International Political Economy of Energy and Climate Change and Brazilian foreign policy.
eduviola@gmail.com

Matías Franchini has a Master and is a PhD candidate in International Relations, University of Brasilia. He is also member of the Research Network on International Relations on Climate Change.
matifranchi@yahoo.com.ar

Alexander Zhebit is Full Professor of International Relations Studies at the Federal University of Rio de Janeiro (Universidade Federal do Rio de Janeiro, Brazil). He

is PhD in History of International Relations and Foreign Policy by the Russian Diplomacy Academy of the Foreign Affairs Ministry.
alex@cfch.ufrj.br

Kathryn Hochstetler is CIGI Chair of Governance in the Americas at the Balsillie School of International Affairs and Professor of Political Science at the University of Waterloo.
hochstet@uwaterloo.ca

Michael Kahn is Senior Research Fellow in the Centre for Research on Evaluation, Science and Technology of Stellenbosch University (South Africa) and Professor Extraordinaire at the Tshwane University of Technology (Pretoria, South Africa).
mikejkahn@gmail.com

Natalia Khmelevskaya is Associate Professor of Department of International Economic Relations and Foreign Economic Ties of MGIMO University, Russia.
Khmelevskaya@mgimo.ru

Printed in the United States
By Bookmasters